OUR

AND

HIS LOVE FOR US

Books by the Author Translated into English

God, His Existence and His Nature: A Thomistic Solution of Certain
Agnostic Antinomies (1914)

Christian Perfection and Contemplation, according to St. Thomas
Aquinas and St. John of the Cross (1923)

The Love of God and the Cross of Jesus (1929)

Providence (1932)

Our Savior and His Love for Us (1933)

Predestination (1936)

*The One God (1938)

The Three Ages of the Interior Life: Prelude of Eternal Life (1938)

The Three Ways of the Spiritual Life (1938)

*The Trinity and God the Creator (1943)

*Christ the Savior (1945)

The Priesthood and Perfection (1946)

Reality: A Synthesis of Thomistic Thought (1946)

Life Everlasting (1947)

*Grace (1947)

The Priest in Union with Christ (1948)

The Mother of the Saviour and Our Interior Life (1948)

*The Theological Virtues—Vol. 1: Faith (1948)

*Beatitude (moral theology, 1951)

Last Writings (spiritual retreats, 1969)

Books by the Author Not Translated into English

Le sens commun: la philosophie de l'être et les formules dogmatiques (1909)

Saint Thomas et le neomolinisme (booklet, 1917)

De Revelatione per ecclesiam catholicam proposita (1918)

De methodo sancti Thomae speciatim de structura articulorum summae
theologicae (booklet, 1928)

Le réalisme du principe de finalité (1932)

Le sens du mystère et le clair-obscur intellectuel: nature et
surnaturel (1934)

Essenza e attualità del Tomismo

Dieu accessible à tous (booklet, 1941)

*De Eucharistia: Accedunt de Paenitentia quaestiones dogmaticae (1942)

Les XXIV Theses Thomistes pour le 30e Anniversaire de leur
Approbation (booklet, 1944)

Verite et immutabilite du dogme (booklet, 1947)

*De virtutibus theologicis (1948)

---

*Commentaries on St. Thomas Aquinas' Summa Theologica.

OUR SAVIOR
AND
HIS LOVE FOR US

By
Fr. Reginald Garrigou-Lagrange, O.P.

Translated by
A. Bouchard

TAN BOOKS AND PUBLISHERS, INC.
Rockford, Illinois 61105

Nihil Obstat: Innocent Swoboda, O.F.M.
                     Censor Librorum

Imprimatur: ✠ Joseph E. Ritter
                     Archbishop
                     St. Louis, Missouri
                     August 13, 1951

This book is a translation of *Le Sauveur et son amour pour nous*. Republished in 1998 by TAN Books and Publishers, Inc. by authorization of Les Éditions du Cerf, Paris.

The type in this book is the property of TAN Books and Publishers, Inc., successor in interest to B. Herder Book Co. of St. Louis, Missouri.

Library of Congress Catalog Card No.: 98-61397

ISBN 0-89555-635-9

Cover illustration by Janssens.

Printed and bound in the United States of America.

TAN BOOKS AND PUBLISHERS, INC.
P.O. Box 424
Rockford, Illinois 61105
1998

TRANSLATOR'S NOTE

Excerpts from St. Thomas' *Summa theologica* are taken from the translation published by Benziger Brothers, 1947.

PREFACE

IN an earlier work, *Providence*, we sought to explain, according to revelation and theology, the nature of divine Providence, its extension and infallibility, and the way we must confidently abandon ourselves to it by fulfilling our duties a little better each day. We have also shown in that work how conformity with God's signified will permit us to abandon ourselves to His will of good pleasure even before it has been manifested to us. Thus, "fidelity and abandonment" is a maxim that preserves the equilibrium of the interior life in the face of two opposing deviations, namely, restless, sterile agitation, and lazy, quietistic indifference.

This book on the Savior is in a sense the sequel to the one mentioned above. Who, indeed, if not the Savior has made the correct notion of Providence, so often expressed in the Old Testament, prevail over the notion of destiny or of an unknown and irresistible linkage of events and causes? Who has liberated men from the clutches of blind fate, spoken of by the Greek poets? Who has enabled us to free ourselves from the bonds of fatality, of chance or ill fortune, of life's countless worries, of slavery to the passions? Who, if not He whom we call the Savior?

The greatest Greek philosophers sought deliverance in contemplation of the Sovereign Good, which they conceived variously, depending on whether they were more or less idealistic. But they admitted that this contemplation of the Sovereign Good was accessible to only a very few men. They themselves attained to it only for a few fleeting moments; and if they spoke of the life to come, it was in terms of a beautiful possibility. Even Plato expressed himself thus in the *Phaedo*, as did Seneca in one of his *Letters to Lucilius* (102).

The problem of men's individual destinies remained obscure, and the necessity resulting from the very nature of things weighed heavily on men's souls. There was nothing to do but to be resigned to it. "The philosophers do not free us from it. Quite the contrary, they buttress by their doctrines the stern necessity of universal laws." [1] According to the Stoics, fate leads those who submit to her, but carries along in spite of themselves those who resist. The determinist doctrines from the Orient added still more to the weight of destiny.

The Savior came not only to deliver us from the stranglehold of fate, from the irresistible chain of known and unknown causes, and from the blows of misfortune; He came also to deliver us from sin, from injustice with respect to God and men. He came to justify us and to promise us, no longer as a beautiful possibility but as an absolute certainty, not only future life in the natural order, but eternal life in the supernatural order, participation in the intimate life of God: a life in which we shall see Him as He sees Himself and love Him as He loves Himself.

Belief in destiny has been superseded by faith in God's love for us and faith in Providence: "God so loved the world, as to give His only-begotten Son; that whosoever believeth in Him, may not perish, but may have life everlasting." [2] The weight of destiny has been lifted, and our individual destinies are brighter. The Savior brings deliverance to all who do not through lust or pride resist the light and the grace of God. It is from this point of view that we shall consider the mystery of the redemptive Incarnation.

On several occasions we have explained to theological students St. Thomas' treatise on the Incarnation, making use of his principal commentators. We judge it useful for our present purpose to extract certain portions of this treatise that bear directly on the personality of the Savior, His interior life, and His love for us, and to present this material in a form accessible to all interior souls. In our presentation we shall go back as much as possible from theology to faith itself, since the latter is far superior to the former.

Theology helps us to discover the innermost meaning of the Gospel. The farther it advances the more, in a sense, it must hide itself. For, like St. John the Baptist, it must somehow disappear after an-

---

[1] Seneca, Ep. 107, 10; *Volentem ducunt fata, nolentem trahunt.* Cf. A. J. Festugière, O.P., *L'Idéal Religieux des Grecs et l'Evangile* (1932), p. 105.

[2] John 3:16.

nouncing the coming of our Lord. It makes known the structure of the body of doctrine, but as is fitting it must express itself as much as possible in the terms of Scripture, that is, in God's own words. Thus theology tends upward toward faith, its source.

We frequently speak of the intimate life of God, which is especially the mystery of the Blessed Trinity. Likewise the interior life of the sacred soul of the Savior derives from the mystery of the Incarnation. We shall therefore consider the Savior's interior life first with relation to the mystery of the Incarnation, and then with relation to the mystery of the Redemption.

In Part One we shall seek to explain Christ's personality according to His own testimony and that of the apostles, His intimate life as it was and is eternally with relation to the fittingness and motives for the Incarnation. We shall consider Christ's sanctity, the fullness of grace that enriched His sacred soul from the first moment of His conception, and that radiates through all His faculties: His intelligence, His will, and His passions.

In Part Two we shall deal with the mystery of the Redemption and of the Savior's love for us, dwelling on His humility, His prayer, His merits, His priesthood, the sacrifice of the Cross and that of the Mass. By thus contemplating at close range the intimate life of Jesus on earth, in heaven, and in the Eucharist, we shall learn how we must go about entering into His close friendship and how the mystery of Christ is bound up with the mystery of our own individual destinies.

We have set out to write neither a treatise on technical theology nor a popularization. Our purpose is to invite interior souls to the contemplation of the mystery of Christ.

To this end, two different pitfalls are to be avoided. Often, even on this subject, the spirit of technical research, when it succeeds in avoiding pedantry, turns the mind to minutiae, and this result is always detrimental to contemplation. Even apart from any defect in theological exposition, a good manual of theology on the solution of the difficulties concerning the communication of idioms, transubstantiation, or the Eucharistic accidents will be of less help in preparing us for contemplation than Bossuet's *Elévations sur les mystères* or his *Méditations sur l'Evangile*. The majority of interior souls do not need to undertake much of the research which is indispensable to theologians. In fact, to understand these matters they would require a philosophical background that they do not possess and that in a sense would encumber them. For, even at the start—in a different way, of course—these theologically untrained souls are on a higher level. This truth was well understood by the great classical theologians who must ever be our models.

On the other hand, many popularizations, and many pious books as well, lack a solid doctrinal foundation. Yet, far from being separated or merely juxtaposed, sacred doctrine and piety ought to be closely united, the latter springing spontaneously from the former.

Inasmuch as popularizations are characterized by excessive simplification, they often fail to examine certain fundamental and difficult problems from which, however, light would burst forth, perhaps even the light of life.

On the contrary, we have purposely laid emphasis on several of these problems, notably the personality of Christ (wherein it is formally constituted), the motive for the Incarnation, considered in terms of the predestination of Christ, the first of the predestined souls. We have also dealt at considerable length with the mystery of the reconciliation of Christ's liberty with His absolute impeccability, as well as several other difficult questions of this nature. These questions, which because of their difficulty are neglected in many works, are none the less important not only for the theologian but for the contemplative who wishes to live by his faith.

That is why at the end of this work we shall discuss Jesus in His relation to different forms of sanctity. In this regard we have made a special study of a problem much under discussion at the present time: the grace of Christ and the non-Christian mystics.

In an effort to enlighten interior souls desirous of becoming more closely united to the Savior, we have sought to explain the doctrine of the Church on the Word made flesh, according to St. Thomas Aquinas, not in the often technical language of his commentators but in words that can be understood by all. We have tried to do this without succumbing to a superficial oversimplification, but in order to attain the superior simplicity of divine revelation as it is expressed in the Gospels, above all in the Gospel of St. John and in the Epistles.

St. Thomas, who was never a popularizer but will remain the great classic of theology, progressed from the learned complexity of the disputed questions to the superior simplicity of the beautiful articles of the *Summa theologica,* a simplicity that possesses a high value which often escapes those who are unaware of the learned complexity that prepared the way for it. This simplicity lights our way even if we do not always know at what price it was achieved.

The Common Doctor of the Church shows us the path to follow, and he followed it so well himself that at the end of his life he was unable to dictate the conclusion of the *Summa.* He could no longer descend to the complexity of the questions and articles that he still wished to compose, because he had risen to a contemplative state that touched the things of the kingdom of God in a much simpler way, above the letter and in the spirit.

Superficial oversimplification and finicky concern with minutiae are two enemies of contemplation very different in nature. Contemplation rises between and above these two opposing deviations like a summit which is the goal of prayerful souls.

If we follow closely the doctrine of St. Thomas on all that relates to the intimate life of the Savior we shall see, as if enlightened from above, that our own spiritual life—allowing for inevitable differences—must be an imitation of our divine Model. Indeed, this is well shown in the masterpiece known to all, the *Imitation of Jesus Christ.* May the Lord bless these pages and make them fruitful for the extension of His kingdom and for the salvation of souls!

CONTENTS

PART ONE

THE MYSTERY OF THE INCARNATION AND THE PERSONALITY OF THE SAVIOR

PART TWO

OUR SAVIOR'S LOVE FOR US AND THE MYSTERY OF REDEMPTION

OUR SAVIOR
AND
HIS LOVE FOR US

PART ONE

THE MYSTERY OF THE INCARNATION
AND THE PERSONALITY OF THE SAVIOR

❊ I ❊

THE INTERIOR LIFE AND THE MYSTERY OF CHRIST

> "For to me, to live is Christ."
> Phil. 1:21

IN ORDER first of all to understand the importance of the mystery of Christ for each one of us at every stage of our interior life, even the lowest, let us inquire what is meant by the interior life in the more general meaning of the term, and then in the more specific and deeper sense.

The Intimate Conversation of Every Man with Himself and the Basic Tendencies of the Will

The words "interior life" at once call forth a mental picture of a state of relatively profound recollection that may seem inaccessible to most of us who live in the world, engrossed in our affairs from which at times we seek recreation in amusements of one sort or another. This commonplace impression contains both truth and error. The interior life, as its name indicates, presupposes a certain recollection in God, but this recollection is not as out of reach as may at first appear.

Every man, whether good or evil, holds a more or less serious conversation with himself at certain hours of the day whenever he is alone and often enough even amid the throngs of a bustling city. On his way home from work in the streetcar a laborer, when he is not joking or talking with his fellow workers, may appear pensive: he is holding an interior conversation with himself. What is he thinking of? Perhaps that within a week he will be out of a job. How, then, will he provide for his wife and his children? The tenor of his interior conversation varies with his age. When he is young, he thinks of the future. When he is old, he carries within himself the accumulated experience of some sixty years which tends to be translated into an over-all judgment on life; and this judgment will vary widely, depending on whether a man's life has been good or bad and on whether he is or is not a Christian.

The interior life is an elevated form of the interior conversation of every man, when this conversation becomes or tends to become a conversation with God.

In this intimate discourse which each man has with himself, the life of the senses, of the imagination, of the sense memory, and of the emotions all take part, as is the case with animals. In addition, there is participation by the mind, the intelligence, which passes judgment on life. There is also a more or less latent act of the will, which is created to love and to desire what is good. In this interior state there is a fundamental love, a basic tendency of the will, that differs widely among men.[1]

A man will judge differently about the ultimate goal to be pursued, according as the basic tendency of his will is or is not rectified, good or evil.[2] All men seek happiness. Some seek it where it is to be found, in the true good; others seek it where it is not, in satisfying their sensuality or their pride.

Many persons, without being willing to admit it, love themselves above all else, and more or less consciously make everything converge upon themselves as if they were the center of the universe. Along with this self-love, and as it were on the side, they also have a somewhat ineffectual love for their family or their country. Such men do not have an interior life, for their interior conversation with them-

[1] Tauler has stressed this point emphatically. He brings it up again and again. Cf. *Sermons de Tauler*, translated by Hugueny-Théry (editions de *La vie spirituelle*, 1927). Cf. *ibid.*, Vol. I, Introduction, pp. 79–82.

[2] St. Thomas often states this principle in the form given it by Aristotle (*Ethics*, Bk. III, chap. 5): Depending on whether a man is virtuous or not, he will judge differently as to the ultimate goal to be pursued, for according to his interior disposition the true good appears to him as fitting or not so. Cf. St. Thomas, Ia IIae, q. 9, a. 2; Ia IIae, q. 58, a. 5; and Cajetan's commentary on the latter passage.

This principle, the portion of truth in the philosophy of action, we have stressed elsewhere: *Le réalisme du principe de finalité*, Part II, chap. 6.

selves is of death rather than of life. Instead of elevating them, it lowers them.

According to the Gospel, these souls are in a state of spiritual death or of mortal sin. The basic tendency of their will is turned away from the true good, away from the Sovereign Good which is the principle of all others. What they are really seeking is not truth and the true good of man, of their family, of their children, of their country. On the contrary, they are seeking perpetual pleasure and the money needed to procure it. According to Christian philosophy they live by the quest of pleasurable good and of the useful, without rising to really desire moral good conceived by right reason as the object of virtue.

Their fundamental will is directed toward death, not toward life. They have no interior life. What they discover deep within themselves is death; and hence they seek to escape from themselves, to externalize themselves in study, in science, in art, or in social and political activity, or to live by their imagination and their senses and thus forget their sad evaluation of life which would lead them to discouragement and pessimism.

In this regard Pascal says that the man who would escape from himself by taking up hunting, for instance, prefers the pursuit of the hare to the hare, and in a more elevated order of activity prefers the search for truth to truth itself. He is ever in need of something new. This is the reverse of changeless contemplation of attained truth. Such a man seeks to escape from himself to avoid boredom, emptiness, discouragement. But sometimes the hour of discouragement can become by the grace of God the moment of conversion. This has happened many times: a despairing man about to seek death remembers the name of God, invokes it, and, perceiving the grandeur of the mystery of Christ and of our Redemption, is converted and thenceforth gives himself wholly to the service of God and to the salvation of souls.

On a lower level and without going that far, souls in the state of mortal sin may at moments entertain some such noble thoughts as these: "Honor is the poetry of duty"; "a beautiful life is a thought of youth realized in maturity." Sometimes an actual grace may illuminate one of these noble maxims and lead souls to seek higher things.

When the basic tendencies of a man's will are directed toward the moral good, the object of virtue, when this man desires the good itself or duty, efficaciously and not merely as a fancy, more than he desires pleasure and what is useful to obtain it, then it can be said of him that he already has an interior life. If such are the basic tendencies of his will, then the interior conversation that he holds with himself in hours of solitude or in crowded streets is a conversation that is directed toward life. In reality this man who genuinely and efficaciously loves the good more than himself is beginning to converse interiorly with God and no longer with himself.

St. Thomas [3] says that when a child, even one who has not been baptized, attains to the full age of reason, he must choose the path of goodness and duty in preference to the path of pleasure. He must efficaciously desire the true good and from that instant on orient his entire life toward it. For one wishes the end, even if it is only dimly understood, before wishing the means. But to desire efficaciously the true good more than self is already to love more than oneself the Sovereign Good, God, the Author of our nature. Fallen man is not capable of such an efficacious love without being regenerated through grace, which cures him of original sin. That is why St. Thomas does not hesitate to teach that a child—even one who has not been baptized— who after he has reached the full age of reason efficaciously loves the good more than self, is justified by the baptism of desire, because this love, which is already the efficacious love of God, is not possible to man in his present state without regenerative grace.[4]

Doubtless if this child is not in a Christian environment he will find it most difficult to persevere; but if he does persevere, he will receive ever richer graces and will be saved. In a Christian environment he will naturally receive much more help. That is why it is such a great grace to have been born in the Church.

We cannot overemphasize this point: the moment the fundamental will of a man is efficaciously directed toward the true good, the man is justified, he is in the state of grace, he possesses within himself the

---

[3] *Summa theol.*, Ia IIae, q. 89, a. 6.   [4] Cf. St. Thomas, Ia IIae, q. 109, a. 3.

seed of eternal life. He already has a certain interior life which is truly alive, even if it is not yet as recollected as might be desirable.

The man who has persevered in the state of grace for a considerable time comes to have especially in moments of solitude, in the silence of a church, or in the midst of a crowd, an interior conversation with himself which is no longer one of egoism and self-love, but which is already in its own way a conversation with God.

As we ride in a crowded bus of an evening we can sometimes, even without having the gift of the discernment of spirits, recognize those men and women who have gone astray in misconduct and are the despair of their families—if they have any—and those who on the contrary live by the thought of the good and gropingly by the thought of God, by a faith that may indeed need to be enlightened but that is nevertheless the pupil of their mind's eye. These persons offer up a short prayer from time to time; and when they are not praying, their interior conversation does not separate them from God. They are the living proofs of the truth of Christ's consoling words to His apostles: "For he that is not against you, is for you." [5] Often they seem happy to meet a priest and sometimes ask him to pray for them and for their families.

They are good at heart. God is hidden in the depth of their hearts, and He draws them to Himself by lights and graces proportioned to their condition. In their own way these men are treading the path toward eternal life. Are there many of them of an evening in a crowded bus? God knows who they are. In any case we should remember that it is never by chance that two spiritual and immortal souls meet, wherever it may be, in a train or elsewhere, especially if one of them is in the state of grace, even more so if one is very closely united to God and can through prayer call down on the other the light of life.

What has just been said gives us a distant glimpse of the interior life, what it must become in a truly Christian soul that is destined to tend ever more rapidly toward God. As a stone falls faster when approaching the earth that attracts it, so must souls tend more rapidly toward God in the measure that they come closer to Him and that He draws them to Himself with increasing force. Their fundamental will

[5] Mark 9:39; Luke 9:50.

must tend with ever-increasing efficacy toward God. They must therefore, especially in moments of solitude whether in a church or in a crowded street, converse ever more intimately, not in a selfish manner with themselves, but generously with God who dwells within them.

Their fundamental will thus rectified and supernaturalized must be more and more victorious over selfishness in all its forms. They must reach out beyond themselves, and instead of seeking to relate everything to themselves they must try to relate everything to God. Their fundamental will must become zeal for the glory of God and for the salvation of souls. Then they will have an interior life that is truly fruitful for themselves and for their neighbor.

Clearly, the interior life is all that really matters for each one of us. It is much more indispensable than what we speak of as the intellectual life. For without a true interior life man is the prey to selfishness and pride and can have no wholesome, lasting, and profound influence on society.

This true interior life is realized in its fullness by the saints, but especially by the Saint par excellence, our Lord Jesus Christ. Hence the necessity of reflecting, and reflecting with love, upon the interior life of Jesus and of not being contented with knowing Him from the outside in a purely historical manner, as the speculative theologian may do when he does not strive hard enough to live what he teaches.

What Christ Must Be to Us

The need of reflecting on the interior life of the Savior is particularly great in the present period of general confusion, when individuals and entire peoples misunderstand the ultimate end of human life and forget the profound difference between perishable, material goods and immutable, spiritual goods. Material goods divide us in the measure that we eagerly seek them; for they cannot belong at one and the same time to everyone as a whole and to each one in particular. A given house and lot cannot belong integrally and simultaneously to several men any more than the same territory can belong to several nations.

On the other hand, as St. Thomas, following St. Augustine,[6] has

---

[6] Cf. St. Thomas, Ia IIae, q. 28, a. 4 ad 2; IIIa, q. 23, a. 1 ad 3.

often remarked: spiritual goods can belong at the same time and in plenitude to all and to each; and they unite us the more in the measure that we seek them. Thus, each one of us can live by the same truth, by the same virtue, by the same God, by the same Christ our Savior.

Every Christian should ultimately be able to say, as did St. Paul: "To me, to live is Christ." [7]

As St. Thomas remarks in explaining these words,[8] a man's life is what interests him most. It is by living that his faculties reach fulfillment. It is to life that his existence is dedicated. For example, the Angelic Doctor adds, for some, to live is to hunt; for others, it is study, intellectual activity; for others still, to live consists in exterior activity. For a soldier, to live is to engage in military service. Finally, to the Christian, to live—once he has become fully conscious of the grandeur of his destiny—is Christ. This is particularly true of the priest, the apostle, whose mission it is to reveal to others the mystery of Christ.

Indeed, it is not enough for us to understand Christ's message. We must also put it into practice. Jesus Himself has told us in the conclusion of His Sermon on the Mount: "Everyone therefore that heareth these My words and doth them, shall be likened to a wise man that built his house upon a rock. And the rain fell and the floods came and the winds blew, and they beat upon that house, and it fell not for it was founded on a rock. And everyone that heareth these My words and doth them not, shall be like a foolish man that built his house upon the sand. And the rain fell and the floods came and the winds blew, and they beat upon that house, and it fell, and great was the fall thereof." [9]

In his commentary on St. Matthew, St. Thomas remarks: The rock on which we must build signifies Christ Himself: as St. Paul tells us, the spiritual rock is Christ.[10] . . . But there are those who listen to Christ's message only in order to know it (without putting it into practice); they build on the intelligence only, and that is to build upon the sand. . . . Others listen to His message in order to put it into practice and to love God and their neighbor; these build on rock . . .

[7] Phil. 1:21. [8] *In Epistolam ad Philipp.*, 1:21.
[9] Matt. 7:24 f. [10] I Cor. 10:4.

and they can ask with St. Paul: 'Who then shall separate us from the love of Christ?' " [11]

These words, written by a man of learning like St. Thomas, are significant.[12] For to St. Thomas, to live was not only to study. To live was Christ, to whom he had consecrated all his labors and his entire life.

Certainly, both intellectual and exterior activity are necessary. But the Christian must love his work not only for the natural satisfaction and the profit he derives from it, but for Christ who must be known and loved, "that a man may live not to himself, but to God." [13] In this way his powers are increased tenfold, even a hundredfold. He is no longer giving only himself, he is giving Christ for the salvation of souls.

To live more and more by Christ we must die to ourselves, that is, to the life of egoism, sensuality, and pride. "For to me, to live is Christ, and to die is gain." We must stop making ourselves the center of existence, and unconsciously relating everything to ourselves. On the contrary, we must relate everything to God. This is the precious fruit of the spirit of sacrifice, which progressively causes to die within us all that is disorderly. The spirit of sacrifice gives us peace and the tranquillity of order by making us give first place in our souls to charity, to the love of God and of souls, a love that is ultimately victorious over all egoism and all disorderly love of self.

As we mentioned at the beginning of this chapter, man since his fall is inclined consciously or unconsciously to relate everything to himself, to think continually of himself, and to love himself in prefer-

[11] Rom. 8:35.

[12] St. Thomas' own words are as follows (*In Matthaeum*, 7:26): "Fundamentum est illud super quod ponit aliquis intentionem suam. Quidam enim audiunt ut sciant, et hi aedificant super intellectum: et haec est aedificatio super arenam. . . . Quidam autem audit ut faciat et diligat; et hic aedificat super petram, quia super firmum et stabile. . . . Istud enim fundamentum est super caritatem. Quis nos separabit a caritate Christi?"

[13] St. Thomas, IIa IIae, q. 17, a. 6 ad 3. In his commentary on the Epistle to the Galatians 2:20, St. Thomas also says: "Homo quantum ad illud dicitur vivere, in quo principaliter firmat suum affectum, et in quo maxime delectatur. Unde et homines qui in studio seu in venationibus maxime delectantur, dicunt hoc eorum vitam esse: quilibet autem homo habet quemdam privavivit quaerens tantum quod suum est, soli sibi vivit. . . . Cum vero quaerit bona aliorum, dicitur etiam illis vivere." In this sense St. Paul could truly say: "For me, to live is Christ."

ence to all else. If, however, he listens to Christ's message and puts it into practice, the day will come when, instead of thinking continually of himself and of relating everything to himself, he will live by Christ, and through Him he will think almost always of God, the Supreme Truth and Goodness, and he will relate everything to Him. Then will the fundamental will of his soul be truly rectified and supernaturalized; his interior life will be founded in the image of God's, in whom the Word, the expression of the thought of the Father, produces Love by spiration and makes all things converge toward the Supreme Good.

It is from this point of view that we must meditate upon St. Thomas' treatise on the Incarnation. When, during the last days of his life, the saintly doctor was so absorbed in superior contemplation that he could no longer dictate the last pages of his *Summa,* he thought that the mysteries hidden in Christ are inexhaustible and that the doctors had discovered only a minute portion of them.

St. John of the Cross tells us the same thing in the *Spiritual Canticle,*[14] in which he calls these mysteries "caverns" to symbolize their unfathomable depth. May the Lord deign to give us a deep and keen understanding of these mysteries so that we may the better see the radiation of His goodness.

[14] Stanza 37.

JESUS, THE SON OF GOD ACCORDING TO THE FIRST THREE GOSPELS

IF WE would fathom the interior life of our Lord, we must first hear the testimony He has given of Himself, of His divine sonship, and of His mission as Redeemer.

We shall begin by examining this testimony as it is presented in the first three Gospels, written between A.D. 50 and A.D. 70. Next we shall observe in the Acts of the Apostles, composed around A.D. 63–64, how St. Peter in his first sermons proclaimed Jesus to be the Son of God. In the third place we shall note St. Paul's testimony on the divinity of Christ as expressed in the first epistles, written between 48 and 59. Finally we shall study on this point the Gospel of St. John, written between A.D. 80 and A.D. 100 precisely to defend Christ's divinity against the denials of the first heretics.

The historical study of the Gospels has its use, especially from the point of view of apologetics, as a means of enlightening unbelievers and of answering their objections. However, such a study is not altogether indispensable. For, even if primitive documents were lost, the living tradition and the living magisterium of the Church would suffice. This oral tradition preceded Scripture, and through it in the first place the word of God was transmitted by our Lord and by the apostles.

We know that many liberal Protestants, and after them the modernists, have maintained that the divinity of Jesus is not expressed in the Gospels, but that it is a dogma deduced by Christian thought from the notion of the Messiah.[1] They further hold that in all the Gospel texts the name "Son of God" is equivalent only to "Messiah" and does not signify that Jesus is in reality and by nature the Son of God.

---

[1] Cf. Denzinger, *Enchiridion*, nos. 2027–2038.

Several rationalists, among them Renan, B. Weiss, H. Wendt, and A. Harnack, have recognized in Christ a certain divine sonship superior to Messiahship. Yet they deny that by reason of this sonship Jesus is truly God. Renan, concluding his *Life of Jesus*, writes: "Rest now in thy glory, noble pioneer! Thy work is done; thy divinity founded. . . . Henceforth, beyond frailty, thou shalt behold from the heights of divine peace the infinite results of thy acts. . . . Between thee and God men will no longer distinguish." [2]

A little further on, Renan adds: "In order to make himself adored to this degree, he must have been adorable. . . . The faith, the enthusiasm, the constancy of the first Christian generation is not explicable, except by supposing, at the origin of the whole movement, a man of surpassing greatness.[3] . . . This sublime person, who each day still presides over the destiny of the world, we may call divine, not in the sense that Jesus has absorbed all the divine, or has been adequate to it (to employ the expression of the schoolmen), but in the sense that Jesus is the one who caused his fellow-men to make the greatest step toward the divine." [4]

Among conservative Protestants, F. Godet in Switzerland, Stevens, Gore, Ottley, and Sanday in England have in recent years defended the divinity of Jesus as expressed not only in the Fourth Gospel and in the epistles of St. Paul but in the Synoptics as well.[5]

To rightly understand the testimony of the Gospels, we must remember that they contain over fifty passages in which Jesus is called the "Son of God." It is important also that we grasp the sense in which these words, "Son of God," must be taken.

In Scripture the word "son" is used with reference to another man either in the strict sense to denote one who is born of another, or in the broader sense to designate a disciple or an adopted heir. Likewise the word "son" is used with respect to God, either in the broad sense that Christians are the children of God and live by His Spirit, or in the strict and exact sense reserved to the Second Person of the Blessed

---

[2] Ernest Renan, *The Life of Jesus* (Everyman's Library, 1934), p. 227.
[3] *Ibid.*, pp. 237 f. [4] *Ibid.*, p. 243.
[5] See the account of their teaching in Rev. Marius Lepin's work, *Jésus Messie et Fils de Dieu*, p. 237.

Trinity, who in the Prologue of St. John's Gospel, is called "the only-begotten Son who is in the bosom of the Father." [6] We shall see that even in the Synoptic Gospels Jesus is called the Son of God in the strict and exact and most elevated sense, inasmuch as He has declared that He not only participates in the divine nature through grace, as we do, but that He possesses the divine nature with all its properties and rights.

Jesus' Reserve in Manifesting His Divinity

It should be noted that Jesus manifested His divine sonship only by degrees. More important still, when in Caesarea St. Peter said to our Lord in the name of the apostles: "Thou art Christ, the Son of the living God," St. Matthew reports: "Then He commanded His disciples that they should tell no one that He was Jesus the Christ." [7] Likewise one day when He was casting out unclean spirits, the latter cried out: "Thou art the Son of God," and St. Mark tells us: "He strictly charged them that they should not make Him known." [8] Again, after the Transfiguration, our Lord said to the three apostles whom He had taken with Him to Thabor: "Tell the vision to no man." [9]

Why this reserve? Because men's souls were not yet prepared to receive such an exalted revelation and they could not have borne it. In fact, Jesus saw that many Jews understood the prophecies only in a material sense, that they were awaiting a temporal Messiah who would restore the kingdom of Israel and set them over the other peoples. Thus, if from the start of His ministry Jesus had declared Himself to be the Messiah, the Son of God, He would have aroused a wholly exterior enthusiasm in this throng which craved wonders and earthly prosperity, and the true meaning of His words would have been lost. Even at the end of His ministry Jesus said to the apostles: "I have yet many things to say to you: but you cannot bear them now." [10] The sublime truth of the mystery of the Incarnation had to be unveiled slowly in the subdued light of the parables, so that little

[6] John 1:18. [7] Matt. 16:20. [8] Mark 3:12.
[9] Matt. 17:9; Mark 9:8. [10] John 16:12.

by little souls might grow and become capable of hearing the divine message.

We have here an example of Christ's humility: although He had infinite treasures of light, love, and power, He remained hidden, never seeking to astonish or arouse admiration. He wished to save souls by working secretly deep within men's hearts. Far from declaring His divine sonship, as He did at the end of His ministry before His death, He at first tended to conceal it so that those whom He wished to enlighten and mold would not be dazzled or blinded by a light that was too powerful. He disposed them progressively to receive greater light. How totally differently are His ways from those of false wonder-workers who would astound and deceive! There is a great lesson here for us: souls must be taught the truth gradually, as much of it as they can bear at a time.

But Christ's testimony, very reserved at first, became more and more articulate until, during the last days of His ministry, it became clear and luminous to all who had ears to hear.

As recorded in the Synoptic Gospels, Jesus first manifested His divinity by claiming certain privileges, and He then affirmed with ever-increasing clarity that He was the Son of God. Let us follow this ascending progression, for it is the accomplishment of all the Old Testament prophecies, the fullness of revelation bearing the authentic mark of God's works, *fortiter et suaviter*, power and gentleness.

The Divine Rights Claimed by Jesus

Jesus has claimed seven major privileges that can belong to God alone.

According to St. Matthew and St. Mark, Jesus proclaimed Himself to be greater than the prophet Jonas, greater than Solomon,[11] greater than David, who called Him his Lord in Psalm 109: "The Lord said to my Lord: Sit Thou at My right hand, until I make Thy enemies Thy foolstool." With respect to this prophecy Jesus said to the Pharisees: "If David then call Him Lord, how is He his son?"

[11] Matt. 12:41 f.

St. Matthew adds: "And no man was able to answer Him a word." [12]

Jesus has also shown Himself to be greater than Moses and Elias, who appeared at His side at the Transfiguration.[13] He is greater than John the Baptist, as we see by His answer to the precursor's disciples who had been sent to ask Him: "Art Thou He that art to come, or look we for another?" [14]

He stands forth even greater than the angels, for we find in St. Mark [15] and in St. Matthew [16] that, after His victory over Satan, "the angels ministered to Him." And He Himself said: "The Son of man shall come in the glory of His Father with His angels: and then will He render to every man according to his works." [17] "And He shall send His angels . . . and they shall gather together His elect from the four winds, from the farthest parts of the heavens to the utmost bounds of them." [18] Neither Isaias nor any other prophet ever spoke of sending *his* angels.

Now, He who is superior to all the prophets and to the angels is superior to all creatures.

Moreover, Jesus demands with regard to Himself faith, obedience, and love, even to the abnegation of all contrary affections and to the sacrifice of one's life. In foretelling the persecutions of the first three centuries, He said: "A man's enemies shall be they of his own household. He that loveth father or mother more than Me, is not worthy of Me; and he that loveth son or daughter more than Me, is not worthy of Me. And he that taketh not up his cross, and followeth Me, is not worthy of Me. He that findeth his life, shall lose it: and he that shall lose his life for Me, shall find it." [19]

Jesus knew, when He spoke thus to His apostles, that they would suffer martyrdom. These words, which were to be fulfilled especially during the persecutions, would bespeak intolerable arrogance if Jesus were not God. What prophet ever dared to say: "He that loveth father or mother more than me is not worthy of me"? As for the saints, the higher they rise the less they speak of themselves; their ego tends to be obliterated before God. How is it, then, that Jesus spoke with

---

[12] Matt. 22:45; Mark 12:36. [13] Matt. 17:3. [14] Matt. 11:3, 11.
[15] Mark 1:13. [16] Matt. 4:11. [17] Matt. 16:27.
[18] Matt. 24:31. [19] Matt. 10:36 f.; Luke 14:26.

such majesty of Himself, He who was so humble that He accepted the deepest humiliations for our salvation? Again, after the rich young man had refused His call to perfection, He said: "Amen I say to you, there is no man who hath left house or brethren or sisters or father or mother or children or lands for My sake and for the gospel, who shall not receive a hundred times as much now in this time . . . with persecutions: and in the world to come life everlasting." [20] "He that is not with Me, is against Me: and he that gathereth not with Me, scattereth." [21]

St. Thomas Aquinas, in his Commentary on St. Matthew, 12:30, sees in these last words a manifestation of Christ's divinity. God alone, he remarks, is the final end toward which every man must tend, and that is why he who is not with God (who does not tend toward Him) is separated (or turned away) from Him. That is why Elias said: [22] "How long do you halt between two sides? If the Lord be God, follow Him." [23] But, St. Thomas continues, a mere man could not say: "He that is not with Me is against Me." While it is permissible to remain neutral or indifferent with regard to a man who is a man and no more, one cannot remain neutral or indifferent with respect to God, our final end. Therefore, since Jesus has spoken these words, it must mean that He is superior to all creatures.

About the very beginning of His ministry, Christ also declared in His Sermon on the Mount: "Blessed are ye when they shall revile you and persecute you and speak all that is evil against you, untruly, for My sake." [24] "For My sake" means to suffer persecution for justice' sake and for the noblest of all causes, an act that will be richly rewarded in heaven.

Jesus calls for obedience and perfect abnegation. He also speaks as the supreme Lawgiver, equal to the Lawgiver of Sinai who gave Moses the ancient law for the chosen people. Since Christ came to complete this divine law and to purge from it the false interpretations of the rabbis, He expressed Himself several times in the following manner: "You have heard it was said to them of old. . . . But I say to you. . . ." [25] Thus He forbade divorce, which Moses

---

[20] Mark 10:29 f.   [21] Matt. 12:30.   [22] III Kings 18:21.
[23] Matt. 5:11.   [24] Matt. 5:11.   [25] Matt. 5:21–48.

had permitted only because of the hardness of the Israelites' hearts.[26] He also proclaimed Himself "Lord of the Sabbath." [27]

In addition, He performed miracles in His own name, using the form of a command. To the paralytic He said: "Arise, . . . and go into thy house." [28] He raised Jairus' daughter by saying to her: "Talitha cumi," that is to say: "Damsel (I say to thee), arise." [29] He also brought back to life the son of the widow of Naim, saying to him: "Young man, I say to thee, arise." [30] He commanded the sea swollen by the storm: "Peace, be still." And St. Mark tells us, "the wind ceased; and there was made a great calm." [31] And they feared exceedingly: and they said to one another: "Who is this (thinkest thou) that both wind and sea obey Him?"

The apostles, on the contrary, performed miracles in the name of Jesus.[32] Peter said: "In the name of Jesus Christ of Nazareth, arise, and walk. . . . By the name of our Lord Jesus Christ of Nazareth . . . this man standeth here before you whole." [33]

In addition, Jesus claims the power to remit sins, to make souls over, to fill them once again with divine life, a power which, the Pharisees recognized, can belong only to God. This calls to mind the scene described in St. Matthew: "And behold they brought to Him one sick of the palsy lying in a bed. And Jesus, seeing their faith, said to the man sick of the palsy: Be of good heart, son, thy sins are forgiven thee. And behold some of the scribes said within themselves: He blasphemeth. And Jesus seeing their thoughts, said: Why do you think evil in your hearts? Whether is easier, to say, thy sins are forgiven thee: or to say, Arise, and walk? But that you may know that the Son of man hath power on earth to forgive sins (then said He to the man sick of the palsy), Arise, take up thy bed, and go into thy house." [34] St. Matthew adds, "And the multitude seeing it, feared, and glorified God that gave such power to men."

Likewise He said: "Come to Me, all you that labor, and are burdened, and I will refresh you." [35] Beyond this, He claimed the right to communicate to others the power to remit sins: He said to His

[26] Matt. 5:32; 19:9. [27] Mark 2:27 f. [28] Matt. 9:6; Mark 2:9.
[29] Mark 5:41. [30] Luke 7:14. [31] Mark 4:39.
[32] Matt. 7:22. [33] Acts 3:6; 4:10. [34] Matt. 9:2–8.
[35] Matt. 11:28.

apostles: "Amen I say to you, whatsoever you shall bind upon earth, shall be bound also in heaven; and whatsoever you shall loose upon earth, shall be loosed also in heaven." [36]

Jesus has claimed not only the power to remit sins, but also the power of judging the living and the dead. He answered Caiphas: "And you shall see the Son of man sitting on the right hand of God, and coming with the clouds of heaven." [37] "And He shall send His angels with a trumpet, and a great voice: and they shall gather together His elect. . . ." [38]

He also promised to send the Holy Ghost, saying to the disciples before the Ascension: "And I send the promise of My Father upon you: but stay you in the city, till you be endued with power from on high." [39] Therefore He is not inferior to the Holy Ghost whom He promised to send.

Finally, Jesus accepted adoration,[40] of which Peter, Paul, and Barnabas—and even the angels, in the Apocalypse—declared themselves unworthy.[41]

Thus it is clear that Jesus, according to the Synoptic Gospels, claimed for Himself seven major privileges which can belong to God alone, namely:

1. He is superior to all creatures: greater than Jonas, than Solomon, than David, than Moses, than Elias, than John the Baptist; and He is superior to the angels, who are "His angels."

2. He demands with regard to Himself, faith, obedience, and love, even to the abnegation of any contrary affection and to the sacrifice of one's life.

3. He spoke as the supreme Lawgiver, in the Sermon on the Mount.

4. He performed miracles in His own name.

5. He claimed the power to remit sins and has conferred this power on others.

6. He claimed the power to judge the living and the dead of all human generations.

---

[36] Matt. 18:18; 16:19.

[38] Matt. 24:31.

[40] Matt. 8:2; 28:9, 17; Mark 5:6.

[37] Mark 14:62; 8:38; 13:26.

[39] Luke 24:49.

[41] Acts 10:25 f.; 14:14; Apoc. 19:10; 22:8.

7. He promised to send the Holy Ghost, and His promise was accomplished on Pentecost.

Jesus can claim these rights and powers only if He is not merely God's envoy, the Messiah, but God Himself. He affirmed His Godhead only in a veiled manner in order to prepare souls little by little to receive a more explicit affirmation, which was to become increasingly clear and powerful up to the moment of His condemnation to death.

The Divine Sonship of Jesus according to the Synoptic Gospels

In the first three Gospels our Lord not only claims privileges and rights that belong to God alone, but on several occasions He declared that He is the Son of God in the strict and proper sense, which is totally different from the meaning of the term applicable to the souls of the just as a whole.

First of all He declared Himself to be the Son of God when speaking of the happiness in store for the humble who answer the divine call. In St. Matthew we read: "I confess to Thee, O Father, Lord of heaven and earth, because Thou hast hid these things from the wise and the prudent, and hast revealed them to little ones. Yea, Father, for so hath it seemed good in Thy sight. All things are delivered to Me by My Father. [He does not say merely 'our Father,' as we do, but 'My Father.'] And no one knoweth the Son, but the Father: neither doth anyone know the Father, but the Son, and he to whom it shall please the Son to reveal Him." [42]

These words are also recorded in St. Luke,[43] and the authenticity of this text is admitted not only by Catholic exegetes but by the majority of Protestant critics as well. What is here affirmed is the equality of the Father and the Son with regard to knowledge and cognoscibility: "No one knoweth the Son but the Father: neither doth anyone know the Father, but the Son." The Father is by nature unknowable, for He is beyond the reach of natural knowledge. The same is true of the Son. Yet they know each other perfectly. This equality in knowledge, as St. Thomas remarks,[44] presupposes consubstantiality,

---

[42] Matt. 11:25 f.   [43] Luke 10:21.   [44] *Comment. in Ev. sec. Matthaeum,* 11:27.

or the possession of the same divine substance. In other words, it is the common substance of the Father and of the Son which is said to be unknowable inasmuch as it is beyond natural cognition. If no one knoweth the Son but the Father, it is because, like the Father, the Son is inaccessible to any created natural knowledge; therefore, it is because He is God.

Loisy, among the Modernists, has conceded this traditional explanation of the text. He even goes on to remark that its meaning is substantially the same as the following words of St. John: "No man hath seen God at any time: the only-begotten Son who is in the bosom of the Father, He hath declared Him." [45] That these texts of St. John and St. Matthew are equal in sublimity, Loisy recognizes. Yet he adds without any basis whatever, and against almost all other critics including the liberal Protestants, that, while this affirmation is contained in St. Matthew and St. Luke, Jesus did not make it Himself, it having merely been attributed to Him by Christian tradition. [46]

Jesus made a similar declaration in His response to Peter's confession at Caesarea: "Simon Peter answered and said: Thou art Christ, the Son of the living God. And Jesus answering, said to him: Blessed art thou, Simon Bar-Jona: because flesh and blood hath not revealed it to thee, but My Father who is in heaven." [47]

Some critics say that it cannot be proved historically that in this confession Peter affirmed anything more than the Messiahship. For Peter's words are reported by St. Mark (8:29) as: "Thou art the Christ"; [48] and by St. Luke (9:20) as: "The Christ of God." [49] It is only St. Matthew who records the words: "Thou art Christ the Son of the living God." As a matter of fact, on the basis of Peter's words alone it would be difficult to prove that they affirm anything beyond the Messiahship. But we also have Jesus' answer: "Blessed art thou, Simon Bar-Jona: because flesh and blood hath not revealed it to thee, but My Father who is in heaven." By these words Jesus showed that Peter had affirmed more than the Messiahship, for the signs of the

---

[45] John 1:18. Cf. Alfred Firmin Loisy, *The Gospel and the Church*, trans. by Christopher Home, 1903.

[46] Against this opinion of Loisy's, cf. Father Lagrange, *Revue biblique*, April, 1903, p. 304; also Lepin, *op. cit.*, p. 323.

[47] Matt. 16:16.   [48] Mark 8:29.   [49] Luke 9:20.

Messiahship had already been manifest since the beginning of the Savior's ministry, and several of the apostles had already recognized Him to be the Messiah. Thus Andrew, Philip, and Nathaniel [50] had already recognized Jesus as the Messiah, and for this reason followed Him.

Jesus had already clearly enumerated the signs of His Messiahship to the disciples of St. John the Baptist.[51] Thus the Messiahship in itself did not require any such revelation as that spoken of by our Lord in His answer to Peter: "Blessed art thou, Simon Bar-Jona: because flesh and blood hath not revealed it to thee, but My Father who is in heaven." These words are equivalent in meaning to the preceding text of St. Matthew: "And no one knoweth the Son, but the Father." [52] Therefore it can be said: If Peter could know only through the Father what he affirmed concerning Jesus, he must have affirmed His divine sonship. It does not, however, follow that Peter was given to know through faith at that moment the nature of this divine sonship as explicitly as it would later be defined by the Church.[53]

In the parable of the vineyard and the wicked husbandmen, there is a third affirmation of Christ's divine sonship. It is recorded by all Synoptics.[54] The authenticity of these texts is conceded by most critics, even by many liberal Protestants. St. Mark tells us: "And He [Jesus in the presence of the scribes and chief priests] began to speak to them in parables: A certain man planted a vineyard . . . and let it to husbandmen; and went into a far country. And at the season he sent to the husbandmen a servant to receive of the husbandmen of the fruit of the vineyard. Who having laid hands on him, beat him, and sent him away empty. And again he sent them another servant; and him they wounded in the head, and used him reproachfully. And again he sent another, and him they killed: and many others, of whom some they beat, and others they killed. Therefore having yet one son, most dear to him; he also sent him unto them last of all, saying: They will reverence my son. But the husbandmen said one to another:

[50] John 1:41, 49.   [51] Matt. 11:4.   [52] Matt. 11:27.
[53] Cf. Lepin, *op. cit.*, p. 332.   [54] Matt. 21:33–46; Mark 12:1–12; Luke 20:1–19.

This is the heir; come let us kill him; and the inheritance shall be ours. And laying hold on him, they killed him, and cast him out of the vineyard. What therefore will the lord of the vineyard do? He will come and destroy those husbandmen; and will give the vineyard to others." [55]

At the conclusion of this parable, Jesus at once added: "And have you not read this Scripture: 'The stone which the builders rejected, the same is made the head of the corner. By the Lord has this been done, and it is wonderful in our eyes.' " [56] St. Mark reports that thereupon Jesus' enemies "sought to lay hands on Him, but they feared the people. For they knew that He spoke this parable to them. And leaving Him, they went their way."

The application of this parable of the wicked husbandmen is in fact evident. The servants of the lord of the vineyard, whom he sent to the husbandmen, were the prophets. A little later, Jesus tells the Pharisees unequivocally: "You are the sons of them that killed the prophets. Fill ye up then the measure of your fathers. You serpents, generation of vipers, how will you flee from the judgment of hell? Therefore behold I send to you prophets and wise men and scribes: and some of them you will put to death and crucify, and some you will scourge. . . . That upon you may come all the just blood that hath been shed upon the earth. . . . Jerusalem, Jerusalem, thou that killest the prophets, and stonest them that are sent unto thee, how often would I have gathered together thy children . . . and thou wouldest not?" [57]

Therefore, if the servants of the Lord of the vineyard are the prophets, His dearly beloved Son is more than a prophet and Messiah, He is truly His Son.

This parable describes exactly the same mystery as that spoken of at the beginning of the Epistle to the Hebrews: "God, who at sundry times and in divers manners, spoke in times past to the fathers by the prophets, last of all, in these days hath spoken to us by His Son, whom He hath appointed heir of all things, by whom also He made the world. Who being the brightness of His glory, and the figure of His

[55] Mark 12:1 f.   [56] Ps. 117:22.   [57] Matt. 23:31-37.

substance, and upholding all things by the word of His power, making purgation of sins, sitteth on the right hand of the majesty on high." [58]

What is more striking about the application of the parable of the wicked husbandmen is that the priests of the synagogue who heard and understood it were the men who by very reason of their function were supposed to know the Scriptures and the signs of the Messiahship best. Therefore they should have been the first to welcome the Messiah. Yet it was they who resisted Him most obstinately. God offered them the fullness of revelation and great glory: participation in Christ's work and entrance with Him into eternal life. They preferred a merely human glory to one that was wholly divine: "to sit in the first chairs in the synagogues" [59] and to remain there. It follows that in trying to resist the majesty of God they were overwhelmed by His glory, which was to have become theirs. As they were too deeply attached to things of least value—their human traditions and their status, to which they clung jealously—their souls did not open up to receive the great gift of salvation that God wished to give them. Thus the apostate priest was crushed beneath the grandeur of his priesthood because he did not receive with humility the immense grace it bestowed on him. "He hath put down the mighty from their seat, and hath exalted the humble." [60] Zaccheus' eyes were opened, whereas the priests of the synagogue were blinded.

There is a fourth affirmation of Jesus' divine sonship in His question to the Pharisees: "What think you of Christ; whose son is He? They say to Him: David's. He saith to them: How then doth David in spirit call Him Lord, saying: The Lord said to my Lord, Sit on My right hand, until I make Thy enemies Thy footstool? If David then call Him Lord, how is He his son?" [61] St. Matthew adds, "And no man was able to answer Him a word: neither durst any man from that day forth ask Him any more questions." [62]

The authenticity of this text is admitted by the principal liberal critics. The Lord referred to in the psalm which Jesus quotes is superior to David, and equal to the highest Lord, God the Father.

[58] Heb. 1:1-3.   [59] Mark 12:39.   [60] Luke 1:52.
[61] Matt. 22:42-45.   [62] Cf. also Luke 20:44; Mark 12:37.

A fifth affirmation of the divinity of Jesus is to be found in His answer to Caiphas during the Passion. In St. Matthew we read: "And the high priest said to Him: I adjure Thee by the living God, that Thou tell us if Thou be the Christ the Son of God. Jesus saith to him: Thou hast said it. Nevertheless I say to you, hereafter you shall see the Son of man sitting on the right hand of the power of God, and coming in the clouds of heaven. Then the high priest rent his garments, saying: He hath blasphemed; what further need have we of witnesses? Behold now you have heard the blasphemy." [63]

It was not merely His Messiahship that Jesus affirmed in His answer to the high priest. For divine sonship and the privilege of being seated at the right hand of the Almighty as well as of exercising sovereign power are not attributes of the Messiah as such. That is why Caiphas tore his garments and cried out "He hath blasphemed," as is recorded in the first three Gospels. The Gospel of St. John throws light on the other three. In St. John we find that after the paralytic's cure ". . . the Jews sought the more to kill Him, because He did not only break the Sabbath, but also said God was His Father, making Himself equal to God." [64] Again in St. John, after Jesus had said "I and the Father are one," we read: "The Jews then took up stones to stone Him." [65] This is the explanation of Caiphas' question to Jesus, for the high priest was aware of Christ's earlier declarations: "I adjure Thee by the living God, that Thou tell us if Thou be the Christ the Son of God." Finally, in St. John there is another text that throws light on the Synoptics: "The Jews answered him: We have a law; and according to the law He ought to die, because He made Himself the Son of God." [66] Certainly it would not have been considered a crime for our Lord to affirm His Messiahship, for everybody was at that time expecting the Messiah, the anointed one, God's envoy. Thus He must have affirmed that He was superior to the Messiah.

In St. Matthew there is a sixth affirmation of Jesus' divinity. It appears after the recital of the Savior's resurrection in the formula of baptism: "And Jesus coming, spoke to them, saying: All power is given to Me in heaven and in earth. Going therefore, teach ye all

[63] Matt. 26:63 f.   [64] John 5:18.   [65] John 10:31.
[66] John 19:7.

nations; baptizing them in the name of the Father and of the Son
and of the Holy Ghost. Teaching them to observe all things whatsoever I have commanded you: and behold I am with you all days,
even to the consummation of the world." [67] Thus ends the Gospel of
St. Matthew.

Loisy denies without valid reason the authenticity of the baptismal
formula, as having been pronounced by Jesus Himself. But he at
least recognizes that the use of this formula is attested to in *Didache*
7:1, and it is probable that it was universally accepted by the Churches
at the beginning of the second century. [68]

Now in this formula of baptism the Son is equal to the Father and
to the Holy Ghost. But if He were not God He would be infinitely
inferior to Them. As to the closing words, "I am with you all days,
even to the consummation of the world," they give promise of divine
assistance which is a fulfillment of Isaias' prophecy: "And they shall
call His name Emmanuel, which being interpreted is God with us." [69]

What are we to infer from these six affirmations? We must conclude, in opposition to the Modernists, that in the Synoptic Gospels
the declarations of Jesus regarding His eminent dignity proclaim far
more than His Messiahship and announce the divine sonship which
is His alone.

Moreover, this divine sonship is superior to Messiahship, not only
in the sense conceded by such rationalists as Harnack, but in the
sense that it places Christ above all creatures, equal to God and Himself God, the Second Person of the Blessed Trinity.

That is the meaning of the words quoted above: "No one knoweth
the Son, but the Father: neither doth any one know the Father, but
the Son." Equality of knowledge. "Going therefore teach ye all
nations: baptizing them in the name of the Father and of the Son
and of the Holy Ghost." And according to the Synoptics as according
to St. John, Jesus was crucified because He had declared He was the
Son of God, equal to His Father. It should be added that in St. Luke
the angel Gabriel declared to Mary: "The Holy which shall be born
of thee shall be called the Son of God." [70] Also, in St. Matthew it is

[67] Matt. 28:18 f.   [68] Loisy, *Les Evangiles Synoptiques*, II, 751.
[69] Isa. 7:14; Matt. 1:23.   [70] Luke 1:23; cf. Matt. 1:20 f.

recorded that when Jesus was baptized by John the Baptist, the Precursor "saw the Spirit of God descending as a dove, and coming upon Him. And behold a voice from heaven, saying: This is My beloved Son, in whom I am well pleased." [71]

What is truly remarkable is that those who should have been the first to recognize Christ's mission failed to do so. This throws a searching light on the meaning of a divine mission. Father Clerissac tells us that "The Incarnation is a mission of the Son of God in the world and is propagated through the multiplicity of ecclesiastical ministries in all epochs." [72] Thus the Church carries on Christ's mission. She has been sent by Him, and she preserves His spirit. Our task is to be docile to her voice, which transmits God's word to us and which leads us, sometimes amid many snares and errors and ruins, toward eternity.[78]

[71] Matt. 3:16 f. [72] *Le mystère de l'Eglise,* chap. 7.

[78] *Ibid.* "The unmistakable sign that we are adhering to the full spirit of the Church is never to admit that we can be made to suffer by the Church any differently than by God."

❋ III ❋

O UR SAVIOR, THE AUTHOR OF LIFE,
ACCORDING TO THE FIRST SERMONS
OF ST. PETER AND OF THE APOSTLES

W E HAVE seen that according to the Synoptic Gospels Jesus
affirmed not only His Messiahship but also His divine sonship, by claiming privileges that belong to God alone, such as perfecting the Mosaic law, remitting sins, judging the living and the dead,
and declaring that "no one knoweth the Son, but the Father: neither
doth anyone know the Father, but the Son." [1] Besides, it was because
He proclaimed Himself to be the Son of God that He was accused of
blasphemy by the high priest and that He was afterward crucified.[2]

Certain rationalists, like Welhausen and Loisy, have maintained
that these declarations in the Synoptics resulted from a progressive
idealization after Jesus' death and were attributed to Him although
He Himself never really pronounced them.

To defend such an interpretation, these rationalists would have to
prove that after Jesus' death there was time for the progressive idealization of His preaching to take place. Yet it is historically certain that
the opposite was the case. For, according to the Acts of the Apostles
and the epistles of St. Paul whose authenticity is not open to doubt,
the apostles began teaching even as early as Pentecost that Jesus had
proclaimed Himself to be not only the Messiah but also the Son of
God.[3]

St. Peter's Discourses in the Acts of the Apostles

The authenticity of the Acts of the Apostles is historically certain. It has been accepted not only by all Catholic critics and conserva-

---

[1] Matt. 11:27. [2] Matt. 26:63.

[3] E. Jacquier, *Les Actes des apôtres* (Etudes bibliques, Paris, 1926); cf. J. M. Vosté,
O.P., *Theses in Actus Apostolorum* (1931), chaps. 1 f.

tive Protestants, but by many rationalists like Renan, Reuss, Harnack, etc., who attribute the entire book to St. Luke, the companion of St. Paul. Very probably the Acts, which close abruptly with the recital of St. Paul's arrival in Rome in A.D. 62, were written around the year A.D. 63–64, and at least before A.D. 70, the year of the destruction of Jerusalem. The rationalist Harnack declared in 1908 that this opinion should be considered plausible.[4]

The Acts of the Apostles record the sermons delivered by St. Peter on Pentecost and the days following. In these sermons Peter, speaking to the Jews, laid particular emphasis on the Messianic character of Jesus, calling to their attention that He was approved of God,[5] for He performed miracles, He rose from the dead,[6] and the prophecies were fulfilled in Him and through Him. But in addition Peter attributed to Jesus a sanctifying role that far surpasses the Messiahship, and ascribed to Him privileges that can belong only to God.

In his Pentecost sermon, St. Peter said: "Ye men of Israel, hear these words: Jesus of Nazareth, a man approved of God among you, by miracles, and wonders, and signs, which God did by Him, in the midst of you, as you also know: this same being delivered up, by the determinate counsel and foreknowledge of God, you by the hands of wicked men have crucified and slain. Whom God hath raised up, having loosed the sorrows of hell, as it was impossible that He should be holden by it. For David saith concerning Him: . . . Thou wilt not . . . suffer Thy Holy One to see corruption. . . . Ye men, brethren, let me freely speak to you of the patriarch David; that he died, and was buried; and his sepulcher is with us to this present day. Whereas therefore he was a prophet, . . . foreseeing this, he spoke of the resurrection of Christ. For neither was He left in hell, neither did His flesh see corruption. This Jesus hath God raised again, whereof all we are witnesses. Being exalted therefore by the right hand of God, and having received of the Father the promise of the Holy Ghost, He hath poured forth this which you see and hear. . . . Therefore let all the house of Israel know most certainly that

---

[4] *Die Apostelgeschichte* (1908), p. 221; cf. P. Batiffol, *Orpheus et l'Evangile* (1910), p. 132.   [5] Acts 2:22.   [6] *Ibid.*, 4:33.

God hath made both Lord and Christ this same Jesus, whom you have crucified." [7]

The apostles often called Jesus "Lord," [8] a term which the Jews, when they spoke Greek, reserved for Yahweh.[9]

In his second sermon, after he had cured in Jesus' name the man born lame, St. Peter said: "Ye men of Israel, why wonder you at this, or why look you upon us, as if by our strength or power we had made this man to walk? The God of Abraham and the God of Isaac and the God of Jacob, the God of our fathers, hath glorified His Son Jesus, whom you indeed delivered up and denied before the face of Pilate, when he judged He should be released. But you denied the Holy One and the Just, and desired a murderer to be granted unto you. But the Author of life you killed, whom God hath raised from the dead, of which we are witnesses. . . . And the faith which is by Him, hath given this perfect soundness in the sight of you all." [10]

The expression "Author of life" can be applied to Jesus only if He is the Son of God in the true sense, and Himself God. For God alone, who is life by essence, can by participation produce the life which pulses in every living creature. Only God can bring a corpse back to life; and above all God alone can give the life of the soul, grace, which is a participation in His intimate life. Therefore, when St. Peter said, "You killed the Author of life," it is the same as if he had said, "Jesus is God." The thought of Jesus especially as the Author and the dispenser of supernatural life, and his words are equal in sublimity to those of St. John: "In Him was life, and the life was the light of men"; [11] "I am come that they may have life, and may have it more abundantly"; [12] "I am the way and the truth and the life." [13]

There is testimony also in St. Peter's beautiful answer to the high priest, when he and St. John were arrested and brought before the Sanhedrin. The high priest of the synagogue, surrounded by the ancients and scribes, asked the two prisoners: "By what power, or by what name, have you done this?" They were referring to the cure of the man born lame. "Then," it is reported, "Peter, filled with the

---

[7] Acts 2:22–36.   [8] Acts 2:20, 21, 36; 3:20; 4:29; 7:58, 59; 10:36.
[9] In the Septuagint see psalms 1–3.   [10] Acts 3:12 f.
[11] John 1:4.   [12] John 10:10.   [13] Ibid., 14:6.

Holy Ghost, said to them: Ye princes of the people, and ancients, hear: If we this day are examined concerning the good deed done to the infirm man, by what means he hath been made whole: be it known to you all, and to all the people of Israel, that by the name of our Lord Jesus Christ of Nazareth, whom you crucified, whom God hath raised from the dead, even by Him this man standeth here before you whole. This is the stone which was rejected by you the builders, which is become the head of the corner. Neither is there salvation in any other. For there is no other name under heaven given to men whereby we must be saved." [14] The record adds that the members of the Sanhedrin "could say nothing against it. . . . And calling them, they charged them not to speak at all, nor teach in the name of Jesus." [15]

In this testimony Peter made three major affirmations. First, he said that the miracle was performed in the name of Jesus. Miracles, however, are not accomplished in the name of a mere prophet, but in the name of God, for He alone can produce a genuine miracle, that goes beyond all natural forces. Secondly, he called attention to psalm 117, as Jesus Himself had done in the parable of the wicked husbandmen: "The stone which was rejected by you the builders, . . . is become the head of the corner." Thirdly, Peter affirmed that Jesus is the Savior of the world, as did the converted Samaritans according to St. John: "Neither is there salvation in any other." This was equivalent to saying that Jesus is the Author of salvation; and, according to the psalms the Author of salvation is God Himself,[16] the Author of grace. This is to say once again that Jesus is the Author of life.

Peter continued to give the same testimony when, after he had been delivered from prison by an angel, the high priest questioned him again. He and the other apostles answered: "We ought to obey God, rather than men. The God of our fathers hath raised up Jesus, whom you put to death, hanging Him upon a tree. Him hath God exalted with His right hand, to be Prince and Savior, to give repent-

[14] Acts 4:8–12.　　　　　[15] Acts 4:18.

[16] "Attend unto my help, O Lord, the God of my salvation" (Ps. 37:23) ; "O Lord, the God of my salvation: I have cried in the day, and in the night before Thee" (Ps. 87:2) ; "O Lord, Lord, the strength of my salvation . . ." (Ps. 139:8).

ance to Israel, and remission of sins. And we are witnesses of these things and the Holy Ghost, whom God hath given to all that obey Him." [17]

Exasperated by what they had just heard, the members of the council wished to have the apostles put to death, but a Pharisee, named Gamaliel, a doctor of the law revered by the entire people, took up their defense, showed the drawbacks to putting them to death, and added: "Refrain from these men, and let them alone; for if this council or this work be of men, it will come to naught: but if it be of God, you cannot overthrow it, lest perhaps you be found even to fight against God." [18] The members of the Sanhedrin followed his advice and were content to scourge the apostles. Then, forbidding them to speak in the name of Jesus, they released them. "And they indeed went from the presence of the council, rejoicing that they were accounted worthy to suffer reproach for the name of Jesus. And every day they ceased not in the temple, and from house to house, to teach and preach Christ Jesus." [19]

At the first Council of Jerusalem, Peter, in order to show that the converted Gentiles were not to be obliged to observe the law of Moses but only the gospel, rose and said: "Men, brethren, you know that in former days God made choice among us, that by my mouth the Gentiles should hear the word of the gospel, and believe. And God, who knoweth the hearts, gave testimony, giving unto them the Holy Ghost, as well as to us; [20] and put no difference between us and them, purifying their hearts by faith. Now therefore, why tempt you God to put a yoke upon the necks of the disciples, which neither our fathers nor we have been able to bear? But by the grace of the Lord Jesus Christ, we believe to be saved, in like manner as they also." [21] Again this is as much as to say that Jesus is the Author of salvation or of the supernatural life.

Several times during his sermons Peter called Jesus "Lord," [22] "Lord of all." [23] To Cornelius the centurion he said: "He commanded

---

[17] Acts 5:29 f. [18] Acts 5:38 f. [19] Acts 5:41 f.

[20] In fact, as stated in the Acts of the Apostles (10:46), some converted Gentiles began "speaking with tongues, and magnifying God," a sign that they, too, had received the Holy Ghost. Cf. also Acts 11:15.

[21] Acts 15:7 f. [22] Acts 2:36; 11:20. [23] Ibid., 10:36.

us to preach to the people, and to testify that it is He who was appointed by God, to be judge of the living and of the dead. To Him all the prophets give testimony, that by His name all receive remission of sins, who believe in Him." [24] The author of the Acts tells us that as Peter was still talking, "the Holy Ghost fell on all them that heard the word," [25] and they began to speak with tongues and to glorify God.

It was also in the name of Jesus that the apostles performed miracles and conferred baptism.

Lastly, there is a twofold testimony in the martyrdom of St. Stephen and in the conversion of St. Paul, both recorded in the Acts.

The Martyrdom of St. Stephen and the Conversion of St. Paul, Signs of the Divinity of Jesus

The account of the martyrdom of St. Stephen says in part: "But he, being full of the Holy Ghost, looking up steadfastly to heaven, saw the glory of God, and Jesus standing on the right hand of God. And he said: Behold, I see the heavens opened, and the Son of man standing on the right hand of God." [26] The Jews then "crying out with a loud voice, stopped their ears, and with one accord ran violently upon him. And casting him forth without the city, they stoned him; [27] and the witnesses laid down their garments at the feet of a young man, whose name was Saul." And as they stoned him, Stephen prayed saying: "Lord Jesus, receive my spirit." "And falling on his knees, he cried with a loud voice, saying: Lord, lay not this sin to their charge. And when he had said this, he fell asleep in the Lord."

As he was dying, Stephen, the saintly deacon, said: "Lord Jesus, receive my spirit," just as Jesus had said to His Father: "Into Thy hands, I commend My spirit." [28] It seems, therefore, that St. Stephen, seeing the Son of man standing on the right hand of God, recognized Him as the Son of God. And it was from Jesus that he received the grace of dying like Him, praying for his executioners.

The prayer of the dying Stephen, said in Jesus' name, had ex-

[24] *Ibid.*, 10:42.   [25] Acts 10:44.   [26] Acts 7:55 f.
[27] Stoning was the punishment reserved for blasphemers.   [28] Luke 23:46.

traordinary efficacy. We read in the Acts: "And Saul [the young man guarding the garments of those who were stoning the holy deacon] was consenting to his death. And at that time there was raised a great persecution against the Church which was at Jerusalem; and they were all dispersed through the countries of Judea and Samaria. . . . But Saul made havoc of the Church, entering in from house to house, and dragging away men and women, committed them to prison." [29]

A few days later, Stephen's prayer was answered. As recorded in the Acts, Saul was converted on the road to Damascus: "Suddenly a light from heaven shined round about him. And falling on the ground, he heard a voice saying to him: Saul, Saul, why persecutest thou Me? Who said: Who art Thou, Lord? And He: I am Jesus whom thou persecutest. It is hard for thee to kick against the goad. And he trembling and astonished, said: Lord, what wilt Thou have me to do? And the Lord said to him: Arise, and go into the city, and there it shall be told thee what thou must do." [30] And in fact, Ananias, one of the Lord's disciples, heard the following words with regard to Saul: "Go thy way; for this man is to me a vessel of election, to carry My name before the Gentiles and kings and the children of Israel. For I will show him how great things he must suffer for My name's sake." [31]

Then Ananias went to Saul and said: "Brother Saul, the Lord Jesus hath sent me, He that appeared to thee in the way as thou camest; that thou mayest receive thy sight, and be filled with the Holy Ghost. And immediately there fell from his eyes as it were scales, and he received his sight; and rising up, he was baptized. . . ." [32] Paul then spent several days with the disciples who were at Damascus, and "immediately he preached Jesus in the synagogues, that He is the Son of God." [33] The Jews then began to persecute Paul and plotted to kill him. But he went to Jerusalem to contact the apostles. Since they were afraid of him, he had Barnabas tell them how on the road to Damascus "he had seen the Lord, and that He had spoken to him." [34]

Thus Saul saw the Lord in His glorified humanity. He bore testi-

---

[29] Acts 7:59 f.   [30] Acts 9:3 f.   [31] Acts 9:15 f.
[32] Acts 9:17 f.   [33] Ibid., 9:20.   [34] Ibid., 9:27.

mony to it in the recital of his conversion [35] and added certain new details to convince his listeners that he had not been the victim of an illusion: "And they that were with me, saw indeed the light, but they heard not the voice of Him that spoke with me." [36] He also recorded the words of Ananias,[37] and the warning that he received from Jesus Himself.[38] He retold the story of his conversion before King Agrippa, who recognized his innocence.[39]

Finally, in the First Epistle to the Corinthians, he wrote: "Am I not an apostle? Have not I seen Christ Jesus our Lord?" [40] And again, a little farther: ". . . He rose again the third day, according to the Scriptures: And that He was seen by Cephas [Peter]; and after that by the eleven. Then was He seen by more than five hundred brethren at once: of whom many remain until this present. . . . After that, He was seen by James, then by all the apostles. And last of all, He was seen also by me, as by one born out of due time. . . . If Christ be not risen again, then is our preaching vain, and your faith is also vain." [41] That is to say, we have no guaranty that God has accepted His death for our redemption. If, on the contrary, Jesus is victorious over death by His resurrection, it is because on the cross He conquered sin, the consequence of which is death, and therefore He is the Savior of the human race.

What are we to conclude from the testimony contained in the Acts of the Apostles concerning the divinity of Jesus? We must conclude that immediately after Pentecost the apostles declared Jesus to be the Son of God, the Author of life, the Savior of the human race, the Judge of the living and the dead.

How could the apostles, who had been, as it were, morally crushed during the Passion, give such steadfast testimony even at the price of martyrdom, had they not been sustained by the One who gave aid to St. Stephen during his martyrdom and who converted Saul on the road to Damascus?

What is particularly evident is that, contrary to the rationalists J. Weiss, Holtzmann, and Loisy, sufficient time did not elapse for

---

[35] Acts 22:6 f.   [36] *Ibid.*, 22:9.   [37] *Ibid.*, 22:14 f.
[38] *Ibid.*, 22:18.   [39] Acts 26:12 f.   [40] I Cor. 9:1.
[41] *Ibid.*, 15:4 f.

a progressive idealization of Jesus' teaching to take place. Jesus was proclaimed the Son of God, the Author of life, and the Savior on Pentecost and consistently thereafter. This was the belief of the first Churches from their very foundation. And when between A.D. 50 and 59 St. Paul wrote his first epistles—to the Romans, to the Corinthians, and to the Thessalonians—he affirmed the divinity of Jesus as a dogma already held by these Churches, which were composed in part of converted Jews who were firm believers in monotheism and therefore scarcely inclined to accept the divinity of the Savior without incontestable divine revelation. Sufficient time did not elapse to permit a gradual idealization of Jesus' teaching. When, a little later on, the Ebionites denied the divinity of Jesus they were unanimously reproved by the Church; and St. John wrote the Fourth Gospel in refutation of their heresy.

✻ IV ✻

THE MYSTERY OF THE INCARNATION ACCORDING TO ST. PAUL

THE epistles of St. Paul corroborate the testimony concerning the divinity of Jesus contained in the Synoptic Gospels and the Acts of the Apostles. St. Paul expressly affirmed the divinity of Jesus, and he spoke of it not as of a belief unknown until then but as of a dogma already accepted by the Churches to which he was writing.

We must not forget that the principal epistles, the two to the Thessalonians, the two to the Corinthians, and those to the Galatians, the Romans, the Ephesians, the Colossians, and the Philippians, were written between 48 and 59, or between 50 and 64, as is recognized by several rationalists, among them Harnack and Julicher.

Let us first view St. Paul's Christology in broad outline, and afterward stress what he said concerning the divinity of Jesus.[1]

St. Paul's Habitual Contemplation and His Christology

The Apostle of the Gentiles did not come to know the Savior in the same manner as the other apostles, by accompanying Him in His ministry, listening to His sermons, witnessing His miracles, and observing His actions. St. Paul was converted after the death of Jesus, on the road to Damascus, and he saw Him only in His glory after His resurrection.[2] He attained this knowledge in a single instant by an extraordinary grace at the moment of his miraculous conversion. The divine words that he heard then were to remain engraved in his

---

[1] Cf. F. Prat, S.J., *The Theology of St. Paul;* M. J. Lagrange, O.P., *Commentaire sur l'Epître aux Romains;* J. M. Vosté, O.P., *Studia Paulina* (1928), chap. 10; *Commentarius in Epistulam ad Ephesios, Commentarius in Epistulam ad Thessalonicenses.*

[2] Acts 9:1 f.

soul forever: "Saul, Saul, why persecutest thou Me? . . . I am Jesus whom thou persecutest." [3] And the Lord had said to Ananias: ". . . this man is to Me a vessel of election, to carry My name before the Gentiles; . . . I will show him how great things he must suffer for My name's sake." [4]

It follows that the object of St. Paul's habitual contemplation was not what Jesus accomplished during His ministry, but His infinite greatness, His divine character as Creator, His action upon redeemed mankind, His mind, His reign in souls. St. Paul almost always contemplated Jesus in His glory. That is why he wrote to the Ephesians: "He . . . ascended above all the heavens, that He might fill all things. And He gave some apostles and some prophets and other some evangelists and other some pastors and doctors, for the perfecting of the saints, for the work of the ministry, for the edifying of the body of Christ: until we all meet . . . unto a perfect man, unto the measure of the age of the fullness of Christ." [5]

Indeed St. Paul thought of Jesus as truly man, born of woman and of the posterity of David,[6] but a man who has never known sin,[7] and who by His love, His humiliations, and His sufferings on the cross, has won for us the eternal life which He Himself enjoys in heaven: "He humbled Himself, becoming obedient unto death, even to the death of the cross. For which cause God also hath exalted Him, and hath given Him a name which is above all names: that in the name of Jesus every knee should bow, of those that are in heaven, on earth, and under the earth: and that every tongue should confess that the Lord Jesus Christ is in the glory of God the Father." [8]

St. Paul proved by Scripture that the Messiah was to suffer and die for us, and then rise from the dead,[9] and that Jesus is the Messiah thus defined.[10] He habitually designated Jesus as "the Lord." [11] In the Septuagint the term "Lord" is the usual translation of the word Yahweh (or Jehovah). Thus, to call Jesus "Lord" is to say that He is God. Like the Latin *Dominus,* the term κύριος implies absolute

---

[3] *Ibid.,* 9:4 f.   [4] *Ibid.,* 9:15 f.   [5] Eph. 4:10–13.
[6] Rom. 8:3; 1:3 f.   [7] II Cor. 5:21.   [8] Phil. 2:8 f.
[9] Acts 17:2 f; 18:4 f.; I Thess.1:10.   [10] Rom. 1:3; 9:4 f.; 15:8 f.
[11] Phil. 2:8 f.

sovereignty not only in the natural order over the world, but in the order of grace over the Church and over consciences. It is in this vein that St. Paul wrote to the Corinthians: "I give thanks to my God always for you, for the grace of God that is given you in Christ Jesus, that in all things you are made rich in Him, . . . so that nothing is wanting to you in any grace, waiting for the manifestation of our Lord Jesus Christ. Who also will confirm you unto the end without crime, in the day of the coming of our Lord Jesus Christ." [12] In his epistles St. Paul calls Jesus "Lord" more than 230 times. But in many passages he affirms more explicitly that Jesus is the Son of God not by adoption but by nature.

The Divine Sonship of Jesus according to St. Paul

The epistles of St. Paul proclaim the divine sonship of Christ Jesus by attributing to our Lord three great privileges that could belong to no creature, however exalted it might be: First, He is the first-born and the head of all the just, even of the angels. Secondly, everything subsists through Him and for Him. Thirdly, at the end of the world all things will be finally placed under His dominion.

Jesus is the first-born and the head of all the just according to the testimony of the Epistle to the Romans: "For whom He foreknew, He also predestinated to be made conformable to the image of His Son; that He might be the first-born amongst many brethren. And whom He predestinated, them He also called. And whom He called, them He also justified. And whom He justified, them He also glorified." [13]

This doctrine is often developed in the other epistles: "But I would have you know that the head of every man is Christ." [14] "In whom we have redemption . . . according to the riches of His grace, which hath superabounded in us . . . that He might make known unto us the mystery of His will . . . in the dispensation of the fullness of times, to re-establish all things in Christ, that are in heaven and on earth, in Him." [15] "The exceeding greatness of His power . . . He wrought in Christ, raising Him up from the dead, and setting Him

[12] I Cor. 1:4 f.   [13] Rom. 8:29 f.   [14] I Cor. 11:3.   [15] Eph. 1:7 ff.

on His right hand in the heavenly places, above all principality and power and virtue and dominion and every name that is named, not only in this world, but also in that which is to come." [16]

"He is the head of the body, the Church, who is the beginning, the first-born from the dead; that in all things He may hold the primacy." [17] "Who is the head of all principality and power," [18] that is, the head of the angelic powers. In fact, Christ has said: "The Son of man shall send His angels" [19] on judgment day to gather together the elect. And during His life on earth He had the power to cast out devils and gave this power to His apostles. Christ's superiority over the angels is explained in its every aspect in the Epistle to the Hebrews, 1:5—2:18.

The second privilege of Jesus Christ, according to St. Paul, is that everything subsists through Him and for Him. To the Colossians, he wrote: "Who is the image of the invisible God, the first-born of every creature [according to eternal generation]. For in Him were all things created in heaven and on earth, visible and invisible, whether thrones or dominations or principalities or powers: all things were created by Him and in Him. And He is before all, and by Him all things consist." [20] ". . . the body of His glory, . . . whereby also He is able to subdue all things unto Himself." [21]

The third privilege attributed to Christ Jesus by St. Paul is that all things will finally be placed under His dominion at the end of the world. In the First Epistle to the Corinthians he writes: "And as in Adam all die, so also in Christ all [the just] shall be made alive. . . . Afterward the end, . . . when He shall have brought to nought all [rebellious] principality and power and virtue. For He must reign, until He hath put all His enemies under His feet. [22] And the enemy death shall be destroyed last: For He hath put all things under His feet. [23] . . . And when all things shall be subdued unto Him, then the Son also Himself shall be subject unto Him that put all things under Him, that God may be all in all." [24]

---

[16] *Ibid.*, 1:19 ff.   [17] Col. 1:18.   [18] *Ibid.*, 2:10.
[19] Matt. 13:41; 14:31; Mark 13:27.   [20] Col. 1:15–17.
[21] Phil. 3:21.   [22] Cf. Ps. 109:1.   [23] Cf. Ps. 8:8.
[24] I Cor. 15:22 ff.

To the Colossians St. Paul likewise wrote: "For I would have you know, what manner of care I have for you and for them that are at Laodicea. . . . That their hearts may be comforted, being instructed in charity, and unto all riches of fullness of understanding, unto the knowledge of the mystery of God the Father and of Christ Jesus: in whom are hid all the treasures of wisdom and knowledge." [25] By reason of these treasures Jesus surpasses the highest choirs of angels.

These three privileges cannot belong to any creature whatsoever. Of no creature, not even the angels, can it be said: "He is the first-born, head of all the just"; "all things subsist through Him and in Him"; "all things will be finally subject to Him at the end of the world."

Moreover, many texts of St. Paul explicitly speak of Jesus as the Son of God in a particular sense that is fulfilled in Him alone.

In the Epistle to the Romans, St. Paul declares he is the apostle of Christ Jesus, to announce "the Gospel of God, which He had promised before by His prophets, in the Holy Scriptures, concerning His Son, who was made to Him of the seed of David, according to the flesh, who was predestinated [26] the Son of God in power, according to the spirit of sanctification, by the resurrection of our Lord Jesus Christ from the dead." [27] In other words, Jesus, true man, born of the race of David, was proven to be the Son of God by the miracle of His resurrection.

Likewise, in Romans: "God sending His own Son, in the likeness of sinful flesh and of sin, hath condemned sin in the flesh; that the justification of the law might be fulfilled in us, who walk not according to the flesh, but according to the spirit." [28]

To the Galatians: "But when the fullness of the time was come, God sent His Son, made of a woman, under the law: that He might redeem them who were under the law: that we might receive the adoption of sons. And because you are sons, God hath sent the Spirit of His Son [that is, the Holy Ghost, promised by His Son], into

[25] Col. 2:1–3.
[26] The Vulgate uses the word "predestinated" instead of "declared," the former being a possible meaning of the Greek but more difficult to explain because of what is said immediately following concerning the miracle of the Resurrection.
[27] Rom. 1:1–4.   [28] Rom. 8:3 f.

your hearts, crying: Abba, Father." [29] This text shows more clearly the difference between the just who are the sons of God by adoption, and He who is truly the Son of God by nature.

St. Paul affirmed this natural divine sonship even more explicitly when he spoke of the eternal pre-existence of the Son of God, or of the divine person of Christ before the Incarnation. In fact, he wrote to the Colossians: "Who is the image of the invisible God, the first-born of every creature [born before all creatures, and not created]: for in Him were all things created in heaven and on earth, visible and invisible, whether thrones, or dominations, or principalities, or powers: all things were created by Him and in Him. And He is before all, and by Him all things consist. And He is the head of the body, the Church, . . . Because in Him, it hath well pleased the Father, that all fullness should dwell; and through Him to reconcile all things unto Himself. . . ." [30]

In the above text the Son of God is manifestly called "Creator" in the same sense that God Himself is so called in the Epistle to the Romans: "For of Him, and by Him, and in Him are all things." [31]

St. Paul often liked to contrast the annihilation of the crucified Jesus with His glory, His power, and His sovereign wisdom as Son of God. In the First Epistle to the Corinthians he wrote: "But we preach Christ crucified, unto the Jews indeed a stumbling block, and unto the Gentiles foolishness: but unto them that are called both Jews and Greeks, Christ the power of God, and the wisdom of God. . . . But of Him are you in Christ Jesus, who of God is made unto us wisdom, and justice, and sanctification, and redemption." [32]

We find the same antithesis in the Epistle to the Philippians: "For let this mind be in you, which was also in Christ Jesus: who being in the form of God, thought it not robbery to be equal with God: but emptied Himself, taking the form of a servant, being made in the likeness of men, and in habit found as a man. He humbled Himself, becoming obedient unto death, even to the death of the Cross. For which cause God also hath exalted Him. . . ." [33]

It would be impossible to express more forcefully the annihilation,

---

[29] Gal. 4:4–6. [30] Col. 1:15–20. [31] Rom. 11:36.
[32] I Cor. 1:23–30. [33] Phil. 2:5–9.

the crushing of the humanity of the crucified Jesus, and at the same time the eternal pre-existence of His divine personality as Son of God, equal with God.

Likewise, Paul said to the Colossians: "For in Him [Christ] dwelleth all the fullness of the Godhead corporeally [really]." [34] And to the Romans: "For I wished myself to be anathema from Christ, for my brethren . . . who are Israelites . . . and of whom is Christ, according to the flesh, who is over all things, God blessed for ever. Amen." [35] This text is similar to the one in the Epistle to the Colossians, cited above, in which it is said that the Son of God created all things and "by Him they consist." [36]

In the New Testament there are several analogous doxologies in honor of Christ,[37] whence comes the "Gloria Patri et Filio et Spiritui Sancto" at the conclusion of the psalms in the Office, affirming the equality of the three persons of the Blessed Trinity, and offering to all three equally the cult of adoration reserved for God alone.

All of St. Paul's testimony concerning the divine sonship of Jesus is summarized at the beginning of the Epistle to the Hebrews, 1:1 ff., which calls to mind the parable of the wicked husbandmen: "God, who at sundry times and in divers manners, spoke in times past to the fathers by the prophets, last of all, in these days hath spoken to us by His Son, whom He hath appointed heir of all things, by whom also He made the world. Who being the brightness of His glory, and the figure of His substance, and upholding all things by the word of His power, making purgation of sins, sitteth on the right hand of the majesty on high. Being made so much better than the angels, as He hath inherited a more excellent name than they." [38]

The remainder of chapter 1 of the Epistle to the Hebrews explains clearly that Jesus Christ is the Son of God by nature, the Creator and Master of all things, the head of the kingdom of God, whereas the angels are only servants of God and His sons by adoption.[39] Thus, if men were required to obey the commands of the angels

---

[34] Col. 2:9. [35] Rom. 9:3-5. [36] Col. 1:16 f.
[37] Cf. Heb. 13:21; I Pet. 4:11; II Pet. 3:18. [38] Matt. 21:33-46.
[39] "For to which of the angels hath He said at any time, Thou art My Son, today have I begotten Thee? And again . . . Thou in the beginning, O Lord, didst found the earth: and the works of Thy hands are the heavens" (Heb. 1:5-10). Cf. also Heb. 2:10.

of the Old Testament, how much more must they obey the word of Jesus Christ who, after having been humbled and humiliated during His passion for our salvation, is now crowned with glory.[40]

This adheres to the general principles of St. Paul's Christology, which derives from the fact that Paul was converted on the road to Damacus after Jesus' death, and thought of Him especially in His glory, risen from the dead. Paul saw Christ in His infinite grandeur, as God's only Son, as Creator and preserver of all things, as the head of the kingdom of God. Let us bear in mind that St. Paul was "caught up to the third heaven . . . and heard secret words, which it is not granted to man to utter." [41]

It was Paul also who wrote: "And lest the greatness of the revelations should exalt me, there was given me a sting of my flesh, an angel of Satan, to buffet me." [42] Paul's enjoyment of very elevated revelations did not prevent his being afflicted by one of those humiliating crosses that all men must drag after them as ceaseless reminders of their nothingness.

Now, in speaking so magnificently about the divinity of Jesus in his Epistles written between A.D. 48 and 59 (or between 50 and 64), St. Paul wrote not as of a dogma hitherto unknown but as of a dogma already accepted by the Churches which he was addressing. We must therefore conclude, contrary to the rationalists J. Weiss, Holtzmann, and Loisy, that this dogma of the divinity of Jesus did not result from a progressive idealization which might little by little have trans-

---

[40] Some liberal Protestants and rationalists, like Sabatier and Guignebert, have maintained that according to several texts of St. Paul it seems that Jesus is inferior to the Father, and that God sent His Son and raised Him from the dead (Rom. 8:3; I Thess. 1:10); that there is only one God, namely, the Father, and one Lord, who is Jesus Christ (I Cor. 8:6; 12:5 f.); everything is Christ's and Christ is God's (I Cor. 3:23); the Son will place His kingdom in the Father's hands and will be subject to Him (I Cor. 15:24–28; 11:3; Eph. 1:17).

The answer to this difficulty is that Jesus possesses two natures, one divine and the other human. As man He is inferior to the Father, and as Son of God He receives His divinity from the Father. This is manifestly the meaning of these texts, which would otherwise contradict the ones cited earlier that affirm the equality of the Father and the Son. The first rule for interpreting an author's texts is not to interpret them in such a way as to make him contradict himself.

[41] II Cor. 12:2–4. The Hebrews called "third heaven" (empyrean) the spiritual heaven where God dwells, above the heaven of air (atmosphere) and the heaven of the stars (ether).   [42] II Cor. 12:7.

formed and transfigured the original teaching of Jesus and of the apostles. Sufficient time did not elapse for such a progressive idealization, since about the year 48 or 59 St. Paul already spoke in his Epistles of the divinity of Jesus as of a dogma accepted by the Christian world. This acceptance was the result of the apostles' teaching from Pentecost onward. Had not St. Peter preached on Pentecost and consistently thereafter that Jesus is the Author of life, the Savior of all, the Judge of the living and the dead? [43]

St. Paul's affirmations on the eternal pre-existence of the divine person of Jesus are equal in sublimity to those in St. John's Gospel, of which we shall speak last.

[43] Acts 3:13–16; 4:10–18; 5:29–31.

❊ V ❊

THE WORD MADE FLESH ACCORDING TO ST. JOHN

OF RECENT years Catholic exegetes have proved at great length that there is no valid argument against the authenticity and the historicity of the Fourth Gospel, unanimously attributed by tradition to the apostle St. John.[1] It has been demonstrated that by reason of both the language and the style in which it is written, this Gospel was composed by a Jew, an eyewitness and a disciple of Jesus. Moreover it has been shown that the author was he who is called "the disciple whom Jesus loved" in this book where the apostle St. John is never mentioned by name. St. John wished to supplement what was lacking in the Synoptics in the matter of factual description especially of events that occurred in Judea, and also in the matter of our Lord's sermons which the first three Gospels often recorded only in substance.[2]

The Fourth Gospel was written between the years 80 and 100, as the rationalist Harnack admits. Its chief purpose is unquestionably dogmatic. It was written in particular to prove, in opposition to the Cerinthians and the Ebionites, that Jesus is really the Son of God, as proclaimed in 20:31. The events recorded are never presented as allegories or parables. They are set forth as facts that really occurred. Nor can it be said that in reporting Jesus' sermons St. John tended to present his own personal views. In several places he has clearly dif-

[1] St. Irenaeus in his book *Adversus Haereses*, written between A.D. 174 and 189, says that the Fourth Gospel was composed by John, the disciple of the Lord who leaned on His bosom at the Last Supper, and that he published it while living in Ephesus. Now, St. Irenaeus had close relations with St. Polycarp and with other direct disciples of the apostles, and he is an exceptional witness inasmuch as he was born in Asia, lived in Rome, and became bishop of Lyons.

[2] Cf. Lagrange, O.P., *Saint Jean* (1925), chaps. 1–3; J. M. Vosté, O.P., *Studia Joannea* (1930), chaps. 2, 6; Batiffol, *L'enseignement de Jésus*, pp. 196 ff.

ferentiated between the words of Christ and the private reflections he was making about them.[3]

The Prologue

The prologue of the Fourth Gospel provides the dogmatic foundation and presents the point of view of the entire work. It explains the meaning of the expression "Word made flesh," and the nature of the relationship between the Word and God (1:1 f.): "In the beginning was the Word, and the Word was with God, and the Word was God; the same was in the beginning with God." That is to say: before the world and before time, the Word was from all eternity. He was with God, as His interior thought. He was in substantial and active communion with God the Father, but distinct from Him, and He was sent by Him. Although He is distinct from the Father, the Word is none the less consubstantial with the Father, for it is said: ". . . and the Word was God." The Word was eternally united to His Father by nature and by His will. In these first verses of the prologue, St. John raises his mind's eye from the Savior's humanity to His divine personality and to His divinity. It is as if someone stood on the shore gazing out over the ocean and became lost in its immensity, though actually seeing but a tiny portion of it. Yet the ocean is finite and limited, whereas the perfection of the Word is infinite.

The relationship of the Word to creatures in general is expressed in the following verse (1:3): "All things were made by Him: and without Him was made nothing that was made."

All things without exception, even matter, were made by Him. The Father possesses the creative power, but nothing comes into existence unless the Word gives it form. The world, before it was created, existed ideally in the Word; for it was eternally present to the divine intelligence wherein all is life.[4]

Finally, the relationship of the Word with men is expressed in verses 4 and 5: "In Him was life, and the life was the light of men.

[3] John 2:21; 12:33; 7:39.
[4] Cf. St. Augustine, *In Evang. sec. Joannem*, chap. 1, §§ 1, 16; St. Thomas, Ia, q. 18, a. 4; Bossuet, *Elévations sur les mystères*, 12th week, 10th elevation.

And the light shineth in darkness, and the darkness did not comprehend it." The natural light of the intelligence and the supernatural
light of revelation and faith that the Word pours upon the earth
shine among men in the darkness of ignorance and sin; and many
men have remained hardened in spite of the miracles performed by
the Word made flesh and they have not received the light He brought
them.

A little further on, the Evangelist says: "He came unto His own,
and His own received Him not" (1:11); and ". . . the light is
come into the world, and men loved darkness rather than the light:
for their works were evil" (3:19).

By contrast, what did He give to those who received Him? "But
as many as received Him, He gave them power to be made the sons
of God, to them that believe in His name" (1:12–13); that is, to all
those who received Him as the Creator and as the Author of eternal
salvation, whether they were Jews or pagans, He gave the power to
become, in the supernatural order, adopted sons of God. This sonship is not the result of natural generation. It is not born "of blood nor
of the will of the flesh [the blind instinct of the senses] nor of the
will of man [enlightened by reason]." It comes directly from God.

It can be said that the adopted sons of God are "born of God"
(1:13) in the sense that Jesus used when He spoke to Nicodemus:
"Unless a man be born again of water and the Holy Ghost, he cannot enter into the kingdom of God. That which is born of the flesh, is
flesh; and that which is born of the Spirit, is spirit." [5] Likewise St.
Peter says that by the grace that sanctifies us we become "partakers
of the divine nature," [6] and we participate in the intimate life of
God.

This is the nature of the relationship of the Word with God the
Father and with men. "The Word was made flesh, and dwelt among
us." [7] "Flesh" in this case means "man," as it often does in biblical
language; [8] it was chosen in order to emphasize the reality of Christ's
human nature and the supreme self-abasement of the Word. All the
heresies concerning Christ Jesus have been shattered by this word

---

[5] John 3:5 f.   [6] II Pet. 1:4.   [7] John 1:14.
[8] "All flesh had corrupted its way upon the earth" (Gen. 6:12; Isa. 40:5; Joel 2:28).

"flesh," whether they denied His divinity or His humanity, or the unity of the two natures in the person of the Word.

What are the sources of this doctrine? [9] They are to be found in our Lord's own teachings, preserved in the apostolic tradition and compared with what the Old Testament tells us of the eternal wisdom of the word of God.[10]

After the prologue, the Fourth Gospel divides naturally into two parts. First, Jesus manifests His mission and His divinity during His public life (1:19 through chap. 12). Secondly, Jesus manifests His mission and His divinity during His passion and after His resurrection (chapters 13 to 20).

Jesus Manifests His Mission and His Divinity during His Public Life

First of all, men of good will acknowledge Jesus as God. Then the unbelief and opposition of many Jews break forth and increase. Finally, Jesus is glorified in His triumphal entrance into Jerusalem. There are the three sections of the first part of the Gospel of St. John.

It was John the Baptist who first designated Jesus as the Messiah and the Son of God (1:29 f.): "Behold the Lamb of God, behold Him who taketh away the sin of the world. . . . I saw the Spirit coming down, as a dove from heaven, and He remained upon Him.

[9] Several rationalists maintain that the doctrine of St. John on the Word or Logos is derived in part from Philo, his Jewish contemporary. Philo indeed speaks of a Logos whom he calls "son of God" and who has a part in the formation of the world and brings to men a celestial revelation. But Philo's Logos is not the Creator; he is the son of God in the same sense as is all creation. He is neither Messiah nor Redeemer. Philo never had any idea of the Incarnation.

[10] In the Old Testament creation is attributed to the word of God. "And God said: Be light made. And light was made" (Gen. 1:3). The word of God is then personified in the Psalms (Ps. 32:6; 106:20; 147:15, 18; 148:8). According to Ecclesiasticus, Wisdom has its origin and seat in God (1:1); it is eternal and is made manifest in the works of creation (1:4, 9, 10); it is an unfathomable abyss of knowledge (24:38 ff.). This doctrine is developed and clarified in 7:24–26; 8:6, 8; 9:4, 9.

The epistles of St. Paul contain several of the elements of the Johannine doctrine of the Logos: Col. 1:15 f.; Phil. 2:5–11; Heb. 1:1–3; 4:12. St. John may have used the word Logos, whose meaning was being distorted by several philosophers, in order to clarify its meaning.

And I knew Him not; but He who sent me to baptize with water, said to me: He upon whom thou shalt see the Spirit descending, and remaining upon Him, He it is that baptizeth with the Holy Ghost. And I saw, and I gave testimony, that this is the Son of God."

On the two succeeding days the first disciples, Andrew, Simon Peter, Philip, and Nathanael, accepted Jesus as the Messiah and even as the Son of God, according to the testimony of John the Baptist (1:35, 41, 45, 49). Then Jesus performed His first miracle at Cana (2:11), and manifested Himself at Jerusalem by driving the traders out of the temple, saying: "Make not the house of My Father a house of traffic" (2:16). Many, seeing the miracles He performed, believed in Him (2:23).

Then He said to Nicodemus (3:13 ff.): "And no man hath ascended into heaven, but He that descended from heaven, the Son of man who is in heaven. . . . So must the Son of man be lifted up: that whosoever believeth in Him may not perish, but may have life everlasting. For God so loved the world as to give His only-begotten Son; that whosoever believeth in Him may not perish, but may have life everlasting."

John the Baptist gave further testimony (3:31–36): "He that cometh from above, is above all. . . . He that cometh from heaven, is above all. And what He hath seen and heard, that He testifieth: . . . for God doth not give the Spirit by measure. The Father loveth the Son: and He hath given all things into His hand. He that believeth in the Son, hath life everlasting."

Jesus then manifested Himself in Samaria, and the Samaritans recognized Him: "We . . . know that this is indeed the Savior of the world" (4:42). In Galilee Jesus cured the son of an officer, and the latter together with his entire household believed in Him (4:53).

Yet scarcely had the men of good will acknowledged the divine sonship of Jesus when the Jews' unbelief burst forth and became increasingly bitter. This opposition found its first outlet when the Savior cured a paralytic on the Sabbath (5:16 ff.). "But Jesus answered them: My Father worketh until now; and I work. Hereupon therefore the Jews sought the more to kill Him, because He did not only break the Sabbath, but also said God was His Father, making Himself equal to God. Then Jesus answered and said to them: Amen, amen, I say unto you, the Son cannot do anything of Himself, but what He seeth the Father doing: for what things soever He doth, these the Son also doth in like manner. . . . For as the Father raiseth up the dead, and giveth life: so the Son also giveth life to whom He will. For neither doth the Father judge any man, but hath given all judgment to the Son; that all men may honor the Son, as they honor the Father. . . . Amen, amen I say unto you, that he who heareth My word, and believeth Him that sent Me, hath life everlasting. . . . For as the Father hath life in Himself, so He hath given to the Son also to have life in Himself."

The Galileans, too, were incredulous when Jesus said that He was the bread of life on which they must feed through faith and that later He would give Himself to them as food (6:48–52).

The opposition in Judea increased at the feast of the tabernacles (chapters 7 to 9). Then Jesus said to the Pharisees: "I am the light of the world. . . . Neither Me do you know, nor My Father: if you did know Me, perhaps you would know My Father also" (8:12, 19). And He added (8:42, 56, 59): "If God were your Father you would indeed love Me. . . . Abraham your father rejoiced that he might see My day: he saw it, and was glad." The Jews answered Him: "Thou art not yet fifty years old, and hast Thou seen Abraham? Jesus said to them: Amen, amen I say to you, before Abraham was made, I am. They took up stones therefore to cast at Him. But Jesus hid Himself, and went out of the Temple." The words "Before Abraham was made, I am," imply that Jesus' life had no beginning and therefore express the eternal and immutable pre-existence of the person of the Word before the Incarnation.

The same opposition was intensified on the occasion of one of Jesus' sermons given at the time of the feast of the dedication. As He walked in the Temple, Jesus said (10:27 ff.): "My sheep hear My voice: and I know them, and they follow Me. And I give them life everlasting; and they shall not perish forever, and no man shall pluck them out of My hand. That which My Father hath given Me is greater than all: and no one can snatch them out of the hand of My Father. I and the Father are one."

The Jews again took up stones to stone Him as a blasphemer "because," they told Him, "that Thou, being a man makest Thyself God" (10:33). Jesus had indeed affirmed His divinity when He said: "I and the Father are one," and by claiming to be almighty like the Father and therefore able to preserve souls in the path of goodness so that no one could snatch them from His hand. The Jews understood so well that He had affirmed not only His Messiahship but also His divinity that they treated Him as a blasphemer and decided to stone Him. They were awaiting a Messiah, but a conquering Messiah who would answer their nationalistic aspirations. A short while later Jesus, after saying "I am the resurrection and the life" (11:25), brought Lazarus back to life. The Jews who witnessed the miracle believed in Him. It was then that the Sanhedrists decided to put Him to death (11:53).

At the end of His ministry, Jesus made a triumphal entry into Jerusalem. There were Gentiles who wished to see Him. A voice from heaven uttered these words: "I have both glorified it [My name], and will glorify it again. . . . Jesus answered, and said: . . . I, if I be lifted up from the earth, will draw all things to Myself" (12:28–32). Nevertheless the Savior's enemies persisted in their unbelief.

Jesus Manifests His Divinity during His Suffering and in His Glory

At the Last Supper our Lord said to His disciples: "You call Me Master, and Lord; and you say well, for so I am" (13:13). In the discourse after the Last Supper, Jesus said: "I am the way and the truth and the life. No man cometh to the Father, but by Me" (14:6). God alone can say not merely "I have the truth and the life," but "I am the truth and the life." For God alone is the eternally subsistent Being. Later, when Philip asked: "Lord, show us the Father, and it is enough for us," Jesus answered him: "Have I been so long a time with you, and have you not known Me? . . . Do you not believe that I am in the Father, and the Father in Me? . . . The Father who abideth in Me, He doth the works," the miracles that I perform (14:9 ff.).

When He promised the Comforter, the Spirit of truth, Jesus added: "He shall glorify Me; because He shall receive of Mine, and shall show it to you. All things whatsoever the Father hath, are Mine. Therefore I said that He [the Holy Ghost] shall receive of Mine, and show it to you" (16:14 ff.; cf. 16:28, 32).

In His prayer for His disciples (John 17:1–5, 9 f.), Jesus said again: "Father, the hour is come, glorify Thy Son, that Thy Son may glorify Thee . . . that He may give eternal life to all whom Thou hast given Him. . . . I have finished the work which Thou gavest Me to do. And now glorify Thou Me, O Father, with Thyself, with the glory which I had, before the world was, with Thee. . . . I pray . . . for them whom Thou hast given Me: because they are Thine: And all My things are Thine, and Thine are Mine; and I am glorified in them."

The divine glory of Jesus was also manifested in His passion, in spite of the hatred of His enemies and the humiliations they inflicted on Him. The soldiers who had come with Judas fell back when Jesus said to them: "Whom seek ye?" "Jesus of Nazareth." "I am He" (18:4–6). And He proclaimed to Pilate: "My kingdom is not of this world. . . . Everyone that is of the truth, heareth My voice" (18: 36 ff.). And when Pilate sought to save Him and said: "I find no cause in Him," the Jews answered: "We have a law; and according to the law He ought to die, because He made Himself the Son of God" (19:6 f.).

Finally, to those who had eyes to see, the glory of Jesus was made manifest in His last words: "It is consummated" (19:30); as well as by the heroism of His death, by His magnanimity toward His executioners, and last of all by His resurrection. His glory was manifested again after the Resurrection in His last commands to His apostles: "Peace be to you. As the Father hath sent Me, I also send you. . . . Receive ye the Holy Ghost. Whose sins you shall forgive, they are forgiven them; and whose sins you shall retain, they are retained" (20:21 ff.). Thomas the apostle, at long last convinced of the reality of the Resurrection, cried out to Him: "My Lord and My God" (20:28).

Later, after the miraculous catch of fish, Jesus fulfilled the promise He had made to Peter and conferred upon him the office of governing the entire Church: "Feed My lambs. . . . Feed My sheep" (21:16 f.). Thus He stood forth ever more clearly as the head of the kingdom of God.

What are we to conclude as to the testimony of the Fourth Gospel concerning the divinity of Jesus? As recorded in that Gospel, Jesus' declarations state explicitly that He is the Son of God by nature and not by adoption: and it is for this very reason that the Jews demanded His death. For they said: "He said God was His Father, making Himself equal to God" (5:18; 10:33; 19:7).

Now, this testimony is the same as that in Matthew 11:27 and Luke 10:22: "All things are delivered to Me by My Father. And no one knoweth the Son, but the Father: neither doth anyone know the Father, but the Son, and he to whom it shall please the Son to reveal Him."

Finally, the affirmations contained in St. Matthew and St. Luke are equal in sublimity to the magnificent prologue of St. John: "In the beginning was the Word, and the Word was with God, and the Word was God. . . . And the Word was made flesh, and dwelt among us (and we saw His glory, the glory as it were of the only-begotten of the Father,) full of grace and truth. . . . No man hath seen God at any time: the only-begotten Son who is in the bosom of the Father, He hath declared Him" (1:1, 14, 18).

St. John also says in his First Epistle, 1:1: "That which was from the beginning, which we have heard, which we have seen with our eyes, which we have looked upon, and our hands have handled, of the word of life. . . . That which we have seen and have heard, we declare unto you, that you also may have fellowship with us, and our fellowship may be with the Father, and with His Son Jesus Christ." This is the tenor of St. John's contemplation, and it is very similar to St. Paul's.

The persecutor converted on the road to Damascus met the disciple that Jesus loved. What St. John tells us in his Gospel around A.D.

80 is what St. Paul wrote in his Epistles around A.D. 53. It is also what St. Peter preached on Pentecost and thereafter when he said that Jesus is the Author of life and the head of the kingdom of God which was announced by the prophets.

❊ VI ❊

THE PROPHETIC ANNOUNCEMENT OF THE SAVIOR

WE KNOW that taken as a whole the prophecies of the Old Testament all contain three fundamental assertions: There is but one God; His spiritual kingdom is to encompass all nations; the Messiah to be sent by Him is to be the head of this kingdom. This general view is clarified and abundantly confirmed by the study of the principal prophecies taken individually, especially if we consider the progressive development of the divine revelations from the promises made to the first man and to the patriarchs, to the prophecies of David and Isaias which describe in detail even the circumstances of the life and passion of the Savior.

It is also well to remember that these patriarchs and prophets included several that prefigure the Christ who was to come. For example, Abraham the Father of believers, Isaac who carried the wood of his sacrifice and allowed himself to be bound in preparation for his immolation, and Joseph who was sold by his brothers and became the savior of his people. Then there were Moses, the liberator, the head and lawgiver of the Hebrews; Job, the figure of the suffering Christ; David, who typified the Messiah by his trials, his kingship, his prayer, and his psalms; and Jeremias who loved and suffered for his people; and then there was Jonas. It was our Lord Himself who pointed out Jonas as the figure of His preaching and His burial.[1]

The Prophecies of the Patriarchal Period

The prophetic revelations of the patriarchal period up to and including Moses announced the Savior of the world who was to be of

---

[1] Matt. 12:39 ff.; Luke 11:29 ff.

the family of Abraham, Isaac, Jacob, and Juda the son of Jacob, who gave His name to one of the twelve tribes of Israel and who was the father of the royal race of David.

Immediately after the sin of the first man, God, at the same moment that He decreed punishment for sin, announced the future Savior who was to be of the race of the woman, and by whom this race would crush the head of the serpent.[2] Lamech announced that the future benediction would pass through Noe,[3] who was in fact saved from the flood together with his family and with whom God renewed His alliance, giving him the rainbow for a sign.[4]

Noe in his turn announced that God would choose the tents of Sem in which to dwell.[5] In fact, it was Abraham, the son of Sem, whom God chose to make the father of His people. He said to him: "Go forth out of thy country . . . and come into the land which I shall show thee. And I will make of thee a great nation, and I will bless thee, and magnify thy name, and thou shalt be blessed." [6] God renewed this promise to Abraham several times,[7] particularly when He told him of the birth of Isaac from whom would come his posterity.

Finally, Abraham was put to the test when the Lord asked him to sacrifice Isaac, the son of the promise. But the angel of the Lord stopped him: "Lay not thy hand upon the boy; . . . now I know that thou fearest God, and hast not spared thy only-begotten son for My sake. . . . Because thou hast done this thing, . . . I will bless thee, and I will multiply thy seed as the stars of heaven. . . . And in thy seed shall all the nations of the earth be blessed." [8]

Then Isaac, by virtue of his father's merits, received the same divine blessing: "Because Abraham obeyed My voice." [9] When Jacob won his brother Esau's birthright away from him, he heard from his father Isaac's lips these words of blessing: "God almighty bless thee, and make thee to increase, and multiply thee: that thou mayst be a multitude of people. And give the blessings of Abraham to thee, and to thy seed after thee." [10] Jacob even heard the Lord tell him: "And thy seed shall be as the dust of the earth: . . . and in

---

[2] Gen. 3:15.   [3] Ibid., 5:29.   [4] Ibid., 9:12.   [5] Ibid., 9:27.
[6] Ibid., 12:1 ff.   [7] Ibid., 13:14 ff.; 17:1 ff.; 18:17 ff.   [8] Ibid., 22:12 ff.
[9] Ibid., 26:5.   [10] Ibid., 28:3 f.

thee and thy seed all the tribes of the earth shall be blessed." [11] It was then that he saw a ladder that touched heaven; on the ladder the angels of God were ascending and descending and above it was the Lord Himself. It was the same Jacob who, on the verge of death, blessed his sons and said in particular to Juda: "The scepter shall not be taken away from Juda, nor a ruler from his thigh, till he come that is to be sent, and he shall be the expectation of nations." [12]

To summarize the prophecies of Genesis: Salvation was to come from the posterity of the woman, from the race of Seth, from the branch of Sem, from the family of Abraham, from the family of Isaac, and of Jacob, and from the tribe of Juda.[13]

Later, Balaam announced: "A star shall rise out of Jacob and a scepter shall spring up from Israel." [14] Finally Moses, the legislator and liberator of Israel, announced: "The Lord thy God will raise up to thee [Israel] a Prophet of thy nation and of thy brethren like unto me: Him thou shalt hear." [15] This promise in its fullest sense clearly includes the Messiah, the prophet par excellence, the universal mediator between God and men, the author of the second alliance as Moses was the mediator of the first alliance. That is why the New Testament relates this promise to Christ and declares that it was fulfilled in Him. Jesus Himself says to the Pharisees: "For if you did believe Moses, you would perhaps believe Me also; for he wrote of Me." [16]

After Pentecost St. Peter said to the Jews: "Moses said: A prophet shall the Lord your God raise up unto you of your brethren, like unto me: him you shall hear according to all things whatsoever he shall speak to you. And it shall be, that every soul which will not hear that prophet, shall be destroyed from among the people. . . . [For] to you first God, raising up His Son, hath sent Him to bless you; that every one may convert himself from his wickedness." [17] St. Stephen, the first martyr, also repeated this prophecy of Moses before he was stoned by the Jews.[18]

---

[11] *Ibid.*, 28:14.   [12] *Ibid.*, 49:10.

[13] For these prophecies cf. Gen. 3:15; 5:29; 9:26; 12:3; 26:1–4; 35:9; 44:10.

[14] Num. 24:17.   [15] Deut. 18:15.   [16] John 5:46.

[17] Acts 3:22.   [18] *Ibid.*, 7:37.

The Period of the Kings

During this period, which was primarily David's, the Messiah was announced as king, Son of God, priest par excellence, and there were even descriptions of His passion and sacrifice.

First of all Anna, Samuel's mother, saluted from afar in her canticle the king and the Christ that God would send: "The Lord shall judge the ends of the earth, and He shall give empire to His king, and shall exalt the horn of His Christ." [19]

Through the lips of the prophet Nathan God promised to David as a reward for building the Temple: "And when thy days shall be fulfilled and thou shalt sleep with thy fathers, I will raise up thy seed after thee, which shall proceed out of thy bowels, and I will establish his kingdom. He shall build a house to My name, and I will establish the throne of his kingdom forever. I will be to him a father, and he shall be to me a son. . . . My mercy I will not take away from him. . . . And thy house . . . and thy throne shall be firm forever." [20]

The title "son of David" given to the Messiah in rabbinical writings presupposes the universal acceptance by the Jews of the Messianic significance of the passage just quoted.

David himself in the psalms announced the universal dominion of God, and he described the glories and sorrows of the Messiah, who was to be the King of all peoples: "And all kings of the earth shall adore Him: all nations shall serve Him. For He shall deliver the poor from the mighty: and the needy that had no helper." [21]

How pregnant with meaning are these words, especially when applied to the feasts of Epiphany and of Christ the King! David called this King "the Anointed of the Lord," "Christ," and even "Son of God," as, for instance, in psalm 2: "The kings of the earth stood up, and the princes met together, against the Lord, and against His Christ," that is, against the One who had received the royal anoint-

[19] I Kings 2:10.

[20] II Kings 7:12–16. This prophecy refers specifically to Solomon (verse 13), but in Solomon are included all his descendants (verses 14–16). St. Peter applied this prophecy to Jesus Christ (Acts 2:30).

[21] Ps. 71:11 f.

ing, the Anointed One par excellence, the Messiah-King. The psalm continues: "He that dwelleth in heaven shall laugh at them: and the Lord shall deride them. . . . But I am appointed king by Him over Sion, His holy mountain, preaching His commandment. The Lord hath said to Me: Thou art My Son, this day have I begotten Thee. Ask of me, and I will give Thee the Gentiles for Thy inheritance, and the utmost parts of the earth for Thy possession." This prophecy has been fulfilled in the catholicity of the Church.

Psalm 109 describes the kingship and the priesthood of the Messiah: "The Lord said to my Lord: Sit Thou at My right hand: until I make Thy enemies Thy footstool. The Lord will send forth the scepter of Thy power out of Sion. . . . The Lord hath sworn, and He will not repent: Thou art a priest forever according to the order of Melchisedech. The Lord at Thy right hand . . . shall judge among nations." St. Paul enlarged on this prophecy in his Epistle to the Hebrews.

Yet David also foretold in psalm 39, verses 7–9, that the Messiah would offer Himself up voluntarily as a victim for sin; "Sacrifice and oblation Thou didst not desire. . . . Burnt offering and sin offering Thou didst not require. Then said I, Behold I come. In the head of the book it is written of Me that I should do Thy will: O My God, I have desired it, and Thy law in the midst of My heart." In the Epistle to the Hebrews, St. Paul says that Christ uttered these words upon coming into the world and offered Himself as a voluntary victim because the sacrifices of the Old Law were powerless to wipe out sin.[22]

Psalm 21 contains the words Jesus pronounced on the cross: "O God, My God, . . . why hast Thou forsaken Me? . . . O My God, I shall cry by day, and Thou wilt not hear: and by night. . . . But Thou dwellest in the holy place. . . . In Thee have our fathers hoped: they have hoped, and Thou hast delivered them. They cried to Thee, and they were saved. . . . But I am a worm, and no man: the reproach of men, and the outcast of the people. All they that saw Me have laughed Me to scorn: they have spoken with the lips, and wagged the head. He hoped in the Lord, let Him deliver Him:

[22] Heb. 10:7–9.

let Him save Him, seeing He delighteth in Him. For Thou art He that hast drawn Me out of the womb: . . . depart not from Me. For tribulation is very near: for there is none to help Me. . . . Fat bulls have besieged Me. . . . I am poured out like water; and all My bones are scattered. . . . My tongue hath cleaved to My jaws. . . . For many dogs have encompassed Me: the council of the malignant hath besieged Me. They have dug My hands and feet.[23] They have numbered all My bones. And they have looked and stared upon Me. They parted My garments amongst them; and upon My vesture they cast lots. But Thou, O Lord, remove not Thy help to a distance from Me; look toward My defense. . . . Save Me from the lion's mouth."

Finally, in psalm 15, verse 10, David announced the fruits of the Messiah's sacrifice and His resurrection: "Thou wilt not leave My soul in hell; nor wilt Thou give Thy Holy One to see corruption."

As Father Lagrange, O.P., shows, the only literal explanation of psalm 16 (15), verse 10, especially according to the Greek, is that made in the Acts of the Apostles: [24] the person who speaks in this psalm hopes to rise from the dead. The apostles, who testified to the resurrection of Christ, quite naturally saw in it the fulfillment of the verse.[25]

Even in psalm 21, which begins with the words "O God, My God, . . . why hast Thou forsaken Me?" David described the glory of the Messiah as being the fruit of His passion: "I will declare Thy name to My brethren: in the midst of the church will I praise Thee. Ye that fear the Lord, praise Him: all ye, the seed of Jacob, glorify Him. Let all the seed of Israel fear Him: because He hath not slighted nor despised the supplication of the poor man. Neither hath He turned away His face from Me: and when I cried to Him, He heard Me. . . . All the ends of the earth shall remember, and shall be converted to the Lord [to the God of Israel]: and all the kindreds of the Gentiles shall adore in His sight." [26]

[23] Likewise in Ps. 68:22 we read: "And they gave Me gall for My food, and in My thirst they gave Me vinegar to drink."

[24] Acts 2:25–32; 13:35–37.

[25] Lagrange, "Le Messianisme dans les Psaumes," in *Revue biblique* (1905), p. 192.

[26] Ps. 21:23–28.

Summing up, David announced the sufferings and the glories of the Messiah. The Messiah was to be the Son of God, He was to be the mighty king, merciful to the humble but dreaded by the wicked, the priest par excellence.[27] At the same time He was to be the voluntary victim for sin; He was to be overwhelmed with anguish and suffer a terrible death; but He would rise glorious from the grave.[28]

After David there was Solomon, who sang of the eternal Wisdom that was to be manifested to the world: "The Lord possessed me in the beginning of His ways. . . . I was set up from eternity. . . . Wisdom hath built herself a house. . . . She hath slain her victims, mingled her wine, and set forth her table. . . . And to the unwise she said: Come, eat my bread, and drink the wine which I have mingled for you, . . . and walk by the ways of prudence."[29] Today we have the Eucharist, the Eucharistic bread, and the precious blood.

Then too, the Canticle of Canticles, according to tradition, sings of the union of Christ with His Church, mention of which is also made in psalm 44:7.

It is clear that the prophecies of the period of the Kings, as well as the earlier ones, always refer to a Messiah who was to be of the race of Israel, but who was also the Son of God, and Himself God: "The Lord said to my Lord." It was by referring to this psalm 109, that our Lord silenced the Pharisees with the words: "What think you of Christ; whose Son is He? They say to Him: David's. He saith to them: How then doth David in spirit call Him Lord, saying: The Lord said to my Lord, Sit on My right hand, until I make Thy enemies Thy footstool? If David then call Him Lord, how is He his son? And no man was able to answer Him a word: neither durst any man from that day forth ask Him any more questions."[30] Thus the prophecies of this period are clear and explicit.

The predictions of the period of the prophets, particularly those of Isaias, shed still more light on the Savior and on the work He was to accomplish.

[27] Ps. 2:7; 71; 110.   [28] Ps. 39:7–9; 21; 48; 15:10.   [29] Prov. 8:22—9:6.
[30] Matt. 22:42–46; cf. Mark 12:35–37; Luke 20:41–44.

The Period of the Prophets

At this period in the history of Israel, it is the origin of the Savior, His qualities, His functions, and His sacrifice that were brought into relief.

Abdias (chap. 21) made the general prophecy that saviors were to come on Mount Sion. Joel predicted the pouring forth of the Spirit of God on all flesh, and he added: "And it shall come to pass, that everyone that shall call upon the name of the Lord shall be saved: for in Mount Sion and in Jerusalem shall be salvation, as the Lord hath said, and in the residue whom the Lord shall call." [31] Osee announced the conversion of Israel and the kingship of the future Messiah.[32] Micheas portrayed the peoples flocking toward Jerusalem the city of salvation,[33] and the Messiah's birth at Bethlehem: "And thou, Bethlehem Ephrata, art a little one among the thousands of Juda: out of thee shall He come forth unto Me that is to be the ruler in Israel: and His going forth is from the beginning, from the days of eternity. . . . Now shall He be magnified even to the ends of the earth." [34] We can see the fulfillment of this oracle in our own time in the progress of the missions or of evangelization.

It was Isaias especially who in his great prophecy described the birth of the Messiah, His divine attributes, His universal kingdom, His sacrifice which was to bring salvation to all peoples, and His triumph.

First, the nativity: "Therefore the Lord Himself shall give you a sign: Behold a virgin shall conceive, and bear a son, and His name shall be called Emmanuel." [35] This isolated text is indeed remarkable, but it is somewhat obscure. Who is this virgin? The answer is made clearer further on, for the name "Emmanuel" is more explicitly defined in the following chapter, in which Emmanuel means "Lord," "Messiah," "God is with us." [36] St. Matthew, and after him Catholic tradition, interpret the "virgin" of Isaias' text to mean the Virgin

---

[31] Joel 2:32; cf. *ibid.*, 2:28–31. [32] Osee 3:5; 11:1.
[33] Mich., chap. 4; cf. also Isa. 2:2 ff.; Zach. 8:20 ff.
[34] Mich. 5:1–3.   [35] Isa. 7:14.   [36] *Ibid.*, 8:8, 10.

Mary, and "Emmanuel" to mean the Word incarnate, the Son of God made man, truly God with us.[37] In St. Matthew 1:20 f., we see how the revelation made to Joseph before the birth of Jesus is the consummation of the one made earlier to Isaias: "Behold the angel of the Lord appeared to him in his sleep, saying: Joseph, son of David, fear not to take unto thee Mary thy wife, for that which is conceived in her, is of the Holy Ghost. And she shall bring forth a son: and thou shalt call His name Jesus. For He shall save His people from their sins." Now all this was to happen, St. Matthew tells us, "that it might be fulfilled which the Lord spoke by the prophet, saying: Behold a virgin shall be with child, and bring forth a son, and they shall call His name Emmanuel, which being interpreted is, God with us."

The functions of the Messiah are described in chapter 9 and those following: "For a child is born to us, and a son is given to us, and the government is upon His shoulder: and His name shall be called Wonderful, Counselor, God the Mighty, the Father of the world to come, the Prince of Peace." [38] The coming of no greater person could be prophesied. The words "God the Mighty" clearly mean that in this child who was to come into the world would rest the fullness of divine power. Very few grasped the meaning of these words when they were written. They have the sublimity of the prologue to St. John's Gospel: "In the beginning was the Word, and the Word was with God, and the Word was God. . . . And the Word was made flesh, and dwelt among us."

In chapter 11 we read: "And there shall come forth a rod out of the root of Jesse [David's father], and a flower shall rise out of his root. And the Spirit of the Lord shall rest upon Him: the spirit of wisdom and of understanding, the spirit of counsel and of fortitude, the spirit of knowledge and of godliness.[39] And He shall be filled with the spirit of the fear of the Lord. . . . He shall judge the poor with justice, and shall reprove with equity for the meek of the earth." These are the gifts of the Holy Ghost that the Messiah was to re-

---

[37] Cf. Lagrange, "La Vierge et Emmanuel," in *Revue biblique* (1892), p. 481; and Knabenbauer, *Comm. in Isaiam*, I, 172.   [38] Isa. 9:6 ff.

[39] According to the Hebrew this verse should read, "fear of the Lord"; but the Septuagint and the Vulgate use the word "godliness," which has almost the same meaning.

ceive in an eminent degree and the just were to receive also by participation.

The Messiah's universal kingdom is proclaimed in 16:5; 18:7; and in chapters 24 to 27. His character as cornerstone is spoken of in 28:16: "Therefore thus saith the Lord God: Behold I will lay a stone in the foundations of Sion, a tried stone, a cornerstone, a precious stone, founded in the foundation. He that believeth, let him not hasten." After Pentecost St. Peter tells the members of the Sanhedrin: "This [Jesus, in whose name the lame man had been cured] is the stone which was rejected by you the builders, which is become the head of the corner. Neither is there salvation in any other. For there is no other name under heaven given to men, whereby we must be saved." [40] Isaias had said that this cornerstone would be "a stone of stumbling. . . . And very many . . . shall stumble and fall, and shall be broken in pieces [against it]." [41] St. Paul also mentions it in the Epistle to the Romans, and he adds: "whosoever believeth in Him shall not be confounded." [42] Similar references are to be found in Ephesians 2:20 and in I Peter 2:4.

Isaias announced that God Himself would come: "God Himself will come and will save you. Then shall the eyes of the blind be opened, and the ears of the deaf shall be unstopped. Then shall the lame man leap as a hart, and the tongue of the dumb shall be free. . . . And a path and a way shall be there, and it shall be called the holy way: the unclean shall not pass over it, and this shall be unto you a straight way, so that fools shall not err therein. . . . They shall walk there that shall be delivered. And the redeemed of the Lord shall return, and shall come into Sion with praise, and everlasting joy shall be upon their heads." [43] Usually the prophets associated the Messianic deliverance with the supreme apparition of God upon earth. [44]

The virtues and works of the servant of God are clearly foretold: "Behold My servant, I will uphold Him: My elect, My soul delighteth in Him: I have given My spirit upon Him, He shall bring forth judgment to the Gentiles. He shall not cry, nor have respect

[40] Acts 4:11. [41] Isa 8:14 f. [42] Rom. 9:32 f.
[43] Isa. 35:4 ff. [44] Cf. ibid., 7:14; 40:5; Mal. 3:1.

to person, neither shall His voice be heard abroad. The bruised reed He shall not break, and smoking flax He shall not quench: He shall bring forth judgment unto truth. He shall not be sad nor troublesome, till He set judgment in the earth. . . . Thus saith the Lord God that created the heavens and stretched them out. . . . I the Lord have called Thee in justice. . . . And I have given Thee for a covenant of the people, for a light of the Gentiles: that Thou mightest open the eyes of the blind, and bring forth the prisoner out of prison, and them that sit in darkness out of the prison house. I the Lord [the One who is], this is My name: I will not give My glory to another, nor My praise to graven things." [45]

According to some rationalists, "servant of God" signifies the people of Israel as a whole. However, most present-day critics and all Catholic exegetes point out that in this prophecy the "servant of God" is clearly differentiated from the people of Israel. The words "The bruised reed He shall not break, and smoking flax He shall not quench: He shall bring forth judgment unto truth," refer to a real person, distinct from the mass of the people. In fact, as St. Matthew tells us,[46] Jesus commanded His apostles not to speak of His miracles so as not to arouse in the populace a craving for marvels, thereby applying the prophecy to Himself.

Isaias placed great stress on the Savior's sacrifice. He described it, even specifying certain details that were accomplished to the letter in the passion of Jesus: "I have given My body to the strikers, and My cheeks to them that plucked them: I have not turned away My face from them that rebuked Me. The Lord God is My helper, therefore am I not confounded: therefore have I set My face as a most hard rock, and I know that I shall not be confounded." [47]

"Behold My servant shall understand, He shall be exalted, and extolled, and shall be exceeding high. As many have been astonished at thee, so shall His visage be inglorious among men, and His form among the sons of men. . . . And there was no sightliness, that we should be desirous of Him. Despised, and the most abject of men, a man of sorrows, and acquainted with infirmity: and His look was as it were hidden and despised, whereupon we esteemed Him not.

[45] Isa. 42:1-9.   [46] Matt. 12:17.   [47] Isa. 50:6 f.

Surely He hath borne our infirmities and carried our sorrows.[48] . . .
But He was wounded for our iniquities, He was bruised for our sins:
the chastisement of our peace was upon Him, and by His bruises we
are healed. All we like sheep have gone astray, every one hath turned
aside into his own way: and the Lord hath laid on Him the iniquity of
us all." [49] Here we have the mystery of the Redemption in its entirety, both in its essential aspects and in some of its details.

"He shall be led as a sheep to the slaughter, and shall be dumb
as a lamb before His shearer, and He shall not open His mouth. He
was taken away [put to death] from distress, and from judgment:
who shall declare His generation? because He is cut off out of the
land of the living: for the wickedness of My people have I struck
Him." [50]

Not even the apostles, with the exception of John, realized at the
moment of the passion and death of our Savior that it was for our
salvation that He was thus offering Himself and dying on the cross.

This prophecy is so extraordinary that it has been called "the Passion according to Isaias." For it is the redemptive Passion in the most
profound sense, in its supreme motive of mercy and justice. It is the
Passion glimpsed in advance in its most inward aspects, as it was in
a measure understood by Mary at the foot of the cross, by St. John,
the holy women, the good thief, and the centurion. It is the Passion,
infinite wellspring of grace, whose true nature was to remain hidden
to the great majority of those who saw Jesus die on the cross.

Finally, after describing the humiliations and sufferings of the
Messiah, the prophet told of His triumph and the conversion of
many: "And the Lord was pleased to bruise Him in infirmity: if He
shall lay down His life for sin, He shall see a long-lived seed, and
the will of the Lord shall be prosperous in His hand [that is to say,
the conversion of all peoples and the coming of the kingdom of God
throughout the world]. . . . Because He hath delivered His soul
unto death, and was reputed with the wicked: and He hath borne
the sins of many, and hath prayed for the transgressors." [51] After the
Resurrection and the Ascension St. Paul writes to the Hebrews: "He

---

[48] Likewise the friends of Job looked upon him as a sinner.
[49] Isa. 52:13 ff.   [50] *Ibid.*, 53:7 ff.   [51] *Ibid.*, 53:10 ff.

[Christ] continueth forever. . . . Whereby . . . always living, to make intercession for us." [52]

Isaias' prophecy comes to a close with a description of the glory of the New Jerusalem that attracts all nations by its light, its holiness, and its splendor: "All you that thirst, come to the waters. . . . And the nations that knew not thee shall run to thee, because of the Lord thy God, and for the Holy One of Israel, for He hath glorified thee. Seek ye the Lord, while He may be found: call upon Him, while He is near. Let the wicked forsake his way . . . for He is bountiful to forgive. For My thoughts are not your thoughts: nor your ways My ways, saith the Lord. For as the heavens are exalted above the earth, so are My ways exalted above your ways, and My thoughts above your thoughts." [53]

"Arise, be enlightened, O Jerusalem: for thy light is come, and the glory of the Lord is risen upon thee. For behold darkness shall cover the earth, and a mist the people: but the Lord shall arise upon thee, and His glory shall be seen upon thee. And the Gentiles shall walk in thy light, and kings in the brightness of thy rising." [54]

Isaias even gives us a glimpse of the celestial Jerusalem: "Thou shalt no more have the sun for thy light by day; . . . but the Lord shall be unto thee for an everlasting light, and thy God for thy glory. Thy sun shall go down no more, and thy moon shall not decrease: for the Lord shall be unto thee for an everlasting light, and the days of thy mourning shall be ended." These texts anticipate what our Lord was so often to speak of as "eternal life." [55]

As Father Condamin, S.J., says in *Le livre d'Isaïe*: "In this magnificent poem Jerusalem is represented as the center of the universal kingdom, extending over all nations, a religious kingdom where everything converges toward the cult of Jehovah composed of the just and the saints, an eternal kingdom (55:3; 60:15, 19, 20; 61:8). The theologians are correct in seeing the realization of these promises in the Church founded by Jesus Christ, since the Servant of Jehovah is Jesus Christ and since the numerous posterity of the Servant, the multitudes of men given to Him at the price of His sufferings and

---

[52] Heb. 7:24 f.   [53] Isa. 55:1, 5–9.   [54] *Ibid.*, 60:1–3.
[55] *Ibid.*, 60:19 f.

death, are to people the New Jerusalem (53:10–12; 54:1–3)." [56]

Isaias is unquestionably the greatest of the prophets because of the importance of his revelations and the majesty of his style. He lived during one of the most troubled periods in the history of Israel, which at that time suffered much at the hands of the Assyrians.[57] As Ecclesiasticus (48:25–28) tells us: "Isaias . . . comforted the mourners in Sion. He showed what would come to pass forever, and secret things before they came." Isaias' style is both simple and sublime, perfectly natural, majestic and powerful. His judgments are concise, penetrating, and stress the salient points, dissipating illusions and emphatically drawing attention to the kingdom of God, giving a presage of the Messiah's greatness and of the majesty of divine glory.

Isaias also had true poetic genius. His vigor and imagination were equal to the great ideas he was called on to express. His poetic genius is particularly evident in the contrasts, the antitheses of his predictions. In his work, the prophecies themselves are always in poetry, some of it in verse; and very beautiful verse it is. His writing is the product of the noblest inspiration, in the truly supernatural sense of the word.

After Isaias, there was Jeremias who foretold the coming of the true pastor whom God would raise from the dead: [58] "Behold the days come, saith the Lord, and I will raise up to David a just branch: and a king shall reign, and shall be wise: and shall execute judgment and justice in the earth." [59] Ezechiel also said in the name of the Lord: "And I will set up one shepherd over them, and he shall feed them; . . . there shall be showers of blessing. . . . And they shall know that I the Lord their God am with them." [60] After the vision of the restoration of life to the dried bones, Ezechiel said: "And My

---

[56] P. 361.

[57] Isaias now appears to us clothed in glory, but during his life he was a simple man even though he came from a noble family (7:3), married only one woman (3:3), and became the father of two children (7:3; 8:3, 18). He was the friend and counselor of a much-harassed king, Ezechias; and after the invasion of Sennacherib (chap. 37 ff.), the prophet whose name was to be known to all succeeding generations retired into obscurity. According to a very ancient tradition he suffered martyrdom, being cut asunder with a wooden saw. St. Paul (Heb. 11:37) speaks of the prophets who were thus put to death. A similar Jewish tradition holds that Jeremias was stoned to death.

[58] Jer. 23:5–8.   [59] Cf. Jer. 33:14.   [60] Ezech. 34:23–31.

servant David shall be king over them, and they shall have one
shepherd." [61]

Later Jesus would say: "I am the good shepherd. The good shepherd giveth His life for His sheep. . . . I am the good shepherd;
and I know Mine and Mine know Me. As the Father knoweth Me,
and I know the Father: and I lay down My life for My sheep. And
other sheep I have that are not of this fold: them also I must bring,
and they shall hear My voice, and there shall be one fold and one
shepherd." [62] The universal kingdom of God announced by the
prophets is realized in the Church militant, suffering, and triumphant.

Daniel saw the little stone flung down from on high that was to
overthrow the colossus with clay feet, the symbol of idolatry. He
saw, too, that "the stone that struck the statue became a great mountain, and filled the whole earth." Then he explained the symbol
by saying: "The God of heaven will set up a kingdom that shall never
be destroyed, and His kingdom shall not be delivered up to another
people, and it shall break in pieces and shall consume all these kingdoms, and itself shall stand forever." [63] This was the announcement
of the indefectibility of the Church.

Daniel also foresaw the power that would be given to the Son of
man: "And He gave Him power and glory and a kingdom: and all
peoples, tribes, and tongues shall serve Him: His power is an everlasting power that shall not be taken away: and His kingdom that
shall not be destroyed. . . . The saints of the most high God shall
take the kingdom: and they shall possess the kingdom forever and
ever." [64]

Finally, Daniel announced in a very mysterious manner in the
prophecy of the seventy weeks the time of the coming of the Messiah (9:24): "Seventy weeks are shortened upon thy people, and upon
thy holy city, that transgression may be finished, and sin may have an
end, and iniquity may be abolished: and everlasting justice may be
brought; and vision and prophecy may be fulfilled; and the saint of
saints may be anointed." The tradition of the Church has understood
this verse to refer to the work accomplished in the world by the com-

[61] *Ibid.*, 37:24.   [62] John 10:11–16.   [63] Dan. 2:34–44.
[64] *Ibid.*, 7:14–18.

ing of Jesus Christ. The seventy weeks are seventy periods of seven years, like those in Leviticus,[65] until the advent of Him who was to wash away the sins of the world.

Among the last prophets, Aggeus promised his contemporaries that the Messiah would enter the new temple they were then building.[66] Zacharias saluted the Messiah on Sion (2:8-13), the "Orient," who will raise up the true temple of the Lord, the king on his humble mount, on an ass, the Savior, the source of grace to Jerusalem.[67]

Malachias, the last of the prophets, announced the forerunner who was to follow him four centuries later; [68] he spoke of the sacrifice that would replace all others: "From the rising of the sun even to the going down, My name is great among the Gentiles, and in every place there is sacrifice, and there is offered to My name a clean oblation: for My name is great among the Gentiles, saith the Lord of hosts." [69] Catholic tradition applies this verse to the sacrifice of the New Law, that is, the Eucharistic Sacrifice which perpetuated in substance the sacrifice of the Cross until the end of the world among all evangelized peoples.

Such was the progressive development of the divine revelations on the Messiah. From the very beginning of the period of the prophets this development was characterized by wonderful unity. All these prophecies announce the establishment of the monotheistic religion, the universal reign of the true God, the God of Abraham, of Isaac, and of Jacob, who was to become the God of all the nations of the earth. The prophecies all announce the Messiah, the head of the kingdom of God, Savior of the world, who was to be of the family of Abraham, Isaac, and Jacob, of the tribe of Juda, the son of David according to the flesh and yet the Son of God and the priest par excellence whose painful sacrifice would wash away the sins of the world and would be an infinite source of grace to all souls of good will.

[65] Lev. 25:8. [66] Agg. 2:1-10.
[67] Zach. 2:8-13; 3:8; 6:9-15; 9:9; 13:1; 14. [68] Mal. 3:1.
[69] Ibid., 1:11-14.

The Power of the Prophecies

Once we understand the true meaning of the divine testimony contained in the Old Testament, telling of the coming of the Savior, we can grasp some of the power of these predictions.

God alone by His foreknowledge could know long before the event (at least 400 years) and even in detail many free acts of the future involving the free will of a number of persons, the free will of the Messiah and that of His disciples and persecutors.

Jesus was born in Bethlehem [70] of the family of Juda and of David,[71] to preach the gospel to the poor and the meek; [72] He opened the eyes of the blind, restored the infirm to health, and led to the light those that languished in darkness.[73] He showed the perfect way and was a teacher to the Gentiles.[74] He was a victim for the sins of the world.[75] He was both the stone of stumbling and the cornerstone.[76] He was also like the little stone which Daniel spoke of [77] that was to grow into a mountain and fill the earth.

He was rejected, misunderstood,[78] betrayed, sold,[79] struck in the face, mocked, covered with spittle,[80] given gall for drink.[81] He was pierced, His hands and His feet were nailed; [82] He died as a result of this brutal treatment,[83] and upon His vesture men cast lots.

He rose from the dead [84] the third day.[85] He ascended into heaven to take His place at the right hand of the Almighty.[86] Kings took up arms against Him.[87] But afterward the kings of many peoples throughout the earth adored Him.[88] And the calling of the Gentiles, through Jesus Christ, foretold by the prophets, was accomplished.

Considering all these prophecies from our vantage point, after they have been abundantly fulfilled, we are aware of something truly remarkable about them.

---

[70] Mich. 5:2.
[71] Gen. 49:10; Isa. 7:13 f.
[72] Isa. 29:18 f.
[73] Ibid., 61:1.
[74] Ibid., 55:4; 42:1–7.
[75] Ibid., 53:5.
[76] Ibid., 8:14; Ps. 117:22.
[77] Dan. 2:35.
[78] Ps. 108:8; Isa. 53:2 f.
[79] Zach. 11:12.
[80] Isa. 50:6.
[81] Ps. 68:22.
[82] Zach. 12:10; Ps. 21:17.
[83] Dan. 9:26.
[84] Ps. 15:10.
[85] Ibid., 109:1.
[86] Ibid.
[87] Ibid., 2:2.
[88] Isa. 60:14.

Only God could forsee all these free acts by men, many of whom were in opposition to one another. Above all, only God could foresee the unquestionably extraordinary facts which depend on His liberty alone and are beyond the natural expectations of men, such as the birth of the Messiah at Bethlehem rather than elsewhere, or His triumph after the annihilation of His passion, or again the evangelization of the entire world, as known to the ancients, by a few poor Galilean fishermen.

Such numerous, confident, and extraordinary predictions cannot be natural phenomena. They surpassed human sagacity, and the natural aspirations of the Jews as well. For the Jews were much inclined to view even religious matters in a materialistic light, and they were little disposed to allow other peoples to participate in their religious privileges.

Nor can these predictions be fortuitous in nature. For blind chance, being accidental, cannot be the first cause of order in the world or of the great events which give history its noblest meaning. If it were, then order would spring from the absence of order, the harmony and beauty of great human lives would derive from an unintelligent cause, and what is more perfect would come from what is less perfect, without any reason whatever.

Lastly, the extraordinary holiness of Jesus which everyone—even Renan and the other rationalists—recognize, can come only from an intelligent and holy cause, and this cause must be God Himself by whom Jesus was sent forth.

Thus Pascal was able to write: "The greatest proofs of Jesus Christ are the prophecies. And God Himself furnished them most liberally. . . . For sixteen hundred years (that is, since Abraham) He raised up prophets; and for the next four hundred years He spread these prophecies, together with the entire Jewish people which held them in custody, throughout the world: [89] it was necessary not only that there be prophecies to make people believe, but that these prophecies be diffused over the face of the earth so that everyone would accept the Gospel." [90]

---

[89] During this period the Jews spread into Alexandria and Asia Minor, and from the latter into Greece and the Roman Empire.   [90] *Pensées*, sect. 11, "Les Propheties."

Pascal, to show more clearly the power of these predictions, emphasizes the multiplicity of prophets who came at different epochs, in various conditions, and yet who were all in agreement with regard to what they were announcing.

"Had even one man written a book of prophecies about Jesus Christ, as to the time and the manner [in which He was to be born, live, and die], and had Jesus Christ come in fulfillment of these prophecies, this would have been evidence of infinite power. But we have much more here: we have a succession of men over four thousand years [that is, since the beginning of the world] who came one after the other and constantly and without variation foretold the same advent. It was an entire people that announced it and that subsisted for four thousand years in order to bear witness as a body to the assurances they had of it, from which neither threats nor persecutions could deter them: this fact has a far greater significance."

The time foretold by Daniel in particular [91] could not have been humanly foreseen because of the complexity of the events involved. Pascal says: "It takes courage to predict one thing in so many ways: the four idolatrous or pagan monarchies (spoken of by Daniel), the end of the kingdom of Juda and the seventy weeks (or seven years) had to be simultaneous and to come before the destruction of the second temple [of Jerusalem]." In fact, Daniel had said: "And after sixty-two weeks [to follow immediately upon the other seven] Christ shall be slain. . . . And a people with their leader that shall come, shall destroy the city and the sanctuary." [92] As it actually happened, a few years after the death of our Lord, in the year 70, the Roman army led by Titus captured and destroyed Jerusalem.

It was also predicted that during this period, before the destruction of Jerusalem, many pagans would be taught and brought to a knowledge of the true God adored by the Jews, and that many would be converted. Pascal adds: "During the fourth monarchy, before the destruction of the second temple, large numbers of pagans adored God and led an angelic life: young girls consecrated their virginity and their lives to God; men gave up their pleasures. What Plato was unable to persuade a few chosen and learned men to do, a secret power

[91] Dan. 2:27; 9:20; 11:2 ff. [92] Ibid., 9:26.

could succeed in urging upon a hundred million ignorant men by virtue of a few words."

In fact, between the time of Jesus' death and the year 70, the date of the destruction of Jerusalem, many notable events occurred including Pentecost, the conversion of St. Paul, his three apostolic voyages, the first council of Jerusalem, the foundation of the different Churches to which St. Paul addressed his letters, his own martyrdom and that of St. Peter.

Indeed, what was the cause of all this? Pascal continues: "The rich give up their possessions, children leave the comforts of their parents' homes for the austerity of the desert. What does all this mean? It is what was foretold long before. For two thousand years (that is, since Abraham) no pagan had adored the God of the Jews; and at the time predicted throngs of pagans turned to adore this one and only God. Temples were destroyed, kings bowed before the Cross. What does all this mean? It is the Spirit of God which has been poured out over the earth."

The prophet Joel, speaking in the name of the Lord, had announced: "I will pour out My Spirit upon all flesh: and your sons and your daughters shall prophesy. . . . Moreover upon My servants and handmaids in those days I will pour forth My Spirit." [93]

And this is what really happened. As Pascal also tells us: "All the peoples of the world lived in infidelity and in concupiscence; the whole earth was aflame with charity. Princes left their honors; girls suffered martyrdom. Whence comes this power? It is that the Messiah has come. These are the effect and the signs of His coming."

Despite persecutions and passions in revolt, this all came to pass: "All the great of the earth unite [against Christ and the apostles], the scholars, the wise men, the kings. The former write, the latter condemn, still others kill [during three centuries]. And, notwithstanding all this opposition these simple and helpless people resist all these powers and conquer even these kings, these scholars, and these wise men, and wipe idolatry from the earth. And all this is accomplished by virtue of the force that had foretold it." [94]

Through the lips of Ezechiel the Lord had announced the king-

[93] Joel 2:28.   [94] Pascal, *loc. cit.*

dom of the Messiah: "I the Lord have brought down the high tree [idolatry], and exalted the low tree. . . . I the Lord have spoken and have done it." [95]

Pascal did not fail to note an objection that comes naturally to mind with respect to these prophecies: "If all this was so clearly foretold to the Jews, why did they not believe it? And why were they not exterminated for resisting something so evident?"

"I answer," he says: "First of all, it was predicted that they would not believe something so clear and that they would not be exterminated. Secondly, nothing brings greater glory to the Messiah; for it was not enough that prophets should exist; it was necessary that their prophecies be preserved without suspicion." That is how everything came to pass. "The Jews, by killing Jesus in order not to accept Him as the Messiah, gave Him the crowning mark of the Messiah. And by continuing to misjudge Him they became the irreproachable witnesses [speaking against themselves though not wishing to be conscious of it]; and by killing Him and continuing to deny Him, they accomplished the prophecies." [96]

In fact, both David and Isaias had announced the Servant of God would be "despised, and the most abject of men, a man of sorrows, and acquainted with infirmity. . . . And we have thought Him as it were a leper, and as one struck by God and afflicted." [97]

Yet the prophets announced not only His sufferings and His death of expiation, but also His elevation and the establishment by Him of a spiritual kingdom of God over all peoples. This has been accomplished by the evangelization of the whole world.

Thus, from all eternity God foresaw the sin of the Jews, but He did not will it in any way. He merely permitted it for the sake of a greater good, for the sake of the heroic patience of the Savior. This divine foresight suppressed neither the free will of Jesus nor that of His persecutors.

Two conclusions come forth from all this. The expectation for the Messiah was distorted, given a materialistic turn by the national prejudices of the Jews. But let us not give a materialistic interpreta-

---

[95] Ezech. 17:24.   [96] Pascal, *loc. cit.*   [97] Isa. 53:3 f.

tion to the Gospel, let us not lower it to our level; but by our fidelity let us rise toward its level, let us allow divine grace to raise us toward the Gospel, and let us truly put it into practice.

The penetrating force of the prophecies must produce its effects not only upon our minds, but also upon our hearts and souls. We must show by our own lives that Christ has really come into the world, that He is the Savior, that His regenerative action is ever at work in the world and must continue until the end of time, just as in the early days of Christianity.

✤ VII ✤

THE DIVINE PERSONALITY OF JESUS

IF WE would glimpse at the intimate life of our Lord as it has been from all eternity, we must pause and contemplate the mystery of His divine personality.

We have seen with what reserve He at first manifested Himself so as not to arouse a wholly external enthusiasm in a crowd craving for marvels and for earthly prosperity. Now we can understand a little better why in the beginning He showed Himself under the veil of the parables as the Sower of divine truth, as the Good Shepherd who gives His life for His sheep, as the only son of the master of the vineyard who was sent after the servants had been ill-treated and killed by the husbandmen. In the last-mentioned parable He announcd that He would be put to death.

In the course of His ministry He gradually showed Himself to be equal to the divine Lawgiver of Sinai, since He came to perfect the divine law. When He cured the paralytic He claimed the power to remit sins, to remake or regenerate men's souls: "Come to Me, all you that labor, and are burdened, and I will refresh you." [1]

Finally, as His passion approached, He declared more openly the fact of His divine sonship. He affirmed it before the Pharisees with an authority that can belong only to God. He who was meek and humble of heart did not fear to tell them: "Amen, amen I say to you, before Abraham was made, I am." He declared: "I and the Father are one." "I am the way and the truth and the life." [2] He did not merely say, as had the prophets, "I have received the truth that I might transmit it to you." He said: "I am the truth and the life," words that God alone can rightfully use.

---

[1] Matt. 11:28.   [2] John 8:58; 10:30; 14:6.

Such was Jesus' teaching with respect to His divinity and it was so understood by the apostles. St. Peter saw in Him "the Author of life." [3] St. Paul spoke of Him as "the Son of His [God's] love, . . . who is the image of the invisible God, the first-born of every creature," in whom "were all things created in heaven and on earth, visible and invisible"; [4] the Son who being equal with God the Father "humbled Himself, becoming obedient unto death, even to the death of the cross." [5] St. John the Baptist looked upon Him as "the Lamb of God . . . who taketh away the sin of the world." [6] And St. John the Evangelist called Him the Word made flesh: "In the beginning was the Word, and the Word was with God, and the Word was God" (John 1:1).

Thus the Church merely repeats the testimony that Jesus gave of Himself when she professes in the Creed that He is "the only-begotten Son of God, light of light, true God of true God, . . . being of one substance with the Father," and that by Him "all things were made" (Nicene Creed).

Such in brief is our Lord's testimony about His divine sonship. With the help of theology, let us meditate on the meaning and scope of this testimony. Let us also ask God to give us the grace of contemplating this mystery. For in this contemplation our souls must find their daily nourishment and they must live by it more and more with each passing day.

In order to penetrate even a little into the mystery of the divine personality of Jesus, we must understand the fittingness of the Incarnation with respect to both God and man. This will give us much light.

Jesus has claimed for Himself the properties of divine nature and those of human nature as well. He has shown Himself to us as truly a man, who was born in time at Bethlehem and died on the cross. At the same time He had told us: "I am the way and the truth and the life." I am the truth and the life in their fullness.

How can one and the same person have two natures that are infinitely apart, divine nature and human nature? We have perhaps ceased to look upon this with astonishment, the holy astonishment

[3] Acts 3:15.   [4] Col. 1:13–16.   [5] Phil. 2:6–8.   [6] John 1:29.

of contemplation. There is, of course, another form of astonishment that leads to negation.

Incredulity objects: A God made flesh would be no longer God or man, but a fabulous being, a myth, half-God, half-man. He would have a hybrid nature, neither divine nor human (this was Eutyches' error).

The incredulous ask: How could the infinite God who governs the world be in person in the body of a helpless little child? An infinite God in the womb of a virgin! Thus does human wisdom speak, seeing only darkness in supernatural truths that are far too lofty and too mighty for it.

Indeed, the union of humanity and divinity in the person of Jesus remains an incomprehensible mystery for the believer, and it will be definitely explained only in heaven. Yet the light of faith shows us even here below that on the one hand God tends to communicate Himself as much as possible to man and that, on the other hand, man tends to be united as much as possible to God. When we place these two truths side by side, we begin to glimpse from afar the union of humanity and divinity in the person of the Savior. We shall strive to develop these two points in what follows.

God Has Given Himself in Person to Humanity

God, on the one hand, tends to communicate Himself as much as possible to man. Why? Because God is the Sovereign Good, and goodness is essentially communicative. The good naturally tends to pour itself out, to share the riches within it.[7] And the more perfect a good is, the more it tends to communicate itself fully and intimately.[8] The sun sheds about it light and heat. Plants and animals having reached adulthood give life to other plants and animals. At a higher level, the artist and the scholar, who have conceived ideas, strive to make them known. The apostle who loves goodness passionately, desires to communicate it to others. Goodness is fundamentally communicative; the higher its level the more abundantly and in-

---

[7] Cf. St. Thomas, IIIa, q. 1, a. 1.

[8] Cf. St. Thomas, *Contra Gentes*, Bk. IV, chap. 11, no. 1.

timately it gives itself. Whereas the friendship of a superficial soul remains totally external and a matter of the affections, the friendship of a noble soul is the generous gift of its innermost self.

Thus, since God is the Sovereign Good, it is highly fitting that He communicate Himself in the highest degree possible to His creatures, both intimately and fully. But this divine communication, fitting as it is, remains free—something that the Neo-Platonists did not understand. It is in no way necessary to the infinite beatitude of God. For He finds His beatitude in the possession of His own sovereign goodness, which is infinitely superior to all created goods and cannot be increased by them.[9] God created all things freely. At the dawn of creation it was through His goodness that He gave His creatures being, life, intelligence. Through a wholly gratuitous love He raised men and angels to the supernatural life of grace, to a participation in His own intimate life. Is this the limit of what God can do?

Why could He not give Himself in person? Is it not the peculiar quality of friendship to inspire us to give our innermost selves? Why could not the Word of God give Himself in person to a privileged soul, in such a manner that the Word, this soul and its body would form only one person, a single self, that of the Word made flesh, in whom would dwell divine perfections and human properties, a person who could truthfully say: "I who speak to you am the way, the truth, and the life."

Thus in a marvelous manner would be realized the principle that God, the Sovereign Good, tends to communicate Himself to man in the highest degree possible. Goodness is essentially communicative, and the nobler it is the more abundantly and intimately it gives itself. This is the most elevated aspect of the mystery of which we are speaking.

The Full Development of the Human Personality and Union with God

The unbeliever objects: But then, since Jesus would possess no human personality, He would not be truly a man. This was the ob-

[9] Cf. St. Thomas, Ia, q. 19, a. 3.

jection once raised by Nestorius and his disciples. Some modern rationalists expand this view by saying that human personality consists
primarily in the consciousness a man has of himself and in the liberty
by reason of which he is his own master.[10] Thus, if Jesus did not have
a human personality,—and this is what the Church teaches—then
He had no human consciousness of Himself nor any human liberty,
but only a divine consciousness and a divine liberty. Hence, they
claim, He was not truly a man, and having no human liberty He
was powerless either to merit or to obey. If on the other hand, these
rationalists add, it is held that He had both a human consciousness and
human liberty coexistent with a divine consciousness and a divine
liberty, then it must be said that there were in Him two personalities,
two persons, doubtless very intimately united by knowledge and love,
but none the less two persons and not a single person. Therefore, the
rationalists conclude, Jesus is only the greatest of the saints who was
intimately united to God in a truly extraordinary degree; but He cannot be called God. In short, if personality is formally constituted by
consciousness or liberty, in order for Jesus to be only one person, He
could have only one consciousness and one liberty. Thus He could not
be at one and the same time truly God and truly a man.

This objection is based on a superficial and false conception of
personality, and it leaves out of consideration the very intimate
relationship between the full development of a human personality
and union with God. We have to lay very much stress on this matter,
for it is the second aspect of the mystery of Christ's divine personality.

To understand how Jesus, without having a human personality,
a human ego, can be truly a man, and how His humanity is glorified
and not lessened by the divine personality of the Word, we must consider for a moment the nature of personality in general. This would
be an easy enough task had not so many errors piled up regarding this
matter. We must therefore clear them away so as to preserve the true
meaning of the words "I" and "me" which everybody uses.

With St. Thomas we must ask ourselves what is personality, and
rise progressively from the lowest degrees of human personality up

[10] Günther and Rosmini erred in thus viewing Christ's personality. Cf. Denzinger,
Enchiridion, no. 1917.

to the most perfect. We shall then be able to glimpse through the twilight of faith at the personality of the Savior, far above that of a St. Paul, a St. Peter, or a St. John.

Personality is a positive thing. It is that which makes every being endowed with reason an independent subject who can say "I," "me"; and which makes him a being who belongs to himself, his own master *sui juris;* and by reason of which are attributed to him a reasonable nature, being, and ability to carry on the operations in which his activity consists. In this sense it is ordinarily said that Peter and Paul are persons, two distinct persons. Each of them is an independent subject and a totality to which we attribute human nature, existence, activity. Each of them says "I," "me." This fact differentiates the person as a primary subject of attribution from all that is fitting to him, and the person cannot be attributed to another subject. We say: "Peter is a man, Peter exists, Peter speaks well." But we cannot attribute Peter to another subject. He himself is the primary subject of attribution existing and functioning as a separate entity.[11]

It follows that our personality, or that by which every being endowed with reason is an independent subject, an entity to which its nature, its existence, and its operations are attributed, cannot be formally constituted by anything which is attributed to it as a part. Our basic personality can therefore not be formally constituted either by our body, or even by our soul, that is, by either of the two parts of the nature which is attributed to us, nor by any one of our faculties or of our acts.

It is therefore clear that our basic personality, from the ontological point of view, cannot be formally constituted by our consciousness. Consciousness of the ego, the "me," is not the ego, the "me." The former presupposes and knows the latter, but does not constitute it. Nor does our liberty formally constitute our personality. It is merely a psychological and moral manifestation of our basic personality, the latter belonging to the ontological order, or the order of being. For the act presupposes being: in order to act, one must first be.

Thus our personality is more fundamental than consciousness and

[11] Cf. St. Thomas, IIIa, q. 2, a. 2; q. 4, a. 2 (Cajetan's commentary, nos. 6–8); q. 17, a. 1 f.

liberty. Personality is what makes each one of us an independent subject to which is attributed all that is fitting to him. And if we can attribute to Jesus as to a single independent subject two intelligences (one divine and the other human) and two liberties, it will follow that there are not in Him two persons, but only one.[12]

All this contains a great mystery which we cannot understand. But it is not unintelligible or absurd. On the contrary, we can progressively rise to it, starting from the lowest degrees of the human personality. It is easy enough to see that from the psychological and moral point of view a human personality grows in the measure that it tends to become more intimately united to God, obliterating itself before Him. This union in self-effacement, far from being servitude, is a glorification.[13] If we study this fact carefully, we shall get a glimpse of what is realized in Christ, not only from the psychological and moral points of view, but from the point of view of being or of the basic personality.

Whereas God, as we were saying earlier, tends to give Himself as much as possible to man, the perfect man tends to become as closely united as possible to God.

Some have thought that personality develops in the measure that man becomes more and more independent in his existence and in his action from all that is not himself, and in the measure that others depend upon him. In this sense, the personalities of Napoleon and Goethe have been glorified.

Such a concept leaves out of account the fact that our personality

[12] When we say with St. Thomas that our personality is that by which every reasonable being is an independent subject to which is attributed his nature, his existence, and his operations, we are not conceding that what formally constitutes our personality is our existence. Existence is a contingent attribute of every created person, and it is not what makes a person a primary subject of attribution. No created person is his own existence, he merely has existence; in this respect he differs from God. The Thomists say: *Persona Petri, imo personalitas Petri, non est suum esse, sed realiter distinguitur ab eo.* And St. Thomas himself wrote (IIIa, q. 17, a. 2 ad 1): "Being is consequent upon person, . . . as upon that which has being." Cajetan has shown with much penetration (*In IIIam,* q. 4, a. 2, no. 8) that without this notion of personality we cannot explain the truth of the following judgments: Peter is a man, Peter exists, but he is not existence. From this it also follows that in Jesus there is only one person, a single subject, and one existence (IIIa, q. 17, a. 2) and that He was truly able to say: "I am the truth and the life," that is, being itself.

[13] Cf. St. Thomas, IIIa, q. 2, a. 2 ad 2.

consists especially in independence with regard not to all things, but to those which are inferior to us and which we dominate by our reason and our liberty, such as the independence of the soul which can subsist after the dissolution of the body.

When we glorify certain human personalities that have disregarded the rights of God, we are forgetting that our special independence with regard to inferior things is based on the very strict dependence of our souls with regard to the superior things, that is, Truth and Goodness, and in the last analysis with regard to God. If our reason rules space and time, the things of the senses, it is because it was created to know God, the supreme Truth. If our liberty conquers the attraction of the things of the senses, it is because it was created to prefer God to them, and to love Him, the universal and total Good above all else.

From these facts derives a noble and neglected law, namely, that the full development of the personality consists in becoming more and more independent of inferior things, but also in becoming ever more closely dependent upon Truth, Goodness, that is, upon God Himself.

False personality, on the contrary, consists in a so-called independence with regard to everything, including God Himself, to whom obedience is refused. This false personality scorns the so-called passive virtues of humility, patience, and gentleness. It is nothing but insubordination and pride, and reaches its fullest development in the devil whose motto is: *Non serviam* ("I will not obey"). As a matter of fact, it leads to the worst of all servitudes. True personality, on the other hand, is realized in the saints, but particularly in our Lord Jesus Christ.

Many false ideas arise about the development of personality because the mystery of the Incarnation is no longer contemplated and because it is forgotten that the full development of the human personality consists in being effaced before that of God, by becoming as united as possible to Him. We must consider this fact most carefully that we may begin to understand how it is that the humanity of Jesus is in no sense diminished because in Him human personality has made way for the divine personality of the Word. This is the culminating point of the lofty law: Human personality grows by effacing itself before that of God.

Indeed, wherein lies the superiority of the good man over the libertine? It is that the good man conforms his will to God's. Whereas the libertine is crushed by adversity, the good man grows with it, ever conforming his will more closely to God's. Whence comes the superiority of the man of genius over the ordinary worker? He is inspired by God; he is closely dependent upon a superior inspiration.

Nobler than the man of genius, a higher and more powerful personality has manifested itself through the ages: that of the saints. Personality is measured by the profound and lasting influence it can exert. Now, the influence of a saint is not limited to his own country or his own time. In a sense it extends to the whole Church in a sphere superior to space and time.

For almost two thousand years millions of souls have been living by the epistles of St. Paul, as if these pages had been written yesterday, whereas almost nobody, except for a few scholars, reads the letters of Seneca. For the past seven centuries thousands of religious have lived by the thought of a St. Bernard, a St. Dominic, a St. Francis of Assisi, of a St. Catherine of Siena and a St. Claire. How is it that these saints have exerted such a tremendous influence on souls? Whence comes their prodigious personality that raises them above the limits of their country and their time?

The secret is that in a sense they were one with God. They had died to themselves in order to live for God. No one but the saints has fully understood that human personality can truly grow only by dying to itself so that God may reign and live ever increasingly within it. That is why the saints, and only the saints,—as St. Catherine of Siena tells us—declared war on their own egos, the ego composed of self-love and pride. They have sought to live more and more not for themselves but for God, and consequently to die to their own judgment and to their own will, in order to live solely by the thought and the will of God. They have willed that God should be their *alter ego*, more intimate than their own ego. They have willed to become the servants of God, just as the hand is the servant of the will. They have willed to become genuinely adopted sons and friends of God, to the point of living continually for Him and of orienting the basic tendencies of their thought and of their will always toward Him. At certain moments of union they were able to say with St. Paul: "I live, now not I; but Christ liveth in me." [14] The full development of human personality consists in losing itself in that of God.[15]

And yet even the greatest saint remains a being distinct from God, a creature. He has indeed substituted divine ideas for his human ideas, and the divine will for his own will, but he is none the less a being distinct from God. Even our Blessed Lady during moments of most intimate contemplation remains a creature.

At the summit of holiness we find our Lord Jesus Christ. In Him God has given Himself in person to the greatest extent possible to humanity, and humanity has been personally united to God to the greatest extent possible, to the point of forming a single ego with the Word of God. In Jesus Christ, God's ideas have been substituted for human ideas, and the divine will has fully subordinated the human will. But that is not all. Something far more fundamental has taken place. At the root of the intelligence and of the will, at the root of the soul itself, in the order of being, the divine person of the Word has assumed the humanity of Jesus. That is why He could say: "I who speak to you, I am the way, the truth, and the life." "The Father and I are one." [16]

---

[14] Gal. 2:20.

[15] This superior impersonality of the saints is the fruit of their interior life. We can see it in St. John the Baptist, who wished ever more ardently to efface himself so that our Lord might be increasingly acknowledged. Likewise St. Thomas Aquinas retired more and more into the background of his books so that only the light and the truth might shine out of them. By this self-effacement the saints make place for God, and at certain moments it is clear that it is God who lives and speaks in them.

[16] We can see here the profound difference between personality and individuality. Individuality derives from matter, which is the principle of individuation. Thus two men are two distinct individuals because in each of them human nature has been received in a determinate portion of matter, at a given point in space and in time. Likewise two drops of water, similar as they may be, are two because the nature of water is received in each in a given portion of matter and in a given quantity. Individuality, deriving as it does from matter, is thus a reality of a very low order.

Personality, on the contrary, is something very lofty. For it is that by which every reasonable being is an independent subject, *sui juris*, the subject of existence and of his operations (IIIa, q. 2, a. 2 ad 2). This fact is true not only of man but also of the angels and of the divine persons of the Blessed Trinity. Each of the three divine persons is a distinct "I" even

That is why Jesus has a unique manner of pronouncing the word "I," a word that the saints rarely use except to accuse themselves of their faults. They know that all the good we do is accomplished through the power of the Lord, whereas evil comes only from ourselves. They know that our egos, composed of self-love, are, as Pascal has said, hateful, whereas the ego of Jesus is adorable: It is the ego of the Word made flesh.[17] He alone has been able to say: "He who loves his father and his mother more than Me is not worthy of Me." No one but God can speak thus.

How is it that Jesus infinitely surpasses all the saints whose model, light, strength, and life He is? It is because in Him, in the strictest meaning of the words, human personality, the human ego, has been replaced from the first moment of His conception and for all eternity by the divine personality of the Word.

In Jesus Christ there is no human personality, no human ego, and yet He is truly a man. His humanity, far from being lessened by personal union with the Word, is glorified by this union. From its union with the Word, Christ's humanity receives, as we shall see, an innate, substantial, uncreated holiness. Similarly, our imagination is nobler than that of the animals because it is united to our intelligence. In us imagination serves a superior faculty, and it is elevated by this sub-

---

though all three possess the same indivisible nature, fully communicated by the Father to the Son and by Them to the Holy Ghost: Goodness is fundamentally diffusive of itself, and the more intimately and fully diffusive it is, the higher the order to which it belongs. (Cf. St. Thomas, *Contra Gentes*, Bk. IV, chap. 11.) It follows that in Jesus the personality, which is that of the Word, is uncreated, whereas in Him, as in ourselves, individuality derives from matter, the principle of individuation, by virtue of which His body is a specific body rather than some other and occupies a given portion of space rather than any other. Thus individuality and personality are quite distinct: to develop one's individuality often means to become ever more egoistical; whereas the real development of personality is to be found, as we have seen, in an ever more intimate union with God.

[17] Here we get the full meaning and scope of the following words of St. Thomas (IIIa, q. 2, a. 2, ad 2): "Personality pertains of necessity to the dignity of a thing, and to its perfection so far as it pertains to the dignity and perfection of that thing to exist by itself (which is understood by the word person). Now it is a greater dignity to exist in something nobler than oneself than to exist by oneself. Hence the human nature of Christ has a greater dignity than ours, from this very fact that in us, being existent by itself, it has its own personality, but in Christ it exists in the Person of the Word. Thus . . . the sensitive part of man, on account of its union with the nobler form which perfects the species, is more noble than in brutes, where it is itself the form which perfects."

ordination, as is strikingly clear in artists of genius. It is the glory of
the inferior to "serve" and thus to contribute to the realization of an
end superior to itself. This has been understood by those who have
associated the words "servitude" and "greatness." "To serve God is
to reign," and no creature ever served Him so well as did the holy
humanity of our Savior.

Innumerable corollaries could be deduced from this doctrine. Let
us merely mention the more important ones.

The Hypostatic Union
The Most Intimate Union after That of the Trinity

We can see that this personal or hypostatic union (that is to say,
the union in a single person or in a single subject of divinity and
humanity) is not merely a moral union born of the conformity of
the human will with the will of God through grace and charity.
Indeed, this moral union with God, which exists especially among the
saints, can become most intimate. In the Old Testament, Abraham
was called the friend of God, but he remained infinitely removed
from God. The same holds for the apostles and for the greatest
saints.

Nor is this personal or hypostatic union a natural and essential
union, for it does not constitute a single nature or essence. The two
natures remain completely distinct, although intimately united. As
a matter of fact, divine nature is absolutely immutable and cannot
convert or change itself into a created nature; and if it could, then
Jesus would no longer be truly God. On the other hand, human
nature cannot be converted or changed into divine nature; and if it
could, Jesus would then not be truly a man. Nor can the two natures
enter into the composition of a third nature, for this would presuppose a modification or alteration of divine nature, which is absolutely
immutable, and which cannot be the incomplete part of a whole that
is more perfect than itself.

The personal or hypostatic union of divinity and humanity in Jesus
does not in any sense involve the confounding of the two natures.
Likewise, in ourselves the union of body and soul does not involve

any confusion of the two. Within limits we might make the following comparison and say that, just as our body is dominated, vivified by our soul, and will be reanimated by it on the day of resurrection, thus in Jesus human nature is completely dominated by God, possessed by the Word.[18] Christ is not a fabulous being, demi-god and half-man. He is true God and true man, without any pantheistic confusion of the two natures united in His divine person.

Thus are supernaturally realized in this sublime mystery God's desire to give Himself as much as possible to man, and man's yearning to be united as much as possible to God.

This is the strongest and most intimate union possible, after the union of the Blessed Trinity. In the Blessed Trinity the three persons are necessarily one and the same divine nature. In Jesus it is a fact that the two natures belong to the same person. This personal or hypostatic union, which constitutes the God-man, is incomparably more intimate than that of our soul with our body. Whereas the body and the soul are separated at death, the Word is never separated either from the soul or from the body which He has assumed.[19] The union is immutable and indissoluble for all eternity.

We do not contemplate enough this ineffable mystery of merciful Love. The sublimity of the mystery derives from the very fact that two natures infinitely remote from each other, one supreme and the other lowly, are so intimately united. Beauty results from unity shining through variety. When the diverse elements are infinitely removed from each other and yet intimately united, we have not merely beauty but the truly sublime. Only divine love is strong enough thus to associate supreme riches and human nature, with all the sufferings which can overwhelm it.

When we make the way of the cross and contemplate Jesus on His painful journey, bowed beneath the weight of our sins, let us remember that He is the way, the truth, and the life, and through Him

[18] Yet there is a notable difference: whereas our body and our soul are the two parts of our human nature, the humanity and the divinity of Jesus are not parts of a single nature, but they are united in the same person.

[19] Even when the body of Jesus was separated from His soul after His death, it was not separated from the person of the Word. There remained on the cross and in the holy sepulcher the sacred cadaver of the Word made flesh. Cf. St. Thomas, IIIa, q. 50, a. 2.

we shall go toward this ocean of divine life where He alone can lead us, by giving us the grace of perseverance.

We love to contemplate the sea and the mountains, and to gaze long at them in admiration. Why do we not contemplate more often this immense mystery of the Incarnation, which brings us salvation? Very simple souls, molded by the Gospel and the liturgy, attain this contemplation, as has happened quite often in the countryside of France, Spain, and Italy.

When we enter a church we often do no more than ask for a special favor for ourselves and for our dear ones. Should we not remember sometimes to thank God for having given us our Lord? The Incarnation surely merits a special act of thanksgiving. This thanksgiving which must begin here below will be continued by the saints for all eternity. This will be the canticle of the elect about which we read in the Apocalypse: "To Him that sitteth on the throne, and to the Lamb, benediction, and honor, and glory, and power, forever and ever." [20]

A soul that thanks God daily, in the intimacy of meditation, for having given us His Son, is certain to attain to a high degree of union with God. Any humble soul, even one lacking in human culture, can thank God for the infinite gift He has given us.

[20] Apoc. 5:13.

Personality

In What It Is Formally Constituted

EVERY theologian knows that personality cannot be formally constituted either by consciousness or by liberty. Consciousness of self presupposes the existence of the self of which one is conscious, but it does not constitute the self. Liberty is also a psychological and moral manifestation of the fundamental personality, to which it is attributed and which it therefore presupposes. Persons are free, but it is not liberty that constitutes them formally. Therefore it is possible for Jesus to be a single person, even though there are in Him two consciousnesses and two liberties, one divine and the other human.

Basic personality is not of the order of the act, as we have said, but of the order of being, for action presupposes being. In order to act, one must first of all be.

This basic personality is, according to natural reason or common sense, that by which every reasonable being is a primary subject of attribution who can say "I," "me," and to whom is attributed all that belongs to him, whereas he himself is attributable to no other person. Thus, Peter and Paul are persons. It is commonly said: Peter is a man, Peter exists, Peter is good, and so on. In each of these affirmative judgments the verb "to be" expresses the real identity of the subject of the proposition and of the attribute. When we say "Peter is a man," we are in fact saying that Peter is the same being who is a man, who exists, and so on.

How can the real identity of the subject and the attribute of each of these propositions be safeguarded? This requires that there exist in Peter, beneath the diversity of the qualities which are attributed to him, something that is "one," that is identical and real, something that formally constitutes him as the primary subject of attribution of all that is fitting to him. That is his basic personality in the ontological order, or the order of being.

According to some, this personality is something negative: Peter would, according to them, be a person because his humanity would not depend either radically or actually upon a divine person, or because it had not been assumed, as was the humanity of Jesus, by a divine person.[1]

Many theologians have rejected this opinion for a number of reasons: 1. What formally constitutes that by which each of us is a primary subject of attribution cannot be something negative. If dependence is a positive thing, independence is all the more a positive perfection, even though we express it in negative terms. In fact, the independence of God in the realm of being is the supreme perfection, positive in the highest degree.

2. The natural personality of each one of us cannot be defined by the absence of a wholly supernatural and exceptional grace, that is, by the absence of the grace of hypostatic union. It is not the absence of a supernatural gift which constitutes the realities of the natural order. If this were so, it would follow that the realities of the natural order are not naturally knowable and definable.

3. In the Blessed Trinity there are three personalities which are not negative but positive realities, and which must have an analogical similarity with created personality; otherwise we could not know them.

4. The real identity affirmed by such judgments as "Peter is a man, Peter exists, Peter is good" cannot be constituted and explained by something negative. There must be something positive that constitutes the subject as such, fundamentally identical in itself, under the diversity of qualities which are attributed to it.

This identity is not assured, either, by the portion of matter which exists in each of us. For, if this were the case my body, inasmuch as it is this individual body constituted by this particular portion of matter, or my hand, inasmuch as it is this individual hand, would each be

[1] Cf. Scotus, *In III Sent.*, d. 1, q. 1, nos. 5 ff.; d. 5, q. 2, nos. 4 f.

primary subjects of attribution. Now this is not true at all, for both my body and my hand are attributed to me as parts of myself. And. with respect to Christ, the individuation of His humanity by matter is infinitely removed from His uncreated personality.

5. Moreover, those who maintain that personality is a negative thing usually refuse to admit that there is, prior to the consideration of our mind, a distinction between every created essence and its existence, between every created person and its existence. Now it is true, prior to the consideration of our mind, that the humanity in us is not its existence and the person of Peter is not his existence, for God alone is His existence. God alone has been able to say: "I am who am." And it is because He is God that Jesus was able to say: "I am the truth and the life." No created person is existence; it merely has existence, which it has received. Of themselves a created essence and a created person are merely susceptible of receiving existence.

6. Those who hold that personality is something negative generally also refuse to admit that in Jesus there is only one existence. Now, as St. Thomas has well shown, the unity of existence follows from the unity of the person.[2] If the humanity of Jesus had its own existence, then it would have in the order of being its ultimate actuality or perfection independently of the Word, and the hypostatic union would be merely an accidental union, so it seems. There is in this view the danger of unconsciously returning to Nestorianism, which held that there were in Christ two accidentally united persons.

For these various reasons most theologians admit that personality consists in something positive. But there remains some divergence of opinion among them.

Some theologians hold that personality is a substantial mode which presupposes existence.[3] The reason for this view is that they, like those mentioned above, make no real distinction (that is, no distinction prior to the consideration of our mind) between created essence and existence. As a result, the substantial mode which constitutes human personality presupposes not only human essence or nature, but the existence which is identified with the essence.

---

[2] *Summa theol.*, IIIa, q. 17, a. 2.
[3] Cf. Suarez, *Disput. Metaph.*, disp. 34, sect. 1 f., 4; *De incarnatione*, disp. 11, sect. 3.

The Thomists answer this objection as they did the preceding opinion: Before the consideration of our mind the humanity in us is not existence, for God alone is His existence. Hence the distinction between the created essence and existence does not follow the consideration of our mind, but on the contrary precedes it. That is to say, it is a real distinction. Indeed it is not a spatial distinction of things which can be separated one from the other. Yet it is a distinction which is real, infinitesimal as it may appear, for it is anterior to the consideration of our mind. The so-called distinction of reason follows the consideration of our mind. And there is no middle ground between the real distinction and the distinction of reason, for a distinction either does or does not precede the consideration of our mind.

Thus personality does not presuppose existence, but the opposite is true, as St. Thomas says: "Being is consequent upon person, . . . as upon that which has being." [4] Existence is attributed to it as to a primary subject of attribution, which is itself not attributable to any other.

In addition, since existence is in all things the ultimate actuality or perfection in the order of being, all that happens to a substance already endowed with its own existence happens to it accidentally. Hence, if Jesus' humanity were to have its own existence, the substantial mode subsequent to existence (spoken of by the second group of theologians) would be only accidentally fitting to it. Thereupon the hypostatic union would become accidental, bringing us unwittingly back toward Nestorianism.

A third opinion holds, in opposition to the two preceding ones, that personality is indeed something positive that does not presuppose existence but is identified with existence, which in turn is distinct from the created essence. Thus Peter's personality would be identified with his created existence, and the personality of Jesus with the uncreated existence of the Word. [5]

Although this opinion is very similar to the doctrine of St. Thomas, it still differs from it on a significant point. St. Thomas wrote: "*Esse*

---

[4] IIIa, q. 17, a. 2 ad 1.
[5] Cf. Billot, S.J., *De Verbo incarnato*, 5th ed., q. 2, pp. 75, 84, 137, 140.

non est de ratione suppositi." [6] On the contrary, personality is what formally constitutes the person.

He also wrote: "Being is consequent upon nature, not as upon that which has being, but as upon that whereby a thing is: whereas it is consequent upon person or hypostasis, as upon that which has being." [7] Being is consequent upon nature, by reason of which Peter is a man; and it is consequent upon the person of Peter, which exists.

Thus if, according to St. Thomas, existence follows the person, it does not formally constitute the person.

It is even absolutely impossible for existence, which is a contingent attribute of every created person, to formally constitute the latter as a primary subject of attribution. That would amount to saying that the personality of Peter is his existence. Now, God alone is His existence. As the Thomists say: "Persona Petri (imo personalitas Petri, qua formaliter constituitur ejus persona) non est suum esse."

Prior to the consideration of our mind, this proposition is true: "Peter is not his own existence." "Only God is His own existence." St. Thomas says: "An angel is composed of *esse* and *quod est.*" [8] "*Quod est*" is the person who exists. There is a real distinction not only between created essence and existence, but between the created person (understood to be fully constituted by its personality) and existence.

Likewise the identification of created personality with existence leads to the denial of the real distinction between created essence and existence, a distinction which is none the less maintained by the partisans of this opinion and which is also a fundamental doctrine of Thomism.

It may be objected: But Peter is not his humanity either, and yet he is not really distinct from it. Why then, since he is not his existence, would he be really distinct from his humanity?

---

[6] *Quodlibet,* II, q. 2, a. 4: *Esse non est de ratione suppositi creati.* On the contrary, "personalitas est de ratione personae seu suppositi rationalis naturae." Moreover, in the *Treatise on the Incarnation,* St. Thomas does not deal with the unity of existence in Christ (IIIa, q. 17) until he has dealt with the hypostatic union and considered its consequences. This consequence (i.e., *est unum esse in Christo*) is therefore not the formal constituent of the personal or hypostatic union of the two natures.

[7] *Summa theol.,* IIIa, q. 17, a. 2 ad 1.   [8] *Ibid.,* Ia, q. 50, a. 2 ad 3.

We answer: Peter is really distinct from his humanity, just as the whole is distinct from its essential part, and he is all the more distinct from his existence, which is in him not an essential part but a contingent attribute.

Prior to any consideration of our mind, the following propositions are true: Peter is not his human nature. Peter is not his existence. In fact, Peter is not his human nature, for it is only the essential part of all that he is. The part, even the essential part, is not the whole. Therefore it is false to say: Peter is his nature. The verb "to be" expresses the real identity of the subject and the attribute, and even the essential part is not really identical with the whole.

Furthermore, Peter is not his existence either, for his existence is for him only a contingent attribute. In fact, Peter could very well not exist. Existence is in him neither an essential attribute nor what formally constitutes his person, since his person is merely susceptible of existing. In all created persons existence is a contingent attribute which, because it is a contingent attribute, cannot formally constitute the person as a primary subject of attribution.

In addition, as St. Thomas says, in God there are three personalities and only one existence: "The three persons have merely one being." [9] Thus the divine persons are not formally constituted by existence; hence they would not be analogically similar to human personality if the latter were formally constituted by existence.

If then personality is (1) something positive, (2) which does not presuppose existence, and (3) is not identical with existence, what is it?

The answer is, as the Thomists teach in general [10] and as Cajetan teaches in particular: Personality, according to natural reason or to common sense, is in every reasonable being that by which he is the primary subject of attribution of individuated reasonable nature, of existence, of accidents. [11]

In other words, personality is required in him to safeguard the real identity affirmed by all of the following propositions: Peter is a

[9] *Ibid.*, IIIa, q. 17, a. 2 ad 3.
[10] Cf. also Jacques Maritain, *Les degrés du savoir*, pp. 845–53.
[11] *In IIIam*, q. 4, a. 2, nos. 6–11.

man, Peter is existent, Peter is good, that is, Peter is the same being or subject who is a man, who is existent, who is good. Beneath the variety of essential and contingent qualities that are attributed to him, there must be in him something real, positive, identical, which is not any of the parts attributed to him and which formally constitutes him as the primary subject of attribution or as the whole. Thus what formally constitutes personality cannot be either individuated nature or existence or consciousness or liberty. It is what constitutes the primary subject of attribution as subject (*suppositum*). In Latin it is called "*subsistentia*," and with respect to beings endowed with reason, "*personalitas*."

This conception which seems too abstract and too subtle for some minds is merely, as Cajetan remarks, the simple explanation of what natural and common sense tell us. This is of major importance.[12]

That by which every reasonable being is the primary subject of attribution is manifestly of the substantial order and not of the accidental order. It is the term in which are united individuated nature,

---

[12] Cajetan (*In IIIam*, q.4, a.2, no. 8) explains admirably how it is necessary to go from the nominal definition of the person, conceded by common sense, to the real definition which he defends and which is nothing but the metaphysical explanation of the nominal definition, an explanation by means of a simple conceptual analysis, without reasoning. It suffices to search for the profound meaning of the personal pronouns: I, me, thou, he. Aristotle had already noted (*Metaph.*, Bk. V, chap. 8) that the so-called primary substance is the primary subject of attribution, in opposition to the so-called secondary substance, which is the nature of the subject. For example, Peter is a primary substance, or more exactly, he is more than the humanity that is attributed to him as his nature. St. Thomas has clarified this notion of the person in his explanation of the mystery of the Incarnation (IIIa, q.2, a.2; q.4, a.2; q.17, a.1 f.) by showing, as we have seen, that personality is in every reasonable being that by which he is a primary subject of attribution of individuated nature, of existence, and of operations. And Cajetan adds (*In IIIam*, q.4, a.2, no. 8): "Accedit ad haec quod nomen hypostasis, aut personae et similiter nomina propria naturarum cum pronominibus, ut hic homo, hic bos, et similiter pronomina demonstrativa personaliter, ut ego, tu, ille, omnes confitemur significare formaliter substantiam, et non negationem aut accidens aut extranea. Si omnes hoc fatemur cur ad quid rei significatae perscrutantes, divertimus a communi confessione?" That is to say: Why, when we seek the real definition of the person, do we turn away from the notion of common sense, or the nominal definition commonly received by all of us, which is the starting point that we all wish to safeguard?

Cajetan is not indulging in a reverie here. This is the metaphysics of what the grammarian calls the personal pronoun: I, me, thou, he. This metaphysics of the personal pronoun (or of the possessive adjective, my, thy) is no less important than that of the noun, the substantive, than that of the verb or of the adverb of time or of place. Cf. Aristotle, *Perihermeneias*, Bk. I, *de nomine, de verbo*, etc.

existence, the operations attributed to the person, as parts of the same entity. Thus, by analogy, the top of a pyramid is the term and the culminating point of the lines which converge toward it. This is in reality quite mysterious for us, for we do not have an immediate intellectual intuition of it, as do the angels. Our knowledge rises only with difficulty from the sensible to the intelligible. Yet what is here affirmed is not any more mysterious than what is commonly affirmed with regard to continuity. As St. Thomas remarks: "If the humanity of Christ were separated from the Word, it would become a distinct person, just as when one separates two parts of a continuous line, each of the two becomes a whole." [13] What is here affirmed is not any more surprising than the commonly accepted fact that the division of a ringed animal like the worm produces two animals instead of one. The division creates a term that did not previously exist. Thus, any *continuum* is divisible *ad infinitum*, without ever being infinitely divided; for it is composed of infinitely divisible parts. (Cf. Aristotle, *Physica*, Bk. III, chap. 1.)

It follows from this that the humanity of Christ, which is completed by the uncreated personality of the Word, is not a human person. For it is not a primary subject of attribution. When Jesus says, "I am the way, the truth, and the life," He attributes to Himself, to the same self, the properties of human nature (I who speak to you) and those of divine nature (I am the truth and the life). That is why St. Thomas says in substance: "Temporal nativity would cause a real temporal filiation in Christ if there were in Him a subject capable of such filiation." [14] He also writes: "If the human nature had not been assumed by a divine person, the human nature would have had its own personality; . . . the divine person by His union hindered the human nature from having its personality." [15] "Si praeestitisset (*personalitas humana*) . . . , desiisset per corruptionem." [16]

Thus, according to St. Thomas, the humanity of Christ does not have its own personality as it would have had if it had not been per-

---

[13] *III Sent.*, dist. V, q. 3, a. 3. "Ad tertium dicendum, quod separatio dat utrique partium totalitatem et in continuis dat etiam utrique esse in actu; unde supposito quod (Verbum) hominem deponeret, subsisteret homo ille per se in natura rationali, et ex hoc ipso acciperet rationem personae." [14] *Summa theol.*, IIIa, q. 35, a. 5 ad 1.
[15] *Ibid.*, IIIa, q. 4, a. 2 ad 3. [16] *Contra Gentes*, IV, 43.

sonally united to the Word. But it does not follow at all that there is something lacking to Christ's humanity, for, as St. Thomas says, it is much nobler to exist in the Word than to exist in oneself.[17]

On the basis of this notion of personality, the truth of the following propositions is proved: Peter is a man, but he is not his humanity, which is the essential part of him; Peter exists, but he is not his existence, which is in him only a contingent attribute.

From this we can also see why there is in Jesus only one personality, only one primary subject of attribution, to which both human nature and divine nature are fitting, as well as both human liberty and divine liberty. There is in Him therefore only one existence,[18] for existence follows the person, which is the subject that exists. The unity of the person thus entails unity of existence.

Finally, the hypostatic union is not accidental, it is substantial, inasmuch as the two natures belong to the same person and exist by the same existence.[19] In this manner is maintained the profound meaning of Jesus' affirmation: "I am the way, the truth, and the life."

[17] Cf. St. Thomas, IIIa, q. 2, a. 2 ad 2.   [18] IIIa, q. 17, a. 2.
[19] IIIa, q. 2, a. 6.

❊ VIII ❊

THE FITTINGNESS OF THE INCARNATION AND OUR INTERIOR LIFE

"Come to Me, all you that
labor, and are burdened,
and I will refresh you."
Matt. 11:28

HAVING considered the fittingness of the Incarnation from the point of view of God, who is inclined to give Himself as much as possible to man, and from the point of view of man, who is disposed to become as united as possible to God, we must now consider this mystery with reference to the loftiest virtues which are, as it were, the soul of our interior life.

These loftiest of virtues are called the "theological virtues," because they have God as their immediate object and because they unite us to Him. Through faith we adhere to what God has revealed of Himself and of His works. Through hope we tend toward God, sustained by His help, in order some day to possess Him and to see Him face to face. Through charity we supernaturally love God more than ourselves, above all things, because He is infinitely lovable, infinitely better than we are, and because He first loved us as a Father.

Undoubtedly these three virtues are the noblest of all; from above they inspire the moral virtues which bear not on our final end but on the means to attain it. Thus faith must inspire prudence; and our charity, our love of God and of souls, must inspire and also quicken from above the virtues of justice, fortitude, and temperance, by making them meritorious with respect to eternal life.

If these are the three most exalted virtues that can dwell in a human soul, what is their relationship to the mystery of the Incarnation? For no other divine intervention could more successfully have snatched us away from evil and more powerfully dispose us toward goodness.

Following the thought of St. Augustine, St. Thomas [1] tells us that after man's fall God could have redeemed us by other means than that of the Incarnation. For example, He might have sent a prophet to explain to us the conditions of forgiveness. But then there would not have been perfect reparation for the offense against God caused by mortal sin, which by turning us away from God actually denies or refuses to God the infinite dignity of final end or Sovereign Good. In order to make perfect reparation for this offense, which has a gravity immeasurable as is the person offended, it was necessary that a human soul offer to God an act of love of infinite value. This could be accomplished only by a human soul which belonged to a divine person, who alone is capable of performing acts of truly infinite value.

Thus the Word made flesh can offer to His Father in reparation an act of love of unlimited value, which can please God more than all the combined sins of men displease Him.

That is why the Incarnation was the most fruitful source of grace to redeem us, and at the same time necessary for perfect reparation to God for the offense committed against Him. No divine intervention could so successfully tear us away from evil. Nothing could have cured us so completely of our three wounds—concupiscence of the flesh, concupiscence of the eyes, and the pride of life—as the sufferings, the poverty, and the humility of our Savior.

At the same time, the mystery has a second aspect which we must insist on particularly because of its bearing on the interior life: The Incarnation, by extricating us from the forces of evil, disposes us powerfully toward goodness. For it offers us the perfect model of all virtues and it increases tenfold, so to speak, our most exalted virtues: faith, hope, and charity.

Faith Increased Tenfold

First of all, faith is given much greater certainty by the Incarnation because of the fact that we believe in God who has come to us in sensible form to speak to us.

[1] IIIa, q. 1, a. 2.

The formal motive of faith, as a theological virtue, is the authority of God who reveals the truths we are to believe.

It is because God is infallible and cannot err or lead us into error that the first man after his fall believed the divine promise of a Redeemer, that Abraham believed that the Messiah would be born of his race, and that the prophets believed that He would come not only for the salvation of Israel but for the salvation of mankind. The authority of God, who makes revelations and seals His revelations by miracles, is a motive in itself very firm and infallible. Yet God remains hidden, and dwells in an inaccessible light. He remains invisible even when He speaks through prophets like Moses, Elias, or Isaias, even when He confirms their preaching by extraordinary miracles.

Very much more certain does our faith become when God comes to us and, taking a body and human lips like our own, speaks to us Himself through the medium of the senses yet in a tone and with an authority which can belong only to God! How much is our faith reinforced when the Word of God is made flesh and comes to tell us: "Amen, amen I say unto you: He that believeth in Me, hath everlasting life"; [2] or again: "I am one that give testimony of Myself," [3] for I am light itself, "I am the way, the truth, and the life." [4]

None of the prophets could speak in these terms. They were able to say: "I have received the truth," but not one of them could affirm: "I am the truth and the life."

Jesus Christ, our Savior, is Himself the prime truth, both revealing and revealed. That is why, as St. Augustine says,[5] He can bear witness to Himself and to the other mysteries, just as light manifests itself by manifesting colors and all that it illuminates.

Primary revealing truth, the formal motive of our faith, in other words, the authority of God the Revealer, is manifested palpably, so to speak, in Christ and in His sublime manner of teaching.

True, we do not see Christ's divinity here below, either with the eyes of our body or with those of the mind, but Jesus speaks with such great authority when He says: "Amen, amen I say to you, be-

---

[2] John 6:47. [3] Ibid., 8:18. [4] Ibid., 14:6.
[5] In Joannem, 8:18.

fore Abraham was made, I am," [6] that there can be no doubt He is the living God become palpable who now speaks to us in order to increase our faith tenfold. In fact, the messengers of the Pharisees could not help saying: "Never did man speak like this man." [7] The Samaritans also said to the woman whom our Lord had converted and who had called them to hear the Messiah: "Now we believe not because of what you have told us but because we have heard Him ourselves and we know that He is really the Savior of the world."

If the tone of the Curé of Ars' voice betrayed his holiness when he preached, how much more must the tone, the authority, and the magnetism of our Lord Jesus Christ have bespoken His holiness! That is why from the time of His first Sermon on the Mount, "the people were in admiration at His doctrine. For He was teaching them as one having power, and not as the scribes and Pharisees," [8] who commented on the scriptural texts without making them live. The simple in heart have an understanding of the greatness of things. They recognized our Lord's greatness from the moment of His first sermon. The fact that the populace afterward condemned Him resulted from their having been misled by perverse men.

What a privilege to have heard even for an instant the Word made flesh preach and to have received directly from His lips His doctrine in all its vigor, simplicity, and grandeur!

St. John has written in his Gospel: "No man hath seen God at any time: the only-begotten Son who is in the bosom of the Father, He hath declared Him." [9] Again, in his First Epistle he said: "That which was from the beginning, which we have heard, which we have seen with our eyes, which we have looked upon, and our hands have handled, of the Word of life: . . . that which we have seen and have heard, we declare unto you." [10]

Our faith is thus supremely confirmed by this highest testimony, which has been made palpable, so to speak, by the Incarnation. Thus St. Paul could write to the Hebrews the following words in order to confirm them in their faith: "God, who at sundry times and in divers manners spoke in times past to the fathers by the prophets, last of all,

[6] John 8:58.   [7] *Ibid.*, 7:46.   [8] Matt. 7:28 f.   [9] John 1:18.
[10] I John 1:1-3.

in these days hath spoken to us by His Son, whom He hath appointed heir of all things, by whom also He made the world." [11]

Let us suppose for a moment that the Incarnation had not taken place and that the loftiest teaching was that of the prophets, of Elias or Isaias. How much diminished would our faith be, how meager the history of humanity, by comparison with what they are in reality! The very greatness of the prophets would vanish, for they were great only inasmuch as they were the precursors of our Lord Jesus Christ. "Those who have ears to hear" cannot be mistaken as to the tone of the Savior's voice nor as to the sublimity of His doctrine. Despite trials, obscurity, temptations, let us believe in the word of Jesus, let us keep it in our hearts, and let us live by it in the spirit of faith. "The just man liveth by faith." [12]

Hope Strengthened

The Incarnation not only confirms our faith; it also greatly arouses our hope.

Through this theological virtue we desire and await the Supreme Good, and we tend toward it supported by the divine assistance promised by God to those who believe. The prime object of hope is a future good and one that is difficult to attain, the Supreme Good which we are to enjoy for all eternity. The formal motive of hope is divine assistance, or, better still, it is God Himself infinitely willing to help us, *Deus auxilians*. He is infinitely willing to help because He is infinitely merciful and all-powerful, and because He has promised to help us to achieve the summit of our destiny. God is true to His promises. This is one of His most beautiful titles: "The Lord is faithful in all His words." [13]

St. Paul was fond of repeating this thought. Anyone who despairs doubts the infinite mercy of the One who is Goodness itself. Judas' greatest sin, after he had been unfaithful, was to doubt the fidelity of God, who has promised His help to the greatest sinners if they asked it of Him.

Yet, although hope is entirely consonant with the deepest aspira-

[11] Heb. 1:1 f.   [12] Rom. 1:17.   [13] Ps. 144:13.

tions of our hearts, there is in us, alas, an inclination toward discouragement, especially after we have for many years been bruised by the
battles and hardships of life.

Now the mystery of the Incarnation is calculated to revive our
confidence, for it brings us not only the divine assistance of grace, but
the Author of grace Himself. It is God infinitely willing to help us
who was given to us at Bethlehem, *Deus auxilians*. He is the formal
motive or the reason for our hope, and He remains with us in the
Eucharist.

Our confidence is increased because God, by coming to us in person, gives a palpable manifestation of His infinite goodness. We tend
to have greatest confidence in our friends and in the measure that they
prove to us that they have a genuine and deep affection for us. But
Jesus is God infinitely willing to help, *Deus auxiliator*, who never
tires of telling us of His merciful love.

He says to all men: "Come to Me, all you that labor and are
burdened, and I will refresh you" (Matt. 11:28). The One who
speaks thus is the Author of salvation, as the liturgy tells us: "God,
the bestower of pardon and the author of human salvation, we implore Thy clemency. . . ."[14]

To the paralytic who thought only of his bodily cure, Jesus said:
"Thy sins are forgiven thee"; that is to say, I am curing your spiritual and immortal soul, which is much more precious than your body
that is destined to return to dust. And as a sign of the spiritual
cure of the soul, Jesus cured this poor man of his paralysis. This miracle was but a sign of something incomparably more wonderful: the
resurrection of the soul to the essentially supernatural life of grace.

St. Paul wrote to the Romans in order to confirm their hope: "If
God be for us, who is against us? He that spared not even His own
Son, but delivered Him up for us all, how hath He not also, with Him,
given us all things?"[15] These words must have strengthened the
Christians in the catacombs during the three centuries of persecution.
St. Paul added: "Who shall accuse against the elect of God? God
that justifieth. Who is he that shall condemn? Christ Jesus that died,

---

[14] Prayer from the Office of the Dead, according to the Dominican rite.
[15] Rom. 8:31.

yea that is risen also again; who is at the right hand of God, who also maketh intercession for us. Who then shall separate us from the love of Christ? Shall tribulation? or distress? or famine? or nakedness? or danger? or persecution? or the sword? (As it is written: For Thy sake we are put to death all the day long. We are accounted as sheep for the slaughter.)" [16]

All these things were fulfilled to the letter in Rome during the ten general persecutions which the Roman emperors inflicted upon the Christians from the days of Nero to those of Diocletian. And the following words of St. Paul were also fulfilled in their entirety: "But in all these things we overcome, because of Him that hath loved us." [17] We overcome in the sense of making the life of grace shine upon and illumine even our adversaries through our love for them. "For I am sure," St. Paul went on to say, "that neither death nor life nor angels nor principalities nor powers nor things present nor things to come nor might nor height nor depth nor any other creature shall be able to separate us from the love of God, which is in Christ Jesus our Lord."

That is to say, no created power whatever can separate us from the love that Christ has for us and that enkindles in us a reciprocating love. No created or creatable power can cause God to abandon the just, those who have been justified by the blood of His Son, unless they themselves abandon Him first. The Colosseum of Rome is a reminder to each succeeding generation of the victory of Christ's love over the blind fury of His persecutors. The imposing ruins of this amphitheater built by Vespasian and Titus bear enduring witness to the hope and the fortitude of the martyrs who were sustained by the promises and the love of the Word made flesh.

Through all their tortures they remained faithful by the efficacy of the grace of Christ. As St. Paul says, they overcame "because of Him that hath loved us." [18] The formal motive of our hope is not our own personal effort, by which we cooperate with divine assistance. The formal motive of our hope is God Himself, infinitely willing to help, *Deus auxilians,* God Himself who through the Incarnation is with us and remains with us in the Eucharist as the daily nourishment

[16] *Ibid.,* 8:33 ff.   [17] *Ibid.,* 8:37.   [18] *Ibid.*

of our souls. It is thus that our confidence in God is greatly strengthened by the Incarnation. The Word did not become incarnate without good reason. It was not for material progress or the advancement of science, but for the sanctification of our souls, and we, too, should ardently yearn for this sanctification.

More Ardent Charity

Finally, this mystery of our faith should enflame to the highest pitch our charity, our love of God and of souls. As St. Augustine says in words that theologians will repeat until the end of time: "For what principal reason did the Word become Incarnate, if not to manifest His love for us? . . . Since we cannot love Him [first], let us at least learn to give Him love for love." [19]

Through infused charity which we receive in baptism we are called on to love God supernaturally more than ourselves. We are called on to love Him as our great friend who loved us first and who is infinitely better in Himself than all His blessings taken together. To love Him thus is to desire efficaciously the accomplishment of His holy will as expressed in His commandments; that is, we must desire that He should truly and completely reign in our souls and that He be glorified by us eternally in the words of psalm 112:1: "Praise the Lord, ye children: praise ye the name of the Lord."

Thus charity is superior to hope. Through hope we desire to possess God, ultimately for God who is the final end of our hope as of all the virtues.[20] Through charity we efficaciously love God, our best friend, formally for Himself alone; and we love Him more than ourselves, desiring for Him all the blessings that are fitting for Him; that His kingdom come and that His goodness be manifested in what we call divine glory. To love God is to conform our entire life to these words of the Our Father: "Thy will be done": Thy will, as expressed in Thy commandments, be done on earth as it is in heaven. To love God is also to say to Him with trusting abandonment: "Into Thy hands I

---

[19] *De catechizandis rudibus*, chap. 4.

[20] As Cajetan says (*In IIam IIae*, q. 17, a. 5, no. 6) : "Per spem, desidero Deum, non propter me, sed mihi (jam finaliter), propter Deum qui est finis ultimus actus spei."

commend my spirit," I offer Thee the marrow of my will, do with it whatever Thou please.

Through charity, by efficaciously loving God more than ourselves, we generally love all His eternal decrees, ordered toward the manifestation of His goodness. So God, the infinitely Good, becomes for us another self, who is in a sense more truly we than we are ourselves. For He possesses within Himself all the good that can exist in each one of us. In this sense God contains more of me than I do, for He is what I am in an eminent degree.

This divine goodness, the formal object of charity, has been manifested to us by the supreme love through which God has given us His only Son: "God so loved the world, as to give His only-begotten Son." [21] We can even say that this is the fundamental truth of Christianity, for it was this act of God's love for us which gave us our Lord Jesus Christ as our Savior.

St. John tells us this in his First Epistle: "By this hath the charity of God appeared toward us, because God hath sent His only-begotten Son into the world, that we may live by Him. In this is charity: not as though we had loved God, but because He hath first loved us, and sent His Son to be a propitiation for our sins. My dearest, if God hath so loved us, we also ought to love one another." [22]

St. Paul writes in the same vein to Titus: "For the grace of God our Savior hath appeared to all men; instructing us, that, denying ungodliness and worldly desires, we should live soberly and justly and godly in this world, looking for the blessed hope and coming of the glory of the great God and our Savior Jesus Christ." [23]

The incarnation of the Word thus greatly strengthens our faith, our hope, and our charity. It gives us the example of all the virtues, and particularly it is the principle of an act of love infinite in value rising upward within the soul of Jesus, a redemptive act of love which is more pleasing to God than all the sins in the world can displease Him.

Let us give thanks to God for this blessing of the redemptive Incarnation which to some extent makes palpable for us primary re-

[21] John 3:16.   [22] I John 4:9-11.   [23] Titus 2:11-13.

vealing Truth, merciful Omnipotence, and supreme Goodness; and which never ceases to pour out to us, especially through the Eucharist, all the graces that we need in our indigence. These three divine perfections, which are the formal motive of the three theological virtues, are for us like three stars of the first magnitude, three lamps of fire, St. John of the Cross tells us, which guide us through the night on our pilgrimage toward the light of eternity.

We can indeed say with St. Paul in profound gratitude: "God (who is rich in mercy) for His exceeding charity wherewith He loved us, even when we were dead in sins, hath quickened us together in Christ (by whose grace you are saved)." [24] This grace is the seed of glory. Let us pray that we may persevere in it and through it, so that it may truly be within us "the beginning of eternal life."

[24] Eph. 2:4 f.

❈ IX ❈

THE MOTIVE OF THE INCARNATION AND THE INTIMATE LIFE OF JESUS

> "I believe in God . . . the Son . . .
> who for us men and for our salvation
> came down from heaven."
>
> Nicene Creed

ONE of the considerations which can help us penetrate deeply into the intimate life of Jesus is the motive of the Incarnation, the motive of His coming into the world, which must always have been present in His mind as the purpose of His earthly life. We should like to call attention, as St. Thomas himself has done, to the three following points: 1. The motive of the Incarnation was a motive of mercy. 2. The Word, in becoming incarnate to redeem us, did not in any sense subordinate Himself to us but on the contrary re-established the primitive order on an infinitely loftier level. 3. In His intimate life Jesus is first of all Savior, priest, and victim.

The Motive of the Incarnation, a Motive of Mercy

The opinion is held by some that in the actual plan of Providence, the Word would have become incarnate even if man had not sinned. Christ would then have come not as a Savior and victim, but as the head of the kingdom of God and as the supreme doctor, in order to give greater glory to God and thus to crown creation. He would have come with an immortal body, not subject to pain. But, champions of this opinion maintain, sin having supervened, Christ came in mortal flesh, *in carne passibili*, as Savior and victim for our salvation.

According to this opinion, it is accidentally, so to speak, that in the

actual plan of Providence Jesus is Savior and victim. He is first of all
the King of kings, the head of the kingdom of God.

St. Thomas has weighed the value of this opinion, which had already been expressed in his own time, and he writes with regard to
this subject: "There are different opinions about this question. For
some say that even if man had not sinned, the Son of man would have
become incarnate. Others assert the contrary, and seemingly our as-
sent ought rather to be given to this opinion. For such things as spring
from God's will, and beyond the creature's due, can be made known
to us only through being revealed in the Sacred Scripture, in which
the divine will is made known to us. Hence, since everywhere in the
Sacred Scripture the sin of the first man is assigned as the reason of
the Incarnation, it is more in accordance with this to say that the work
of the Incarnation was ordained by God as a remedy for sin; so that,
had sin not existed, the Incarnation would not have been. And yet the
power of God is not limited to this; even had sin not existed, God
could have become incarnate." [1]

In other words, according to St. Thomas, Thomists in general, and
many other ancient and modern theologians, the motive of the Incarnation was above all a motive of mercy, to liberate fallen humanity
from its misery. From this point of view Jesus is first of all Savior and
Victim rather than King, and therein lies the primordial trait of His
spiritual physiognomy.

This interpretation is based on many passages of Scripture and on
some very weighty testimony of tradition. Both Daniel [2] and Zacharias [3] declared that the Messiah would come "that sin may have an
end, and iniquity may be abolished." Jesus Himself said: "The Son
of man is come is seek and to save that which was lost." [4] Likewise,
in St. John He said: "God so loved the world as to give His only-
begotten Son; that whosoever believeth in Him may not perish, but
may have life everlasting. For God sent not His Son into the world,
to judge the world, but that the world may be saved by Him." [5]

St. Paul wrote: "Christ Jesus came into this world to save sinners." [6] To this St. John added in his First Epistle: "The blood of

---

[1] IIIa, q. 1, a. 3.   [2] Dan. 9:24.   [3] Zach. 3:9.
[4] Luke 19:10.   [5] John 3:16 f.   [6] I Tim. 1:15.

Jesus Christ His Son cleanseth us from all sin." [7] And "If any man sin, we have an advocate with the Father, Jesus Christ the just: and He is the propitiation for our sins: and not for ours only, but also for those of the whole world." [8] Finally, "God . . . hath first loved us, and sent His Son to be a propitiation for our sins." [9]

Moreover, the name "Jesus" does not mean King or Doctor, but Savior, and the names God gives always express the primordial trait of the spiritual physiognomy of those who receive these names. The angel Gabriel, sent by God, said to Mary: "Behold thou . . . shalt bring forth a son; and thou shalt call His name Jesus." [10] To Joseph the angel said: "Thou shalt call His name Jesus. For He shall save His people from their sins." [11] Thus the motive of the Incarnation is that reason for which it was necessary: to save us through perfect reparation for offense against God by means of an act of reparative love which would be more pleasing to God than He is displeased by all the sins of the world, and which would be an infinite source of grace for us.

Tradition is no less affirmative than is Scripture, as we can see in the Nicene Creed: "I believe . . . in one Lord Jesus Christ, the only-begotten Son of God. . . . Who for us men, and for our salvation, came down from heaven." This is the meaning of the entire liturgy of Advent and of the Nativity, which for many centuries has prepared the faithful for the celebration of the birth of the Savior.

The Fathers of the Church also teach in general that according to the actual plan of Providence the Word would not have become incarnate if men had not been in need of redemption. This is the doctrine in particular of St. Irenaeus,[12] St. Athanasius,[13] St. Gregory Nazianzen,[14] St. John Chrysostom who was the greatest of the Greek Fathers, and St. Augustine, the most illustrious of the Fathers of the Latin Church.

[7] I John 1:7. [8] *Ibid.*, 2:1. [9] *Ibid.*, 4:10.

[10] Luke 1:31. [11] Matt. 1:21.

[12] "If flesh had not been in need of being redeemed, the Word should not have become Incarnate (*Adv. haereses*, V, xiv, 1)."

[13] "The Word would not have become man if it had not been necessary to redeem us" (*Adv. Arian.*, or. 2, no. 56).

[14] "Why did God assume humanity, united to divinity (in Jesus)? Without any doubt, in order to prepare our salvation. What other reason can be given?" (Oratio 3, no. 2.)

St. John Chrysostom says explicitly: "There is no other cause for the Incarnation than this: God saw us fallen, abject, oppressed by the tyranny of death, and He had mercy." [15] St. Augustine likewise says: "If man had not fallen, the Son of man would not have come." [16] The motive of the Incarnation was a motive of mercy. This is repeated by St. Thomas, all the Thomists, and many other theologians.

The Thomists in particular add this reason: Once God has determined the plan of Providence, He does not modify it because of some unforeseen accident. He has foreseen all things. No good can occur unless He has willed it, and no evil unless He has permitted it for a greater good. Therefore, it cannot be said that God modified His actual plan as the result of the sin of the first man. The efficacious divine decree on the world extended from the start to everything that was to happen, in a positive manner with respect to the good and in a permissive manner with respect to evil.[17] Now, in actuality the Word came in flesh that was mortal and subject to suffering, which fact, as universally admitted, presupposes sin. Therefore, by virtue of the primitive decree, the Word would not have become incarnate if man had not sinned. This is, as we have seen, what the Scriptures and tradition tell us clearly. In other words, the motive of the Incarnation has been a motive of mercy. As our Lord told us Himself: "The Son of man is come to seek and to save that which was lost." [18] There is much consolation for us in this fact. For even the greatest sinners who cry out to the Savior are saved.

God Has Permitted Evil, Man's Sin, Only in View of a Greater Good

There is another aspect of this mystery which makes it possible to answer the sometimes agonizing question that is called the problem of

---

[15] *In Epist. ad Hebr.*, hom. 5, no. 1.   [16] *Sermon* 174, 2.

[17] The efficacious divine decree of the Incarnation bears from the outset not only on the substance of this fact, but also on the circumstances *hic et nunc* under which it was realized, particularly on the circumstance in a passible and mortal flesh; a circumstance which by common consent presupposes the prevision of Adam's sin.

[18] Luke 19:10.

evil. Why did God permit evil, especially moral evil, the sin of the first man, foreseeing as He did that it would spread to all men, who would because of it be deprived of grace and of the privileges of the state of innocence?

St. Thomas presents very well this second aspect of the mystery, which some of his commentators have neglected [19] but which happily others have emphasized.[20] He says: "There is nothing to prevent human nature from having been raised after sin to a level above its original state. For God permits evil only in view of a greater good. This is why St. Paul wrote to the Romans, 5:20: 'Where sin abounded, grace did more abound.' And the Church sings during the benediction of the paschal candle: 'O happy fault, that merited so great a Redeemer!' "[21]

It is indeed clear that God cannot permit evil, especially sin, except in view of a greater good. Otherwise the divine permission which allows sin to occur would not be holy. It would be impossible to say *a priori* for what great good God permitted the sin of the first man. But after the fact of the Incarnation we can and we must say with St. Paul: God has permitted sin to abound only so that grace might more abound in the person of our Savior and through Him in us.

Thus, when the Word became incarnate to redeem us He did not subordinate Himself to us in any way whatever (He remains infinitely superior to us, and the Incarnation is of greater value than our redemption); but He stooped down toward us to raise us up to Himself. For it is the nature of mercy to incline the superior person toward the inferior one, not to subordinate the former to the latter but to elevate the inferior person. In this way, when the Word became incarnate He bent down in order to restore the primitive order, the original harmony, and even to raise this primitive order far above its original level by uniting Himself personally to human nature and

---

[19] For example, John of St. Thomas and Billuart.

[20] See the explanation of this point of doctrine by the Carmelites of Salamanca and by the Dominicans Godoy and Gonet. See also Cajetan's excellent presentation (*In Iam*, q. 22, a. 2, no. 7): (Si non esset peccatum a Deo permissum) "deesset universo hostia illa divini suppositi, quam in cruce obtulit; quod adeo bonum fuit et est, ut excedat in bonitate omne malum culpae non solum hominum, sed daemonum. . . . O felix culpa."

[21] St. Thomas, IIIa, q. 1, a. 3 ad 3.

thus manifesting to us in the most perfect manner possible His omnipotence and His goodness.[22]

God permits evil only for a greater good, and He would not have permitted the immense evil which is original sin if He did not have in view the greater good which is the redemptive Incarnation. Thus it is that divine mercy, far from subordinating to us the Word made incarnate for us, is the highest manifestation of the power and goodness of God. It sings the glory of God more loudly than all the stars in the firmament.

The Word made flesh, our Savior, is infinitely greater than the first innocent man. Making necessary allowances, Mary is also incomparably superior to Eve. And when Mass is celebrated in the poorest village church, a worship is offered to God which is infinitely superior to that offered to Him by the first innocent man in the Garden of Eden.

The Primordial Trait of the Spiritual Physiognomy of Jesus

It follows that it was not accidentally that Christ is Savior, priest, and victim. This is the chief aspect of His life. He is not first of all a king and a sublime doctor who became accidentally, because of man's sin, a victim and the savior of humanity.[23] As His name "Jesus" signi

[22] It has been objected that it would be perverse to order the superior with respect to the inferior. But the Incarnation is superior to our redemption. Thus it would be perverse to order the former to the latter.

The Thomists have always answered as follows: It would certainly be perverse and even absurd to order the superior to the inferior as to a principle of perfection and to a final end. However, it is not perverse to order the superior to the inferior as to a perfectible subject which must be perfected. Thus, although our body is made for our soul, God orders the soul in a certain manner to the body in order to vivify it, and He would not create the soul of a particular child unless the body of that child were about to take shape. Likewise, although we exist for Christ, who is our end, yet He came to save us and He would not have come if we had not needed to be saved. As there is a mutual dependence between the body made for the soul and the soul which vivifies the body, *"causae ad invicem sunt causae, sed in diverso genere,"* there is also a mutual dependence between the Incarnation in view of which original sin was permitted, and to deliver us from this sin the redemptive Incarnation was willed by divine mercy.

[23] Even in the Mass and the Office of Christ the King, mention is repeatedly made of Christ as the Savior, for He is king both by right of birth and by right of conquest.

fies, He is first of all the Savior, and His entire life was ordered to His heroic death on the Cross, through which He accomplished His mission and His destiny as Redeemer. The motive of the Incarnation was our redemption by the heroic act of love on Calvary. The stigmatics like St. Francis must have penetrated very deeply into this truth.

As a result, Christ appears greater and the unity of His life much more profound. His life was ordered completely toward the act of love by which, in offering Himself up on the cross, He conquered sin, Satan, and death, an act of love which is more pleasing to God than He is displeased by all the sins of men.

This is what St. Thomas says: "God loves Jesus Christ not only more than the entire human race but also more than all creatures taken as a whole. For He willed for Him a greater good by giving Him a name above all other names. He willed that He be truly God. This supreme excellence of Christ has not been diminished by the fact that His Father delivered Him up to death for our salvation. On the contrary, Christ thus became the glorious victor (over sin, Satan, and death), 'the government is upon His shoulder' " (Isa. 9:6).[24]

Now we can understand why the thought of the redemption by the Cross, together with the thought of the glory of God, were uppermost in the mind of our Lord when He came into the world and remained so throughout His life.[25] As St. Paul says: "Wherefore when He cometh into the world, He saith: Sacrifice and oblation Thou wouldest not: but a body Thou hast fitted to Me. . . . Then said I: Behold I come . . . that I should do Thy will, O God." [26]

This oblation was ever living in His heart. It was the soul, as it were, of His preaching and of His sacrifice. The first three Gospels report that Jesus said: "The Son of man is not come to be ministered unto, but to minister, and to give His life a redemption for many." [27]

In one of His most beautiful parables, the parable of the Good

---

He conquered this universal kingship during the Passion when He was crowned with thorns before He received the crown of glory in heaven.   [24] Ia, q. 20, a. 4 ad 1.

[25] On this point see the beautiful book written in the seventeenth century by Chardon, O. P., *La croix de Jésus*.   [26] Heb. 10:5–7.

[27] Matt. 20:28; Mark 10:45; Luke 1:68; 2:38; 21:28.

Shepherd, He said: "I am the Good Shepherd. The good shepherd giveth his life for his sheep. . . . Therefore doth the Father love Me: because I lay down My life, that I may take it again. No man taketh it away from Me. But I lay it down of Myself." [28]

Again He said: "I am come to cast fire on the earth: and what will I, but that it be kindled? And I have a baptism wherewith I am to be baptized: and how am I straitened until it be accomplished?" [29] He was speaking of the baptism of blood, the most perfect of all.[30]

He expressed the purpose of His mission in still different words: "And I, if I be lifted up from the earth, will draw all things to Myself. (Now this He said, signifying what death He should die.)" [31]

This thought was continually in our Savior's mind when He was training the apostles, when, for instance, He told Peter that he could not bear to hear of the coming Passion: "Thou savorest not the things that are of God, but the things that are of men." [32] Likewise, when He said to the sons of Zebedee: "Can you drink of the chalice that I drink of: or be baptized with the baptism wherewith I am baptized?" [33] This was His underlying thought also at the Last Supper, at the moment when He instituted the Eucharist: "This is My body, which is given for you. . . . This is the chalice, the new testament in My blood, which shall be shed for you." [34] "Greater love than this no man hath, that a man lay down his life for his friends." [35]

Finally, Jesus on several occasions spoke of the hour of His passion as "His hour," [36] for it is the hour above all others to which His whole earthly life was dedicated.

Jesus is above all else Savior, priest, and victim. This is the primordial trait of His spiritual physiognomy, the fundamental character of His interior life. What are the consequences of this for us?

It follows that in the actual plan of Providence, it is not by accident that souls must, in order to be sanctified, carry their crosses in union with the Savior. He Himself has told us so: "And He said to all: If any man will come after Me, let him deny himself, and take up his cross daily and follow Me. . . . For he that shall lose his life for

---

[28] John 10:11–18. [29] Luke 12:49 f. [30] Cf. St. Thomas, IIIa, q.46, a.12.
[31] John 12:32 f. [32] Matt. 16:23. [33] Mark 10:38. [34] Luke 22:19 f.
[35] John 15:13. [36] John 2:4; 12:23; 13:1; 16:21, 25, 32; 17:1.

My sake, shall save it." [37] This was magnificently fulfilled by the martyrs who, by uniting their sufferings to those of the Savior, in turn saved souls, sometimes even the souls of their persecutors.

It follows also that in order to be a saint, and even a great saint, it is not necessary to be a doctor or a man of action. It is enough to be genuinely configured to the crucified Christ, as was St. Benedict Joseph Labre who could call his own only his poverty and his heroically supported pain, and who appeared to be the living image of our Lord Jesus Christ.

Finally, it follows (as St. Thomas explains with great profundity [38] in speaking of the effects of baptism) that while the sanctifying grace which the first man in the state of innocence possessed is a participation in divine nature and makes us children of God, the specifically Christian grace which was communicated to us after the fall by Christ the Redeemer makes us "living members of Christ." That is why Christian grace as such inspires us to suffer following the example of Jesus in order to expiate, to make reparation for the outrages committed against God, in order to collaborate for our salvation and that of our neighbors, just as the members of a single body must help one another.

That is why no Christian idea can win acceptance, and no Christian work can persevere, until it has passed through trials and tribulations. "Unless the grain of wheat falling into the ground die, itself remaineth alone. But if it die, it bringeth forth much fruit." [39]

This is how Christians are profoundly configured to their head, who said concerning Himself to His disciples of Emmaus, although they did not yet understand it: "Ought not Christ to have suffered these things, and so to enter into His glory?" [40] Isaias had announced it in his prophecy of the Passion.[41] It is required every day in the Holy Sacrifice of the Mass, and it will be repeated until the end of the world.

[37] Luke 9:23 f.
[39] John 12:24.
[38] St. Thomas, IIIa, q. 62, a. 2.
[40] Luke 24:26.
[41] Isa., Chap. 53.

THE PREDESTINATION OF CHRIST

THE light that illumines from above the whole life of a saint is his predestination, that is, the act of intelligence and love by which God has from all eternity ordered or destined him to a given degree of glory and has decided to grant him for the attainment of this glory all the graces he will need, from the very first to that of final perseverance.[1] Through many bitter trials perhaps, the servant of God will with the help of these graces merit the beatitude of eternal life, to which he has been predestined from all eternity.[2]

As for children who die after baptism without having had time to merit, they have been predestined to glory without having to strive for its attainment.

What is true of all the elect, angels and men, adults and children, is that they have been predestined to glory, i.e., eternal life.

The Exceptional Nature of Christ's Predestination

The predestination of Christ, the first among predested souls, is absolutely exceptional. His is not only the predestination to glory or eternal life. His is predestination to the unique grace of personal union with the Word, a grace that is incomparably superior to that possessed in heaven by all the angels and saints.

As man, Christ was predestined to become not the son of God by adoption but the Son of God by nature.[3]

[1] Cf. St. Thomas, Ia, q. 23, a. 1, 4.   [2] *Ibid.*, a. 5.

[3] Cf. St. Thomas, IIIa, q. 24, a. 1 f. Thomists who have meditated at length on the articles of St. Thomas bearing on the motive of the Incarnation and on the predestination of Christ know that for St. Thomas these two questions balance each other and that the second permits us to insist on what in the preceding chapter we called the

St. Paul wrote to the Romans: "For whom He foreknew, He also predestinated to be made conformable to the image of His Son; that He might be the first-born among many brethren." [4] Jesus is thus the first of the predestined souls. From all eternity God has willed Him to be His Son by nature, and He has desired to make of the elect, angels and men, His sons by adoption. The first-mentioned sonship vastly surpasses the latter.

In the Epistle to the Colossians, we read: "Who is the image of the invisible God, the first-born of every creature: for in Him were all things created in heaven and on earth, visible and invisible. . . . He is before all, and by Him all things consist. And He is the head of the body, the Church, who is the beginning, the first-born from the dead; that in all things He may hold the primacy." [5]

It was first of all to divine sonship by nature that Jesus as man was predestined, and all the gifts that He received derived from this first one, which is the noblest of all. It is from this sonship by nature that springs the beatitude of His saintly soul, the light of glory that permits Him to see the divine essence with a penetration which is superior to that of all the blessed. Not only does Jesus see God face to face as do all the saints in heaven, but He Himself is God. And it is certainly much greater to be God than to see Him.

Christ's Predestination, the Cause of Our Own

It follows that Christ's predestination is the supreme model of our own, [6] as our divine sonship by adoption is a participating likeness of the divine sonship by nature. In this sense, as St. Paul says, we have been "predestinated to be made conformable to the image of" [7] God's only-begotten Son. But we receive only a participation in the divine nature, sanctifying grace, whereas the only-begotten Son of

---

second aspect of the mystery: God permitted the sin of the first man for a greater good, which is the redemptive Incarnation. He permitted sin to abound that grace should more abound. We thus grasp better the meaning of the *"felix culpa quae talem ac tantum meruit habere redemptorem."*   [4] Rom. 8 :29.   [5] Col. 1 :15–18.

[6] Cf. St. Augustine, *De praedestinatione sanctorum,* chap. 13. Cf. also St. Thomas IIIa, q. 24, a. 3.   [7] Rom. 8 :29.

the Father has received from Him divine nature in its entirety by eternal generation. He is "God of God, Light of Light, true God of true God," as is said in the Nicene Creed. He is the Word of God made flesh, and, being the Son of God by nature, He cannot become His son by adoption and by participation. For a father does not adopt someone who is already his own child.[8]

Lastly, in predestining the elect from all eternity, God decided that Christ the Redeemer would be the cause of their salvation,[9] and that He would merit for them all the effects of predestination: grace, final perseverance, and eternal life. This is brought out in all the texts of Scripture in which Jesus is called "Savior," "author of salvation." For instance: "He that believeth in the Son, hath life everlasting"; [10] "I am come that they may have life, and may have it more abundantly"; [11] "My sheep hear My voice: and I know them, and they follow Me. And I give them life everlasting; and they shall not perish forever, and no man shall pluck them out of My hand. That which My Father hath given Me, is greater than all: and no one can snatch them out of the hand of My Father. I and the Father are one." [12]

As God, Jesus predestines the elect. As man, He has merited for the elect all the effects of predestination: habitual grace, actual graces, final perseverance, and glory.[13] Thus all the elect are subordinated to Him, according to the words of St. Paul: "All are yours; and you are Christ's; and Christ is God's." [14]

This gives us an insight into the grandeur of the prologue to the Epistle to the Ephesians: "Blessed be the God and Father of our

[8] Cf. St. Thomas, IIIa, q. 23, a. 4: "Christ, who is the natural Son of God, can nowise be called an adopted son." [9] Cf. *ibid.*, q. 24, a. 4.

[10] John 3:36; 5:24, 40; 6:47. [11] *Ibid.*, 10:10. [12] *Ibid.*, 10:27–30.

[13] As God, Jesus has predestined all the elect, angels as well as men. As man, He has merited for men grace and glory, and He merited for angels at least the accidental graces by which they serve Him as His ministers in the kingdom of God. They are His angels, as the Gospels tell us on several occasions: "And then shall He [the Son of man] send His angels, and shall gather together His elect from the four winds, from the uttermost part of the earth to the uttermost part of heaven" (Mark 13:27). Cf. also Matt. 13:41; 24:31. Cf. St. Thomas, IIIa, q. 8, a. 4: Christ is the head of the angels, who are part of the Church triumphant; IIIa, q. 59, a. 6: Christ judges the angels, His ministers, and He is terrible to the demons. [14] I Cor. 3:23.

Lord Jesus Christ, who hath blessed us with spiritual blessings in heavenly places, in Christ: as He chose us in Him before the foundation of the world, that we should be holy and unspotted in His sight in charity. Who hath predestinated us unto the adoption of children through Jesus Christ unto Himself: according to the purpose of His will: unto the praise of the glory of His grace, in which He hath graced us in His beloved Son. In whom we have redemption through His blood, the remission of sins, according to the riches of His grace, which hath superabounded in us in all wisdom and prudence. . . . In whom [Jesus Christ] we also are called by lot, being predestinated according to the purpose of Him who worketh all things according to the counsel of His will; that we may be unto the praise of His glory, we who before hoped in Christ." [15]

This lofty doctrine of the predestination of Christ throws light on the predestination of Mary to be the Mother of God. The predestination of Christ, as man, to be the Son of God by nature is in fact identical with the eternal decree of the Incarnation. Now this decree bears upon this fact as it was to be realized *hic et nunc,* in certain given circumstances. And therefore it includes not only Jesus, but Mary as well. From all eternity it had been decided that the Word of God made flesh would be born miraculously of Mary ever virgin, united to Joseph the just by the bonds of a genuine marriage. The execution of this providential decree was expressed thus by St. Luke: "The angel Gabriel was sent from God into a city of Galilee, called Nazareth, to a virgin espoused to a man whose name was Joseph, of the house of David; and the virgin's name was Mary. And the angel being come in, said unto her: . . . the Most High shall overshadow thee. And therefore also the Holy which shall be born of thee shall be called the Son of God." [16]

We see therefore that Mary's predestination is intimately bound up with that of Jesus, and since our Lord is not the adopted son of the Most High, since He is His Son by nature, Mary is, in the order of dignity, the first adopted daughter of God, far higher than the

<hr>

[15] Eph. 1:3-12.   [16] Luke 1:26-35.

angels through the degree of grace she received at the moment of the Immaculate Conception, in view of her unique mission as Mother of God and Mother of men. Her predestination is all of a piece, so to speak, with that of her Son, as are their lives here on earth and in heaven.

❊ XI ❊

THE SANCTITY OF JESUS

Innate, Substantial, Uncreated Sanctity
and the Fullness of Created Grace

> "And we saw His glory, the
> glory as it were of the only-
> begotten of the Father, full
> of grace and truth."
>
> John 1:14

HAVING considered the motive of the Incarnation, which is our salvation, we must, in order to penetrate deeper into the intimate life of our Savior, consider His sanctity. This will help us to understand ever better the meaning of these words of St. Paul: "Where sin abounded, grace did more abound." [1] Jesus is infinitely more perfect that Adam was in his innocence; and while there are obstacles to grace since the fall which did not exist in man's innocent state, yet the grace which comes to us from Jesus is more abundant, if we do not resist it, than that which the innocent Adam would have transmitted to us. The grace we receive through Jesus introduces saints into a more profound intimacy with God, the intimacy of the Eucharistic Communion, which did not exist in the earthly paradise.

Let us therefore consider the radical perfection of Jesus which permeates His entire soul and which shines forth in all His faculties and virtues. We refer to His sanctity and to the fullness of grace that He has received.

As St. Thomas shows [2] holiness in general has two essential characteristics: first, absence of all stain, of all sin, and of all directly or

---

[1] Rom. 5:20.   [2] IIa IIae, q. 81, a. 8.

indirectly voluntary imperfection; and second, a firm union with God. The latter is, in fact, the principal trait of sanctity, from which the former derives. For it is in the measure that one is firmly united to God that one avoids directly or indirectly voluntary sin, sins of commission as well as sins of omission or negligence. These two aspects of supernatural perfection have often been expressed as follows: Sanctity is separation from all that is impure, from all that is earthly in the pejorative sense of the word,[3] and it is also the immutable and fundamental consecration of the soul to God. This separation and this consecration are perfected in heaven, but they exist to a lesser degree here below, sometimes even in children who have the sanctity of their age, such as St. Tarcisius and Blessed Imelda.

But where shall we find here below perfect sanctity? A Greek philosopher once asked: "Where shall we find the ideal man?" We have the answer in the life and death of Jesus.

Let us contemplate these two aspects of sanctity as they exist in Jesus. Whereas in us, who come from below, a progressive separation from the world leads to union with God, in Jesus, who comes from above, it is the personal union of His humanity to the Word which leads to a separation of all that is impure or even merely less perfect.

The better to understand this radical perfection of the Savior, let us progressively rise from our earthy regions toward those where He dwells. Let us first inquire what the absence of sin and of imperfection means with relation to Him. We shall then be better able to grasp the most positive characteristic of His sanctity and its uniqueness.

Jesus Was without Sin

Unbelievers are forced to admit on the basis of the history of Christ's life that no man as perfect as He ever walked the earth. Even those who, like Renan, spent their lives denying the divinity of Jesus—something terrible in its consequences—even they have been obliged to concede that He is incomparably superior to all the pagan sages, that the virtue of Socrates pales before His goodness, His pa-

---

[3] In Greek ἅγιος (holy) comes from ἀ γῆ (unattached to earth).

tience in tribulation, His gentleness toward His tormentors. Several rationalists have gone so far as to say: There will never be any higher moral perfection on earth; Jesus will always remain the unequaled model, the ideal man of wisdom.[4]

In actual fact, no one was able to discover any sin or imperfection in Jesus. Certain mealymouthed humanitarians have reproached Him with His anger against the Pharisees and the money-changers in the Temple, but it is clear that this anger was the holy indignation of zeal. Only those can disapprove who through their egoism have become totally indifferent to the rights of God and to the salvation of souls.

Not only has it been impossible to discover any fault in Jesus, but even before His birth heaven was gathering testimony in favor of His absolute innocence.

Isaias announced: "And His name shall be called Wonderful, Counselor, God the Mighty, the Father of the world to come, the Prince of Peace." [5] And: "Behold My servant, I will uphold Him: My elect, My soul delighteth in Him: I have given My spirit upon Him, He shall bring forth judgment to the Gentiles. He shall not cry, nor have respect to person, neither shall His voice be heard abroad. The bruised reed He shall not break, and smoking flax He shall not quench: He shall bring forth judgment unto truth. He shall not be sad, nor troublesome, till He set judgment in the earth." [6]

Later, on the day of the Annunciation, the archangel Gabriel said to Mary: "The Holy which shall be born of thee shall be called the Son of God." [7]

An angel said to Joseph: "Fear not to take unto thee Mary thy wife, for that which is conceived in her, is of the Holy Ghost. And she shall bring forth a son: and thou shalt call His name Jesus. For He shall save His people from their sins." [8] Jesus, virginally conceived

---

[4] A young woman who did not have the faith but who was seeking truth began to read Renan's *Life of Jesus* upon the advice of her unbelieving father. The result was the opposite of what her father expected. In reading what Renan had been forced to say about the greatness of Jesus in order not to contradict the truth too obviously, she received a great interior light, believed at once in the divinity of the Savior, and from that day became an excellent Christian and a soul of prayer. She finally obtained the conversion of her father. [5] Isa. 9:6.

[6] *Ibid.*, 42:1–4. [7] Luke 1:35. [8] Matt. 1:20 f.

in the womb of Mary, was thus exempt from original sin; and it was in prevision of His merits that His Mother was preserved from this stain.

The aged Simeon, divinely enlightened, saw in the child Jesus "the salvation . . . of all peoples: a light to the revelation of the Gentiles, and the glory of Thy people Israel." [9]

St. John the Baptist at first refused to baptize our Lord, and said to Him: "I ought to be baptized by Thee, and comest Thou to me?" Jesus answered him: "Suffer it to be so now. For so it becometh us to fulfill all justice." And that day the Holy Ghost descended upon Jesus in the form of a dove, and a voice from heaven was heard to say: "This is My beloved Son, in whom I am well pleased." [10]

Later on, the Pharisees spied upon our Lord, seeking some excuse to make an accusation against Him. Jesus, with supreme dignity which equaled His humility, answered them: "Which of you shall convince Me of sin? . . . He that is of God heareth the words of God. Therefore you hear them not, because you are not of God." [11] In defense of the woman taken in adultery, who was about to be pitilessly stoned, Jesus said: "He that is without sin among you, let him first cast a stone at her." But no one felt himself pure enough to cast that first stone, and so they "went out one by one." [12]

During the Passion, Pilate declared: "I find no cause in Him." [13] He washed his hands before the crowd, saying: "I am innocent of the blood of this just man: look you to it." [14] The Jews could say only one thing: "We have a law; and according to the law He ought to die, because He made Himself the Son of God." [15]

The centurion, seeing Jesus' gentleness toward His persecutors during the crucifixion and the signs which accompanied His death, cried out: "Indeed this was the Son of God." [16]

Finally, Christ's resurrection is the glorious manifestation of His sanctity, as the apostles never tire of proclaiming. St. Peter, calling attention to one of Isaias's prophecies, wrote in his First Epistle: "Christ . . . suffered for us, . . . who did no sin, neither was guile found in His mouth, . . . who His own self bore our sins in His body

[9] Luke 2:30–32.   [10] Matt. 3:14–17.   [11] John 8:46 f.   [12] Ibid., 8:7–9.
[13] Ibid., 18:38.   [14] Matt. 27:24.   [15] John 19:7.   [16] Matt. 27:54.

upon the tree: that we . . . should live to justice: by whose stripes you were healed." [17]

The Epistle to the Hebrews tells us: "For it was fitting that we should have such a high priest, holy, innocent, undefiled, separated from sinners, and made higher than the heavens; who needeth not daily (as the other priests) to offer sacrifices first for His own sins, and then for the people's: for this He did once, in offering Himself." [18]

All these testimonials from heaven and earth attest that Jesus is without sin. He was never grazed by original sin, and He never committed even the slightest personal sin.

Far more, not only did our Savior never actually commit sin, but He was absolutely impeccable. As is commonly taught by the Fathers and by theology, our Lord was impeccable on three grounds: by reason of His divine personality, by reason of the inamissible plenitude of grace that is His, and by reason of the immediate vision He had of Supreme Goodness, from which He could not turn away. Just as a mass of red-hot iron which is kept in the fire cannot grow cool, so it was that Jesus' soul, personally and indissolubly united to the Word and thereby enriched with the fullness of grace, and always illumined by the light of glory, could not sin.

It is absolutely impossible to attribute sin to the Word made flesh. That would amount to saying: God has sinned. He could die for our salvation, but not sin. God cannot turn away from Himself, outrage Himself. This is crystal clear.

Likewise, a soul which has received the fullness of grace in an inamissible manner cannot sin; for this would involve losing this plenitude, or at least diminishing it.

Finally, a soul which sees God immediately, as do the saints in heaven, cannot turn away from Him or cease for a single moment to love Him.

Jesus Free from All Imperfections

Apart from sin, there was never in Jesus the slightest involuntary disorder of the emotions, nor any moral imperfection. There was

[17] I Pet. 2:21-24.   [18] Heb. 7:26 f.

never in Him a focus of covetousness and lust such as exists in us as
one of the consequences of original sin. Indeed, He was not exempt
from the attacks of the world and the devil. He even allowed temptation to rise up against Him, in order to teach us how to conquer it.
"[Jesus] was led by the Spirit into the desert, for a space of forty
days; and was tempted by the devil." [19] These were temptations of
vainglory and pride, to which He made answer with words from
Scripture and acts of humility.

There was no moral imperfection in our Savior which might have
diminished His sanctity. He was never unfaithful or slow to respond
to the slightest inspiration from His Father. "He that sent Me, is
with Me, and He hath not left Me alone: for I do always the things
that please Him." [20] He never had any other purpose than to "glorify
God" by saving souls, in accordance with the fullness of His mission. [21]

Such is what is sometimes called the negative aspect of Christ's
sanctity: the absence of all sin. But since sin is itself a privation, a
disorder, this aspect—that is, the absence of disorder—is already
very positive and it manifests to us to a certain extent the intimate
union with God which formally constitutes the sanctity of Jesus.

Before entering upon this great subject of the holiness of Jesus,
with particular emphasis on the aspect of separation from the spirit
of the world, from the spirit of covetousness and pride, let us come
back to what we mentioned at the beginning of this chapter: namely,
the difference between the Savior who comes from heaven and ourselves who come from below.

The sacred soul of Jesus is separated from the spirit of the world
by His very elevation, because He comes from above, because He is
the Word made flesh, come down from heaven to save us. It is His
inward greatness that separates Him from all that is inferior. He
cannot become attached to these things. By reason of His very elevation He is detached from earthly pleasures, from honors, from
worldly affairs. He is a perfect model of poverty: He "hath not where
to lay His head." For the same reason He was detached from the
pleasures of the world, and He was free from family responsibilities

[19] Luke 4:1 f.   [20] John 8:29.   [21] Cf. John, chap. 17.

because He came to found a universal family, the Church. Hence He is the perfect model of religious chastity. His elevation also separates Him from any spirit of willfulness. When He was twelve years old He declared that He had come to tend to His Father's business,[22] and He obeyed even unto death, and to the death of the cross. St. Thomas tells us that He had no need to make the three vows of poverty, chastity, and obedience because from the first moment of His conception His will was strengthened and immutably fixed not only upon the good, but upon the best.

Since our Lord comes from above, it is His greatness which separates Him from all that is inferior, not to isolate Him but so that He may act upon the world from a great height, and so that in consequence His action may be more universal and more profound. Such is the action of the sun upon the earth when it is at its zenith, at the highest point above the horizon. Because our Lord was by His very elevation free from the bonds that attach men to earthly goods, to their family, to their own little ideas, to their own will, He was able to act not only on the men of one nation or of one era, but upon the whole human race, to whom He has brought eternal life. It is because of the greatness of the Savior that the Gospel is accessible to all, even the most humble, while at the same time surpassing the understanding of the greatest geniuses. It is for the same reason that the Gospel has never grown old and that it will always be timely with an immutable timeliness, superior to that of the fleeting moment.

Jesus was not of the world, but He was given to the world by God's infinite mercy that He might redeem it. This is brought out by the first aspect of His sanctity, freedom from all sin and imperfection.

There is a vast difference between our Lord and ourselves in this respect. Since He comes from above, He is separated by His very elevation from all that is inferior, evil, or less good. As for us, we come from below, from the world of sin, of lies, of covetousness and pride. So we have to separate ourselves progressively from the spirit of the world, from all that is disorderly in it, and progressively rise toward God. This is the meaning of the Commandments and of the three evangelical counsels.

[22] Luke 2:49.

At this point some may at times be tempted to think that in this work which is so hard for us we have more merit than our Savior. This is an aberration, for our merits would not exist without the grace which comes from Him. Besides, this would be forgetting that by reason of His very elevation our Lord suffered more acutely from sin than we shall ever suffer from it. The fullness of grace increased considerably in His soul the capacity of suffering from the greatest of evils, namely, mortal sin, about which we are not sufficiently grieved because the disorder which it involves is too deep-seated for us to perceive. Our Lord suffered because of sin in the measure of His love for His Father whom sin offends, and in the measure of His love for our souls which sin ravages and kills.

Thus, whereas we must struggle and suffer in order to free ourselves from sin, our Lord has suffered from it infinitely more than we, in the measure of His purity and of His love.

To understand better this most consoling aspect of the sanctity of Jesus, let us repeat the beautiful prayer recommended as a thanksgiving after Holy Communion: "Soul of Christ, sanctify me. Body of Christ, save me. Blood of Christ, inebriate me. Passion of Christ, fortify me. O good Jesus, hear me. Hide me in Thy sacred wounds. Never permit me to be separated from Thee. Defend me from the evil spirit. At the hour of death, call me and command me to come to Thee, so that in the company of Thy saints I may praise Thee for all eternity. Amen."

Let us now enter the sanctuary of the Savior's soul and contemplate the most positive aspect of His sanctity, which constitutes it formally.

The Innate, Substantial, Uncreated and Inamissible Sanctity of Jesus

Through its personal union with the Word, the soul of Jesus has an innate, substantial, uncreated sanctity which is in consequence absolutely perfect and inamissible. This sanctity is constituted especially by the grace of union with the Word and it infinitely surpasses the sanctity of even the greatest servants of God.[23]

[23] Cf. St. Thomas, IIIa, q. 6, a. 6: "The grace of union is the personal being that is

No doubt, when we read the lives of these privileged beings, the saints, we are struck by the splendor of their virtues, of their goodness, of their generosity, of their ardor in sacrifice. Next to them, the most radiant integrity is dull, and the lives of pagan heroes seem external and without depth.

The outstanding trait of the saints is that they have given themselves not merely to an earthly ideal of the intellectual or moral order, but they have given themselves fully to God, they are taken and possessed by Him, and they live only for Him and for the sake of saving souls. They interpret the counsels of God's love as commands, and they allow themselves to be guided by divine inspiration, even when it leads to the greatest sacrifices. And, the more they abandon themselves to God, the more the Lord showers His gifts upon them; and the more they receive, the more they give, bringing life to their fellow men.

Withal, this sanctity of the greatest of God's servants is infinitely inferior to that of the Savior. The sanctity of the saints gradually frees itself from many imperfections; it is not an innate perfection; it is the crowning of a long and painful effort, the fruit of the workings of grace and of their merits. It is the end of a slow ascent during which even the guides sometimes stumble, as did Peter during the passion of his Master. It is easier of course to walk in the plain on the beaten paths than to make this ascent, especially where there is no trail to follow and no firm footing. Sometimes one turns back. It seems as if one is lost and will be caught without shelter in the darkness and cold. As St. John of the Cross remarks, there are ups and downs in this ascent. For three steps forward one makes two backward, but one advances none the less; and after long periods of tribulation during which the servant of God is not free from committing sin, he progressively arrives under the illumination of faith to union with God. His sanctity, alloyed now with impetuosity and again with cowardice, is a slow and laborious task, the work of grace and of personal coopera-

---

given gratis from above to the human nature of the person of the Word." *Ibid.*, IIIa, q. 22, a. 2 ad 3; q. 24, a. 1 f., on whether Christ was predestined to be the Son of God; q. 26, a. 1 f., on Christ as Mediator. Cf. John of St. Thomas, *De incarn.*, disp. 8, a. 1; Gonet, *De incarn.*, disp. 11; Billuart, *De incarn.*, disp. 8, a. 1.

tion, and it has still many signs of human fragility, as we see in the lives of the greatest saints, namely, the apostles.[24]

Besides, the holiness of the servants of God is in their case an accidental perfection, in the sense that it is superadded to their being. It consists in the higher degree of sanctifying grace which they have received and in the charity that has blossomed in them. This perfection is also accidental in the sense that while still here below they can lose it, as Adam lost it for himself and for us. Finally, it is a perfection which always leaves room for a greater perfection, for a deeper understanding of the mysteries of God, and for a more burning charity, the fruit of greater graces and greater efforts.

The sanctity of Jesus, on the other hand, did not progressively free itself from manifold imperfections: it is innate in Him. Jesus was born holy. He was holy even from the first moment of His conception, by the personal union of His humanity with the Word. Thus His soul was from the start sanctified by the divinity of the Word, by the grace of personal union with the only-begotten Son of the Father. It is therefore incomparably better consecrated than a chalice, than the soul of a priest marked with the sign of priesthood. Jesus is above all others the "Anointed of God." [25] He is given exclusively to His Father's "business," as He said at the age of twelve when He was found among the doctors. His sacred soul was supremely pleasing to the Father from the first moment; within it the kingdom of God is realized in its absolute fullness.

The sanctity of Jesus is thus innate and anterior even to His birth. And, by reason of His merits, His mother, the Virgin Mary, received the grace of innate sanctity through the grace of the Immaculate Conception.

But what belongs to Christ alone and what is not to be found in any other human soul or in any angel is the fact that His sanctity is not merely innate, but substantial and uncreated. This is not an accidental perfection, superadded to His being. It is the sanctity of the eternal Word that substantially sanctifies the soul of Jesus in giving it sub-

[24] Although the just can avoid each venial sin taken individually, they cannot avoid them all taken as a whole or continually. To do that, they would need the very special grace received by the Blessed Virgin.   [25] Ps. 44:8.

sistence. The sanctity of the Word thus penetrates His soul in the highest degree possible. If the saints are beings taken by God, possessed by Him, how much more so is "the Anointed of God," who has received the fullness of the divine unction and who subsists by it? For, as we have seen, there is in Jesus only one subject of attribution, a single person, and thus a single subsistence or personality, that of the Word, and a single existence, by reason of which He said: "Before Abraham was made, I am." [26]

That is the same as saying that the sanctity of Jesus, like the grace of union with the Word, is not only substantial, but it is uncreated. For it is formally constituted by the uncreated personality of the Word, which has united itself for all eternity with the soul of the Savior, so that in Jesus the two natures exist through the uncreated existence. This is what makes it possible for Him to say: "I am the truth and the life" or "I am who am." [27]

Isaias spoke of Jesus when he said: "I saw the Lord sitting upon a throne high and elevated. . . . Upon it stood the seraphims: the one had six wings, and the other had six wings: with two they covered His face, and with two they covered His feet, and with two they flew. And they cried one to another, and said: Holy, holy, holy, the Lord God of hosts, all the earth is full of His glory." [28]

St. John likewise records these words in the Apocalypse: "Holy, holy, holy, Lord God Almighty, who was, and who is, and who is to come." [29]

This substantial and uncreated sanctity of Christ is therefore the most perfect sanctity conceivable, the most intimate, and the most steadfast. Because of it He is the Saint of saints. Can a divine person be more intimately and indissolubly united to a soul, to a created nature, than by communicating to it Its own subsistence, or personality, and Its existence? A greater sanctity than this cannot be conceived. In fact, we can say that while the apostles Peter and Paul are saints,

[26] John 8:58.
[27] Cf. St. Thomas, IIIa, q.6, a.6: "The grace of union is the personal being that is given gratis from above to the human nature of the Person of the Word, and is the term of the assumption. Whereas the habitual grace pertaining to the spiritual holiness of the man is an effect following the union." IIIa, q.17, a.2: "Whether there is only one being in Christ." [28] Isa. 6:1–3. [29] John 4:8.

Jesus is sanctity itself, just as He is God Himself and the Deity. This sanctity is therefore inamissible, for Christ cannot cease being Christ, the Anointed of God. This He will always be, *in aeternum*. By the same token He is a priest for all eternity.

In a word: the sanctity of Jesus is constituted above all by the grace of uncreated union, which consists in the possession forever of the Savior's humanity by the person of the Word.

Jesus continually lives, therefore, in an order superior to that of nature, and to that of grace, that is, of supernatural created sanctity. His soul lives in a special order, the order of the hypostatic union, the order of the personal and substantial life of God, wherein He is placed by the grace of His union with the Word.[30]

The saints, especially those who are in heaven, enjoy the ecstasy of knowledge and of love. Their intelligence and their will are, as it were, lost in God, taken away by the divine object. The blessed soul of Jesus, on the other hand, enjoyed from the first moment of its creation an ecstasy superior to that of contemplation and of love. It enjoyed, as we have said, the ecstasy of being or of existence, an habitual, tranquil, permanent ecstasy. For the soul of the Savior subsists only by the personality and by the uncreated existence of the Word.[31]

Such is the innate, substantial, and uncreated sanctity of Jesus, formally constituted by the personal union of His humanity to the Word. Taking up this affirmation by the Church that the sanctity of Christ is innate, some unbelievers have said that in consequence His sanctity is without difficulties and without merit. Though Jesus' sanctity is not the fruit of merit, it is the source of all His merits and of ours as well.[32] Besides, if anyone has faced here on earth hardship, contradic-

---

[30] The Virgin Mary touches this hypostatic order by reason of the grace of her divine maternity, inasmuch as she is the Mother of God, or the mother of Jesus who is God. That is why she is entitled to the worship of hyperdulia.

[31] As the soul separated from the body subsists after death and will on the day of resurrection communicate its existence to the body which it will once again vivify, so the Word communicated His uncreated existence to the humanity of the Savior at the moment of the Incarnation.

[32] As St. Thomas explains (IIIa, q. 19, a. 3), it is true of Christ as of ourselves that it is nobler to have something through merit than without merit. Thus Jesus merited the glory of His body, His Resurrection, His Ascension, the exaltation of His name, and the sal-

tion, combat, it was our Savior. Shall we say that the saints, endowed with special graces from their childhood, have less merit than we? The principle of merit is charity or love of God. Therefore he who has a greater love of God has more merits, and he also suffers much more than others from the greatest of all evils, namely, sin. We can see, therefore, that we cannot even surmise how much our Savior suffered. His innate, substantial, and uncreated sanctity considerably increased the capacity of His soul to suffer here on earth from sin, which is an offense against God and which brings us death by turning us away from Him.

The Fullness of Created Grace

From His substantial and uncreated sanctity our Lord derived created sanctifying grace, and this He received in its fullness. And from grace derive the supernatural virtues and the gifts of charity, wisdom, piety, humility, patience, meekness in a proportionate degree, which is far superior to that of the saints and to that which was realized within the soul of Mary.

Was it possible that the soul of the Savior, which was united in the highest degree possible to God, the source of all grace, should not have been full of grace? Was it possible that His soul, which was to make us participants of all the supernatural gifts, should not itself have been adorned with all of them? [33]

Created grace is a participation in divine nature which, like a second nature, increases the stature of our souls to produce connaturally [34] supernatural and meritorious acts. It is like a divine graft in us which elevates us to a superior life. The soul of Jesus received this grace in its absolute plenitude. That is what St. John meant when he wrote: "And we saw His glory, . . . full of grace and truth." [35] A few

---

vation of our souls. But we must make one exception to this principle if the temporary deprivation of something would diminish our Savior's perfection more than the merit which presupposes this deprivation would increase His perfection. Thus Jesus did not merit the beatific vision, for the temporary deprivation of this vision would diminish His perfection more than the merit would increase it. Christ could merit only what was in Him the principle of merit: His divine personality and the fullness of grace.

[33] Cf. St. Thomas, IIIa, q. 7, a. 9.
[34] That is to say: as if it were naturally.   [35] John 1:14.

great saints, such as St. Stephen the first martyr, and above all Mary, received a relative plenitude of grace, proportioned to their mission in the Church. Thus the archangel Gabriel said to Mary: "Hail, full of grace." [36] Jesus, however, received grace in its absolute fullness, that is to say, in its supreme degree.

According to the actual plan of Providence, this grace cannot be any loftier, for it is morally proportioned to the highest dignity, that of the person of the Word made flesh.[37] Furthermore, in the soul of Jesus this grace cooperates in supernatural and meritorious acts which are, by reason of the personality of the Word, of infinite value.

Finally, this grace possesses the maximum of extension, for it corresponds to the most universal of all missions, that of the Savior of all men. It extends to all supernatural effects, and it contains within itself in an eminent degree, as a superior well-spring, all the graces necessary to the apostles, the martyrs, the confessors, and the virgins of all lands and of all times. As St. Thomas tells us,[38] the soul of Jesus received habitual grace just as the sun receives light, with the greatest intensity and radiance. And since there is probably in the physical world a center of light of even greater intensity and radiance than the sun, let us use it as a feeble symbol of the fullness of created grace within the soul of our Savior. This is to say that the habitual grace within the soul of Jesus surpasses in intensity and splendor that of all the saints and angels together, as the light of the sun excels that of the planets and their satellites.

Christ received this fullness of grace from the first moment of His conception, for it is an immediate consequence of the personal union with the Word. And even in this first instant He received it freely; for His holy soul was created as were those of the angels not in a state of sleep but in a waking and freely acting state.[39]

This plenitude was so perfect even from the first moment that it could not increase during the course of the earthly life of our Lord.[40]

---

[36] Luke 1:28.   [37] St. Thomas, IIIa, q. 7, a. 9 ad 3; a. 12 ad 2.
[38] Ibid., a. 9-12.
[39] Cf. ibid., q. 34, a. 3. Thus the justified adult freely receives sanctifying grace, the principle of merit. Likewise the angels were created in the state of grace. Cf. St. Thomas, Ia, q. 62, a. 3.
[40] The Second Ecumenical Council of Constantinople (553) defined, in opposition

But with the same degree of grace, He accomplished works that were ever more perfect as He grew in years, until the consummation of His mission on the cross.[41] Thus we might say that the sun's light, while maintaining an unchanging degree of intensity, lights and warms the earth more as it approaches the zenith, the highest point in the sky.[42]

This plenitude of grace was from the first moment of Jesus' life the source of the virtues and gifts which are reconcilable with the beatific vision and with personal union to the Word.[43] And these virtues and gifts proceed from it in a proportionate degree, that is, the supreme degree.[44] This fact gives us an insight into the charity of Christ, even from the first moment, and into His love for His Father and for souls, His wisdom, His prudence, His piety, His justice, His fortitude, His patience, His humility, His meekness.

From the first moment of His earthly life, He possessed in the supreme degree all the virtues excepting those which fundamentally admit of an imperfection that cannot be reconciled with the beatific vision. For He received the beatific vision from that first instant. Thus it was that He had neither faith nor hope, both of which will disappear in us to make way for the vision of God.[45] Nor did He have contrition, which presupposes personal sin, but He took upon Himself the punishment which our sins demanded.[46]

This shows us the falsity of saying that Christ, having received so

---

to Theodore of Mopsuestia, that the blessed soul of Christ was not subject to the passions and that it did not become better through progress in virtue and good works: "ex perfectu operum non melioratus est Christus." (Cf. Denzinger, no. 224.)

[41] Cf. St. Thomas, IIIa, q. 8, a. 12 ad 3.

[42] In Mary, on the contrary, there was an increase in grace and in charity, from the initial plenitude at the moment of the Immaculate Conception until the moment of final plenitude at her death, before the Assumption.

[43] Cf. Isa. 11:1: "And there shall come forth a rod out of the root of Jesse, and a flower shall rise up out of his root. And the spirit of the Lord shall rest upon him: the spirit of wisdom and of understanding, the spirit of counsel and of fortitude, the spirit of knowledge and of godliness. And he shall be filled with the spirit of the fear of the Lord."   [44] Cf. St. Thomas, IIIa, q. 7, a. 2.

[45] From this it follows that there was never faith or hope greater than Mary's. Her heroic faith and hope, especially at the foot of the cross, far surpassed the faith and hope of the angels while they were still in their transitory state.

[46] For the same reason Mary did not have contrition, although in union with her Son she bore the punishment for our sins.

much, could not suffer. Quite the contrary. As we have already remarked, the fullness of grace in Christ's soul greatly increased His capacity for suffering here on earth from the worst of all evils, namely, sin. The nobler and purer a soul is here on earth, the more it suffers from mortal sin, the radical disorder that turns souls away from God, their final end.

This spiritual suffering began in our Lord's soul from the instant He knew of His mission as Savior.[47] It was then that He offered His first act of love, in union with those which were to follow until His death. From the start He offered up His whole life in an incomparably more perfect manner than does the religious when at his profession he promises obedience until death.[48]

This fullness of grace is manifested in the marvelous harmonizing of apparently opposed virtues. Harmony, which is unity in diversity, is all the more beautiful in the measure that there is a more profound unity in a vaster diversity, and that there is a deeper intimacy between widely separated elements.

In Jesus are admirably reconciled the loftiest supernaturality and the simplest and most spontaneous naturalness. But when we try to be natural, we often forget the exigences of grace and fall into the practical naturalism of indifference. If, on the other hand, we try to attain supernatural perfection without passing through the indispensable intermediaries, we fall into a state of arrogant rigidity, reminiscent of the Jansenists, or into a false supernatural exaltation which borders on eccentricity. In Jesus, nature and grace are wonderfully harmonized because He possesses the fullness of grace and because His nature is completely docile.

In Jesus also the most sublime wisdom and the most astute practical sense are also harmonized. As for us, we are usually either too abstract, lost in vague generalities, or, on the contrary, we put undue emphasis on details, without viewing things from a sufficient height.

---

[47] St. Paul says: "Wherefore when He [Christ] cometh into the world, He saith: Sacrifice and oblation Thou wouldst not: but a body Thou hast fitted to Me: . . . Behold I come: . . . that I should do Thy will, O God" (Heb. 10:5–7).

[48] This explains why the first meritorious act of Christ, although of infinite value, did not render the succeeding acts superfluous. He offered up the first united to all the others, as destined to lead Him to the death of the cross.

Within Jesus are also united perfect justice and boundless mercy, whereas in us justice often turns to severity, and mercy to weakness. Let us call to mind our Savior's forgiveness of the adulterous woman: what firmness and yet what generosity!

Likewise in Him are harmonized a supreme dignity and the deepest humility. Among men, however, magnanimity is frequently accompanied by haughtiness, and souls that are naturally modest often remain pusillanimous and without energy.

Finally in Jesus are reconciled the most heroic strength and the greatest meekness, as witnessed by the smile of the Crucified praying for His executioners: "Father, forgive them, for they know not what they do." [49]

Nowhere else can we find a loftier or deeper moral harmony, more far-reaching in its scope, or of greater splendor, couched in terms of such noble sobriety.

The Consequences for Us

Jesus is the sun of sanctity, eager to shower His splendors upon us. He received holiness as the universal principle of all graces, graces of light, of attraction, of power. He is not a vessel, a brook, or even a river of sanctity: He is its living source.

St. John tells us: "And of His fullness we all have received, and grace for grace." [50] Let us contemplate the radiation of this sanctity in the lives of the saints, of the apostles, martyrs, confessors, and virgins of all times, including our own.

Let us remember that when we were baptized we received from the Savior the same emanation of supernatural life. If we have fallen back into the death of sin, we have been spiritually revivified by absolution, Christ's own pardon, and our souls have been placed once again beneath the living waters of grace, beneath the torrent of divine mercies. If we face tribulation, let us remember that the grace offered to us is proportionate to the sacrifices demanded of us. Let us allow ourselves to be drawn to the Savior, to be illumined, warmed, and vivified by Him. Let us allow ourselves to be loved by His pure and

[49] Luke 23:34.　　　　　[50] John 1:16.

powerful love, which will purify us more and more. If He makes us suffer, it is to make us like Himself, and to associate us with the mystery of the Redemption through suffering. Let us ever ask Him for new graces, including the grace of final perseverance. And, without resisting, let us allow these graces to inspire us to ever greater acts of generosity, for our own salvation, for that of our neighbor, and for the glory of Christ. Let us also pray for saints who will tell the men of our time what they most need to hear, saints who by their lives will reveal to them Christ's love for us.

Even in the Old Testament the Lord said to His ministers: "Be holy because I am holy." [51] Now that we have received the One who is the Saint of saints, let us say to Him: "Lord, sanctify us, so that we may sanctify Thy name, that we may bear witness to Thy mercy, and that Thy kingdom may become more firmly established within us." This is the first prayer that children learn from their mothers, for these are the first words of the Our Father: "Our Father who art in heaven, hallowed be Thy name," that is, may His name be glorified, may its holiness be recognized, not only by our words but by our acts, by our whole life, which should be a song of glory for the Creator in recognition of His goodness.

[51] Lev. 11:44.

❈ XII ❈

THE HUMAN INTELLIGENCE OF THE SAVIOR AND HIS CONTEMPLATION

> "Never did man speak like this man."
>
> John 7:46

WE HAVE inquired into the nature of the innate, substantial, uncreated sanctity of our Lord and into the absolute fullness of grace which derives from this sanctity and radiates upon the souls of all men.

We must now consider the supernatural riches of the Savior's intelligence, will, and heart. We shall speak first of His human intelligence, for there can be no doubt that Jesus has a human intelligence, the property of His human nature, as well as a divine intelligence, the property of His divine nature. This point has been defined by the Church in opposition to Apollinarianism. To maintain that He has only a divine intelligence is to claim that He has no soul and that the Word takes its place. If this were the case, Jesus would not be truly a man, since He would possess only the least important part of human nature, namely, the body.

To gain some insight into the spiritual riches of Jesus' human intelligence, let us first of all consider Him in His actual role as teacher, and then inquire into the nature of His contemplation of the truths which He taught.

What Kind of Teacher Was Jesus?

Modern rationalists are willing to see in Him a profound moralist of great delicacy and charm, who translated into figurative and highly popular language the maxims of ancient Judaic wisdom, "giving

them a new life by filtering them through His impressionable soul,"
as one of these rationalists puts it.[1] But they are generally agreed
that Jesus never had any doctrine; that He never taught a body of
truths or of dogmas that no one could knowingly and willfully reject
without turning away from God and losing his soul. According to
them, it was only much later, by a slow process of elaboration, by the
union of the Christian religion with Greek philosophy, that Catholic
dogma was constituted.

To make Jesus seem more like one of us, liberal Protestants and
modernists have held that He was ignorant of many matters relative
to the kingdom of God and that He did not have from the beginning
of His life the consciousness of His Messiahship. Both groups admit
that He bore within Himself a ferment that brought forth a new
religious movement, but they hold that He did not teach a doctrine
and a truth which no one can refuse to believe without turning away
from the way of salvation.

What on the other hand do we see in the Gospel? In St. Luke
(2:46–49), we read that when Jesus was twelve years old He was
found by Mary and Joseph "in the Temple, sitting in the midst of the
doctors, hearing them and asking them questions. And all that heard
Him were astonished at His wisdom and His answers. . . . And
He said to them [Mary and Joseph]: How is it that you sought Me?
Did you not know, that I must be about My Father's business?"[2]

Thus, long before His public ministry, Jesus knew His mission.
During this ministry He spoke repeatedly of His doctrine, of the
truths to which He came to bear witness, of the light He was bringing into the world, of the faith to be given to His words. As St. Mark
reports, He began His ministry by preaching the gospel of the kingdom of God and saying: "The time is accomplished, and the kingdom
of God is at hand: repent, and believe the gospel."[3] St. Matthew
says that "when Jesus had fully ended these words [the Sermon on

---

[1] To a believer, this word "impressionable" seems to have been chosen in order to de-
nature as much as possible the lofty inspiration here in question. This word robs it of all
that it is, while apparently conceding to it a certain poetic grandeur of the order of the
imagination and of sensibility. To think that such words have been spoken with regard
to Him who is "the way, the truth, and the life"!

[2] Luke 2:46–49.   [3] Mark 1:15.

the Mount], the people were in admiration at His doctrine. For He was teaching them as one having power, and not as the scribes and Pharisees." [4] St. Matthew also reports that Jesus said to His apostles before leaving them: "All power is given Me in heaven and in earth. Going therefore teach ye all nations: baptizing them in the name of the Father, and of the Son, and of the Holy Ghost; teaching them to observe all things whatsoever I have commanded you: and behold I am with you all days, even to the consummation of the world." [5] St. Mark reports these words even more fully: "Go ye into the whole world, and preach the Gospel to every creature. He that believeth and is baptized, shall be saved: but he that believeth not shall be condemned." [6] This is indeed the doctrine necessary for salvation.

In the Gospel, Jesus continually appears as the Master and continually speaks of His doctrine. On Holy Thursday, having washed His apostles' feet, He said to them: "Know you what I have done to you? You call Me Master and Lord, and you say well, for so I am. If then I, being your Lord and Master, have washed your feet. . . . I have given you an example, that as I have done to you, so you do also. . . . If you know these things, you shall be blessed if you do them." [7]

Jesus often said: "My doctrine is not Mine, but His that sent Me. If any man will do the will of Him, he shall know of the doctrine, whether it be of God, or whether I speak of Myself." [8] In the Gospel of St. John, Jesus says as many as six times: "He that believeth in Me [with a faith quickened with love], hath everlasting life." [9] And to the Pharisees, He said: "If I do [the works of My Father], though you will not believe Me, believe the works: that you may know and believe that the Father is in Me, and I in the Father." [10] And: "Whilst you have the light, believe in the light." [11]

The apostles also preached everywhere that Jesus' word was divine. St. Paul declared that he had received his doctrine from Jesus Himself, when he wrote to the Galatians: "I give you to understand,

---

[4] Matt. 7:28 f.   [5] Matt. 28:18–20.   [6] Mark 16:15 f.
[7] John 13:12–17.   [8] *Ibid.*, 7:16 f.
[9] John 3:15, 36; 5:24; 6:47; 7:38; 11:25 f.   [10] *Ibid.*, 10:38.
[11] *Ibid.*, 12:36.

brethren, that the gospel which was preached by me is not according to man. For neither did I receive it of man, nor did I learn it; but by the revelation of Jesus Christ." [12] At this point St. Paul calls to mind his conversion and the fact that his doctrine conforms with that of the other apostles, and that it was approved in a conference with them at Jerusalem. It is by this evangelical doctrine that the entire primitive Chuch lived, without any concern at all about reconciling it with Greek philosophy. We see, therefore, that Jesus presented a unified doctrine, whatever the rationalists may say to the contrary.

Far more than this, the sublimity of Jesus' doctrine is apparent the moment one hears it preached, especially when one compares what it tells us of God and of human life with what the philosophers or even Moses and the prophets have said. A person easily finds in Jesus' teaching the loftiest dogmas and the purest morality. And the more it is put into practice, the more does its grandeur impress itself upon us. The more anyone lives by it the more he loves it, the more he sees its eternal timeliness, whereas the works of even the greatest geniuses always grow old in some particular.

The most eminent philosophers of antiquity, Plato and Aristotle, had certainly risen above the materialism and skepticism of their predecessors. Indeed, they had affirmed the existence of God, the Supreme Intelligence and the Sovereign Good. But they had not been able to attain the explicit idea of creation *ex nihilo*, which presupposed no pre-existing subject to be transformed. Especially they had not been able to grasp the idea of a free creation, the idea of the creative *Fiat* expressed in the first lines of Genesis. They could not arrive at an understanding of the extent to which this world's beings depend upon God. In consequence their idea of Providence remained very timid. They dared not affirm that divine Providence can extend to the smallest details of the lives of each of us. They spoke with even greater timidity of the life to come, of its rewards and punishments. When they did affirm it, their affirmation, as they said, was in terms of a beautiful possibility.[18] Their moral teaching, beautiful in certain respects, remained marred by some rather gross errors. They did not even think it was possible to abolish slavery, and their personal lives

[12] Gal. 1:11 f.   [18] Life to come was thus presented even in the *Phaedo*.

were far below the level of their teaching; in fact, their lives sometimes were the negation of their teaching.

How different is the Gospel, in which Jesus speaks with absolute
certainty of God, His Father and ours, of Providence, and of eternal
life! Did He train Himself naturally, as has been claimed, by the
simple meditative reading of the Old Testament, of Moses and the
Prophets?

Moses and the Prophets certainly far surpassed the ancient philosophers inasmuch as they affirmed, through the light of revelation
and with absolute certainty, that God is the One who is, that everything has been created from nothing, that God made man holy and
good in the beginning, and that after our fall He labored mercifully
for the restoration of His people, to whom He had promised a Savior.

Yet, in the teaching of Moses and the Prophets the intimate life
of God, the Blessed Trinity, remained hidden, and the omnipotence
of the Creator inspired especially fear, the beginning of wisdom. The
Lord's commandments had taken into account the imperfection of
men's souls, which were going through the hard experience of being
in need of redemption, and which had to be slowly guided toward the
new era of the promised Savior.

Jesus, on the other hand, taught with the most absolute certitude,
without any timidity whatever, not only the truths of creation and of
the soul's immortality, but the dogma of eternal life which was far
beyond any conception of the life to come that the philosophers talked
about. And He made eternal life known not merely by symbols like
that of the promised land, which were used in the Old Testament;
but even in His first words on the beatitudes, He declared: "Blessed
are they that hunger and thirst after justice: for they shall have their
fill. . . . Blessed are the clean of heart: for they shall see God. . . .
Blessed are they that suffer persecution for justice' sake: for theirs
is the kingdom of heaven. . . . Be glad and rejoice, for your reward is very great in heaven." [14] In the parable of the talents the faithful servant was told: "Enter thou into the joy of thy Lord." [15] That
is to say: See God as He sees Himself, and love Him as He loves
Himself.

[14] Matt. 5:6-12.   [15] Ibid., 25:21, 23.

From the start of His ministry, in the Sermon on the Mount, Jesus did not merely tell us, as Moses did, that God is the Creator and Master of all things, but that He is our Father. Accordingly Jesus taught us to pray thus: "Our Father who are in heaven, hallowed be Thy name. Thy kingdom come. Thy will be done." [16] What loftier idea of God can be given to men, and what more sanctifying power for their lives? This is the essence of the whole of Christian dogma and morality.

This eternal Father, Jesus continued, has an only Son, begotten from all eternity, and "God so loved the world, as to give His only-begotten Son; that whosoever believeth in Him, may not perish, but may have life everlasting." [17] Jesus increasingly manifested Himself to be this only-begotten Son, come to save us, to redeem us by His mission and by His death: "The Son of man is not come to be ministered unto, but to minister, and to give His life a redemption for many" (Matt. 20:28).

He declared that He would rise from the dead, ascend into heaven, but that He would still be present in the Church until the end of time in the form of the Eucharist,[18] and through the Holy Ghost whom He would send and who would dwell in us in order to make us grasp the meaning of the gospel and thus lead other souls to eternal life.[19] Thenceforth eternal life is seen to be indissoluble union with the Father, the Son, and the Holy Ghost in the radiance of the beatific vision: "Blessed are the clean of heart, for they shall see God."

Can we fail to endure patiently anything that is said untruly about us when we remember that it has been said of Him who is the Teacher of teachers, who is "the truth and the life," that He never had a doctrine?

His teaching includes not only the dogma of creation which had been so clearly enunciated in the Old Testament, but also those of the Blessed Trinity, the Incarnation, the Redemption, the Eucharist, and eternal life. These are all, of course, unfathomable supernatural mysteries, but mysteries which answer our most deep-seated natural

---

[16] *Ibid.*, 6:9 f.   [17] John 3:16.
[18] Matt. 26:26; Mark 14:22; Luke 22:19.
[19] John 14:16, 26; 15:26; 16:7; Acts 1:8.

aspirations and which arouse in us nobler ones. They are mysteries which harmonize admirably with one another, and it is in vain that the incredulous seek to find any contradiction in them. How superior is this doctrine to the timid affirmations of the philosophers and to the often obscure predictions of the prophets!

In its simplicity this doctrine is sublime in the true sense of the word. The sublime is indeed what is most elevated, most extraordinary in the order of the beautiful. And as the beautiful is a splendid harmony, the splendor of unity in diversity, so the sublime is the loftiest and most intimate harmony of most diverse and separated elements, in appearance irreconcilable. The sublime is particularly the intimate union of supreme goodness and the deepest wretchedness. When divine mercy bows to this extent, gratitude must find expression not merely in words but in tears: the sign of a relationship that is so profound that it is beyond expression in human terms. Now the mysteries of the Incarnation, the Redemption, the Eucharist, are the union of the infinite riches of divine mercy with the universal wretchedness of man, the union of man's poverty with the infinite grandeur of God.

This sublimity is no less apparent in the moral teaching of Jesus than in the mysteries He revealed.

How petty the maxims of the pagan sages seem, compared to the Gospel! They say, as Socrates did: "Know thyself"; "be manly"; "The measure of goodness is the good man," who lives by right reason. Jesus came to say: "Be you therefore perfect, as also your heavenly Father is perfect." [20] Be you perfect, not merely as the angels are, but as the heavenly Father is perfect. For you have been made participants not only of the angelic life, but of the intimate life of God, the seed of eternal life, which will consist in seeing God as He sees Himself, and in loving Him as He loves Himself. "Blessed are the clean of heart: for they shall see God."

The wise men of antiquity said with pride: "The strong man grappling with adversity is a divine spectacle." Jesus said with humility, simplicity, and depth: "Blessed are they that mourn [their sins], Blessed are they that suffer persecution for justice' sake: for theirs is

[20] Matt. 5:48.

the kingdom of heaven," it is already realized within them. Such words had never been heard. So lofty are they that even believers are often slow to understand when persecution comes to them. They are astonishing words, and yet so simple when spoken by our Savior.

There is no affinity between the highest moral teaching of the pagans and that of Jesus. The philosophers spoke of acquired virtues, which are often unstable. The virtues our Savior spoke of are the infused virtues which must grow with merit until the supernatural life of eternity.

The new law of the Gospel, which is a law of love, is likewise far superior to the law of fear promulgated by Moses: "You have heard that it was said to them of old: Thou shalt not kill. . . . But I say to you, that whosoever is angry with his brother, shall be in danger of the judgment." [21] "You have heard that it hath been said, Thou shalt love thy neighbor, and hate thy enemy. But I say to you, Love your enemies: do good to them that hate you: and pray for them that persecute and calumniate you: that you may be the children of your Father who is in heaven, who maketh His sun to rise upon the good and bad, and raineth upon the just and the unjust. For if you love [only] them that love you, . . . do not even the publicans this? . . . Be you therefore perfect, as also your heavenly Father is perfect." [22] These words summarize the entire Sermon on the Mount, spoken at the beginning of our Savior's ministry.

As we have said before, Jesus substituted for the petty nobility of the human virtues the highest nobility of sanctity. He preached hunger and thirst for the justice of God, that is, for union with God. [23]

It is difficult to know what in this doctrine is most to be admired: its loftiness, its depth, its scope, its intimate understanding of the heart's secrets, [24] its infallible views on the future. All these supernatural splendors harmonize wonderfully with the most complete naturalness in expression and with the most astute practical sense.

---

[21] *Ibid.*, 5:21 f.   [22] *Ibid.*, 5:43–48.   [23] *Ibid.*, 5:6.

[24] *Ibid.*, 9:4. Before curing the man sick of the palsy, Jesus said to the Pharisees: "Why do you think evil in your hearts?" On several occasions He showed that He knew the heart's most intimate secrets. Cf. Matt. 12:25; 22:18; 26:10; John 2:25; 4:19; 6:65; 7:20; 13:11.

Nowhere can there be found a more perfect harmony between nature and grace. Here natural aspirations are not merely filled but surpassed, and the word of Christ inspires far superior aspirations which are united in the efficacious and powerful desire for the supernatural life of eternity, for the glory of God and the salvation of souls. These were words completely ignored by the pagan sages, and the Old Testament prophets could only lisp them.

Here indeed the plenitude of divine revelation is given to us here on earth in a still obscure manner, in order to lead us to the definitive and dazzling revelation of eternity.

By its sublimity and its conformity with our highest aspirations, the doctrine of Jesus so far surpasses all other doctrines, even that which the chosen people rightly gloried in having received from God, that we cannot fail to recognize in it a powerful and superhuman originality. But this is not the originality of an innovator who is breaking with the past. Jesus said: "Do not think that I am come to destroy the law, or the Prophets. I am not come to destroy, but to fulfill." [25]

We can well understand that the astonished Jews asked: "How doth this man know letters, having never learned?" [26] And the messengers of the Pharisees, daring not to lay hands on Him, admitted: "Never did man speak like this man." [27]

It cannot be maintained, therefore, that Jesus merely bore within Himself a ferment which became the principle of a new religious movement, but that He did not have a doctrine. The entire *Credo* is to be found in His teaching and can be expressed in His own words, not only in the words reported by St. John, but in those of the first three Gospels, words which are bound up with the whole fabric of the story, with all the facts of His life, His passion and death.

How Jesus Taught

The manner in which Jesus taught is no less sublime in its simplicity than the object of His doctrine. It has been said that "A man's style is the man." Christ Jesus has indeed His own style. In order to have

[25] Matt. 5:17.   [26] John 7:15.   [27] *Ibid.*, 7:46.

even a vague notion of His ascendancy over souls, it would be necessary to have heard the sermons of great saints like St. Bernard, St.
Dominic, and the holy Curé of Ars.

St. Thomas tells us that the apostle [28] must express himself in such
a manner that the word of God may enlighten the intelligence, stir
the heart, and arouse the will to the accomplishment of the Commandments. The apostle, therefore, must speak with authority, in the name
of God, with simplicity so as to be understood by every soul, with
supernatural unction to stir hearts, and with power to turn wills toward God.

Jesus' method of teaching reveals a sovereign authority which is
equaled only by the simplicity and unction with which He communicates the loftiest truths; whence the power of the Gospel and the profound influence it has exerted for almost two thousand years, in spite
of its austerity and its demands.

The incomparable authority of Jesus is manifested through His
power in affirmation and through the influence of His sanctity. How
did He affirm? He did not make use of the procedures of human
eloquence which flatter the hearer, seeking to please him and to gain
his admiration rather than enlighten him. There is not the least bit of
oratorical artificiality in the sermons of the Master. He also avoided
the abstract considerations of the philosophers and the scriptural dis-
cussions of the scribes, who scrutinized the sacred texts without bringing out their true meaning. Jesus did not argue. He spoke in brief,
clear, penetrating formulas: "If thy right eye scandalize thee, pluck
it out; . . . and if thy right hand scandalize thee, cut it off." [29]
"Love your enemies: . . . and pray for them that persecute and
calumniate you." These are formulas that jostle unruly passions,
amaze the reason, but that address themselves directly to souls of
good will, and arouse this good will in those who are seeking the
truth. As for unreasonable and rebellious spirits, these formulas sink
deep into them like streaks of light and condemnations.

"All things therefore whatsoever you would that men should do to
you, do you also to them." [30] "If one strike thee on thy right cheek,
turn to him also the other. And if a man will contend with thee in

---

[28] IIa IIae, q. 177, a. 1.   [29] Matt. 5:29 f.   [30] Ibid., 7:12.

judgment, and take away thy coat, let go thy cloak also unto him." [31] For in this manner you will win the soul of your brother, you will enlighten and save him. These maxims are so new and so beautiful that they are not easily forgotten. They remain within us like the light of conscience which inspires us toward goodness and chides us for our selfishness.

Jesus affirms with the authority of the supreme Master: "You call Me Master and Lord; and you say well, for so I am." [32] He considers Himself above any human judgment, above any cross-examination, any criticism, any contradiction. No one else has ever used His formulas: "For this was I born, and for this came I into the world; that I should give testimony to the truth. Everyone that is of the truth, heareth My voice." [33] "Amen, amen I say unto you: . . . I speak that which I have seen with My Father." [34] "You believe in God, believe also in Me." [35] "I am the light of the world: he that followeth Me, walketh not in darkness, but shall have the light of life. . . . Although I give testimony of Myself, My testimony is true: for I know whence I came, and whither I go." [36] "I am the way and the truth, and the life." [37] There is no loftier doctrinal authority.

The authority of His life confirmed that of His intelligence. As for the philosophers, their conduct was often in contradiction to their moral teaching. Even Moses was not as perfect as the Lord demanded of him, and because of this he did not enter the Promised Land.[38] Jesus, on the other hand, began by practicing in all perfection everything that He taught: "Jesus began to do and to teach." [39] Because He had accomplished perfectly all the commandments and counsels, without the slightest flaw, He was able to say: "Which of you shall convince Me of sin?" [40] "For I have given you an example, that as I have done to you, so you do also." [41] "If you keep My commandments, you shall abide in My love; as I also have kept My Father's commandments, and do abide in His love." [42] His teaching was but the reflection of His conduct, and He asks incomparably less

[31] *Ibid.*, 5:39 f. [32] John 13:13. [33] *Ibid.*, 18:37.
[34] *Ibid.*, 8:34, 38. [35] *Ibid.*, 14:1. [36] *Ibid.*, 8:12–14.
[37] *Ibid.*, 14:6. [38] Deut. 32:51. [39] Acts 1:1.
[40] John 8:46. [41] *Ibid.*, 13:15. [42] *Ibid.*, 15:10.

from us than what He Himself has done for us: "He humbled Himself, becoming obedient unto death, even to the death of the cross." [43] The authority of a man's life has never so well confirmed the authority of his doctrine.

What is no less remarkable is the fact that this sovereign authority was coupled with the greatest simplicity. Among many human teachers simplicity is destroyed by pompousness born of pride, which is in reality foolishness. Jesus is too great to feel the least pride in His intelligence and in His life. In His greatness, He is the model of humility: "My doctrine is not Mine, but His that sent Me." [44] He cares neither for titles nor honors, nor for the role of learned doctor. Of the scribes and Pharisees He said: "They love the first places at feasts, and the first chairs in the synagogues, and salutations in the marketplace, and to be called by men, Rabbi. But be not you called Rabbi. For one is your master; and all you are brethren." [45]

And while the Pharisees loved to sit in the chair of Moses, to whom did He choose to preach the Gospel? The poor, the poor who were so despised by the pagan sages. This, together with the miracles, is actually a sign of His Messiahship: "The poor have the gospel preached to them." [46] Isaias had declared that He would "preach to the meek" and "heal the contrite of heart." [47] Thus it was that Jesus preached throughout the countryside, on the shores of Lake Genesareth, in Solomon's portico, always in a simple unstudied manner. There was nothing about Him that bespoke artistic or human effort. As He told His listeners, "the words that I have spoken to you, are spirit and life." [48]

One of the most extraordinary things about our Lord's preaching is that the more sublime the object He spoke of, the calmer was His language. There was never the slightest tinge of exaltation in His words. As Bossuet has well said: "Who can fail to admire the condescension with which He tempered the loftiness of His doctrine? It is at once milk for infants and bread for the strong. One can see that He is filled with God's secrets, but it is evident that He is not astonished by them as are other mortals to whom God reveals Himself:

[43] Phil. 2:8.   [44] John 7:16.   [45] Matt. 23:6–8.

[46] Matt. 11:5.   [47] Isa. 61:1.   [48] John 6:64.

He speaks about them naturally, as one being born into these secrets and into this glory. And what He possesses beyond measure,[49] He pours forth by measure, so that our weakness may be able to bear it." [50]

After the Last Supper, He said to the apostles: "I have yet many things to say to you: but you cannot bear them now. But when He, the Spirit of truth, is come, He will teach you all truth." [51] Finally, it was with the utmost simplicity that He recommended humility to His apostles: ". . . calling ùnto Him a little child, [He] set him in the midst of them. And said: Amen I say to you, unless you be converted, and become as little children, you shall not enter into the kingdom of heaven.[52] Whosoever therefore shall humble himself as this little child, he is the greater in the kingdom of heaven." [53] For such a man enters into intimacy with God through mental prayer and through love. Thus are admirably reconciled in Jesus's manner of teaching the highest authority, along with simplicity and humility. How complicated does the abstract doctrine of the philosophers seem beside this eminent simplicity!

Lastly, Jesus spoke with an unction that was truly divine, despite the austerity of His counsels. His own words were realized within Himself: "Out of the abundance of the heart the mouth speaketh." [54] He preached continually of the love with which God first loved us, when we were still sinners. One could feel that He Himself was overflowing with charity and wished ardently for our salvation. He said: "I am come that they may have life, and may have it more abundantly." [55] His preaching was one of glad tidings: "Come to Me, all you that labor, and are burdened, and I will refresh you." [56]

This unction, the expression of His mercy, was particularly palpable in His conversation with the Samaritan woman: "If thou didst know the gift of God, and who He is that saith to thee, Give Me to drink; thou perhaps wouldst have asked of Him, and He would have

[49] *Ibid.*, 3:34.　　　[50] *Discours sur l'histoire universelle*, Part II, chap. 19.
[51] John 16:12 f.
[52] Clearly the reference here is to the second conversion, for the apostles were in the state of grace, three had been on Mount Thabor, and all of them were to receive Communion before the Passion. Peter's second conversion took place at the end of the Passion, immediately after his denials. It was then that he began to enter into the intimacy of the kingdom of God, and even more so on Pentecost.　　　[53] Matt. 18:2–4.
[54] *Ibid.*, 12:34.　　　[55] John 10:10.　　　[56] Matt. 11:28.

given thee living water." [57] This unction was also noticeable in His preaching of the beatitudes and in His last conversation with the disciples before the Passion. During His last discourses it was as if sheets of light, luminous waves, descended from heaven to become diffused in ever wider circles upon the generations to come.

This divine unction, which was the effect of grace, gave foreknowledge of the Holy Ghost of whom it has been said: "His unction teacheth you of all things." [58] There is no romantic sentimentalism about it. It is accompanied by renunciation, it fights against sin, against the spirit of the world and the spirit of evil: "If any man will come after Me, let him deny himself, and take up his cross, and follow Me." [59] While Jesus tells us often that He brings us peace, union with God, He also says that in order to attain this peace we must know how to fight against all within us that would lead us to evil. It is with this in mind that He said: "I came not to send peace, but the sword." [60] Those most beloved of God have been called on to suffer most cruelly from the persecution of those who would not hear the joyful tidings of the Gospel.

In St. Luke we read: "The father shall be divided against the son, and the son against his father, the mother against the daughter." [61] And in St. Matthew: "And a man's enemies shall be they of his own household. He that loveth father or mother more than Me, is not worthy of Me." [62] These family rifts were frequent during the three centuries of the persecutions. One can sense here the exigencies of the divine law.

It is this saintly austerity united to humility which demonstrates the wholly supernatural origin of the Savior's unction. He has sometimes told His saints: "Do not lay too much store on the favorable judgments of men, for I love thee with a perfect love. I spent My earthly existence in humiliations and scorn and in a hidden life. It was thus that I glorified My Father, laid the foundations of My Church, and remedied the evils of pride. This is the path that thou must follow." [63] This is truly Christ's own style, His own manner.

[57] John 4:10.
[58] I John 2:27.
[59] Matt. 16:24; Luke 9:23; 14:27.
[60] Matt. 10:34; Luke 12:51.
[61] Luke 12:53.
[62] Matt. 10:36 f.
[63] Cf. *Vie de la Vénérable Marie-Céleste Crostarosa* by Rev. J. Favre, C.SS.R., p. 152.

As Father Grou, S.J., says very well: "A humble teacher can teach great things, but he will teach them with humility. . . . If he speaks with emphasis and authority, it will not be for his own glory but to extol the one in whose name he speaks and to make a deeper impression on the minds of his listeners. This is how Jesus Christ taught. . . . It is impossible to say such lofty and divine things in a simpler manner. . . . This is how those who have an interior spirit teach. . . . They speak with assurance and at the same time with humility, because they are not speaking of themselves. . . . Their discourses exert upon well-prepared hearts a persuasion, an efficacy that can come only from the grace which prompted their words." [64]

These are the reasons why the Gospel has such power and such a profound attraction upon our souls. It both jostles and captivates them. It jostles our unruly passions and captivates our good will. And yet this book was not written directly by our Lord. As St. Thomas says: [65] "It was fitting that Christ as the most excellent of teachers should adopt that manner of teaching whereby His doctrine is imprinted on the hearts of His hearers," by the grace of light and strength which He granted them. This is the highest magisterium, the living magisterium. And this is why, as St. Thomas also remarks,[66] the new law of the Gospel is first of all written spiritually in the hearts of the faithful by the grace of the Holy Ghost, before being materially written on stone or parchment. Jesus was content to write in the souls of His apostles a living letter that they have made known to the world: "Going therefore teach ye all nations." And in actual fact, His doctrine spread, in spite of innumerable obstacles, to the limits of the world known to the ancient peoples.

Today, after twenty centuries, this power of communication continues to exert its influence, thus verifying the affirmation: "Heaven and earth shall pass, but My words shall not pass." [67] As St. Peter said, these are "the words of eternal life." [68] Until the end of the world our Savior will raise up new priestly vocations so that the gospel may ever be preached for the salvation of souls.

---

[64] L'Intérieur de Jésus, chap. 24: "Manière d'enseigner."
[65] IIIa, q.42, a.4.   [66] Ia IIae, q.106, a.1.   [67] Matt. 24:35.
[68] John 6:69.

While the books of the Greek philosophers stay on library shelves, consulted by a handful of scholars, the Gospel has been for twenty centuries the spiritual food of millions of souls. Even the modern societies which reject the Gospel are none the less impregnated with it in spite of themselves. Whereas the more sincere among the philosophers admit that they are powerless to change the interior dispositions of men, Jesus, with but a few poor Galilean fishermen and in spite of three centuries of persecutions succeeded in changing the moral ideas of humanity.[69] Through His grace He gave to multitudes of souls the love of goodness, to many He gave a supernatural ardor for sacrifice, and He dispersed among all peoples marvelous flowers of sanctity. The Christian martyrology which is read daily in the Office after Lauds is a great motive of credibility, a notable sign of the divine origin of Jesus' doctrine.

No one else has been able to keep a doctrine ever living down the centuries through an immortal race of disciples, so that after two thousand years we still accept it as "the words of eternal life."

When we read the Gospel in a recollected manner we wonder how our Savior was able to unite in His teaching and in His manner of preaching such diverse qualities: the supreme authority of His doctrine and of His life together with such perfect simplicity and humility, an unction which moves men's hearts together with an austerity which makes heavy demands on human nature. The intimate union of such different qualities cannot be explained naturally. Our temperaments are in a sense determined by nature, and must be completed by virtue. The profound union in Jesus of such diverse qualities can be the effect only of very high virtue and of very lofty contemplation, in other words, the effect of the most extraordinary grace.

Our Savior's Contemplation Superior to All Others according to the Gospel of St. John

In what light did Jesus contemplate the things He taught? In an effort to understand this, let us raise our minds progressively toward Him, starting with a less sublime teaching. Then we shall see what

[69] Cf. St. Thomas, *Contra Gentes*, Bk. I, chap. 6.

Jesus has Himself told us in the Gospel of St. John concerning his vision of divine things.

The greatest geniuses of the pagan world, such as Plato and Aristotle, contemplated their doctrine in the natural light of the intelligence, in the light of first principles abstracted from sensible things, and in the mirror of these things the power of their vision discovered a reflection of divine perfections. Thus they taught that God is the primary Being, the supreme Intelligence who ordained all things and who is the sovereign Good. Yet there remained in their affirmations much obscurity and uncertainty.

The prophets of the Old Testament contemplated the doctrine that they announced in the light of prophecy united to the supernatural light of faith. This light was incomparably superior to the natural light of the intelligence with which the greatest Greek philosophers were endowed. Thus Isaias foresaw the promised Savior: "A child is born to us, and a son is given to us, and the government is upon his shoulder: and his name shall be called, Wonderful, Counselor, God the Mighty, the Father of the world to come, the Prince of Peace." [70]

However, the light of prophecy and that of infused faith are still obscure in the sense that they do not give us the evidence of the supernatural mysteries. They merely lead us to adhere to the infallible testimony of God. Just as the most distant stars cannot manifest to us the outermost limits of the firmament, so the infused light of prophecy and that of faith do not suffice to shed light on what St. Paul calls "the deep things of God," [71] namely, His intimate life which we shall clearly understand only in heaven. Beyond doubt the gifts of the Holy Ghost, gifts of knowledge and wisdom, give us a living, quasi-experimental knowledge of the supernatural mysteries, helping us to penetrate and enjoy them. Yet these gifts do not bring us out of the obscurity of faith.

The apostles, as had the prophets before them, received the light of prophecy and that of infused faith in a high degree. One of them, St. Paul, in view of his exceptional ministry, received even a special and extraordinary grace of light which he described as follows: "I know a man in Christ above fourteen years ago (whether in the body, I

[70] Isa. 9:6. [71] I Cor. 2:10.

know not, or out of the body, I know not; God knoweth), such a one caught up to the third heaven. And I know . . . that he was caught up into paradise, and heard secret words, which it is not granted to man to utter." [72] In this passage St. Paul seems to be recalling the ravishment mentioned in the Acts of the Apostles, where these words of the great convert are recorded: "And it came to pass, when I was come again to Jerusalem, and was praying in the Temple, that I was in a trance, and saw Him saying unto me: Make haste, and get thee quickly out of Jerusalem; becasue they will not receive thy testimony concerning Me." [73]

When St. Paul says that he was ravished to the third heaven he meant, as did the Hebrews, the spiritual heaven where God dwells, the empyrean above the heaven of the air (the atmosphere) and even above the heaven of the stars (the ether). It is therefore probable that, in accordance with the thought of St. Augustine [74] and of St. Thomas, [75] St. Paul means that for a short moment he was raised up to the beatific vision of the divine essence. These great doctors, who had themselves received extraordinary graces of contemplation, [76] say it seems that in that brief moment Paul contemplated what "eye hath not seen, nor ear heard . . . what things God hath prepared for them that love Him." [77]

After this ravishment the great Apostle was so profoundly convinced of the truth of the divine doctrine which he was preaching that his conviction was always far beyond even the loftiest words that came to his lips. Sublime words flowed from his pen, sometimes pouring forth like a torrent rushing down a mountainside, and yet they cannot express what he saw. His noblest words are but the inadequate means of expressing, in terms suited to our intelligence, an intuition far above us. Sometimes, alas, a preacher may have more on his lips than exists in the faith of his own heart, and then his preaching becomes theatrical, affected, and bombastic. St. Paul, on the contrary, knew far more than he could tell. There was always much more

---

[72] II Cor. 12:2–4. [73] Acts 22:17 ff.
[74] *De Genesi ad litteram*, 12, 28, etc. [75] IIa IIae, q. 175, a. 3, 4, 5.
[76] The authority of those who reject this opinion is very slight compared to that of Augustine and Thomas Aquinas.
[77] I Cor. 2:9.

within his soul than on his lips; the spirit dominated the letter and vivified it.

St. Paul spoke of what he had contemplated in God. St. Thomas says that "preaching must derive from the fullness of contemplation" [78] if it is to be living and sanctifying and in any way resemble the words of fire that are referred to in the psalms (118:140).[79] We cannot hope to describe the magnificence of a mountain view unless we have actually been up there ourselves. It will not suffice merely to page through a travel guide. That Paul might speak with the greatest possible light and vigor concerning God and the redemptive Incarnation, he had been raised at least for an instant to the summit of divine contemplation. That is why he was the great Doctor of the Gentiles, charged with transmitting to them for the first time the teaching of the Master.

But if Paul was raised for at least one moment to the contemplation of the divine essence, what are we to say of Jesus Himself?

It is true of course that through His divne intelligence Jesus never ceased seeing God. Far more than this, His divine intelligence which is common to the three persons, is identical without any real distinction whatever with the divine essence known from all eternity; and the person of the Word is "the brightness of eternal light," [80] "the brightness of His [the Father's] glory." [81]

However, with respect to His human intelligence, was it only in the obscurity of faith that Jesus ordinarily attained the supernatural mysteries of which He spoke, the deep things of God which He teaches us to know dimly? Did Jesus have but a few moments of ecstasy, as St. Paul did, remaining ignorant of many things relating to the kingdom of God?

The infallible magisterium of the Church has given a partial answer to this question. It has been defined, in refutation of the heresy of the Agnoetes, that Jesus as man was not ignorant of anything whatever relating to the kingdom of God,[82] that will be consummated in

[78] IIa IIae, q. 188, a. 6.   [79] Ps. 118:140.   [80] Wisd. 7:26.
[81] Heb. 1:3.
[82] Cf. Denzinger, *Enchiridion*, no. 248. Declaration of Gregory I (A.D. 600): "Omnipotens Filius nescire se dicit diem (judicii) quem nesciri facit, non quod ipse nesciat, sed quia hunc sciri minime permittat . . . Diem ergo et horam judicii scit Deus et homo;

heaven and that includes all the elect, both angels and men. Can He who even as man is the head of the kingdom of God be ignorant of anything that relates to His function? Can He be ignorant of the day of judgment and the number of the elect for whom He is meriting salvation? The Church tells us that such ignorance could not have been in Him.

But in what light did Christ's human intelligence know here below everything concerning the kingdom of God? Was it only in the light of prophecy united to the light of faith? Or was it in a higher light? Was the sacred soul of our Savior deprived during His life on earth of the light of glory by which the saints in heaven see God face to face? If it is probable that St. Paul while here on earth received this light for at least one instant, what are we to say of the sacred soul of Christ?

The theologians answer in unison: Jesus saw what He taught in the light of the beatific vision.[83] Jesus possessed throughout His earthly life and in a far higher degree the contemplation which St. Paul seems to have attained for an instant during an ecstasy. The contemplation of Jesus even here on earth was not inferior to that which the saints enjoy in heaven. This has been the common teaching of theologians particularly since the twelfth century, and the Church has declared that it would be rash to deny it.[84]

What is the foundation for this doctrine which is commonly accepted in the Church? It is founded first of all on several of Jesus' statements. In St. John He said to Nicodemus with regard to spiritual regeneration: "Amen, amen I say to thee, that we speak what we

---

sed ideo, quia Deus est homo. Res autem valde manifesta est, quia quisquis Nestorianus non est, Agnoita esse nullatenus potest . . . Scriptum est: 'Sciens Jesus, quia omnia dedit ei Pater in manus' (Joan., 13:3). Si omnia, profecto et diem judicii et horam. Quis ergo ita stultus est, ut dicat quia accepit Filius in manibus quod nescit?"

[83] It is no slight matter that on this point all theologians agree, whether they be Thomists, Scotists, Suarezians, or Molinists. Their disagreement on controversial matters shows the value of their agreement on those that are not controversial.

[84] Cf. Denzinger, *Enchiridion*, nos. 2183 ff. The Holy See declared by a decree of June 5, 1918, that it would be foolhardy to teach the following propositions: "Non constat fuisse in anima Christi inter homines degentis scientiam, quam habent beati seu comprehensores.—Nec certa dici potest sententia quae statuit animam Christi nihil ignoravisse, sed ab initio cognovisse in Verbo omnia, praeterita, praesentia et futura, seu omnia quae Deus scit scientia visionis."

know, and we testify what we have seen, and you receive not our testimony. If I have spoken to you earthly things, and you believe not; how will you believe, if I shall speak to you heavenly things? And no man hath ascended into heaven, but He that descended from heaven, the Son of man who is in heaven." [85]

The words "what we know" in this passage are synonymous with "what we have seen," as is said immediately afterward. Now, Jesus spoke as a man. It was therefore as a man that He saw God and the things of heaven. Must not testimony correspond to the knowledge from which it derives?

And as at the particular moment when Jesus was saying these words the souls of the deceased just were awaiting their entry into heaven, He said as we have just seen: "No man hath ascended into heaven but He that descended from heaven, the Son of man who is in heaven." Thus Jesus was already in heaven not only as the Son of God, by reason of His divinity and of His divine intelligence, but as the Son of man, by reason of His human intelligence. Not only was He to be in heaven after His death, resurrection, and ascension, but He was there already at that moment. This was the same as saying that as of that instant through His human intelligence He already saw God face to face, without any intermediary whatever. For what is heaven if not the spiritual homeland where the blessed enjoy the immediate vision of God or of eternal life, which consists in seeing God as He sees Himself and in loving Him as He loves Himself?

Tradition commonly holds, therefore, that Jesus even while here on earth was at once *viator et comprehensor*, that is, He was a wayfarer toward eternity and a comprehensor or blessed, already in possession of eternal life.[86]

Jesus also said in St. John: "Every one that hath heard of the Father, and hath learned, cometh to Me. Not that any man hath seen the Father; but He who is of God, He hath seen the Father. Amen, amen I say unto you: He that believeth in Me, hath everlasting life." [87] Jesus was here saying that the believers have heard the Father, His word, but have not seen Him; whereas He, Jesus, "who is of God, He hath seen the Father." Therefore this can mean only that

[85] John 3:11 ff. [86] Cf. St. Thomas, IIIa, q. 15, a. 10. [87] John 6:45 f.

He was more than a believer, that He was not reduced to believing in God, to believing in His own divinity and in His own divine personality. For He had more than faith; He had the vision that the blessed possess in heaven.[88] There is an immense difference between believing and seeing.

Likewise, in His priestly prayer, Jesus in praying for His disciples said again: "Father, I will that where I am, they also whom Thou hast given Me may be with Me; that they may see My glory which Thou hast given Me, because Thou hast loved Me before the creation of the world." [89]

These last words are singularly expressive: "I will that where I am [that is to say, in heaven], they also whom Thou hast given Me may be with Me." The apostles already had supernatural faith. Jesus was asking for them the beatific vision, the vision of the divine essence and of the glory which had been given to Him as man, and which derives from the uncreated glory or essential beatitude which He enjoys as God. He asked for His apostles the perfect grace which He Himself already had, that is, eternal life, which consists in seeing God and Him whom God has sent.[90]

This is how St. John the Baptist and after him St. John the Evangelist understood the testimony of the Master. St. John the Baptist said to Jesus' disciples: "I am not Christ, but . . . I am sent before Him. . . . He must increase, but I must decrease. He that cometh from above, is above all. He that is of the earth, of the earth he is, and of the earth he speaketh.[91] He that cometh from heaven, is above all. And what He hath seen and heard, is above all. And what He hath seen and heard, that He testifieth: and no man receiveth His testimony. . . . For He whom God hath sent, speaketh the words of

---

[88] It follows from this that the loftiest faith that ever existed was Mary's, especially when she stood at the foot of the cross. It was a faith superior to that which the angels had during their short journey toward eternity.

[89] John 17:24.

[90] Cf. John 17:3: "Now this is eternal life: that they may know Thee, the only true God, and Jesus Christ whom Thou hast sent."

[91] "He that is of the earth, of the earth he is," is the principle of contradiction or of identity applied to the order of spiritual things, to show how much they differ from the things of earth. Flesh is flesh, spirit is spirit. They must not be confused.

God: for God doth not give the Spirit by measure.[92] The Father loveth the Son: and He hath given all things into His hand. He that believeth in the Son, hath life everlasting," that is, he has entered upon eternal life.[93]

The testimony of St. John the Baptist given above is as lofty as that of St. John the Evangelist in the prologue of the Fourth Gospel: "No man hath seen God at any time: the only-begotten Son who is in the bosom of the Father, He hath declared Him." [94] Is this not saying that in contrast to the prophets who had not seen God, the only-begotten Son had seen Him, and that He had seen Him as man, for it was as man that Jesus made God known? This vision is the source of His testimony, infinitely superior to all those that preceded.

In his First Epistle St. John also says: "Dearly beloved, we are now the sons of God; and it hath not yet appeared what we shall be. We know that, when He shall appear, we shall be like to Him: because we shall see Him as He is." [95] Then will Jesus' priestly prayer be answered: "Father, I will that where I am, they also whom Thou hast given Me may be with Me; that they may see My glory which Thou hast given Me." [96]

The more deeply one contemplates in the real sense of the expression these words of Christ, the more one grasps in the obscurity of faith the truth that our Savior possessed even here on earth the light of glory. It was this light that He manifested to three of His disciples on Mount Thabor when for a few moments His body was transfigured.

Finally, is this not what St. Paul tells us: "In Him, it hath well pleased the Father, that all fullness should dwell; [97] . . . in whom [Jesus] are hid all the treasures of wisdom and knowledge." [98] "That . . . you may be able to comprehend, . . . what is the breadth and length and height and depth . . . also the charity of Christ." [99] "God, who, at sundry times and in divers manners, spoke in times past to the fathers by the prophets, last of all in these days

[92] God would have given Him the Spirit with measure if here on earth Jesus as man had had only the obscure and limited knowledge of infused faith, and not the knowledge of vision.

[93] John 3:28–36.

[94] Ibid., 1:18.

[95] I John 3:2.

[96] John 17:24.

[97] Col. 1:19.

[98] Ibid., 2:3.

[99] Eph. 3:18.

hath spoken to us by His Son, whom He hath appointed heir of all things, by whom also He made the world. Who being the brightness of His glory, and the figure of His substance, . . . being made so much better than the angels, as He hath inherited a more excellent name than they." [100] Since Jesus was "appointed heir of all things" even here on earth, He also enjoyed here below the eternal heritage. Otherwise His human intelligence would have been less enlightened than that of the angels whom He already called "His angels" or His ministers in the kingdom of God. Lastly, if Jesus did not already possess the beatific vision here on earth He would have been made more perfect when He received it after His death, His charity would have increased with His knowledge of God. But this is contrary to the teaching of the whole Catholic tradition, according to which Christ did not become better or more perfect.[101] Therefore He did not make the transition from faith to the vision of the divine essence. For, if that had been the case His charity or love of God at the moment of transition would have increased as would habitual created grace, and this is contrary to all traditional teaching concerning the absolute plenitude of grace that Jesus received from the very first instant of His conception.[102]

The Savior's Contemplation according to Theology

Can theology make even more explicit the meaning of the scriptural passages that we have just quoted? It can and does indeed by means of highly fitting arguments which St. Thomas has admirably presented.[103]

St. Thomas says that Jesus must have possessed even here on earth the vision which thousands of blessed souls have in heaven. Every intelligent being must have the knowledge fitting to his state. This is true of the physician, the magistrate, and the priest. Too often incapable and improvident persons occupy high posts, to the detriment

---

[100] Heb. 1:1–4.

[101] Cf. *Concilium Constantinopolit.* II (A.D. 553); Denzinger, no. 224.

[102] Cf. St. Thomas, IIIa, q.7, a.12: "The grace of Christ cannot be increased . . . since Christ as man was a true and full comprehensor from the first instant of His conception."   [103] IIIa, q.10, a.4.

of those whom they are guiding. However, this cannot be the case of those directly chosen by God to be His extraordinary ministers in the transmission of revelation. Thus Providence owed it to itself to give Jesus the science or knowledge proportionate to His mission.

Jesus' mission is that of the Teacher of humanity, charged with leading it to eternal life. He was constituted for all time as the Teacher of teachers, the Master of the apostles, the doctors, the greatest contemplatives. After Him no one will come who is more enlightened or who will teach us better the way that leads to eternal blessedness. Must not the perfect Master, then, possess the evidence of what He is teaching, especially if He is Himself "the way, the truth, and the life"?

The great Sower of truth, charged with telling all human generations until the end of time "the words of eternal life," must have known this eternal life even while He was still on earth. He knew the divine essence not "through a glass in a dark manner" but "face to face" according to St. Paul's words.[104]

The divine essence that St. Paul probably saw for a brief moment in an ecstasy, Jesus saw continually here on earth through His human intelligence, without needing to interrupt His conversation with His apostles. He was above ecstasy, and His words were so luminous precisely because His intelligence was perpetually illumined by this spiritual sun which never suffered eclipse even while He slept, even during the dark hour of His passion.

Millions of souls in heaven enjoy this contemplation, and they have attained it only through the merits of Jesus Christ. Could He, then, have been deprived of that which He gave to others through His merits? The Master of all humanity must have had the vision of the goal toward which He was leading it. This is the principal reason given by St. Thomas.

There is a second reason. It was fitting that He should have this vision so that He might possess a clear knowledge of His own divinity and not merely believe in it obscurely. We do not yet fully grasp the immense difference between believing and seeing. We shall have a clear knowledge of this difference the moment we enter heaven.

[104] I Cor. 13:12.

Finally, the third reason is that Jesus is the natural heir of God, as St. Paul tells us.[105] Even as man, Jesus is the Son of God by nature, and not by adoption as we are. But the natural heir enjoys his heritage from the start. Jesus has therefore had eternal life as a birthright. The fullness of grace which He received at the moment of His conception must have blossomed forth at that very instant, otherwise Jesus would have become more perfect afterward. This, as we have seen, is contrary to the Second Council of Constantinople.[106] For had this been the case, His charity, His love of God, would have increased later on when He emerged from the obscurity of faith and received the light of glory.

The fact that the upper reaches of Christ's soul enjoyed the beatific vision even here on earth is not irreconcilable with the fact that Jesus was still in a sense a wayfarer toward eternity. He was proceeding toward eternal life in His mortal body which was still subject to suffering and in His soul as well, inasmuch as it too was still capable of suffering and like ourselves knew through acquired knowledge, which is the fruit of experience and reflection. Thus Jesus was at once wayfarer and comprehensor. He enjoyed beatitude in the highest reaches of His soul, and He was a voyager in its less elevated parts which were in contact with the hardships of His life as Savior and victim.[107]

Even during His passion He did not lose the beatific vision, but He freely prevented the irradiation of the light of glory upon His lower reason and sense faculties. He did not wish this light and the joy that proceeds from it to lessen in any way by their radiance the sorrow which was invading Him from all sides. He completely yielded Himself up to suffering, so that the holocaust might be perfect.[108] Thus, although in a much less perfect manner, did the martyrs in the midst of their sufferings rejoice, as they gave their blood in testimony of their faith in Christ.

What did Jesus' human intelligence contemplate under the light of glory? The divine essence, the Blessed Trinity, which He already

---

[105] Heb. 1:2: "[God] hath appointed [Jesus] heir of all things."
[106] Cf. Denzinger, no. 224.   [107] Cf. St. Thomas, IIIa, q.15, a.10.
[108] Cf. *ibid.*, q.46, a.8 ad 2.

knew in a more perfect manner than did the angels inasmuch as His sacred soul through its personal union with the Word was nearer to God than they. He also contemplated in the divine essence everything that related to His universal mission as head of the kingdom of God, as leader of men and of angels, as judge of the living and of the dead. This is to say that in God He already knew all creatures, all souls, all that they have done, are doing, and will do. He knew the number of the elect, on what day and at what hour this number will be complete: in other words, at what hour the world will come to an end. Nor is there anything about the angelic world that He did not know, for the angels are His ministers in the kingdom of His Father, and He has said that they are "His angels" whom He will send on judgment day to gather the elect.[109]

We can now understand what St. John of the Cross wrote for contemplatives in his *Ascent of Mount Carmel* (Bk. II, chap. 22): "In the law of Scripture the inquiries that were made of God were lawful. . . . But now that the faith is founded in Christ, and, in this era of grace, the evangelical law has been made manifest, there is no reason to inquire of Him in that manner. . . . For, in giving us, as He did, His Son, which is His Word—and He has no other—He spoke to us all together, once and for all. . . . And this is the sense of that passage with which St. Paul begins . . . 'God, who, at sundry times and in divers manners, spoke in times past to the fathers by the prophets, last of all, in these days hath spoken to us by His Son [Heb. 1:1]. . . .' Wherefore he that would now inquire of God, or seek any vision or revelation, would not only be acting foolishly, but would be committing an offense against God, by not setting his eyes altogether upon Christ, and seeking no new thing or aught beside. . . . Set thine eyes on Him alone, for in Him I have spoken and revealed to thee all things, and in Him thou shalt find yet more than that which thou askest and desirest. For thou askest locutions and revelations, which are the part; but if thou set thine eyes upon Him, thou shalt find the whole; for He is My complete locution and answer,

---

[109] Mark 13:27: "And then shall He [the Son of man] send His angels, and shall gather together His elect from the four winds, from the uttermost part of the earth to the uttermost part of heaven."

and He is all My vision and all My revelation; so that I have spoken
to thee, answered thee, declared to thee and revealed to thee, in giving Him to thee as thy brother, companion and master, as ransom and
as reward. For since that day when I descended upon Him with My
Spirit on Mount Thabor, saying: 'This is My beloved Son, in whom
I am well pleased: hear ye Him [Matt. 17:5],' I have left off all
these manners of teaching and answering, and I have entrusted this
to Him. Hear Him; for I have no more faith to reveal, neither have
I any more things to declare." [110]

Jesus is the Master of teachers, the Master of the greatest contemplatives. He saw immediately in the divine essence what He
taught. That is why the more souls advance the more they forsake all
other books and seek nourishment only in the Gospel or in the words
of our Savior.

In an order inferior to the beatific vision, Jesus also had the infused
knowledge which is possessed by the angels and which is sometimes
granted in a measure to the saints, as when, for example, the apostles
after Pentecost preached in foreign languages without having learned
them. Jesus also knew the various dialects better than did the apostles
through the grace of Pentecost. [111]

Finally, Christ Jesus, like all other men, had the knowledge of experience which He rapidly gained through the exercise of His senses
and of His intelligence. This was one more of His perfections, which
was not made useless by reason of His superior knowledge, for even
though experience taught Him the same things He already knew by

[110] *The Complete Works of St. John of the Cross*, I, 173 f.

[111] According to several theologians, it was this infused knowledge which made it
possible for Christ to merit from the first moment of His life when He did not yet have
any acquired knowledge, and also later on to merit while He slept, for this infused
knowledge does not necessarily require the participation of the imagination (IIIa, q. 11,
a. 2).

As said by John of St. Thomas (*De incarn.*, d. 17, a. 3, n. 14) and the Salmanticenses
(*De incarn.*, disp. 27, dub. 3, 55), Jesus was able to merit even by acts of love which
were the immediate consequence of the beatific vision. For the beatific vision allows
the liberty to love God, if not in Himself and for Himself, at least inasmuch as He is
the reason for loving creatures. Thus God necessarily loves Himself and freely wills to
create in order to manifest His goodness. Thus, too, the blessed in necessarily loving
God whom they see face to face freely pray for us. See below, chap. 13: "The Liberty
of Christ."

other means, it taught Him to know them in a different way. He foresaw far in advance and infallibly that He would be crucified at a given hour on a certain day. Yet when the moment of the crucifixion came, the experience of pain taught Him in a way something new that no prevision could reveal to Him in the same degree. Thus, St. Paul tells us: "And whereas indeed He [Jesus] was the Son of God, He learned obedience by the things which He suffered: and being consummated, He became, to all that obey Him, the cause of eternal salvation." [112]

Thus did Christ's human intelligence contemplate even here on earth, under the illumination of His divine intelligence. Let us meditate on the light of His sacred soul, and the supernatural riches which it possessed from the very first moment of His life. He knew us beforehand and He knows our entire existence as it is in the book of life. He knew then and He knows now all the hereditary influences that have contributed to form our temperaments. He knows all our natural aptitudes, all the supernatural graces we have received and those we have refused. He sees all our acts, past, present, and future. He sees the state of our souls thirty years from now, three hundred years and three thousand years from now. He knows our faults much better than we do; and what deep humility this should inspire in us! He knows the exact moment and the circumstances of our death, and what will follow for each one of us.

Lord Jesus, give us Thy light when we pray, lead us from reasoned meditation on Thy perfections to the prayer of the heart which will unite us more intimately to Thyself. Thou art the Good Shepherd who leads His sheep into eternal pastures. Make Thy words come to realization within us: "The sheep hear his [the shepherd's] voice: and he calleth his own sheep by name, and leadeth them out. . . . I am the Good Shepherd; and I known Mine, and Mine know Me. . . . My sheep hear My voice: and I know them, and they follow Me. And I give them life everlasting; and they shall not perish forever, and no man shall pluck them out of My hand. That which My Father hath given Me, is greater than all: and no one can snatch them out of the hand of My Father. I and the Father are one." [113]

[112] Heb. 5:8 f.   [113] John 10:3–14, 27–30.

XIII

THE HUMAN WILL OF OUR SAVIOR

"As the Father hath given Me commandment, so do I."
John 14:31

NOW that we have spoken of the human intelligence and of the contemplation of Jesus, we must consider His human will and the eminent perfection of His liberty.

The Church has defined that Jesus has two wills, as He has two intelligences: a divine and uncreated will, the property of His divine nature, and a human will, the property of His human nature.[1] If our Savior did not indeed have a human will beneath His divine will, He would not be truly a man, and He would not have been able to obey or to merit. For obedience and merit presuppose the submission of a will inferior to another that is more elevated.

The Mystery

The human will of Jesus possesses a very high perfection and a great mystery: His will was even here on earth impeccable, and yet it was perfectly free in obeying and in meriting.

Not only did Jesus never disobey His Father in actual fact, but He could not disobey Him. He was impeccable by reason of His divine personality, by reason of the inamissible plentitude of grace and of the beatific vision which were His. For these three reasons He was absolutely impeccable. Yet He obeyed freely, with perfect liberty, which is not merely spontaneity but the absence of necessity in mak-

[1] Cf. Third Council of Constantinople, against the Monothelites, definition of the two wills of Christ. (Denzinger, no. 289.)

ing a choice (*libertas non solum a coactione, sed a necessitate*).[2]

How can obedience be free and meritorious when disobedience is not possible? This mystery is so great in the eyes of some theologians who have been unable to avoid contradiction, that they have claimed that Jesus had not received from His Father the commandment, the obligation to die for us. His Father, according to their reasoning, merely suggested or counseled this sacrifice, without requiring it of Him, and Jesus accepted it freely.

This manner of thinking, which is foreign to the doctrine of the great masters, has no foundation whatever in Scripture. On the contrary, Jesus in the Gospel speaks several times of the commandment He received from His Father, the commandment to die for us: "I lay down My life, that I may take it again. No man taketh it away from Me: but I lay it down of Myself, and I have power to lay it down: and I have power to take it up again. This commandment have I received of My Father." [3]

Likewise, after the Last Supper and just before the Passion Jesus said again: "I will not now speak many things with you. For the prince of this world cometh, and in Me he hath not anything. But that the world may know, that I love the Father: and as the Father hath given Me commandment, so do I. Arise, let us go hence" (John 14:30 f.). When St. Paul told the Philippians (2:8) that "Christ

---

[2] Animals act spontaneously when they go toward food that they like, but they do not act freely. Their action is necessitated by instinct. In another, infinitely superior, order of things, God loves Himself spontaneously but necessarily, not freely. The blessed who see God love Him spontaneously, but necessarily, with a love superior to liberty, for they are infallibly ravished by divine goodness immediately known as it is in itself. Cf. St. Thomas, Ia IIae, q.4, a.4: "The will of him who sees the essence of God, of necessity loves whatever he loves, in subordination to God."

Merit, which no longer exists in heaven, presupposes not only spontaneity but true liberty, the absence of necessity in making choices and in loving. That is why the Church has condemned the following Jansenist proposition: "Ad merendum et demerendum in statu naturae lapsae non requiritur in homine libertas a necessitate, sufficit libertas a coactione" (Denzinger, no. 1094). Psychological free will is not moral liberation from disorder either, for the former can exist without the latter and vice versa, as in the love that the blessed have for God whom they see face to face.

[3] John 10:17 f. In this text of St. John are affirmed both the commandment to die for us and, immediately preceding, the liberty with which Jesus accomplished this commandment. St. Augustine even says that by these words Jesus demonstrated that He gave His life because He willed to, when He willed to, and in the manner He willed. (*De Trin.*, Bk. IV, chap. 13, no. 16.)

Jesus . . . humbled Himself, becoming obedient unto death, even to the death of the cross," he was speaking of this commandment and not of a mere counsel.

Besides, Jesus spoke of other divine commands that constituted an obligation for His human liberty: "If you keep My commandments, you shall abide in My love; as I also have kept My Father's commandments, and do abide in His love." [4]

How, then, are we to reconcile this free and meritorious obedience of Jesus with His absolute impeccability? This will always remain a mystery for us here on earth, but it appears impossible only to those who conceive of liberty after the manner of the world and not after the manner of saints. Liberty, in the eyes of the world, is freedom to disobey as well as to obey, freedom to do evil as well as to do good. True liberty, according to the saints, is not freedom to disobey but only to obey, it is not freedom to do evil, but only freedom to do good. Now this liberty of goodness is supreme in Jesus.

Liberty in the eyes of the world is the power to choose between good and evil, between duty and selfish whims, between obedience and revolt. It is the power to say with Satan: "I will not obey." One might as well claim that reason is the faculty for knowing what is false as well as what is true.

If liberty is thus understood, clearly it is impossible to see how Jesus was free, He who never rebelled against divine authority or the commandments of His Father, and who could not rebel against them.

But as reason is the faculty for knowing the true and not the false (although it can be put to bad use by incorrect thinking), so true liberty, according to God and the saints, is the power to choose not between good and evil but between several goods whose attraction does not necessitate the will. [5] It is this free will that exists in God, in the sacred soul of our Savior, and among the blessed in heaven. In order

---

[4] John 15:10.

[5] Cf. St. Thomas, Ia, q.62, a.8 ad 3: "Free will in its choice of means to an end is disposed just as the intellect is to conclusions. Now it is evident that it belongs to the power of the intellect to be able to proceed to different conclusions, according to given principles; but for it to proceed to some conclusion by passing out of the order of the principles, comes of its own defect. Hence, it belongs to the perfection of its liberty for the free will to be able to choose between opposite things, keeping the order of the

to understand it, let us rise for a moment to the contemplation of God's impeccable liberty. We will then realize that the human liberty of Jesus is the purest image in the created order of God's own liberty.

God's Impeccable Liberty

It is clear that God is both sovereignly free and absolutely impeccable. He is in no sense free to sin, that is, to turn away from Himself, from His divine goodness that he necessarily loves. Yet He enjoys sovereign liberty in the order of goodness, inasmuch as His divine goodness leads Him to love the creatures which He can create or fail to create as He wills. It is with perfect liberty that He created us to manifest His goodness. This is the dogma of divine liberty.[6]

There is indeed a mystery in all this, but there is no contradiction: whereas it was truly fitting that God should create, yet He did so with perfect liberty, so that there would have been no disadvantage to Him had He not created. The theologians say with great exactness: "*Creatio ita conveniens est ut non creatio non sit inconveniens.*" Contrary to Leibnitz' view,[7] God would not have been less good and less wise if He had not created, for as Boussuet says, "God is no greater for having created the universe." Before creation, God was already infinite, so that after creation there is not any more being but only several beings, there is not more life but only many living beings. As St. Thomas says, "since the goodness of God is perfect, and can exist without other things inasmuch as no perfection can accrue to Him from them, it follows that His willing things apart from Himself is not absolutely necessary." [8]

Likewise God has freely raised angels and men to the life of grace,

---

end in view; but it comes of the defect of liberty for it to choose anything by turning away from the order of the end; and this is to sin."

[6] Cf. Council of the Vatican: "Deus bonitate sua et omnipotenti virtute, non ad augendam suam beatitudinem nec ad acquirendam, sed ad manifestandam perfectionem suam per bona quae creaturis impertitur, liberrimo consilio simul ab initio temporis utramque de nihilo condidit creaturam, spiritualem et corporalem, angelicam videlicet et mundanam ac deinde humanam quasi communem ex spiritu et corpore constitutam." Cf. Lateran Council IV, *ibid.*, no. 428.

[7] Leibnitz erred on this point when he said that God would be neither good nor wise if He had not created.

[8] Cf. St. Thomas, Ia, q. 19, a. 3, c. and ad 5; *Contra Gentes*, Bk. I, chaps. 76 and 82.

and He could without any disadvantage to Himself not have so raised them. Furthermore, God has freely willed the Incarnation, and He might well not have willed it and have remitted sin in some other way.

So, too, God sows the divine seed in men's souls in greater or less abundance, according to His good pleasure. "The Spirit breathes where He will." It is with perfect liberty, of course, that God has chosen one race of people rather than another which by its patriarchs and prophets would prepare the way for the mystery of Redemption. It is with perfect liberty that He chose within this people Mary rather than some other virgin to become the Mother of the Savior, and Joseph rather than any other just man to be the foster father of Jesus. It is with complete liberty also that God chose one century rather than another for the coming of the Messiah, just as He freely chose a given hour for the creation or beginning of the universe and another hour for the end of the world when the number of the elect will be complete.

This is the sovereign liberty which is admirably reconciled with absolute impeccability. God cannot turn away from Himself. He is absolutely impeccable, but He is perfectly free with regard to all created things. He does not have the liberty of evil, which is a form of our defectiveness, but He has the liberty of goodness in its absolute fullness.

Christ's Impeccable Liberty, the Perfect Image of God's Liberty

The sacred soul of our Savior enjoys now and enjoyed while on earth through grace a human liberty superior to that of the angels. No created liberty ever was or ever will be more conformable to divine liberty. Our Savior's human liberty was from the first moment the living image of God's liberty.

As we have just said, God is free, not to love His own divine goodness, but to desire to manifest His goodness by creating us who had no right whatever to existence. And as God is infinitely good and wise from all eternity He did not become any better by freely creating the universe. Thus God enjoys both absolute impeccability and the sovereign liberty which can be exercised only in the order of goodness.

Now, Christ's human will is the pure image of the uncreated will, since it is the human will of the Word of God made flesh, superior to the angels and to all the blessed in heaven.

We must conclude, therefore, that Christ's human will is like God's, of which it is the image, at once absolutely impeccable and perfectly free, possessing a liberty which can be exercised only in the order of goodness.

Like God, the sacred soul of Christ while here on earth was free, not to love divine goodness in itself, which He clearly saw in the light of the beatific vision, but to love the manifestation of divine goodness in creatures.[9]

Christ's sacred soul while here on earth loved God seen face to face with a love superior to liberty, just as God loves Himself necessarily; but Christ loved creatures freely, as finite manifestations of God's infinite goodness.

So it was that Jesus was free to call to the apostolate His first twelve disciples rather than other Galilean fishermen. He was free to choose Peter rather than another of His apostles to become His vicar, the head of His Church. He was free to call John to a friendship of predilection. He was free to convert Saul on the road to Damascus on a given day and at a given hour, and to make him or not to make him the Apostle of the Gentiles. He was free to choose among several goods within the order of goodness itself, but He was not free to will evil. His impeccable liberty could not deviate, just as His human intelligence, always enlightened by divine light, could not err.

Can a Command Requiring a Free Act Destroy the Liberty of That Act?

A precept or commandment in the true sense certainly takes away the moral liberty to act otherwise, since it constitutes a moral obliga-

[9] St. Thomas says (Ia, q. 19, a. 3): "God wills His own goodness necessarily. . . . Hence, since the goodness of God is perfect, and can exist without other things inasmuch as no perfection can accrue to Him from them, it follows that His willing things apart from Himself is not absolutely necessary. Yet it can be necessary by supposition, for supposing that He wills a thing, then He is unable not to will it, as His will cannot change."

tion. For the contrary act is illicit and forbidden. But no commandment takes away the psychological liberty to act in conformity with
its demands. On the contrary, a free act of obedience is required, and
if the precept destroyed the psychological liberty of this act, it would
destroy itself as a precept. For example, the commandment to love
our neighbor makes the contrary act of hatred illicit or forbidden,
but far from destroying the liberty of our act of love for our neighbor, it demands a free and meritorious act.[10]

Our Savior had during His life and still has an impeccable psychological liberty, the pure image of God, with regard to all goodness
whose attraction did not necessitate His will. We must conclude,
therefore, that this impeccable psychological liberty was not destroyed
by the divine command to die for us. Otherwise this precept which
demanded a free act of love and obedience would have destroyed itself.[11]

Faced with the command to die for us, Jesus was free in the accomplishment of this inevitable duty. His freedom with respect to
this duty was the freedom of goodness and not the freedom of evil.
He could not disobey, but as St. Paul tells us, He freely obeyed "unto
death, even to the death of the cross." He had given expression to
this liberty Himself when He said: "I lay down My life. . . . No
man taketh it away from Me: but I lay it down of Myself. . . . This
commandment have I received of My Father."[12]

[10] Thus man is not free to choose the religion that pleases him. He must choose the
true religion, but he chooses it freely.

[11] Jesus necessarily loved only God as seen face to face. This fact is necessarily and
intrinsically connected with supreme beatitude. Thus the soul necessarily wishes to exist,
to live, and to know, otherwise it would not see God. But Jesus freely chose the means
that had only an accidental connection (by virtue of an extrinsic precept) with the final
end, for example, death on the cross. This form of death, terrible in one of its aspects
and salutary for us in another of its aspects, did not necessarily attract our Lord. The
precept which demanded this death, did not change its horrible nature, and did not
destroy the liberty of the free act that it required.

Cf. St. Thomas, IIIa, q. 18, a. 4 ad 3: "The will of Christ, though determined to good,
is not determined to this or that good. Hence it pertains to Christ, even as to the blessed,
to choose with a free will confirmed in good." Cf. also IIIa, q. 15, a. 1. See also among
St. Thomas' commentators, John of St. Thomas, the Carmelites of Salamanca, Gonet,
Billuart, and others.

[12] John 10:18.

Precisely wherein lies the liberty of this heroic obedience? In order to truly grasp it, we must consider two things. First, this death on the cross, under one aspect is terrible. Secondly, under another aspect it is eminently salutary for us, for the deliverance of souls. This death does not invincibly attract the human will of our Savior, as the goodness of His Father whom He sees face to face attracts Him. On the one hand, this horrible death is repugnant to Christ's sensibility and to every fiber of His human nature. On the other hand, it attracts our Savior as being the consummation of His mission. The commandment that is also related to it does not change the nature of this death, at once dreadful and salutary. Nor can this commandment destroy the liberty of the free act which it demands.

Under these conditions, what will be the deciding factor causing one or the other of these contrary aspects of a death at once horrible and attractive to prevail? The will of Jesus intervenes here freely, giving the preference to the good, to heroic sacrifice; but as this will is fundamentally righteous, it always intervenes in the correct manner. It intervenes freely because death on the cross is not in itself a good that invincibly attracts. Quite the contrary. Still, the human will of Jesus intervenes infallibly and impeccably because it is the will of the Word made flesh, because it is enlightened by the beatific vision, because it is full of grace and continually receives a very powerful and very gentle actual grace which, far from doing violence to liberty, actualizes it or puts it into action as is fitting.

Thus Jesus obeyed freely, although He could not have disobeyed. One catches a glimpse of this mystery when, for example, an act of painful obedience is required of a good religious. He obeys freely, without even thinking that he could, if he chose, disobey. He might be forbidden, for instance, to go to the bedside of a loved one who is dying, since the trip would be too long and another priest could just as well perform the last rites. This may be a most painful act of obedience required of him, but he accomplishes it freely. The idea does not even occur to him that he might disobey. As the virtue of obedience develops, it leads a soul further and further from the contrary act. It takes away the liberty of evil, but certainly not the liberty

of goodness. In Jesus' soul this virtue, like the virtue of charity, is
absolutely eminent and inamissible.[18]

In heaven Jesus retains this liberty of goodness, even though He
can no longer merit, since the hour for merit has passed. He has
reached the end of His journey, He is no longer a wayfarer. Yet He
retains the liberty of goodness, if not in the act of loving God seen
face to face, at least in His love for creatures. The same is true of the
saints. St. Dominic in his heavenly abode loves God whom he clearly
knows with a love superior to liberty, but it is freely that he prays
for one or another of his sons to obtain certain graces for them. If this
is true of each of the blessed in heaven, it is much more true of our
Savior.[14]

In addition, our Lord's sensibility while He was on earth was perfectly obedient to His infallible intelligence and to His impeccable
will. His emotions or passions, such as melancholy, fear, sensible joy,

[18] In this sense the Thomists say: "Christus non potuit non obedire privative, scilicet
recusando mortem ut praeceptam; sed potuit non obedire negative, recusando mortem
secundum se." Thus the good religious freely obeys a very hard command without even
thinking for a moment that he might disobey this command. He feels that the order is
hard in itself, but the idea does not even occur to him to go against the order he has
received.

[14] The Thomists have wondered whether Christ while on earth freely accomplished
the commandment to love God. They have divided into two main schools of thought
on this point.

Capreolus, Ferrariensis, Medina, and Soto declare that Christ's love of God, ruled by
the beatific vision, was necessary, above liberty, but that in Him the act of love of God
ruled by infused knowledge, comparable to the natural knowledge of the angels, was
free. These theologians hold that these were two distinct acts, as are the acts of knowledge from which they derived. Therefore, according to this view, it is probable that
Jesus merited not only in loving creatures for God but in loving God Himself whom
He knew through infused knowledge, as distinct from the beatific vision. This solution
does not exclude the following one, which appears to be more probable.

Alvarez, John of St. Thomas, the Salmanticenses, and Gonet think that Jesus' love
of God, ruled by the beatific vision, is necessary, above liberty inasmuch as it related to
divine goodness in itself, and that this love was free inasmuch as it related to divine
goodness as a reason for loving creatures. They hold with St. Thomas: "Although God
necessarily wills His own goodness, He does not necessarily will things willed on account of His goodness; for it can exist without other things" (Ia, q. 19, a. 3). God necessarily loves His divine goodness considered in itself; He freely wills the manifestation
of His goodness. It is probable that the same thing applied to the sacred soul of Christ
while He was still on earth. And the blessed in heaven, although they necessarily love
God whom they see face to face, yet freely pray for certain sinners still on earth in order
to obtain graces for them.

never went beyond the bounds of moderation. These emotions never took precedence over reasoned judgment and the consent of the will, as happens with us, but always followed them. When Jesus became angry with the merchants in the Temple, it was because it was His considered judgment that He must manifest to them His holy anger, the zeal for the glory of God. And if He was "sorrowful even unto death" at Gethsemane, it was because He willed to know this over-whelming misery so that the holocaust might be complete.[15]

What a great lesson there is for us in this doctrine of the impeccable liberty of Christ! It teaches us that true liberty consists in being able to choose the good, not evil, just as reason is the faculty of knowing the true, not the false, though it may at times go astray. When the Church has condemned some error such as Jansenism or Modernism, there have been persons who have said: "We must either submit or depart." On the contrary, there is absolutely one thing only to do: obey and not disobey.

This doctrine also teaches us that the more we love God, as our Lord and the saints do, the freer we shall be with respect to all created goods to dominate the attraction of worldly goods and not to fear the threats of the impious. The martyrs have demonstrated the power of Christian liberty, which endures all kinds of torture rather than be unfaithful to God, and which is more concerned with union to God than with union to the body.

Let us ask our Lord that He continually decrease our inclination toward evil by making virtue thrive in us, and by confirming our will in the direction of goodness, so that it may one day be definitely con-firmed in goodness in heaven, when sin will no longer be possible and when we shall have become through the power of Christ impeccable and truly free, enjoying the liberty of the children of God.

[15] Cf. St. Thomas, IIIa, q. 15, a. 4, 6, 9.

PART TWO

OUR SAVIOR'S LOVE FOR US AND THE MYSTERY OF REDEMPTION

❀ XIV ❀

THE TESTIMONY OF JESUS ON THE MYSTERY OF THE REDEMPTION

IN THE preceding pages we have dealt with the mystery of the Incarnation, with the personality of Jesus, His sanctity, the contemplation of His human intelligence, His human will that is at once free and impeccable. We are now about to consider the mystery of the Redemption according to the testimony of the Gospel and of the Epistles, in order to determine the relation to this mystery of our Savior's interior life as priest and victim.

In our Lord's teaching, the mystery of the Incarnation is intimately bound up with the mystery of the Redemption. For the name "Jesus" means Savior or Redeemer, and, as the Creed proclaims, it was to redeem us that the Word was made flesh. "I believe in one God, the Father almighty . . . and in one Lord Jesus Christ, the only-begotten Son of God . . . who for us men, and for our salvation, came down from heaven, and was incarnate . . . and was made man" (Nicene Creed).

We know, of course, that the Modernists have claimed that the doctrine concerning the expiatory character of Christ's death is not evangelical, but merely Pauline, that is, the fruit of St. Paul's personal reflections on the death of Jesus.[1]

How were the Modernists led to entertain such a notion? Because, following in the footsteps of the liberal Protestants who had almost become rationalists, they sought to suppress all supernatural elements in the mystery of the Redemption and to reduce it to the level of a truth of the natural order. Following this trend of thought, they have

---

[1] Among the Modernist errors condemned by Pope Pius XI in the decree *Lamentabili*, the thirty-eighth is this one: "Doctrina de morte piaculari Christi non est evangelica, sed paulina" (Denzinger, no. 2038).

claimed that the Redemption as the Catholic Church has always understood it, is contrary to God's mercy and justice.

The Catholic concept of the Redemption is contrary to God's mercy, they have held, because an infinitely merciful God cannot demand as reparation for sin such rigorous satisfaction as is far superior to anything man can offer Him. The answer to the objection is that this view leaves out of consideration the fact that, while God had demanded such a reparation, He has in His infinite mercy given us His own Son to redeem us. He has loved the world so much as to deign to give to it not only grace and pardon but the Author of grace Himself.

The Modernists further hold that the Redemption as conceived by the Catholic Church, is contrary to divine justice, for it is unjust and cruel to strike an innocent person in place of those who are guilty. Is this not to forget that our Savior is a voluntary victim, who generously offered Himself up for us?

By thus deviating from the fundamental truths of Christianity the Modernists and the liberal Protestants have entirely removed from the death of Jesus on the cross its supernatural character. In their eyes Jesus is only a wise man, a saint who was not understood by His contemporaries, and who courageously died rather than renounce His ideas. He did not die to make reparation in our place, to redeem us, to give us supernatural grace, to merit eternal life for us. His death, as they see it, has value only as an example, such as had the death of Socrates or Leonidas. His death is the greatest example of strength and greatness of soul amid the most terrible trials.

This is what becomes of a supernatural mystery when viewed with the eyes of human wisdom, which in seeking to explain everything naturally finds only darkness in the faith of the Church, the faith of all the martyrs, and of all the saints.

We shall see that contrary to these naturalistic views this doctrine of the Church has been clearly expressed in the words of our Lord preserved in the four Gospels. We shall then see that this doctrine is also to be found in the Acts of the Apostles and in St. Paul's writings.

The Mystery of the Redemption
in the First Three Gospels

First of all, let us bear in mind that Jesus manifested the mystery of the Incarnation only by slow degrees, because men's souls would not have been able to bear all at once such a lofty revelation. The same is true of His announcement of His painful passion, for it was even more difficult to bear the revelation of this mystery, especially for the Jews who, because of their national prejudices, were awaiting a temporal and conquering Messiah who would have made them dominant over other peoples.

Let us bear in mind also that Jesus began to announce His painful passion to His disciples only after He had brought them to believe in His divine sonship, in His divinity. Only after Peter's confession at Caesarea, in which he professed his belief that Jesus was "the Son of the living God," did our Lord begin "to show to His disciples, that He must go to Jerusalem, and suffer many things . . . and be put to death." [2] This mystery which had been announced repeatedly by the prophets, especially in certain Messianic psalms [3] and by Isaias, [4] was difficult to accept. It required a great spirit of faith.

Let us see how our Lord manifested this mystery progressively, according to the first three Gospels and also according to St. John. It is like a leitmotif, at first soft but powerful, which gradually grows louder and finally bursts forth and is dominant. [5]

At the start of His ministry, in the synagogue at Nazareth Jesus read in the book of the prophet Isaias: [6] "The Spirit of the Lord is upon Me, wherefore He hath anointed Me to preach the gospel to the poor, He hath sent Me to heal the contrite of heart: to preach deliverance to the captives, and sight to the blind, to set at liberty them that are bruised, to preach the acceptable year of the Lord, and the day of reward." [7] This is more than an example of high virtue.

---

[2] Matt. 16:21.   [3] Ps. 39, 21, 68.   [4] Chaps. 50, 53.

[5] Thus, in the overture to *Tannhauser* the leitmotif of the Pilgrims' Chorus is at first almost imperceptible, but it gradually rises above the leitmotif of sensuality and evil, until it dominates all.   [6] Isa. 61:1.   [7] Luke 4:18 f.

The announcement is general, but it is certainly clear, and it was to become progressively clearer.

A little later, as we read in St. Matthew,[8] after Matthew the publican is called to the apostleship, as Jesus was at table in Matthew's house together with many publicans and sinners who had joined Him and His disciples for the feast, the Pharisees said to the disciples: "Why doth your master eat with publicans and sinners? But Jesus hearing it, said: They that are in health need not a physician, but they that are ill. Go then and learn what this meaneth, I will have mercy and not sacrifice. For I am not come to call the just, but sinners." [9] But mention was not made of the cruel passion He was to suffer. It was too early for that.

It was only after Peter had confessed at Caesarea that Jesus was "Christ the Son of the living God," [10] that "Jesus began to show to His disciples, that He must go to Jerusalem, and suffer many things from the ancients and scribes and chief priests, and be put to death, and the third day rise again." Peter, drawing Him aside, began to rebuke Him, saying: "Lord, be it far from Thee, this shall not be unto Thee." But Jesus, turning to Peter, said: "Go behind Me, Satan, thou art a scandal unto Me: because thou savorest not the things that are of God, but the things that are of men." [11]

Peter indeed had so little understanding of the things of God when he said these words that he was speaking without knowing it against all of God's plans for the salvation of mankind, against the motive of the Incarnation or of the coming of the Word made flesh into the world. And he spoke thus because his natural affection for Jesus was so great that he could not bear the announcement of His cruel passion. By contrast, the words of the *Stabat Mater* are: "Grant that I may bear the death of Christ, following Mary's example who remained standing at the foot of the cross."

We should note that it was after the first prediction of His passion that Jesus said: [12] "If any man will come after Me, let him deny himself, and take up his cross, and follow Me." [13] This expression,

---

[8] Matt. 9:10–13. [9] Cf. Mark 11:17. [10] Matt. 16:16.

[11] Matt. 16:21–23. Cf. Mark 8:31–33.

[12] Matt. 16:24; Mark 8:34–39; Luke 9:23–27.

[13] It is in this sense that someone has said: "Any destiny that does not have its calvary is

"take up one's cross," was then still obscure to His hearers, but it would become increasingly clear.

Again alluding to His sacrifice and to its fruits, Jesus said: "I am come to cast fire on the earth: and what will I, but that it be kindled? And I have a baptism wherewith I am to be baptized: and how am I straitened until it be accomplished?" [14]

He announced His passion again even more precisely as He was going up to Jerusalem, before His triumphal entry. It is recorded in St. Matthew: "And Jesus . . . took the twelve disciples apart, and said to them: Behold we go up to Jerusalem, and the Son of man shall be betrayed to the chief priests and the scribes, and they shall condemn Him to death, and shall deliver Him to the Gentiles to be mocked and scourged and crucified, and the third day He shall rise again." [15] The apostles must have been struck by these words, and yet they forgot them during the Passion.

It was then that the mother of the sons of Zebedee approached Jesus with her sons and asked that they might sit, the one on His right and the other on His left in His kingdom. Jesus, alluding to His passion which He had just announced, answered: "Can you drink the chalice that I shall drink?" [16] He then added that, whereas the princes of the Gentiles lord it over them, "the Son of man is not come to be ministered unto, but to minister, and to give His life a redemption for many." [17] Here we have the mystery of the Redemption enunciated by Jesus Himself. It would therefore be difficult to claim, as the Modernists do, that this was the personal notion of St. Paul, born of his reflection on the life and death of Jesus. Our Lord has told us Himself that He came "to give His life a redemption for many."

Likewise, in St. Mark we read: "The Son of man . . . is not come to be ministered unto, but to minister, and to give His life a redemption for many." [18] This certainly bespeaks the expiatory character of Jesus' death.

The Passion was also foretold in the parable of the wicked hus-

---

a punishment from God." "Life disappoints only those who do not expect enough from it." [14] Luke 12:49 f.

[15] Matt. 20:17–28; cf. Mark 10:34; Luke 18:31 ff.   [16] Matt. 20:22.

[17] *Ibid.*, 20:28.   [18] Mark 10:45.

bandmen: "And last of all he sent to them his son. . . . But the husbandmen seeing the son, said among themselves: This is the heir: come, let us kill him, and we shall have his inheritance. And taking him, they cast him forth out of the vineyard, and killed him." [19]

Finally the Passion was foretold for the last time during the Last Supper, as recorded in St. Matthew,[20] in St. Mark,[21] and in St. Luke.[22] In St. Matthew we read: "And whilst they were at supper, Jesus took bread, and blessed, and broke: and gave to His disciples, and said: Take ye and eat: This is My body. And taking the chalice, He gave thanks, and gave to them, saying: Drink ye all of this. For this is My blood of the New Testament, which shall be shed for many unto remission of sins."

This was very clear, especially after the preceding predictions of the Passion, and inasmuch as Jesus had already said during the Last Supper: "The Son of man indeed goeth, as it is written of Him: but woe to that man by whom the Son of man shall be betrayed." [23]

In order to give further warning to His apostles, He added as they proceeded to the Garden of Olives: "All of you shall be scandalized in Me this night. For it is written: I will strike the shepherd, and the sheep of the flock shall be dispersed. But after I shall be risen again, I will go before you into Galilee." [24] And St. Luke adds that our Lord said to Peter: "Simon, Simon, behold Satan hath desired to have you, that he may sift you as wheat: [25] But I have prayed for thee, that thy faith fail not: and thou, being once converted, confirm thy brethren." [26]

This last announcement of the Passion was singularly clear, and by the words of the consecration at the Last Supper, especially those referring to "My blood of the New Testament, which shall be shed for many unto remission of sins," [27] it was manifest that during His passion and crucifixion which He had foretold, Jesus would offer His blood as a sacrifice of reparation or of redemption.

None the less, in spite of all these predictions which confirmed

---

[19] Matt. 21:37 f. [20] *Ibid.*, 26:26–28. [21] Mark 14:24.
[22] Luke 22:19 f. [23] Matt. 26:24. [24] *Ibid.*, 26:31 f.
[25] Just as he had desired holy Job (cf. Job 1:11). [26] Luke 22:31 f.
[27] Matt. 26:28.

those of the Messianic psalms and those of Isaias [28] about the suffering Messiah, the man of sorrows—in spite of all this light, when the sacrifice began at Gethsemane the apostles fell asleep, and as soon as the Passion started they fearfully forsook our Lord. At the moment when the mystery of the Redemption was accomplished on the cross, at the moment of the *Consummatum est,* they did not understand that this was the realization of Christ's promises. Many of them even thought that all was lost. And if the apostles behaved in this manner during the dark night of the Passion, how might we expect to react if we were placed in comparable circumstances?

The mystery of the Redemption was clearly announced in the Synoptic Gospels, as we have seen. In one of these Gospels it is also reported that after His resurrection Jesus said to His disciples of Emmaus: "O foolish, and slow of heart to believe in all things which the prophets have spoken. Ought not Christ to have suffered these things and so to enter into His glory?" [29]

The Testimony of Jesus in the Fourth Gospel

The mystery of the Redemption has been expressed even more perfectly in the Gospel of St. John. In this Gospel, Jesus repeats insistently that He is sent by the Father to do His will and to perfect His work.[30] But this work consists in bearing witness to the truth,[31] and in saving men's souls and giving them eternal life. According to this Gospel, Jesus said to Nicodemus: "So must the Son of man be lifted up: that whosoever believeth in Him may not perish, but may have life everlasting. For God so loved the world, as to give His only begotten Son; that whosoever believeth in Him, may not perish, but may have life everlasting." [32]

To this end, Jesus, the Good Shepherd, gave His life for His sheep. There is no simpler or greater expression of the mystery of the Redemption than the parable of the Good Shepherd: "I am come that they may have life, and may have it more abundantly. I am the

---

[28] Chap. 53.
[30] John 4:34; 5:30; 6:38 ff.
[32] *Ibid.,* 3:14–16.

[29] Luke 24:25 f.
[31] *Ibid.,* 18:37; 17:8; 14, 26.

Good Shepherd. The Good Shepherd giveth His life for His sheep.
. . . I am the Good Shepherd; and I know mine, and mine know
Me. . . . I lay down My life for My sheep. And other sheep I
have, that are not of this fold: them also I must bring, and they shall
hear My voice, and there shall be one fold and one Shepherd. Therefore doth the Father love Me: because I lay down My life, that I
may take it again. No man taketh it away from Me: but I lay it
down of Myself, and I have power to lay it down: and I have power
to take it up again. This commandment have I received of My Father." [33]

This is indeed the spontaneous oblation of the voluntary victim,
and this victim is the Good Shepherd Himself, the Priest above all
others, who was to pronounce the priestly prayer before He died.[34]
Jesus did not die as the result of unforeseen circumstances, as did
Socrates, rather than renounce His ideas. Jesus was sent by God to
offer Himself up for us.

At the time of His triumphal entry into Jerusalem, Jesus announced to His disciples that His death would be a triumph, but
that before the triumph He would have to be immolated. He told
them in fact: "The hour is come, that the Son of man should be
glorified. Amen, amen I say to you, unless the grain of wheat falling
into the ground die, itself remaineth alone. But if it die, it bringeth
forth much fruit. . . . Now shall the prince of this world be cast
out. And I, if I be lifted up from the earth, will draw all things to
Myself." St. John adds: "Now this He said, signifying what death
He should die." [35]

A little later, Jesus said: "Greater love than this no man hath, that
a man lay down his life for his friends." [36] Then, during His priestly
prayer, He added: "And for them do I sanctify Myself, that they
also may be sanctified in truth." [37]

Through the fruits of our Savior's death, Satan was defeated, he
lost the rights and the power he had over a sinful humanity,[38] and
grace was given back to men. Jesus is the vine, we are the branches:
"He that abideth in Me, and I in him, the same beareth much

---

[33] *Ibid.*, 10:10–18.   [34] *Ibid.*, chap. 17.   [35] *Ibid.*, 12:23–25, 31 f.
[36] *Ibid.*, 15:13.   [37] *Ibid.*, 17:19.   [38] *Ibid.*, 12:31.

fruit." [39] St. John speaks in the same vein in his First Epistle: "We have fellowship one with another, and the blood of Jesus His Son cleanseth us from all sin. . . ." [40] He is the propitiation for our sins: and not for ours only, but also for those of the whole world. . . ." [41] By this hath the charity of God appeared toward us, because God hath sent His only-begotten Son into the world, that we may live by Him." [42]

St. John develops this doctrine of the precious blood in an admirable manner in the Apocalypse, in the canticle sung to the Lamb: "Thou wast slain, and hast redeemed us to God, in Thy blood, out of every tribe and tongue and people and nation. And hast made us to our God a kingdom and priests, and we shall reign on the earth." [43]

This is the same teaching that we find in St. Peter's first discourses after Pentecost, as reported in the Acts of the Apostles: "This [Jesus] is the stone which was rejected by you the builders, which is become the head of the corner. Neither is there salvation in any other. For there is no other name under heaven given to men, whereby we must be saved." [44] "Him hath God exalted with His right hand, to be Prince and Savior, to give repentance to Israel, and remission of sins." [45]

Finally, St. Peter says in his First Epistle: "You were not redeemed with corruptible things as gold and silver, . . . but with the precious blood of Christ, as of a lamb unspotted and undefiled." [46] "Who His own self bore our sins in His body upon the tree: that we, being dead to sins, should live to justice: by whose stripes you were healed." [47]

Such is the testimony of the Gospels, of the Acts of the Apostles, and of St. Peter's Epistles on the mystery of the Redemption. Hence it cannot be held that the expiatory character of Christ's death is not evangelical, that it is merely the result of St. Paul's personal reflections on the death of Jesus, which he compared with the sacrifices of the Old Law. Our Savior's own words as recorded by St.

---

[39] *Ibid.*, 15:5.
[40] I John 1:7.
[41] *Ibid.*, 2:2.
[42] *Ibid.*, 4:9.
[43] Apoc. 5:9 f.
[44] Acts 4:11 f.
[45] *Ibid.*, 5:45; cf. *ibid.*, 8:37; 10:43; 15.
[46] I Pet. 1:18 f.
[47] *Ibid.*, 2:24.

Matthew and St. Mark tell us that He gave His life "a redemption for many." And St. John the Baptist, before St. Paul, saluted Jesus as "the Lamb of God, . . . who taketh away the sin of the world." [48] Even if we did not have St. Paul's epistles, this testimony would suffice to make us know in the obscurity of faith the very essence of the mystery of the Redemption.

[48] John 1:29.

✸ XV ✸

THE REDEMPTION ACCORDING TO ST. PAUL

The Meaning of This Dogma and the Contrary Errors

THE testimony of the Gospel, completed by that of the Acts of the Apostles, shows us clearly, as we have already seen, that Jesus "gave His life a redemption for many," [1] that His blood was shed "for many unto remission of sins," [2] and that He is "the Lamb of God, . . . who taketh away the sin of the world." [3] Let us now consider what St. Paul tells us with regard to this dogma of our faith, and seek to grasp its true meaning.

The Testimony of St. Paul on the Redemption

It is false, of course, to pretend that the expiatory character of Christ's death is not evangelical, but merely the fruit of St. Paul's personal reflections. The truth of the matter is that the great apostle has made known the full glory of this doctrine. Innumerable passages in his epistles show that the Redemption and sanctification of men were accomplished by the death of Jesus. In fact, he tells us that God delivered His Son up for us, [4] for our sins, [5] for all men, [6] even for the ungodly. [7] This death was an act of obedience, [8] a voluntary gift of Jesus' love. In the Epistle to the Ephesians we read: "Walk in love, as Christ also hath loved us, and hath delivered Himself for us, an oblation and a sacrifice to God for an odor of sweetness." [9] "Christ . . . loved the Church, and delivered Himself up for it;

---

[1] Matt. 20:28; Mark 10:45.   [2] Matt. 26:28.
[3] John 1:29.   [4] I Thess. 5:10; Rom. 5:9.
[5] I Cor. 15:3.   [6] Gal. 2:20; II Cor. 5:14; Rom. 8:32.
[7] Rom. 5:6 f.   [8] Phil. 2:8; Rom. 5:19.   [9] Eph. 5:2.

that He might sanctify it, cleansing it by the laver of water in the word of life: that He might present it to Himself a glorious Church, not having spot or wrinkle, or any such thing; but that it should be holy, and without blemish." [10] "Christ our pasch is sacrificed"; [11] in other words, Jesus is the paschal Lamb whose immolation has taken away the sins of the world, as John the Baptist had announced He would.

St. Paul specifies that he is speaking of a sacrifice of expiation. In fact, he wrote to the Romans: "For all have sinned, and do need the glory of God. Being justified freely by His grace, through the Redemption, that is in Christ Jesus, whom God hath proposed to be a propitiation, through faith in His blood, to the showing of His justice, for the remission of former sins." [12]

St. Paul also shows that the death of Jesus on the cross was a redemption by substitution: "You are bought with a great price." [13] "Christ hath redeemed us from the curse of the law, being made a curse for us." [14] This is the same idea that Jesus expressed in St. Mark: "The Son of man . . . is not come to be ministered unto, but to minister, and to give His life a redemption for many." [15]

St. Paul again affirms this doctrine: "For there is . . . one mediator of God and men, the man Christ Jesus: who gave Himself a redemption for all," [16] that is, who delivered us for a ransom, at the price of His own blood, [17] the supreme expression of His love.

Contrary to the opinion of a number of Protestant liberals, [18] St. Paul holds that the dying Christ substituted Himself for sinful mankind, since he says: "Christ hath redeemed us from the curse of the law, being made a curse for us" [19] on the cross. "Him, who knew no sin, He hath made sin for us, that we might be made the justice of God in Him." [20] That is to say, God treated Him like sin for us, and Jesus had in actual fact taken all our sins upon Himself in order to expiate them. "Jesus Christ, our Lord . . . was delivered up

[10] Eph. 5:25f.   [11] I Cor. 5:7.   [12] Rom. 3:23–25.   [13] I Cor. 6:20; 7:23.
[14] Gal. 3:13.   [15] Mark 10:45; cf. Matt. 20:28.   [16] I Tim. 2:5 f.
[17] Cf. Prat, *The Theology of St. Paul*, Vol. I, note 50: Expiation, propitiation, redemption.
[18] Sabatier, *L'Apôtre Paul*, 3rd ed., p. 328: *La doctrine de l'expiation et son evolution historique*. Paris, 1903.   [19] Gal. 3:13 f.   [20] II Cor. 5:21.

[to death] for our sins, and rose again for our justification." [21]

Thus by His death Christ delivered us from sin,[22] from the snares of the devil.[23] He freed us from the Mosaic Law which was an occasion of sin.[24] The result of all this is the attainment of true liberty [25] by all Christians, "so that we should serve in newness of spirit, and not in the oldness of the letter." [26]

Moreover, Christians are reconciled with God: [27] by Christ's blood they are cleansed, sanctified, justified,[28] accepted as adopted sons of God, and heirs of heaven.[29] The victory will be complete at the end of the world, when death will be thoroughly vanquished by resurrection.[30] Then, too, will the Redemption be fully accomplished, "when this mortal hath put on immortality. . . . Thanks be to God, who hath given us the victory through our Lord Jesus Christ." [31]

The doctrine of the expiatory nature of Jesus' death on the cross is not the fruit of St. Paul's personal reflections. It is an evangelical doctrine which was clearly formulated on several occasions by Jesus Himself. But it was St. Paul's mission to bring out all its glory, not only through the texts which we have just quoted but also through his teaching on the sacraments, especially baptism [32] and the Holy Eucharist,[33] inasmuch as the Mass perpetuates in substance in an unbloody manner the Sacrifice of the Cross, so that its fruits may be applied to each succeeding generation until the end of the world.

The Doctrine of the Redemption and Its Theological Explanation

From St. Paul's testimony, which completes and clarifies that of the Gospel, the real meaning of the Redemption is clearly revealed.

In the general sense of the word, redemption or repurchase is the act by which a person acquires again by paying the required price what

---

[21] Rom. 4:25.   [22] *Ibid.*, 4:25; 6:1–12.   [23] II Tim. 2:26; Col. 2:15.
[24] Rom. 7:4; Gal. 3:13; 4:5–7; Col. 2:13 f.   [25] Gal. 4:31.
[26] Rom. 7:6.   [27] *Ibid.*, 5:10 f.   [28] Rom. 3:24; 5:9, 10, 11 ff.
[29] Rom. 8:14–17; Gal. 3:26—4:4–7.   [30] I Cor. 15:24–27.
[31] *Ibid.*, 15:54–57.
[32] Eph. 4:5; 5:26; Tit. 3:5; Rom. 6:3–12; Gal. 3:27; I Cor. 12:13.
[33] I Cor. 10:15–21; 11:17–34.

he formerly possessed but no longer possesses. Thus we speak of the repurchase of a house or of a piece of property, as captives and prisoners of war are ransomed.

The redemption of the human race can therefore be defined as follows: It is the act by which our Savior, at the price of His own blood (an expression of His love), snatched the human race from slavery to sin and to the devil, and reconciled it with God. In other words, to use the terms dear to both St. Anselm [34] and to St. Thomas: [35] He made satisfaction for our sins, He payed the debt to divine justice, and He merited our salvation. The Council of Trent defines this dogma as follows: "The meritorious cause of our justification is the only-begotten Son of God, our Lord Jesus Christ, who when we were enemies of God,[36] because of His great love for us,[37] has by His very holy passion on the wood of the cross merited our justification and has made satisfaction for us to God the Father." [38]

The Redemption thus conceived was necessary after the fall of man, if God wished to raise us up again and exact reparation equivalent to the gravity of the offense which is mortal sin. It was fitting, of course, that after the fall God should wish to raise us up again. For man's sin, being less grave than that of Satan, is not irremissible, and moreover original sin was voluntary only in the first man.

Yet God could very well have raised us up again by forgiving us and exacting only an imperfect reparation.[39] He might have been content to send us a prophet who would have made known to us the conditions of pardon.

God has done infinitely more for us. In exacting a reparation equivalent to the gravity of the offense, He has given us His own Son as Redeemer. If His justice has exacted this reparation, His mercy has given us the Savior who alone was capable of making full reparation for the offense or disorder of mortal sin.

The injury is all the more grave in proportion to the greater dignity of the person offended. It is more serious to insult a magistrate than

[34] St. Anselm, *Cur Deus Homo*, P.L., 158, 361–430.

[35] St. Thomas, IIIa, q. 1, a. 2; q. 46, a. 1–4.   [36] Rom. 5:10.

[37] Eph. 2:4.   [38] Cf. *Concilium Trid.*, Sess. VI, chap. 7. Denzinger, nos. 799, 820.

[39] St. Thomas, IIIa, q. 1, a. 2.

to insult a passer-by on the street. Mortal sin, by which man with full knowledge and consent scorns divine law on a serious matter by disobeying that law, mortal sin by which man turns away from God, thus has infinite gravity. For mortal sin practically denies God the infinite dignity of being our final end, and falsely sets a wretched created good as our final end. If an offense increases in gravity with the dignity of the person offended, the injury done to God by mortal sin is limitless in gravity; it denies Him the infinite dignity of Sovereign Good.[40] In order to understand in full the gravity of this injury, it would be necessary to have seen God. The angels and saints understand this far better than the devils and even the most perverse beings.

To repair this disorder, an act of love of God of infinite value was necessary. But no creature that is a creature and no more can give infinite value to its acts of love. Even if such an act is supernatural, the fruit of grace and of infused charity, it remains finite, like the creature from which it proceeds, like created grace and charity, even though this act has an infinite object, namely, God Himself. We can love God who is infinite, but we cannot love Him infinitely. He alone is capable of loving Himself in this manner.

Therefore, for a human soul to make an act of love of God infinite in value, that human soul had to belong to a divine preson. Such was the soul of the Word made flesh. Our Lord's soul drew from the divine personality of the Word infinite capacity for satisfying and meriting. It was the act of love of a human soul, but also that of a divine person. For this reason, it is called a theandric act, both divine and human.

This is the essence of the mystery of the Redemption, which St. Thomas expresses in these terms: "He properly atones for an offense who offers something which the offended one loves equally, or even more than he detested the offense. But by suffering out of love and obedience, Christ gave more to God than was required to compensate for the offense of the whole human race. First of all, because of the exceeding charity from which He suffered; secondly, on account of the dignity of His life which He laid down in atonement, for it was

---

[40] Cf. St. Thomas, IIIa, q. 1, a. 2 ad 2; also *De veritate*, q. 28, a. 2.

the life of one who was God and man; thirdly, on account of the extent of the Passion, and the greatness of the grief endured, as stated above.[41] And therefore Christ's passion was not only a sufficient but a superabundant atonement for the sins of the human race; according to I John 2:2: 'He is the propitiation for our sins: and not for ours only, but also for those of the whole world.' "[42]

In short, the love of Christ dying on the cross for our sakes was more pleasing to God than the totality of all men's sins can displease Him. It is on this point above all others that we should pause in contemplation. Everything else converges toward the contrast expressed in the two words: Sin and redemptive love.

The Depth of This Mystery and the Errors Opposed to It

Here indeed is a great mystery. As the Catechism of the Council of Trent [43] tells us: "If the human mind finds difficulties elsewhere, it is incontestably in the mystery of the Redemption that it meets the greatest difficulties of all. It is hard for us to conceive that our salvation depends upon the Cross and upon Him who let Himself be nailed to it for love of us.[44] But it is in this very fact that, according to the teaching of the Apostle, we must admire the sovereign providence of God. For, 'seeing that in the wisdom of God the world, by wisdom, knew not God, it pleased God, by the foolishness of our preaching, to save them that believe. . . . We preach Christ crucified, unto the Jews indeed a stumbling block, and unto the Gentiles foolishness: but unto them that are called, both Jews and Greeks, Christ the power of God, and the wisdom of God.' "[45]

The Catechism of the Council of Trent continues: "It can be said that the mystery of the Cross, humanly speaking, is more than any other outside the conceptions of reason. That is why, since Adam's sin, God has never ceased announcing the death of His Son, at times

---

[41] Q. 46, a. 6.   [42] St. Thomas, IIIa, q. 48, a. 2.   [43] Part I, article 4 of Symbol 1.
[44] It is hard for us to believe that life issues from death and that victory proceeds from annihilation.   [45] I Cor. 1:21–24.

through figures of speech, and again through the oracles of the prophets."

There is a most powerful chiaroscuro in this mystery, especially when we also consider the application of our Savior's merits.

On the one hand, it is clear that God's mercy bends down toward us to raise us up. But what is obscure is the intimate reconciliation of this most tender mercy with the exigencies of infinite justice. We firmly believe both are united in God and in the bruised heart of Jesus, a voluntary victim dying through love of us. We believe this, but we do not see it; and to our superficial gaze it seems that such rigorous justice places limits upon infinite mercy. We do not yet see how they are two forms or two virtues of uncreated love, which are identified in it without any real distinction.[46] Still we can perceive that avenging justice is itself a proclamation of the rights of the Sovereign Good to be loved above all else.

If we stray from the straight path that leads toward these heights, we deviate toward two errors each opposed to the other: either the error of the first Protestants, or the error of their successors who reacted against them.

The first Protestants, Luther, Calvin, and their disciples, falsified the mystery of the Redemption by saying: Christ took our sins upon Himself to the point of becoming odious to His Father, and both on the cross and in His descent to hell, He suffered the torments of the damned. Thenceforth they have added, there remains nothing for us to do and to suffer for salvation, but only to believe in the merits of Christ.

This interpretation of the Redemption makes of it a mystery not superior but contrary to right reason. How could the Word of God made flesh have become odious to His Father? How could He who is God Himself, who is the truth and the life, have endured in the uppermost regions of His soul the torment of the damned, the privation of God? Luther and Calvin have sought to find in the Redemption a penal compensation, a physical torment, rather than a work of spiritual love, and they also suppressed the necessity of love in our

[46] Cf. St. Thomas, Ia, q. 20 f.

life, by saying that all that is necessary is to believe. How could faith without love, without obedience to the precepts, suffice for salvation? [47]

These manifestly inadmissible excesses of the first Protestants provoked the reaction of present-day liberal Protestants, who fall into the contrary error when they say: Christ did not die to expiate our sins and to obtain for us grace and eternal life; but He saved us solely through His doctrine and His example, like the prophets and the martyrs, though His heroism did surpass theirs.

The Catholic doctrine rises like a mountain peak above these two contrary errors. It tells us that Jesus has redeemed us not merely by His example and His doctrine, but by making satisfaction for our sins and by meriting for us grace and eternal life. He offered Himself up for us, especially on the cross, like a veritable host.

There is certainly a profound mystery in all this. Yet this dogma, in affirming the exigencies of divine justice, is in no respect contrary to God's mercy, as the liberal Protestants claim. Conversely, we shall see that God the Father in asking His Son to die for us as a victim has loved Him with a supremely great love, since He has wished thereby to make Him the victor over sin, the devil, and death. Those who have accepted suffering for the salvation of souls enter into the depths of this mystery. At the same time God has wished to proclaim the rights of the Sovereign Good to be loved above all else and to forgive us our sins because of the love of His Son, who was a voluntary victim for us.

[47] One day, after I had given a conference in a Protestant city on sanctifying grace, the beginning of eternal life, a man with searching eyes came to me and said: "I belong to a Lutheran family. My father and grandfather were pastors. I have followed your talk with great interest." I turned to him and asked: "How can you explain that Luther should have written: 'Sin boldly and believe even more boldly?' How could he have so completely misunderstood the precept of love which is the soul of the Gospel: Thou shalt love the Lord thy God with thy whole heart, with thy whole soul, with all thy strength, and with all thy mind?" The man answered: "It is very simple. It was diabolic." I should not have dared to tell him this, and I understood that this son of a Lutheran family was about to enter the Catholic Church, after having gone through great trials.

On the other hand, the devil is sometimes obliged to tell the truth. Thus he admitted during an exorcism that the value of suffering derives from love, and that Christ's sufferings would have been valueless if He had not endured them for love of God and for love of us. This is what "he who does not love," as St. Theresa calls him, is at times forced to admit.

Far from destroying each other in being thus united on the cross, divine mercy and justice rest in a way upon each other, like the two arcs of a circle that form a pointed arch, and the exigencies of justice are revealed to be the consequences of love's own exigencies. Love of the good requires that evil be atoned for, and it gives us the Redeemer, so that this reparation may be offered up and that we may regain eternal life.

The full grandeur of this mystery is manifest in St. Paul's letter to the Ephesians: "God (who is rich in mercy) for His exceeding charity wherewith He loved us, even when we were dead in sins, hath quickened us together in Christ (by whose grace you are saved) and hath raised us up together, and hath made us sit together in the heavenly places, through Christ Jesus, that He might show in the ages to come the abundant riches of His grace, in His bounty toward us in Christ Jesus." [48]

[48] Eph. 2:4–7.

❊ XVI ❊

GOD'S LOVE FOR HIS SON IN THE MYSTERY OF THE REDEMPTION

"And I, if I be lifted up from
the earth, will draw all things
to Myself."

John 12:32

WE HAVE seen what the exact meaning of the dogma is according to St. Thomas: The love of Christ dying for us on the cross pleased God more than the totality of all men's sins can displease Him.[1]

In order to delve more deeply into this mystery, we must consider how it is the manifestation of the uncreated love of God for His Son and for us.

At first blush it might seem that God the Father appears to be cruel to His Son by striking down an innocent person in place of the guilty. This is what the liberal Protestants hold, in their reaction against the thought of Luther and Calvin. It might also seem that God the Father loves us more than He loves His Son, since He has delivered up His Son for us.

This is not so at all, but is but a very inferior view of the matter. This mystery is incomparably superior to any such contentions.

God Has Wished for His Son
the Glory of the Redemption

St. Thomas Aquinas has written these profound words: "God's loving one thing more than another is nothing else than His willing for that thing a greater good: because God's will is the cause of good-

---

[1] IIIa, q.48, a.2, 4.

ness in things; and the reason why some things are better than others, is that God wills for them a greater good. Hence it follows that He loves more the better things. God loves Christ not only more than He loves the whole human race, but more than He loves the entire created universe: because He willed for Him the greater good in giving Him a name that is above all names, so far as He was true God. Nor did anything of His excellence diminish when God delivered Him up to death for the salvation of the human race; rather did He become thereby a glorious conqueror: the government was placed upon His shoulder, according to Isa. 9:6." [2]

In his treatise on the Incarnation, St. Thomas develops this lofty idea when he inquires: [3] Did God the Father Himself deliver up His Son to His passion and death? He answers by explaining St. Paul's words: "He that spared not even His own Son, but delivered Him up for us all." [4]

In his explanation St. Thomas says: "In three respects God the Father did deliver up Christ to the Passion. In the first way, because by His eternal will He preordained Christ's passion for the deliverance of the human race, according to the words of Isaias: 'The Lord hath laid on Him the iniquities of us all'; [5] and again: 'The Lord was pleased to bruise Him in infirmity.' [6] Secondly, inasmuch as, by the infusion of charity [so that it might pour out upon us], He inspired Him with the will to suffer for us; hence we read in the same passage: 'He was offered because it was His own will.' [7] [This was in order that He might accomplish His redemptive mission.] Thirdly, by not shielding Him from the Passion, but abandoning Him to His persecutors: thus we read (Matt. 27:46) that Christ while hanging upon the cross, cried out: 'My God, My God, why hast Thou forsaken Me?' [8] Because, to wit, He left Him to the power of His persecutors, as Augustine says." [9]

What we must consider here is the love of God the Father for His Son, even at the moment that He delivered Him up for us. In this there is a very lofty truth that often passes unnoticed because of its

[2] Ia, q. 20, a. 4, c. and ad 1. [3] IIIa, q. 47, a. 3. [4] Rom. 8:32.
[5] Isa. 53:6. [6] *Ibid.*, 53:10. [7] *Ibid.*, 53:7.
[8] Matt. 27:46. [9] Ep. 140.

elevation and that must be the object of contemplation for souls whose vocation is one of atonement.

Despite appearances to the contrary, the cross on which Jesus seemed to be vanquished is the trophy of His victory. Jesus said: "If I be lifted up from the earth, I will draw all things to Myself." [10] God the Father, through love of His Son, has from all eternity willed for Him this painful triumph, this victory over sin and the spirit of evil. But this far surpasses our human ideas, and we can scarcely find here upon earth even a symbol of this sublime divine love.

Yet, during wartime when a general must sacrifice a handful of men to save his country, who are those that he chooses? He chooses the bravest and those he loves most. He sends for his best lieutenant and tells him categorically: You must be killed to save our country and our army. He embraces the young man and sends him to his death, a death that is all the more glorious because the peril is greater and because there is no escape from it. The young officer leaves, happy that he has been chosen. His general could not have given him a greater proof of his esteem. He accomplishes his destiny as a soldier.

The story is told that under similar circumstances a Japanese general chose his own son among his lieutenants and asked him to go to his death to save the army. The young man understood how great was his father's love for him and immediately sacrificed himself.

Similarly, what officer is chosen to carry the flag into battle? One of the bravest, for he is the chief target of the enemy and he cannot defend himself. He cannot return blow for blow, because he is holding the flag.[11]

These examples of human heroism give us a faint glimpse of our Savior's heroism and of His Father's love for Him when He delivered Him up for our salvation.

After sending His prophets, of whom several were put to death, God sent His only-begotten Son, as the parable of the wicked husbandmen tells us. God the Father sent His Son to the glorious death

---

[10] John 12:32.

[11] It would be a far too materialistic conception of a soldier to think that he is first of all a man who kills. The real soldier is a man who offers his life to save his country, to defend its homes and its intellectual and moral heritage.

of the cross for the salvation of mankind. And, as St. Paul says: When Christ came into the world He said, "Behold I come. . . . Sacrifices and oblations and holocausts for sin Thou wouldest not. . . . Behold I come to do Thy will, O God." [12]

Through Love of His Son, God Asked of Him the Most Heroic Love

It is easy to love one's country when such love costs nothing. It is heroic to love it when under fire. It is easy to love God when everything is going our way. It is heroic to love Him when everything goes against us, when friends abandon us, and when heaven itself seems to be closed to us. Let us now consider what was demanded of our Savior?

Love of the good demands the reparation of evil. The stronger the love, the more it demands. God's love of the good demands the reparation of sin which ravages souls, which turns them away from their final end, and plunges them into the concupiscence of the flesh, and of the eyes, into the pride of life, and ultimately into eternal death.

When God the Father gave us His Son to redeem us, He could have been content with the smallest act of charity by the Word made flesh. For the least of Jesus' acts derived from the divine personality of the Word an infinite value to satisfy and to merit. But then we would not have understood the abysmal chaos which is sin. Even now we understand it so little, after all the sufferings which our Savior endured for our sakes.

God the Father did not retreat before the prospect of the painful death of His own Son, and He asked His Son to expiate our sins by terrible sufferings, and by enduring these sufferings through love to make reparation for all criminal sensuality. He called upon His Son to show us by His own absolute denudation all the shame of the concupiscence of the eyes and pleasure-seeking egoism, to make us realize through His own humiliations the utter folly of pride, and to blot out by His heroic love the disorder of hatreds which divide persons, families, classes, and peoples.

[12] Heb. 10:5-9.

By thus making the utmost demands of His justice, God was not taking pleasure in punishing. On the contrary, He showed how great is His love of the good and His holy hatred of evil, which is merely the reverse of love. No one can sincerely love the good without hating evil. No one can love truth without hating lies. God cannot love the good with infinite love without hating evil with holy hatred. That is why the exigencies of justice are identified with those of love: "Love is strong as death, jealousy as hard as hell," says the Canticle of Canticles.[13]

It is this uncreated love of the good united to holy hatred of evil which required of our Savior the most heroic of all acts and sent Him to the glorious death of the cross.

This brings us once again to the very essence of the mystery of the Redemption: God the Father asked of His Son an act of love which would please Him more than the totality of all men's sins can displease Him, an act of redemptive love, of infinite and superabundant value.

This was to be the *Consummatum est,* the crowning glory of Christ's life, victory over sin and over the spirit of evil. This victory of Good Friday is far superior to the victory of Easter, for the Resurrection or victory over death is merely the sign of Christ's triumph over sin.

Thus it was indeed through love for His Son that God the Father asked Him to die for us. He predestined His Son through love to the glory of the Redemption. What would Jesus' life have been without Calvary? Similarly but on a far humbler level, what would the life of St. Joan of Arc have been without her martyrdom? And for that matter, what would have been the life of all the others who have been called to shed their blood in testimony of the truth of the Gospel? Without this consummation, their lives would now seem to us merely mutilated. And we can understand without too great difficulty that it was a predestination of love that sent them to their martyrdom.

The liturgy sings eloquently of this victory of Christ on Good Friday:

[13] Cant. 8 :6.

Sing, my tongue, the Savior's glory;
Tell His triumph far and wide;
Tell aloud the famous story
Of His Body crucified;
How upon the Cross a Victim,
Vanquishing in death, He died.

Thus did Christ to perfect manhood
In our mortal flesh attain:
Then of His free choice He goeth
To a death of bitter pain;
And as a lamb, upon the altar
Of the Cross for us is slain.

Faithful Cross, O tree all beauteous,
Tree all peerless and divine: . . .
Tree which solely wast found worthy
Earth's great victim to sustain,
Harbor from the raging tempest,
Ark, that saved the world again,
Tree with sacred blood anointed
Of the Lamb for sinners slain.

The depths of the mystery of the Redemption help us to understand why God through love sends such great sufferings to certain souls, to make them labor in union with our Lord, and in a small way like Him, for the salvation of sinners. This is the loftiest of all vocations, superior to the vocation of teaching, just as Jesus was greater on the cross than when He was preaching the Sermon on the Mount.

What greater proof of His love can God give a soul than to make of it a victim of love, in union with the crucified Savior? As the first cause does not obviate the secondary cause, but communicates to it the dignity of causality, so our Savior's sufferings do not render ours useless but raise them up and make us participate in His life.

Let us call to mind, among many others, the example of St. Catherine de Ricci. From 1542 to 1554, a period of twelve years, she experienced each week an ecstasy of suffering lasting twenty-eight hours, from Thursday at noon until Friday at four in the afternoon, an ecstasy in which she relived every moment of our Savior's passion.

Motionless, her face either pale or radiant, her eyes and arms reaching out toward the Beloved, who remained invisible to others present, she followed Him step by step and heart to heart, in each of the stations of this long sacrifice.[14] The witnesses of this fact were aware of the saint's sufferings because her whole being quivered and trembled during this painful way of the cross. When these sufferings began again on the following Thursday, nature must have begged for respite, but our Lord gave this great soul to understand that she must thus unite herself to His passion for the salvation of a certain sinner who was dear to Him or the deliverance of a particular soul in purgatory. It is in this manner that Jesus initiates the souls He loves most into the depths of the mystery of the Redemption.

One of these beloved souls who had offered herself up and who after her oblation saw everything go against her, so to speak, cried out one day when she had been overwhelmed by a new misfortune: "But Lord, what have I done to Thee?" In answer she heard these interior words: "Thou hast loved Me." She then thought of Calvary and understood with greater clearness that the seed must die in order to bear abundant fruit.

Divine Providence calls forth these extraordinary occurrences not for us to consider with curiosity but to make us understand better the grandeur of Jesus' passion. Indeed we should meditate upon it every day. These occurrences also remind us that, if the saints have accepted such sufferings in union with our Savior, we in turn should each day learn to accept better life's daily ups and downs in atonement for our sins, for our sanctification, and so that we too may labor in a measure for the salvation of souls. These extraordinary occurrences are meant to help us understand how much depth there is in the ordinary course of a genuinely Christian life, from early morning Mass and Communion throughout the day until night prayers are said at the close of the day.

We should grasp a little better each day the splendors of the liturgy of the Passion, those sublime verses which express lofty contemplation and great love:

[14] Cf. the chapter dealing with this ecstasy of the Passion in the excellent *Vie de St. Catherine de Ricci* by Rev. C. Bayonne.

Forth comes the Standard of the King.
All hail, thou Mystery ador'd!
Hail, Cross! on which the Life Himself
Died, and by death our life restored!

This is the habitual object of contemplation of the saints.

We can see, therefore, that the demands of justice are ultimately identified with those of love, and mercy wins out because it is the most immediate and deepest expression of God's love toward sinners.[15] The terrible justice of God which first holds our attention is but the secondary aspect of the Redemption, the latter being above all a work of love and mercy.

Divine justice has been appeased by the Just One who bore the burden of human sin in its totality, by the Victim of love who was struck down in our place, by the Word made flesh who died for us.

But mercy also triumphs: God the Father is reconciled through Jesus with sinners, and restores grace to them. He offers eternal life to all, even to the most perverted, and He glorifies the Redeemer by giving Him victory over sin, over the devil, and over death. It is with this in mind that St. Paul says: "All is yours; and you are Christ's; and Christ is God's." [16]

This idea has been beautifully rendered by a great painter in the Oratory of the Dominican Superior General at Rome. Above the altar Jesus is represented dying on the cross and offering His life to His Father for our salvation. The Father appears directly above the Savior, receiving His last sigh. In this painting the artist sought to show the harmony between the wills of the Father and of the Son on Calvary. He desired to bring out the fact that on the cross our Lord not only accomplished the will of His Father, but also continued to

---

[15] Cf. St. Thomas, Ia, q. 21, a. 4: "Now the work of divine justice always presupposes the work of mercy; and is founded thereupon. For nothing is due to creatures, except for something pre-existing in them, or foreknown. Again, if this is due to a creature, it must be due on account of something that precedes. And since we cannot go on to infinity, we must come to something that depends only on the goodness of the divine will—which is the ultimate end. . . . So in every work of God, viewed at its primary source, there appears mercy. In all that follows, the power of mercy remains, and works indeed with even greater force; as the influence of the first cause is more intense than that of second causes."   [16] I Cor. 3 :23.

express His love for the Father. Conversely, it was out of love for His
Son and for us that the Father sent Jesus to the heroic death of the
cross, in order to make Him the glorious victor over sin, the devil,
and death, the Savior of all men.

That is why in this beautiful painting there is only one gesture:
the Father has His arms outstretched to sustain and accept the sacrifice
of His Son, and it is on His Father's heart and in His arms that our
crucified Lord expires: "Father, into Thy hands I commend My
spirit." [17] The expression of the Father is full of mercy and nobility,
the Son's expression manifests the full heroism of His love for the
Father and for us.[18] This is the very essence, so far as it can be expressed in human terms, of the mystery of the Redemption.

[17] Luke 23:46.

[18] There is a fine reproduction of this painting in the quarterly review of religious art
edited by Dom Gaspar Lefebvre, O.S.B.: *L'Artisan liturgique*, October–December, 1932,
p. 571: "Trois tableaux du Pere M.-A. Couturier, O.P.," and in *L'Année Dominicaine*,
June, 1933.

❊ XVII ❊

CHRIST'S REDEMPTIVE LOVE

"Love is strong as death."
Cant. 8:6

WE HAVE spoken of the mystery of the Redemption in terms
of the love of God the Father for His Son, whom He sent
to the glorious death of the cross, in order to make Him our Savior
and the victor over death. It is fitting now to delve deeper into this
mystery and to consider Christ's redemptive love, as expressed by
His pierced heart whose last drop of blood was shed for us.[1]

What is perhaps most striking in Jesus' love, whether directed toward His Father or toward our souls, is that it intimately unites the
greatest tenderness and the most heroic strength in suffering and
death. These two qualities of love are too often separated in men's
hearts, and yet they are completely interdependent. Tenderness without strength becomes merely languor and affectation. Strength without mercy becomes severity and bitterness. Unlike men, God orders
all things with might and sweetness.[2]

The Tenderness and Strength
of Jesus' Love for His Father

Jesus' love for His Father began at the instant of His conception,
in all the fullness of its tenderness and strength. For the rest of us,
on the other hand, spiritual love of God usually awakens only very
slowly. The life of the senses and of the imagination develops in us
before spiritual life, and too often our first tendency is to enjoy the

---

[1] The inspiration for this discussion of doctrine comes from a sermon by Father
Monsabre which we have remembered for many years.   [2] Wisd. 8:1.

pleasures of the senses which surround us. It sometimes takes many years for generous love to blossom even between members of the same family. This is the love that desires the welfare of another, which gives itself, lavishes itself, forgets itself, the love that consummates the perfect union of hearts. The progress of our love for God, beyond the reach of the senses, is even more gradual as a rule. The human will is, of course, naturally inclined to love the Author of human nature more than itself, and to love the true and the good.[3] Little by little, we also learn that God is the supreme and wholly supernatural beauty. Yet the efficacious love of God, the desire for His kingdom and His glory, wins out only with great difficulty over our selfishness, and our more or less unruly love of creatures. It succeeds only by slow degrees in inspiring all our affections, vivifying and ennobling them. Our poor hearts are slow to give themselves to God for all eternity.

Christ's heart, on the other hand, did not hesitate a moment to give itself entirely to His Father. From the first instant of His existence, His heart possessed the fullest generosity. As St. Paul says: "When He [Christ] cometh into the world, He saith: Sacrifice and oblation Thou wouldest not: but a body Thou hast fitted to Me. . . . Behold, I come to do Thy will, O God."[4]

No one knows how tender was the filial love of the child Jesus for His Father. Indeed, He loved His Holy Mother and St. Joseph deeply, and from the first moments of His life He loved souls ardently. But how much more did He love His Father in heaven, His one and only Father!

This powerful love derived from the start from the supernatural love that always enlightened His sacred soul. This light revealed to Him without any obscurity the infinite splendor and the infinite goodness of the heavenly Father. This light guided His preferences, and so He could not err in His choices of affection.

This tender and enlightened love of Jesus for His Father inspired and continues to inspire in Him adoration and thanksgiving. As He Himself told us: "God is a spirit; and they that adore Him, must adore Him in spirit and in truth."[5]

[3] Cf. St. Thomas, Ia, q. 60, a. 5.   [4] Heb. 10:5–9.   [5] John 4:24.

Adoration springs spontaneously from His heart. He is happy to acknowledge that God is infinitely good in Himself, that He is our Creator and our Father. He acknowledges this in practice by bowing with love before His infinite majesty. Jesus even rejoices in His own abasement, in His hidden life, ignored by men. He annihilates Himself, to some extent, in terms of His human nature, so that He may better recognize God's infinite sanctity. Thus we bow and fall to our knees upon entering a church, to acknowledge our own nothingness before the infinite greatness of the Most High. But this is only a momentary attitude on our part. We have hours of adoration and hours of forgetfulness and indifference. Christ, for His part, never for a moment ceased adoring His Father, from the first instant of His life until His death on the cross. And this adoration continues now and will continue forever within His sacred soul, in acknowledgment of His Father's infinite goodness and as a song of praise to Him. Christ the Savior is the praise of God.

This tender love also ceaselessly inspires Christ to acts of thanksgiving; for God is not merely good in Himself, He is our benefactor, and no one will ever receive more from Him than did Christ. What manner of thanksgiving has Christ made? He thanks God for Himself and for all creation, for the treasure of supernatural life given to souls: "I confess to Thee, O Father, Lord of heaven and earth, because Thou hast hid these things from the wise and the prudent, and hast revealed them to little ones. Yea, Father; for so hath it seemed good in Thy sight." [6]

The strength and generosity of Jesus' love are as great as its tenderness. From the first moment, this love inspired in Him not only adoration and thanksgiving, but reparation as well. In fact, while God is a benefactor, He is also a Father who has been outraged by His children. He is the Creator and Master that thousands of souls refuse to acknowledge, even though they have been created to sing His praises more perfectly than do the stars in the firmament.

Besides, in saying to His Father, "Behold, I come," [7] Jesus from the first moment of His life offered Himself up as a victim of reparation in the place of the guilty, in the place of entire people who

[6] Matt. 11:25 f.   [7] Heb. 10:9.

through pride and error are unwilling even to pronounce God's name when they need His help most.

Many saints have been enlightened from their childhood with regard to their providential mission, whether apostolic or reparative. Why, then, should not Jesus not have been enlightened regarding His own mission? And from the first moment Jesus, foreseeing Calvary, loved His Father and offered Him in advance His entire life and His death on the cross. This is the strongest and most generous love. It is the love of the Word made flesh which pleases God more than all of men's sins displease Him.

Heart of Jesus, burning furnace of charity, have mercy on us! What is sweeter or more tender than divine charity? What is stronger than the fire in a furnace which burns and consumes all? Hell makes furious efforts against the Savior, but its rage merely arouses His love to even more heroic acts which change the opprobrium that envelops Him into an incense of adoration. Heart of Jesus, loaded down with opprobrium, have mercy on us! This is strength in the highest degree united to the most profound humility and the greatest tenderness. "Love is strong as death, jealousy as hard as hell." [8] Jesus, most powerful, have mercy on us! Jesus, meek and humble of heart, have mercy on us! This love is the source of all virtues, of all energy. Heart of Jesus, abyss of all virtues, have mercy on us! Whether the Savior's heart is touched by an angel or a man, even when the devil strikes it, it always answers with love of God. This created love within Christ's sacred soul is the highest manifestation of the uncreated love of God.

The Strength and Tenderness
of Our Savior's Love for Us

Christ's love descends upon our souls from the summit of the beatific vision, and in Jesus' love for us we find the same two qualities which are so different: the deepest tenderness and the most heroic strength. Our Lord's tender mercy for souls did not lessen for a moment, in spite of all the ingratitude, the opposition, and the hatred that He met on His path.

[8] Cant. 8:6.

We human beings find it easy to love with tender affection a few persons in our family or among our friends, but often this tenderness is entirely a matter of superficial feelings. Such affection does not often reach the soul of those whom we love. Do we pray much for them? Do we earnestly desire that they attain eternal life? Moreover, often this affection is as narrow as it is superficial: we save it for a few intimates. Feeble as it is, it would lose much of its purely relative intensity by being diffused. Our hearts are poor, miserly with their affection: the indifferent remain outside, and all the more so those who have offended or wounded us. Toward the latter we are even hard and sometimes pitiless.

The supernatural tenderness of Christ for souls is deep, because its primary object is the soul and the desire for its eternal happiness. At the same time, it is universal, immense, and extends to everyone.

Jesus is, as He Himself says, the Shepherd of souls; all can become the sheep of His fold, and He knows each of them by name.[9] He is concerned about those that are absent, He rushes forth to seek them and takes them up on His shoulders.

One of the greatest signs of His coming is this: "The poor have the gospel preached to them."[10] The poor, as well as children, have a chosen spot in His heart. He does not fear to compromise His dignity by admitting them to His side. He explains to them with kindness the doctrine of salvation, and He even waits upon them. He chooses His apostles among the poor and the humble. On Holy Thursday He humbled Himself before them: He washes and kisses their feet, to make them better understand the precept of fraternal love. Heart of Jesus, delight of all the saints, have mercy on us!

What does He say to sinners? "Come to me, all you that labor and are burdened, and I will refresh you" (Matt. 11:28). He has pity for the terrible wretchedness to which sin has brought them, and He inspires them to repent without judging them severely. He is the father of the prodigal son, He embraces the child who is unhappy through his own fault. He forgives the adulterous woman who was about to be stoned. He receives repentant Mary Magdalen, and at

---

[9] John 10:3: "The sheep hear His voice: and He calleth His own sheep by name, and leadeth them out."　　　　[10] Matt. 11:5; Luke 7:22.

once opens to her the mystery of His intimate life. He speaks of eternal life to the Samaritan woman in spite of her unsavory past. He promises prompt entry into heaven to the good thief. The words of Isaias the prophet are truly accomplished in Jesus: "The bruised reed He shall not break, and smoking flax He shall not quench." [11]

Indeed He sharply rebukes the Pharisees who are obstinately rooted in their pride, but it is only because He desires to preserve souls from error, remove them from Pharisaical influences. He also wishes to give the Pharisees a last warning which would still save them if they were not hardened in their pride. In thus warning them, Jesus still loves them. He even gives them grace which makes it possible for them to accomplish their duty.

Christ's love loses none of its tenderness in embracing all souls. It encompasses all nations and all eras. While He certainly has His preferences, for example, for St. John, for Zacheus, for the good thief, He remains accessible to all. "Christ died for all," says St. Paul.[12] Many turn from Him, but He drives no one away. And even when many have turned away from Him, He intercedes for the ingrates, as when He prayed for His executioners. This is the supreme degree of mercy, sweetness, and humility. He tells Peter that he must forgive "seventy times seven," that is, always, and He is the first to do it.

At the same time Jesus' love for us has such power that His is the greatest of all hearts. Heart of Jesus, king and center of all hearts, have mercy on us! It is not only for the glory of His Father but also for our salvation that He has chosen to be a victim in our stead. Heart of Jesus, victim of sin, have mercy on us!

The strength and generosity of His love for us is manifested with increasing force from Bethlehem to the cross. As St. Paul tells us, "The Son of God . . . loved me, and delivered Himself for me." [18] Each of us can repeat these words. The unbelievers wish to see in the dying Christ only a great man crushed by jealous mediocrities. He is infinitely more than that. He is the voluntary victim who offered Himself up to save us. "Greater love than this no man hath," Jesus Himself has told us, "that a man lay down his life for his friends." [14]

[11] Isa. 42:3; Matt. 12:20.　　[12] II Cor. 5:15.　　[18] Gal. 2:20.　　[14] John 15:13.

Generous souls sometimes offer themselves as victims to obtain the conversion of a sinner or to shorten the torments of purgatory for a loved one. Jesus offered Himself as a victim for millions of souls, for all without exception and for each one in particular; and no adult is shut out from the benefits of the Redemption unless he refuses them through pride or to satisfy his passions. Jesus bore the punishment that each of us should have borne. He suffered because of sin in the measure of His love for God whom sin offends, and in the measure of His love for our souls which sin ravages and kills. Heart of Jesus, bruised for our offenses, have mercy on us! The sorrowful and immaculate heart of Mary was intimately associated with this heroic oblation, and helps us to fathom this mystery.

No one has ever loved us or ever will love us as Christ does. That is why, when the faithful of Corinth were divided among themselves, —some of them saying they belonged to Paul, or to Apollo, or to Cephas, or to Christ—St. Paul wrote to them: "Was Paul then crucified for you?" [15]

Jesus has consented to take for Himself the loathsome chalice of Gethsemane, so that He might give us the chalice of His precious blood which is raised up every morning on the altar. These two chalices represent the whole history of the world of souls. They are as it were the two pans of the scales of good and evil, and it is good that prevails. The precious blood of Christ can obliterate all crimes if their perpetrators beg forgiveness.

Jesus, by His victory over sin on the cross, is the source of life and of holiness, the source of all consolation, the salvation of those who hope in Him, the hope of the dying, the delight of the saints, as the Litany of the Sacred Heart reminds us. Finally, He has left us the Eucharist so that He might remain with us until the end of the world and give Himself as food to each and every one of us.

To His privileged friends who follow His example, He says: "It is My love which keeps open the wound of My heart. I desire to prove to souls that My heart is never closed. On the contrary, My greatest wish is that souls may enter through My wounded heart, which is an abyss of charity and mercy. It is only in the heart of God that they

[15] I Cor. 1:13.

will find solace for their sufferings and strength for their weakness. If they will but hold out their hands to Me, I will lead them to it Myself."

We remain selfish because our love is too weak, too poor, too narrow, and because it is pitifully engrossed with our own selves. The heart of Jesus will dilate our hearts by teaching us to love above all else the glory of God and the salvation of souls.

Why do we let ourselves fall prey to jealousy or passion? Because our love does not reach high enough, to the Supreme Being whom we may all possess together and still possess individually. Instead of giving in to jealousy, let us rather thank the Lord for having given to our neighbors qualities that we do not have, and let us rejoice, just as the hand profits by what the eye sees.

Why are we cowards? Because we do not love enough, because our hearts are cold, because we rely far too much on our own strength when our helplessness is obvious, and because we do not depend enough on the heart of Jesus, on His love for us.

The heart of Jesus is able and desires to give us the saintly powers we need, confidence and love, which inspire adoration, thanksgiving, and atonement, by placing the glory of God above all else.

Heart of Jesus, of whose fullness we have all received, have mercy on us! Let us go to the Father, by Him, with Him, and in Him.

✻ XVIII ✻

J ESUS' HUMILITY AND HIS MAGNANIMITY

"Learn of Me, because I am meek,
and humble of heart."

Matt. 11:29

THE mystery of the Redemption, as we have said, is especially the manifestation of our Lord's love for us. Supernatural love or charity contains virtually all of the virtues which rank below it. Charity vivifies the other virtues, inspires them and orders their action to the supreme end, which is its own object: to the love of God above all else. Among these other virtues of our Lord, humility is one that merits special attention because through it in particular Jesus cures us of pride, which according to Scripture is "the beginning of all sin." [1]

The ancient philosophers who have described at length nearly all the moral virtues, have never spoken of humility because they ignored its twofold foundation: namely, the dogma of creation *ex nihilo* (we have been created out of nothingness), and the dogma of the necessity of actual grace for even the smallest salutary act.

Worldly wisdom often maintains also that humility is nothing but an air of virtuousness that is affected by the weak, the cowardly, the discouraged. In its eyes, humility hides a lack of intelligence, ability, and energy. According to the world, the prudent and determined man must know what he is worth in order to assert himself and command respect. He can have no use for a humble attitude that would denote a lack of vigor and dignity. Thus are humility and cowardice confused.

Our Savior, He who was the strongest of the strong and who could

[1] Ecclus. 10:15.

say to His disciples, "Have confidence, I have overcome the world," [2] Jesus, true God, the Word made flesh, who could awe everyone by the power of His intelligence and of His character, by the splendor of His miracles, Jesus, the greatest man in mind and heart that ever walked the earth, tells us: "Learn of Me, because I am meek, and humble of heart; and you shall find rest to your souls." [3] God wishes that we learn this virtue of self-effacement through Him whose greatness surpasses anything here below.

The reason for this is that our Lord's humility, far from being an indication of a lack of intelligence or of energy, derives from a very elevated knowledge of God and is united to a very high dignity. Pascal, wishing to show how infinitely superior Jesus is to all human heroes and geniuses, was content to write: "He gave us no invention, He did not reign; but He was humble, patient, holy, holy to God, terrible to demons, without any sin whatever! Oh! in what magnificence was He clothed to the eyes of the heart which see Wisdom!" [4]

Let us inquire into the principle of Jesus' humility, how He practiced this virtue, and how it was united in Him to magnanimity or greatness of soul.

The Principle of Christ's Humility

True humility does not arise from any lack of clear-sightedness or ability; it springs from a profound understanding of God's infinite greatness and of the nothingness of creatures which cannot exist by themselves. This twofold knowledge becomes ever more unified, for God's infinite majesty manifests the frailty of creatures, and inversely our helplessness reveals to us by contrast God's immense power. St. Catherine of Siena tells us that these two truths are, as it were, the highest and lowest points on the circumference of a circle which grows continually in size. When anyone knows where the lowest point is, he can see by contrast where is the diametrically opposite point. The ever-growing circle is the symbol of contemplation.

Humility is born of the realization of the abyss which separates God from creatures. God the Father, desiring to instill this thought

[2] John 16:33.   [3] Matt. 11:29.   [4] *Pensées*.

into the soul of St. Catherine of Siena, said to her: "I am who am, thou art who art not." This is what He had said to Moses.

God is Being. He cannot not be, having existed from all eternity, without beginning and without any limitation whatever, the infinite ocean of being. God is also sovereign wisdom, who knows everything that is to happen in the most remote future, and for whom there is no mystery. He is love, never-failing and impeccable. He is power, before whom nothing can resist without His permission.

On the other hand, no matter how gifted a creature may be, by itself it is not, that is, it is not self-existent. If a creature has received its existence from God it is gratuitously on His part, because He has most freely loved it, by creating it out of nothingness. The ancient philosophers never rose in their thinking to the explicit idea of creation *ex nihilo*. The thought of the absolute liberty of the creative act never occurred to them. God might very well not have created us. He had no need of us, He who is infinite goodness and beatitude.

Creatures by themselves are nothing, and once they exist they are still nothing in comparison to God. The glow of a candle is something, minute as it may be, in comparison to the blazing sun. However, even the noblest creature is nothing compared to God's infinity, compared to the infinite perfection of His wisdom and His love. Since creation, there have been more beings, but there is no more being, no more life or wisdom or love. Likewise, in relation to the Most High, angels, men, and grains of dust are equally infinitesimal, for between all creatures and God there is always an infinite distance.

Moreover, intelligent creatures depend upon God for the direction of their lives, for He assigns to them their final end, eternal life. "What doth it profit a man if he gain the whole world and suffer the loss of his own soul?" And what is the best path to attain eternal life? The path that divine Providence has mapped out for us from all eternity. It is incumbent on us humbly to recognize this path. It is not for us to determine it ourselves. It may be a hidden way, to preserve us from pride and from forgetting God. Perhaps it is a path of suffering, one that is richer than any other in the fruits of life. The apostolate of prayer and of suffering is no less fruitful than the apostolate of teaching, and it even fecundates the latter by inspiring the search of doctrine not only in books but from the source of life. We must humbly accept the path, which may be hidden and painful, that our Lord has chosen for us in His mercy, the path that is indicated to us by circumstances and by those that our Lord has given us as guides.

Finally, in order to advance in this path which leads to eternal life, what can a creature accomplish of itself? Nothing. Even if a creature has received an abundance of sanctifying grace, it cannot accomplish the slightest salutary act or make the smallest step forward without God's actual help. This help is offered to each creature, but it cannot benefit by this help if it falls prey to the attraction of pleasure or to the temptation of pride. Those who best understand the sublimity of the goal to be attained, are also best aware of their own frailty. Who knew this better than the saints? They mistrusted themselves and placed their confidence in God.

This is the principle of humility: the realization of God's infinite greatness and of our own nothingness. What then, was the nature of Jesus' humility?

In order to understand Christ's humility, we would need to fathom as He did the mystery of the creative act and the mystery of grace. Both here on earth and in heaven Jesus is even humbler than Mary and than all the saints, for He understands better than they the infinite distance that separates every creature from its Creator and He knows better than anyone else the greatness of God and the frailty of every human soul and of every created spirit.

As we said earlier, Jesus enjoyed the beatific vision while He was still here on earth. He saw God face to face through His human intelligence, enlightened by the splendor of the Word. Instead of having to use His reason, as we do, and to use human words to express the idea that God is Being, Wisdom, and Love, Jesus saw the divine essence, the Deity, directly. The most elevated portion of His sacred soul was as in a perpetual ecstasy, captivated by the splendor of God. And with the same vision, which is superior to reason and to faith, He saw the nothingness of all creatures and of His own humanity. Like a painter of genius who can at once tell a masterpiece from a paltry reproduction, Jesus could see continually, even while here on earth, the infinite distance separating time from eternity.

Whereas men who undertake difficult human tasks on their own initiative often take on a determined and dominating attitude, Jesus thought only of humbly accomplishing under His Father's guidance the divine mission He had received: "Father, . . . not as I will, but as Thou wilt." [5]

Jesus was also perpetually aware that by His human powers alone He could accomplish absolutely nothing toward the divine goal He was seeking: namely, to lead souls to eternal life. He rejoiced in this powerlessness, for it glorified God and demonstrated how lofty is the supernatural end to which Providence has destined us: "My doctrine is not Mine, but His that sent Me." [6] "The Father who abideth in Me, He doth the works," [7] that is, the miracles that Jesus worked in His name.

There is a particular act of humility which consists in recognizing not only our nothingness but our wretchedness as the result of sin. This act is necessary for contrition, for sorrow at having offended God, and naturally our Lord, who is impeccable, never made such an act of humility. But He who was innocence itself wished to take upon Himself all our sins. He understood the gravity of mortal sin better than anyone else, and He suffered from it more than anyone else in the measure of His love for God who has been offended and of His love for our souls. He more than anyone else felt inexpressible disgust before such an accumulation of defilement, before so many acts of cowardice and injustice, so much treachery and sacrilege. At Gethsemane this disgust almost overwhelmed Him with nausea: "My Father, if it be possible, let this chalice pass from Me." [8]

The Union of Humility and Magnanimity in Jesus

Jesus understood better than any creature, even while He was still on earth, the greatness of God, man's weakness, and the gravity of the sin He came to wipe out. That is why He was the humblest person that ever lived. This humility, far from being a cloak for a lack of

[5] Matt. 26:39.   [6] John 7:16.   [7] *Ibid.*, 14:10.   [8] Matt. 26:30.

intelligence and energy, was the sign of the loftiest contemplation and the condition of a unique spiritual power. Moreover, it was united to the most perfect dignity, to the noblest supernatural magnanimity which inspires to great things, regardless of the sufferings and humiliations that must be encountered.

These two virtues, humility and magnanimity, in appearance so opposed, are reality related and mutually support each other like the two sides of a pointed arch. They rise together. No one is deeply humble unless he is magnanimous, and it is impossible to be truly magnanimous without great humility.[9] In the spiritual physiognomy of our Savior these two virtues are wonderfully united.

Let us call to mind St. Thomas' description of magnanimity, enlarging upon Aristotle's. Magnanimity seeks only great things worthy of honor, but places little value on honors in themselves. It does not dread scorn if it must be borne for a great cause. It is not elated by success or discouraged by failure. Material goods mean little to it, and it is not greatly disturbed at losing them. The magnanimous man gives freely what he can to all. He is truthful and takes no stock in any opinion that is opposed to truth, no matter how formidable it may become. He is ready to die for the truth.[10]

This greatness of soul is to be found in all the saints, intimately united to their profound humility. It was, of course, present in an eminent degree in Jesus.[11] And He was never greater than during His passion, in the hour of His last humiliations. Let us call to mind His answer to Pilate who had asked Him if he was a king: "My kingdom is not of this world. . . . Thou sayest, that I am a king. For this was I born, and for this came I into the world; that I should give testimony to the truth. Everyone that is of the truth, heareth My voice." [12]

[9] Cf. St. Thomas, IIa IIae, q. 129, 1, 3; q. 161, a. 1 f. ad 3. Humility prevents presumption and pride; magnanimity strengthens us against discouragement. Humility turns us toward God and before what there is of God in our neighbor. Magnanimity inspires us to great things, to those which the Lord wishes us to accomplish even at the cost of men's censure. Alfred de Vigny perceived this when he said: "Honor is the poetry of duty." In his *Servitude et grandeur militaires*, he called to mind the oft-hidden heroism of the best soldiers.   [10] Cf. St. Thomas, IIa IIae, q. 129, a. 1-8.   [11] John 18:36-38.
[12] In the most magnanimous saints, like St. Paul, we discover deep humility, and in the most humble saints, like St. Vincent de Paul, we find great magnanimity.

These two virtues of humility and magnanimity are always united in the life of our Savior. He willed to be born in the humblest condition, although He belonged to a royal race. He was the son of a virgin, but He was thought by men to be the son of a carpenter. He who was the Word of God and could awe everyone, chose to live for thirty years a hidden life working at the most commonplace trade, in order to show us that nothing is accomplished without recollection and humility. Yet we often tend to complain because we are given work beneath our abilities.

After He had emerged from His hidden life, Jesus—innocence itself—sought out John the Baptist to ask him for the baptism of penance, just as if He had been a sinner. But John at first refused, saying: "I ought to be baptized by Thee, and comest Thou to Me?" [13] Jesus' answer was: "Suffer it to be so now. For so it becometh us to fulfill all justice." [14] By this he meant that it was fitting that the Lamb of God who takes away the sins of the world should voluntarily place Himself in the ranks of the sinners. When John heard this, he resisted no more, and when Jesus had been baptized the Spirit of God descended upon Him in the form of a dove, and a voice from heaven was heard, saying: "This is My beloved Son, in whom I am well pleased." [15]

After His baptism, Jesus willed to be tempted in the desert so that He might be more like us. This was still another proof of His humility, and it also taught us to conquer the spirit of evil and to answer his seductive offers with the word of God.

At the very outset of His ministry, what were His first words? "Blessed are the poor in spirit," the humble. To them He promised great things: the kingdom of heaven.

Whom did He choose as His apostles? Unlettered fishermen, a publican like Matthew, and He made of them "fishers of men," than which there is nothing greater.

How did He teach them, when they were wondering among themselves who was the greatest? He called a little child to Him and, placing him in their midst, He said: "Amen I say to you, unless you be converted, and become as little children, you shall not enter into

[13] Matt. 3:14.   [14] *Ibid.*, 3:15.   [15] *Ibid.*, 3:17.

the kingdom of heaven. Whosoever, therefore, shall humble himself as this little child, he is the greater in the kingdom of heaven." [16] Here indeed is the union of humility and supernatural magnanimity which reached up for the great things which are obtained only through the grace of God humbly prayed for each day. As a great Catholic writer, E. Hello, once said, "It is time to become humble, for it is time to become proud," or magnanimous in the sense God wished us to be.

These two virtues are also united in the words Jesus spoke to His apostles on Holy Thursday when He was washing their feet as a supreme mark of humility: "You call Me Master and Lord; and you say well, for so I am. If then I being your Lord and Master, have washed your feet; you also ought to wash one another's feet. . . . The servant is not greater than his lord; neither is the apostle greater than He that sent him." [17]

His glory and one of the signs of His mission is to preach the gospel to the poor. He allowed the publicans to approach Him, and also Magdalen the sinner, and He made of her a great saint.

Although He did indeed enter Jerusalem in triumph, He came mounted on an ass and opposed by the Pharisees. He permitted this opposition. Let us, then, not be irritated when we meet with contradictions.

The Passion was the hour of supreme humiliations accepted for our salvation, to cure us of our pride. Barabbas, the outcast of his people, was preferred to the Word of God made flesh. Men sneered at our Savior, they struck Him and spat in His face, they insulted Him until He breathed His last upon the cross. Yet His greatness shone forth to the centurion, who could not help crying out: "Indeed this was the Son of God." [18]

Never was deeper humility united so closely to a loftier magnanimity. It is in recognition of this fact that St. Paul said to the Philippians: "For let this mind be in you, which was also in Christ Jesus: who being in the form of God, thought it not robbery to be equal with God; but emptied Himself, taking the form of a servant, being made in the likeness of men. . . . He humbled Himself becoming obedi-

---

[16] *Ibid.*, 18:2–4.   [17] John 13:13–16.   [18] Matt. 27:54.

ent unto death, even to the death of the cross. For this cause God also hath exalted Him, and hath given Him a name which is above all names: that in the name of Jesus every knee should bow, of those that are in heaven, on earth, and under the earth: and that every tongue should confess that the Lord Jesus Christ is in the glory of God the Father." [19] Humility and magnanimity, self-abasement and a wholly supernatural greatness, these two virtues are to be found, in an attenuated form in all the saints.

Likewise the Church is unceasingly humiliated, and she seems to be vanquished although she is always victorious. It is necessary that certain interior souls should be particularly united to these humiliations of the Church and should work for the salvation of sinners, always seeming to fail. This is the path of pure love.

There are certain works that will always be a source of humiliation and of graces for those who undertake them. These souls must not complain if things go well in the eyes of the Lord, although they do not seem to succeed. For the Lord Himself has placed His hand on these works and accepts the oblation of reparation which through these works is offered up to Him each day. St. Philip Neri used to say: "I thank Thee, O my God, that things are not going as I should like them to."

These humiliations and sufferings are good, and were all the consolations of earth to come at such moments, they would not console. The Lord does not will it. For there is a certain dose of suffering that we must bear, and if it were taken away from us, we should have lost the better part.

We sometimes complain at the lowliness of our state in life and we desire the appearances of greatness. God loves us much more than we dream. He has already given us great things through baptism, absolution, and Holy Communion. These blessings are infinitely superior to those which we are foolish enough to desire. And even greater blessings have been promised to us: to see Him for all eternity as He sees Himself, and to love Him as He loves Himself.

[19] Phil. 2:5-11.

❊ XIX ❊

Our Savior's Prayer

LET us now speak of the way Christ prayed, so that we may penetrate even deeper into His sacred soul and into the mystery of the Redemption. We feel a need of praying, especially when we are in trouble, because it has been said to us: "Ask and you shall receive, knock and it shall be opened unto you." Yet we also feel that our prayers are too often unworthy of being answered, as it is written in the *Dies irae:*

> Worthless are my prayers and sighing;
> Yet, good Lord, in grace complying,
> Rescue me from fires undying.

Our prayers often lack the necessary humility, trust, and perseverance. They remain superficial and do not cry out from the depths of our souls. That is why we often feel the need of relying on a deeper and stronger prayer than our own, and we ask the Blessed Virgin and the saints to intercede for us. Especially we feel the need of depending on Christ's great prayer, as does the Church at the end of each of the prayers at Mass: *per Christum Dominum nostrum.* And in reality, it is Christ's own prayer that is continued in the Church until the end of time, each morning at Mass and in the Divine Office.

Let us inquire how Jesus prayed while He was on earth, and whether He continues to pray in heaven.

How Jesus Prayed While on Earth

St. Luke tells us that before Jesus chose the Twelve, He "went out into a mountain to pray, and He passed the whole night in the

prayer of God." [1] A little earlier in the same Gospel,[2] we read that
He retired into the desert for the same purpose. We all know His
priestly prayer after the Last Supper, as recorded by St. John,[3] and
also His prayer in the Garden of Olives: "My Father, if it be possible,
let this chalice pass from Me. Nevertheless not as I will, but as Thou
wilt." [4] A little later on, He implored His Father's mercy for His
executioners. And His last breath was a prayer of adoration, of supplication for us, of reparation and of thanksgiving.

It is certain that Jesus prayed not as God but as man, for prayer is
the lifting up of the soul toward God and the expression of a desire
that we ask Him to grant us. As man Jesus knew divine Providence
had ordered from all eternity that certain graces would be obtained
only through His prayer. He knew that it was through His prayer
that He would obtain the conversion of Mary Magdalen, of the good
thief, and of the centurion. It was fitting also that He should pray in
order to give us an example of humble, filial, trusting, and confident
prayer. For He told us: "We ought always to pray, and not to
faint." [5] He wished us to pray unceasingly, as we breathe. When He
taught us to say the Our Father, He said it with us and for us, thus
reminding us that God is the author of all good.

For what great intentions did Jesus pray? Did He pray for Himself? He certainly did at Gethsemane, when He cried out as He lay
prostrate on the earth: "My Father, if it be possible, let this chalice
pass from Me. Nevertheless not as I will, but as Thou wilt." [6] That
is, not as My emotions and the inclination of My nature desire, for
death—and particularly such a terrible death—is repugnant to them;
but as Thou desirest. It is a prayer of supplication which expresses a
conditional desire, "if it be possible," a desire dominated by full conformity of the free will with the will of God. "My Father, if this
chalice may not pass away, but I must drink it, Thy will be done." [7]

Since our Lord had already announced several times that He
would be put to death and that He would rise again,[8] He knew very
well that this conditional prayer would not be answered. Yet He said
this prayer to show that He was truly human and that we are per-

---

[1] Luke 6:12.   [2] Ibid., 5:16.   [3] John, chap. 17.   [4] Matt. 26:39.
[5] Luke 18:1.   [6] Matt. 26:39.   [7] Ibid., 26:42.   [8] Ibid., 16:21.

mitted to express the suffering which our nature feels, while conforming our will to that of God.

But whatever Jesus asked in an absolute and not a conditional manner, He always obtained. Whenever His prayer was the expression of His deliberate and absolute human will, it was always answered.[9] In this prayer He asked what He saw was manifestly within the intentions of God and what He was inspired to ask for earnestly: namely, the graces which according to the plan of Providence were to be obtained through His intercession. For instance, we all believe in the infallible efficacy of His prayer for Peter, of which He spoke to him before His passion: "Simon, Simon, behold Satan hath desired to have you, that he may sift you as wheat. But I have prayed for thee, that thy faith fail not: and thou, being once converted, confirm thy brethren." [10] And after his defection which Jesus then foretold, Peter was indeed converted by a very powerful grace which Christ's prayer obtained for him and which led him to martyrdom. No one in the Church doubts that it is in virtue of this same prayer which Christ said for Peter that each of Peter's successors confirms his brethren in the faith.

The disciples knew the power of the Savior's prayer. After Lazarus' death, Martha said to Jesus: "Lord, if Thou hadst been here, my brother had not died. But now also I know that whatsoever Thou wilt ask of God, God will give it Thee." Jesus answered her: "Thy brother shall rise again. . . . I am the resurrection and the life." [11] At the moment of Lazarus' resurrection, Jesus raised His eyes to heaven and said: "Father, I give Thee thanks that Thou hast heard Me. And I knew that Thou hearest Me always." [12] St. Paul, in his Epistle to the Hebrews, wrote that Jesus "was heard for His reverence. . . . And being consummated, He became, to all that obey Him, the cause of eternal salvation." [13] In this respect His prayer is answered every day and will continue to be answered until the end of the world.[14]

---

[9] Cf. St. Thomas, IIIa, q. 21, a. 4.   [10] Luke 22:31 f.

[11] John 11:21–24.   [12] Ibid., 41 f.   [13] Heb. 5:7–9.

[14] This distinction between conditional and unconditional prayer applies to us also, making all necessary allowances. Thus we must unconditionally ask for the graces which are manifestly necessary for our salvation, and we must ask conditionally for temporal blessings in the measure that they are useful for our salvation.

How did Jesus while here on earth pray for His apostles and for the Church? We have an example of it in His priestly prayer after the Last Supper and just before the Passion. As recorded by St. John, this prayer begins with these words: "Father, the hour is come, glorify Thy Son, that Thy Son may glorify Thee." [15] Why did the meek and humble of heart ask to be glorified? He asked this at the moment of His last humiliations, so that He might glorify His Father by His death, by His very humiliations which, because He accepted them with love, were to make Him victorious over sin and Satan.

This prayer asked for the spreading of God's glory, and it was answered during the Passion, for never was Jesus greater than at this supreme hour. His prayer was answered by the conversion of the good thief and of the centurion, by His own glorious resurrection, and later by the conversion of the world to the Gospel.

Jesus continued His priestly prayer by beseeching His Father to keep His apostles: "Holy Father, keep them in Thy name whom Thou hast given Me; that they may be one, as We also are. While I was with them, I kept them in Thy name. Those whom Thou gavest Me have I kept and none of them is lost, but the son of perdition, that the Scripture may be fulfilled. And now I come to Thee; and these things I speak in the world, that they may have My joy filled in themselves. . . . I pray not that Thou shouldst take them out of the world, but that Thou shouldst keep them from evil. . . . Sanctify them in truth. . . . And for them do I sanctify Myself, that they also may be sanctified in truth." [16]

Jesus foresaw the profound dejection of His disciples a few hours later, during His passion. Yet His prayer would sustain them. It would be answered and it would win for them the strength to remain faithful until their martyrdom.

Jesus also foresaw the great persecutions that would come. Indeed, He had already announced them: "And you shall be betrayed by your parents and brethren, and kinsmen and friends; and some of you they will put to death. And you shall be hated by all men for My name's sake. But a hair of your head shall not perish. In your patience you shall possess your souls." [17]

---

[15] John 17:1.   [16] *Ibid.*, 17:11–19.   [17] Luke 21:16–19.

In His priestly prayer Jesus also besought His Father for all those who would believe in Him through the preaching of the apostles and of their successors, "that they all may be one, as Thou, Father, in Me, and I in Thee; that they also may be one in Us; . . . that the world may know that Thou hast sent Me, and hast loved them, as Thou hast also loved Me." [18] Thus Jesus asked two things for His Church: unity here on earth and the vision of glory in heaven.

He asked the multitude of believers should become but a single heart and soul. This was to be accomplished in the new-born Church, as we learn from the Acts of the Apostles.[19] He asked that the Church, despite the diversity of races, languages, customs, and human institutions, should appear as a permanent moral miracle, through the unity of faith, worship, hope, charity, and hierarchy. This is being accomplished in the Church, especially in the most saintly souls of each generation, whatever their nation or race. Human weaknesses do exist in the Church, but she always has within her holy souls whose great spirit of faith, of trust, and of love is in each generation the realization of our Lord's expressed desire.

Finally, He asked for His Church the glory of heaven: "Father, I will that where I am, they also whom Thou hast given Me may be with Me; that they may see My glory which Thou hast given Me, . . . that the love wherewith Thou hast loved Me, may be in them, and I in them." [20]

Jesus wishes us to be the members of His mystical body and, after we have participated here on earth in His hidden life and in a measure in His life of sorrow, to participate in His glorious life for all eternity.

Our Savior's Prayer for Us in Heaven

St. Paul wrote to the Romans: "Christ Jesus . . . that is risen also again . . . is at the right hand of God, . . . also maketh intercession for us. Who then shall separate us from the love of Christ?" [21] That is to say, who will separate us from the love which Christ has for us and which arouses in us a reciprocating love?

In the Epistle to the Hebrews, the great Apostle also says: "For

[18] John 17:21-23. [19] Acts 4:32. [20] Ibid., 17:24-26. [21] Rom. 8:34 f.

that He [Jesus] continueth forever, hath an everlasting priesthood, whereby He is able also to save forever them that come to God by Him; always living to make intercession for us." [22]

Before leaving us, Jesus Himself assured us that He would pray for us: "If you love Me, keep My commandments. And I will ask the Father, and He shall give you another Paraclete, that He may abide with you forever." [23]

Some theologians [24] have said Jesus in heaven no longer prays for us in the real sense of the word, but that He simply shows to His Father His humanity and His glorious wounds, signs of His past merits.

In the eyes of many other theologians,[25] followers of St. Augustine and St. Thomas, this interpretation attenuates without reason the inspired words that we have just called to mind. When St. Paul says that Christ always living continues to make intercession for us, there is no reason to say that this is no longer a prayer in the true sense of the word. If our Lord continues to ask that His past merits be applied to certain specified souls, there is no imperfection in this. On the contrary, it is a new expression of His love for us.[26]

We are certain that the Blessed Virgin and the saints in heaven pray for us. When we say litanies we ask them to intercede on our behalf, and St. Thomas remarks on this subject: "Since prayers offered for others proceed from charity, . . . the greater the charity of the saints in heaven, the more they pray for wayfarers, since the latter

[22] Heb. 7:24 f.   [23] John 14:15 f.   [24] Medina and Vasquez.

[25] Cf. Gonet, *De incarnatione*, disp. 22, a. 2, likewise Salmanticenses, Billuart, Tolet, Suarez, etc.

[26] In *In Epistolam ad Hebraeos*, 7:25, St. Thomas says with regard to this text: "Semper vivens . . . : Aliter enim sacerdotium ejus fineretur. . . . Excellentiam pietatis ostendit, quia dicit: Ad interpellandum pro nobis, quia licet sit ita potens, ita altus, tamen cum hoc est pius, quia interpellat pro nobis. Advocatum habemus apud Patrem, Jesum Christum (I Joan. 2:1). Interpellat autem pro nobis, primo humanitatem suam, quam pro nobis assumpsit, repraesentando. Item sanctissimae animae suae desiderium, quod de salute nostra habuit exprimendo, cum quo interpellat pro nobis."

St. Thomas also says (*In Epist. ad Romanos*, 8:34) concerning this text: "Jesus, qui est ad dexteram Dei, qui etiam interpellat pro nobis: Nunc autem ejus interpellatio pro nobis est voluntas ipsius de nostra salute: Volo ut ubi sum ego, et illi sint mecum" (Joan. 17:24).

See also *In IV Sent.*, dist. 15, q.4, a.6, qa2, ad 1: "Christus, in quantum homo, orat pro nobis; sed ideo non dicimus: Christe ora pro nobis, quia Christus supponit suppositum aeternum, cujus non est orare, sed adjuvare; et ideo dicimus: Christe audi nos vel miserere nobis, et in hoc etiam evitamus haeresim Arii et Nestorii."

can be helped by prayers: and the more closely they are united to God, the more are their prayers efficacious: . . . Wherefore it is said of Christ (Heb. 7:25): 'Going to God by His own power . . . to make intercession for us.' " [27]

St. Ambrose also says: "He is ever pleading our cause before His Father, and His prayer cannot go unheeded." [28]

St. Augustine speaks in the same vein: "He still prays for us now inasmuch as He is our priest and our head; and inasmuch as He is God, He is prayed to for us." [29] St. Gregory the Great expresses the same view: "*Quotidie orat Christus pro Ecclesia.*" [30] He remains ever our advocate and our mediator.[31]

There is no doubt, of course, that Jesus does not pray in heaven as He did in the Garden of Olives, prostrate and overwhelmed with sadness. The perfect holocaust has been offered up. But He continues to ask that its fruits be applied to us at the opportune moment, especially at the hour of death.[32]

If when we recite litanies we do not say "Christ, pray for us," but "Christ, have mercy on us; Christ, hear us," it is to remind us that Jesus is not man only but that He is also God, and when we address ourselves to His divine person, it is God Himself whom we are addressing, begging Him to grant our requests.[33]

---

[27] IIa IIae, q. 83, a. 11.   [28] *In Epist. ad Rom.*, 8:34.   [29] *In Psalm.* 85.

[30] *In V Psalm. poenitent.*   [31] Cf. I John 2:1.

[32] As Gonet says (*De incarn.*, disp. 22, a. 2), there is no reason why Christ even now that He is in heaven should not pray for us in the true sense of the word. If it were impossible for Him to pray because He is God, then He could not have prayed while here on earth. If He could not pray because He is blessed, then the Blessed Virgin Mary could not pray either. On the contrary, it is fitting that He should make this act of religion to honor God and to obtain for us what is necessary to our salvation, by the application of His past merits.

Jesus remains a priest for all eternity, and one of the principal functions of a priest is to pray for the people who have been placed in his care.

He prays not through indigence but so that the superabundant redemption which has already been accomplished may be applied to us. The infinite merits of Christ do not prevent the Blessed Virgin and the saints from praying so that the fruits of the Passion may be applied to us, nor do they prevent Christ from continuing to pray for us.

Beyond doubt, Christ, now that He has fulfilled His mission, no longer merits. Therefore His prayer, like that of the saints and of Mary, is no longer meritorious (the time for merit has passed), but it is eminently worthy of being answered.

See likewise Salmanticenses, *De incarn.*, *de oratione Christi.*

[33] Cf. St. Thomas, IV dist. 15, q. 4, a. 6, qa 2a, ad 1.

Besides, it is absolutely certain that in the heart of the glorious Christ, adoration and thanksgiving are ever alive. These prayers are, as it were, the soul of the Holy Sacrifice of the Mass. Far more, this prayer of adoration and of thanksgiving will continue for all eternity, even after the last Mass has been said. This is what is said every day in the Preface: "It is truly meet and just . . . that we should at all times and in all places give thanks unto Thee, O holy Lord, Father almighty and everlasting God, through Christ our Lord. Through whom the angels praise Thy majesty, the dominions worship it, the powers stand in awe." This worship of adoration and of thanksgiving will continue eternally, even after the prayer of petition has ceased with the last Mass at the end of the world.

What a consolation to think that Christ "always living" never ceases "to make intercession for us," that this prayer and this oblation is, as it were, the soul of the Holy Sacrifice of the Mass, and that we can always unite our own prayer to it! Our prayer often lacks the necessary humility, trust, and perseverance. Let us rest it upon Christ's prayer. Let us ask Him to inspire us to pray as is fitting, in accordance with God's intentions, to make prayer spring from our hearts and to present it to His Father, so that we may be one with Him for all eternity. Let us thus ask Him for ourselves and for the dying the grace of graces, the grace of a happy death, or of final perseverance, which is the prelude to eternal life.

❊ XX ❊

THE PRIESTHOOD OF CHRIST

THE Savior's sacerdotal prayer which we have just spoken of can be understood only in relation to the priesthood of Christ. We must first of all call to mind St. Paul's teaching on this point in the Epistle to the Hebrews, then what the Church says about it in its Councils, and finally what theology adds in order to help us to penetrate the meaning and the scope of this teaching which is so spiritually fruitful.

St. Paul's Testimony

The Epistle to the Hebrews shows us the full splendor of Christ's priesthood in the light of ideas expressed by St. Paul in the Epistles to the Romans, to the Corinthians, and to Timothy on Christ the Redeemer, the universal mediator, and the head of the Church, and on the necessity of believing in Christ in order to be saved: "For there is one God, and one mediator of God and men, the man Christ Jesus: who gave Himself a redemption for all." [1]

The first part of the Epistle to the Hebrews sets out to show the superiority of the priesthood of Jesus Christ, the mediator of the new alliance, over all the organs used by God in the Old Testament to manifest Himself to men. Jesus, as Son of God, is declared to be superior to all the priests of the Old Law, superior to all the prophets who announced Him, superior to Moses, superior even to the angels who are only God's servants whereas Jesus is the Son of God by origin and by nature, the Creator and Master of all things. [2]

St. Paul says: "For it was fitting that we should have such a high priest, holy, innocent, undefiled, separated from sinners, and made

[1] I Tim. 2:5 f.   [2] Heb. 1:5, 13; 2:18; 4:12; 7:24.

238

higher than the heavens; who needeth not daily (as the other priests) to offer sacrifices first for his own sins, and then for the people's: for this He did once in offering Himself." [3] He did this by offering Himself up not for His own sake but for all sinners, for all men.

To enlighten the recently converted Jews who were at times tempted to return to the rites of the Levitical priesthood, St. Paul showed them that, while the sacrifices of the Mosaic worship were many and varied and at times of great exterior magnificence, yet they remained of themselves without efficacy. These sacrifices, he explained, were but the figure of the great sacrifice to come which was to be accomplished not in exterior magnificence but in the perfect denudation of Golgotha.

In St. Paul's words, "Christ, being come a high priest of the good things to come, . . . neither by the blood of goats or of calves, but by His own blood, entered once into the holies, having obtained eternal redemption. For if the blood of goats and of oxen, . . . [offered up to God] sanctify such as are defiled, to the cleansing of the flesh: how much more shall the blood of Christ, who by the Holy Ghost offered Himself unspotted unto God, cleanse our conscience from dead works, to serve the living God?" [4] Such is the efficacy and the infinite value of Christ's sacrifice.

Finally, whereas the priests of the Old Law succeeded one another as death struck them one after the other, Christ "continueth forever, hath an everlasting priesthood; whereby He is able also to save forever them that come to God by Him; always living to make intercession for us." [5] It is Christ who remains the chief priest of the Eucharistic Sacrifice, the commemoration of the Passion which will be offered up until the end of the world.

This lofty doctrine on Christ's priesthood has been clearly formulated by the Church at the Council of Trent: "Since the work of the Redemption could not be accomplished under the Old Testament, because of the weakness of the Levitical priesthood, it was necessary, according to the mercy of God the Father, that another priest . . . arise, Jesus Christ, our Lord, who could lead to salvation and perfection all who were to be sanctified. Our God and our Lord Himself

---

[3] *Ibid.*, 7:26 f.   [4] Heb. 9:11–14.   [5] *Ibid.*, 7:24 f.

was to offer Himself up once and for all to His Father on the altar of
the cross for our redemption, . . . and at the Last Supper He left
to His spouse, the Church, a visible sacrifice which until the end of
time will commemorate the bloody sacrifice of the cross and apply its
fruits to us." [6]

Christ's Priesthood, the Most Perfect Conceivable

On the basis of St. Paul's testimony, St. Augustine [7] and theologians
as a whole, especially St. Albert the Great [8] and St. Thomas,[9] have
demonstrated that Christ's priesthood is the most perfect that can be
conceived. The reason they give is as simple as it is profound. It derives from St. Paul's own definition of the priesthood: "For every
high priest taken from among men, is ordained for men in the things
that appertain to God, that he may offer up gifts and sacrifices for
sins." [10] As St. Thomas explains,[11] the function of the priest is to be
a mediator between God and men, to offer up to God the prayers of
the people, particularly sacrifice, which is the most perfect act of the
virtue of religion, and also to give to the people the things of God
(*sacerdos* means *sacra dans*): through preaching, the light of truth,
and through the sacraments, the grace necessary for the accomplishment of God's law.

This twofold ascending and descending mediation is accomplished
especially through sacrifice, the supreme sacred act. Ascending mediation is accomplished by the oblation of the sacrifice of a victim. Descending mediation is accomplished by giving to the faithful a part
of the victim offered up, so that they may thus communicate with our
Lord.

The external oblation and immolation of the victim must be a
visible expression of the interior oblation of the priest, of his adoration, his supplication, the sentiments of his "contrite and humbled" [12]

---

[6] Sess. XXII, chap. 1.   [7] *De Trinitate*, Bk. IV, chap. 14.
[8] *De Eucharistia*, dist. 5, chap. 3, ed. Borgnet, XXXVIII, 347.
[9] *Summa theol.*, IIIa, q. 22, a. 1–4; q. 48, a. 3; q. 50, a. 4 ad 3; q. 83, a. 1 ad 3.
[10] Heb. 5:1.   [11] IIIa, q. 22, a. 1.   [12] Ps. 50:19.

heart, as well as of his thanksgiving. Thus through the sacrifice, which is an exterior and public act of the virtue of religion, the adoration, the supplication, the reparation, and the thanksgiving of the entire people rise up to God. For the prayer of the people is united to that of the priest and to a certain extent is one with his.

What follows from this with regard to the perfection of the priesthood, and particularly the priesthood of Christ? As St. Augustine has shown,[13] it follows that the priesthood is all the more perfect in the measure that the priest, the mediator between God and men, is more united to God, more united through interior oblation and immolation to the victim offered up, and more united to the men for whom the victim is offered up.

It is clear, of course, that the more closely united to God the priest is, that is, the holier he is, the more perfect will be the sacrifice he offers up as the principal act of his priesthood. For the priest, in his role as mediator, must make up by his own sanctity for the imperfection of the adoration, the gratitude, the reparation, and the supplication of the people.

Likewise the more closely the priest and the victim are united, the more perfect will the sacrifice be. For the external oblation and immolation of the victim are but the symbol of the inward oblation and immolation of the priest who is accomplishing the greatest act of the virtue of religion. Also the more the victim is pure, precious, and entirely consumed in God's honor, the more perfect will be the sacrifice. That is why the holocaust was the most perfect sacrifice of the Old Law: the entire victim was consumed in God's honor, to signify that man must offer all of himself up to God.

Finally, the more the priest and the people are united, the more perfect is the sacrifice. For the priest must bring together all the adorations, petitions, reparations, and thanksgivings of the faithful in one elevation toward God, rising up as the soul of the whole people. Consequently the more people are thus united to the priest, the greater will be the homage, the worship of adoration given to God, and the more universal or widespread will be the effects of the sacrifice.

It is enough for us to consider the priesthood of our Savior in the

[13] *Loc. cit.*

light of these principles in order to see at once that no greater priesthood can be conceived.

Christ Jesus is a priest not as God but as man. For the mediator must be an intermediary between God and men, and in that capacity inferior to God. Yet no soul can be more closely united to God than the sacred soul of Christ. We have seen that His sanctity was innate, substantial, and uncreated.[14] Jesus is not only absolutely free from any original and personal sin and from any imperfection whatever; He is sanctity itself. He is the Word of God made flesh. His humanity is sanctified first of all by its personal union with the Word, by the Word Himself who possesses it intimately and for all eternity. That is why Jesus' priestly actions, which proceed from His human intellect and will, had while He was here on earth an infinite value in terms of merit and reparation. This infinite value derived, of course, from the divine personality of the Son of God. And even now it is the Word made flesh who through His human soul makes "intercession for us."[15]

It is impossible to conceive of a priest more intimately and indissolubly united to God, or holier than Jesus. Moreover, our Lord, as head of the Church, has received the fullness of created grace which must overflow upon us, and a power of excellence to institute the sacraments, to give them the power to produce and augment divine life, and also to institue a priesthood that will be indefectible until the end of the world, a priesthood that is a participation in His own.[16]

"Behold the Lamb of God, behold Him who taketh away the sin of the world"[17] by His perfect sacrifice. If sin continues, it is not because the virtue of this sacrifice is insufficient, as was that of the sacrifices of the Old Law, but because men often refuse to receive its fruits. We cannot conceive of a holier priest than Jesus.

In addition, Christ's priesthood cannot be more perfect by reason of the union of the priest and the victim, and of the dignity of the latter. Jesus could not offer to His Father for us any victim but Himself. The boy Isaac, a figure of Christ, had consented to let himself be offered up as a sacrifice. Jesus offered Himself up when He was cruci-

---

[14] Cf. chapter 10 *supra*.   [15] Heb. 7:25.
[16] Cf. St. Thomas, IIIa, q. 64, a. 4, and Supplement, q. 35, a. 2.
[17] John 1:29.

fied. As He said: "Therefore doth the Father love Me: because I lay down My life, that I may take it again. No man taketh it away from Me: but I lay it down of Myself, and I have power to lay it down: and I have power to take it up again. This commandment have I received of My Father." [18]

We have become so accustomed to this idea that we cannot picture to ourselves our Lord immolating merely a lamb distinct from Himself, or a dove. He Himself is the victim.

This purest of victims is of infinite value, for it is the body of the Word of God, which, torn and nailed to the cross, sheds all its blood. The union of priest and victim cannot be more perfect, since Jesus is a victim to the depths of His soul, plunged in sorrow and in universal abandonment: "My God, My God, why hast Thou forsaken Me?" It is complete immolation, a perfect holocaust in reparation for the pride of life, the concupiscence of the flesh, and that of the eyes. Priest and victim cannot be more perfectly united than in our Lord, immolated for us.

Finally, the union of priest and faithful cannot be closer. Jesus is the head of the mystical body of which we are the members. The fruits of the sacrifice of the Cross, the life of grace, pour down incessantly from Him to us. At the same time, through Him, our prayers rise up to God united to His at the moment of the Mass which perpetuates in substance the sacrifice of the Cross.

It is particularly at Mass, at the moment of the Consecration and Communion, that the words of St. Paul are verified: "Christ is the head of the Church. He is the Savior of His body." [19] "Now you are the body of Christ, and members of member." [20] "That . . . we may in all things grow up in Him who is the head, even Christ." [21] Our Savior is, therefore, the priest of the entire human race, for He "died for all," [22] for the men of all times and places. And all men can become progressively incorporated in Him through the succession of human generations, and remain members of His mystical body for all eternity.

Thus Christ has made satisfaction and merited for all men. He con-

[18] *Ibid.*, 10:17 f.   [19] Eph. 5:23.   [20] I Cor. 12:27.
[21] Eph. 4:15.   [22] II Cor. 5:15.

tinues to pray for us; and His humanity, as an instrument ever united to His divinity, communicates to us all the graces we receive. The vital influx of grace thus passes continually from Him to us.[23]

We are unable to conceive of a more perfect priesthood, of a priest more closely united to God, more united to the most pure victim that is offered up every day on the altar, and lastly more united to the body of the Christian faithful which is ever renewing itself until the end of time and whose living members are to remain incorporated to Him forever. Our Savior is a priest for all eternity. His adoration and His thanksgiving will never cease, and the glory of the elect will be the consummation of His sacrifice.[24]

What Formally Constitutes Christ's Priesthood

What is there in Christ which corresponds to the priestly character which is indelibly stamped on the souls of His ministers? Some theologians, among them the Carmelites of Salamanca,[25] have thought that Christ's priesthood is formally constituted by habitual created grace (through which He is the head of the mystical body), so far as this grace presupposes personal union to the Word. Thus Christ would be a priest by the very grace which constitutes Him head of the Church and through which He exerts direct influence upon us.

Other theologians in increasing numbers, including several Thomists,[26] think—and, it seems, on solid grounds—that what formally constitutes the priesthood of Jesus Christ is the substantial grace of union with the Word by reason of which He is holy, as well as a sanctifier and mediator able to offer up a sacrifice of infinite value.

The latter approach is being increasingly accepted by theologians at the present time, and was in a way approved by Pope Pius XI in an allocution given on December 28, 1925.[27] It derives from the

[23] Cf. St. Thomas, IIIa, q. 62, a. 5.   [24] Cf. *ibid.* q. 22, a. 5.

[25] *Cursus theologicus, de incarnatione,* disp. 31, dub. 1, §4, no. 16.

[26] Cf. Gonet, O.P., *Clypeus thom. theol., de incarnatione,* disp. 22, a. 3. Hugon, O.P., *De Verbo incarnato,* 2nd ed., pp. 628 ff.

[27] Pope Pius XI says: "E unicamente perché l'Omoousios di Nicea si è incarnato . . . che si effuse e si effonde, inesauribile ed infinita, in Gesù Christo, quella che i teologi chiamano unzione sostanziale, che lo consecrava sacerdote" (*Civilta Cattolica,* 1926, p. 182).

doctrine which has prevailed on the substantial and uncreated as well as innate sanctity of Jesus.[28]

Indeed it it the substantial grace of union to the Word that first of all sanctifies the humanity of our Savior. This grace does not merely give Him an accidental sanctity as does the grace which in us—and in the greatest saints including Mary—proceeds from habitual created grace, an accident of our nature, a divine graft upon our souls. Personal union with the Word gives to Jesus' humanity a substantial and uncreated sanctity [29] which is the source of the infinite value of His human meritorious and propitiatory acts. This uncreated sanctity subsists in heaven, now that the hour of merit and of painful expiation has passed.

In His formal role as universal priest and mediator, Jesus must offer up not a sacrifice of limited value such as those of the Old Law, but a sacrifice of infinite value. The priestly acts of His sacred soul must have a theandric value. And a priest capable of offering up a sacrifice of such value must be more than "the head of humanity." Adam, in his innocent state, was the head of humanity (*caput naturae elevatae*). Yet he was not able, as priest and mediator, to offer up a sacrifice of infinite value.

Therefore what formally constitutes Christ's priesthood seems to be the grace of substantial union to the Word which makes of Him the Lord's Anointed One.[30] This grace of union which is uncreated, for it is the Word Himself who completes and possesses the humanity of our Savior,[31] implies a unique priestly vocation and is the source of the habitual created grace by which Christ, the head of the Church, has immediate influence upon its members or communicates supernatural life to them. All these gifts are necessary to His priesthood, but the first-mentioned is its formal constituent.

This is what St. Thomas seems to think of the matter.[32] In discuss-

---

[28] See chap. 10 *supra;* cf. John of St. Thomas, *De incarn.*, d. 8, a. 1; Gonet, *De incarnatione*, disp. 11.

[29] Jesus' humanity also exists through the uncreated existence of the Word (cf. St. Thomas, IIIa, q. 17, a. 2).   [30] Ps. 44:8.

[31] Cf. St. Thomas, IIIa, q. 6, a. 6: "The grace of union is the personal being that is given gratis from above to the human nature in the person of the Word."

[32] St. Thomas IIIa, q. 22, a. 2 ad 3.

ing Jesus as priest and victim, he says that His humanity was sanctified by the grace of union. The same is true when he speaks of the predestination of Jesus not only to glory, as in the predestination of the saints, but of His predestination to natural divine sonship, which is infinitely superior to adopted divine sonship.[33] Lastly, according to St. Thomas, Jesus as man is the mediator between God and all men through the grace of the hypostatic union.[34] For, by reason of this hypostatic union, He touches the two extremes to be reunited and reconciled: God and humanity.[35]

This is what Bossuet tells us in his *Elevations sur les mystères* (13th week, 1st and 6th elevations), in which he expounds the priesthood of Jesus Christ: "O Christ! O Messiah, who art awaited and given under this sacred name which signifies the Anointed of the Lord! Teach me, in the excellence of Thy unction, the origin and foundations of Christianity. . . . It is a matter of explaining the unction which makes Thee Christ." "Come, Jesus, eternal Son of God. . . . Thou dost receive the powers of the priesthood from Him alone who has said to Thee: 'Thou art My Son, this day have I begotten Thee.' [36] For this divine priesthood, one must be born only of God, and Thou hast Thy vocation 'according to the power of an indissoluble life.' [37] . . . The law of this priesthood is eternal and inviolable. Thou art alone: yet Thou hast left after Thee priests who are only Thy vicars who can offer up no other victim than the one Thou hast Thyself offered up on the cross and that Thou offerest eternally at the right hand of Thy Father."

Thus Jesus is priest by reason of the Incarnation. His priesthood is

---

[33] *Ibid.*, q. 24, a. 1 f.   [34] *Ibid.*, q. 26, a. 2; q. 58, a. 3.

[35] Theologians have at times placed too much emphasis on the distinction between Jesus as God and as man, without always giving enough consideration to what is fitting to Him as God-man, or what is fitting to His humanity by reason of the divine personality of the Word. Jesus, as God and not as man, created all things. As man and not as God, He suffered and was sorrowful even unto death. As God-man, He has loved us with a theandric love which, though it is a human act, has infinite value by reason of the divine personality from which it proceeds.

St. Thomas has made these distinctions very clearly, in particular in IIIa, q. 58, a. 3, in explaining that Jesus sits at the right hand of the Father: first, as God; secondly, as God-man, *secundum gratiam unionis;* thirdly, as man, by reason of the fullness of created grace.   [36] Ps. 2:7.   [37] Heb. 7:16.

substantial as is His sanctity, and it is from His priesthood that derives the priestly character of His ministers, impressed indelibly in their souls. And in these priestly souls He will raise up vocations until the end of time.

✸ XXI ✸

THE INFINITE MERITS OF CHRIST

> "And of His failure we all
> have received, and grace for
> grace."
>
> John 1:16

NOW that we have discussed the priesthood of Christ, it is fitting that we consider the source in Him of the infinite value of the meritorious and satisfactory acts that He accomplished for our salvation. This brings us to the very essence of the mystery of the Redemption, that is, to the source of all the graces we have ever received or ever will receive.

We shall consider Christ's merit rather than His satisfaction.[1] This difference is to be noted between the two: satisfaction relates to the right of the offended person who demands reparation, whereas merit relates to the reward to be obtained and therefore to the good of the one who merits or of those for whom he merits. Thus we can distinguish between merit and satisfaction, although both are intimately united in Christ's acts of love, and in Him the infinite value of His merit and of His satisfaction derives from the same principle.

Let us first inquire what revelation tells us of the value of Christ's merits. We shall then discuss the explanation generally given by the theologians.

The Testimony of St. Paul

St. Paul wrote to the Romans: "God commendeth His charity toward us; because when as yet we were sinners, according to the time,

[1] We have already spoken of satisfaction in chapters 8, 13–16; and we shall discuss it again with reference to the sacrifice of the Cross (chap. 25).

Christ died for us; much more therefore, being now justified by His blood, shall we be saved from wrath through Him. For if, when we were enemies, we were reconciled to God by the death of His Son; much more, being reconciled, shall we be saved by His life. . . . Wherefore as by one man sin entered into this world, and by sin death; . . . if by the offense of one, many died; much more the grace of God, and the gift, by the grace of one man, Jesus Christ, hath abounded unto many. . . . For as by the disobedience of one man, many were made sinners; so also by the obedience of one, many shall be made just." [2]

The Apostle then shows [3] that the Christian who is united to Christ by baptism is dead to sin and has risen to a new life, in the measure that he believes in Christ's merits with a lively faith united to charity. "But now . . . the justice of God is made manifest, . . . by faith of Jesus Christ, unto all and upon all them that believe in Him." [4]

In the Epistle to the Ephesians, St. Paul develops the same idea in a sublime manner: "We all conversed in time past, in the desires of our flesh, fulfilling the will of the flesh and of our thoughts, and were by nature children of wrath, even as the rest. But God (who is rich in mercy), for His exceeding charity wherewith He loved us, even when we were dead in sins, hath quickened us together in Christ (by whose grace you are saved) and hath raised us up together, and hath made us sit together in the heavenly places, through Christ Jesus.[5] That He might show in the ages to come the abundant riches of His grace, in His bounty toward us in Christ Jesus. For by grace you are saved through faith, and that not of yourselves, for it is the gift of God; . . . For we are His workmanship, created in Christ Jesus in good works, which God hath prepared that we should walk in them." [6]

---

[2] Rom. 5:8–19.   [3] *Ibid.*, 6:1–11.   [4] *Ibid.*, 3:21 f.

[5] Here St. Paul contemplates the supreme unfolding of the grace received in baptism, which is the seed of glory.

[6] Eph. 2:1–10. The mention of good works in this context shows that in order to be justified faith is not enough. Love of God and of neighbor is also necessary, that is, the accomplishment of the two great commandments. Luther's great error was that he denied this.

It is this doctrine that the Church sums up as follows: Our Lord Jesus Christ, the Son of God, through the great love He had for us,[7] when we were enemies or sinners,[8] has merited our justification by His sacred passion on the cross.[9]

Pope Clement VI said that "the merits of Christ are infinite, and that a single drop of His blood, because of the [personal] union with the Word, would have sufficed for the redemption of the human race." [10] This is what St. Thomas proclaims in the *Adoro Te:*

> O loving Pelican! O Jesu Lord!
> Unclean I am, but cleanse me in Thy
>   blood!
> Of which a single drop for sinners
>   spilt,
> Can purge the entire world from
>   all its guilt.

This amounts to saying, as the Church generally teaches, that the least act of love that Jesus performed while still a child had infinite meritorious value to obtain for all men of the past, the present, and the future, sanctifying grace, eternal life, and all the assistance necessary to attain them. That is all the more reason why the most heroic act of charity which Jesus accomplished in dying for us on the cross, has merited for us justification and salvation. "Where sin abounded, grace did more abound." [11] "And of His fullness we all have received, and grace for grace." [12]

It should give us great strength and consolation to contemplate these infinite merits of our Savior, which are the source of our entire spiritual life. There is no better way than this to revive our confidence in periods of lassitude and depression, or when we see souls we love adrift and feel the need of praying for them with greater ardor.

To understand revealed doctrine on this point, as proposed by the Church, let us lift our gaze progressively from the most ordinary

---

[7] *Ibid.*, 2:4.   [8] Rom. 5:10.

[9] Council of Trent, Sess. VI, chap. 7: Denzinger, no. 799; also nos. 795, 812, 820.

[10] Cf. Denzinger, nos. 550, 552: "Gutta ejus sanguinis modica, . . . propter unionem ad Verbum pro redemptione totius humani generis sufecisset."

[11] Rom. 5:20.   [12] John 1:16.

things, from our imperfect merits, to the infinite merits of Christ. We shall then begin to grasp the influence of Christ's merits on our whole lives.

Merit in General. Its Conditions

Merit in general, or meritorious action, consists in any act worthy of a reward. Merit in the exact sense of the word—condign merit— is that for which a recompense is due in justice or at the very least in virtue of a promise. Thus, in the natural order, the officer merits his pay. As to congruous merit, this is an act for which a reward is due not in justice or because of a promise, but for reasons of fittingness such as friendship, esteem, liberality. So in the natural order the valiant soldier deserves to be decorated.

In the supernatural order there is an incomparably superior form of merit. It is an act that gives one the right to a supernatural reward, which is far more precious than all the world can offer us in the way of honor and glory. This reward is even far superior to the natural life of the most gifted minds, even to the intellectual life of the angels, that is, to the life they possess by reason of their nature, which is very inferior to grace.

Supernatural merit is a supernatural act accomplished through love of God, an act which, according to a divine ordination, gives one the right to a supernatural reward. Thus it is that every Christian in the state of grace merits by his acts of love of God and of his neighbor, and by the exercise of all the virtues duly inspired by charity, an increase in sanctifying grace and eternal life. This is condign merit properly so-called. It is in this sense that St. Paul says: "For that which is at present momentary and light of our tribulation, worketh for us above measure exceedingly an eternal weight of glory." [18] And so it was that Jesus, when He preached the beatitudes, proclaimed the merits of the just and their reward: "Blessed are the poor in spirit: for theirs is the kingdom of heaven. . . . Blessed are they that hunger and thirst after justice: for they shall have their fill. . . . Blessed are the clean of heart: for they shall see God. . . .

[18] II Cor. 4:17.

Blessed are they that suffer persecution for justice' sake: for theirs is the kingdom of heaven. . . . Be glad and rejoice, for your reward is very great in heaven." [14]

Such is the grandeur of supernatural merit correctly understood. In addition to this, from congruous merit, based not on justice or on a promise but on God's friendship, a just man can obtain the conversion of a friend, a holy Christian mother like Monica can win the conversion of her son.

What is the source of the immense value of supernatural merit? Let us delve into the secret recesses of our souls where our acts of love of God and of our neighbor are formed. Then by degrees we shall be able to rise to the contemplation of Christ's merits, the eminent source of our own.

What are the conditions necessary to make an act supernaturally meritorious, so that it will give us a right to a supernatural reward? The conditions of supernatural merit in the true sense of the word are generally considered to be as follows: It must be a free act, proceeding from charity, performed during one's earthly life, for which God has promised a reward. The meritorious act must be free, proceeding from free choice.[15] The soul must freely give of its own and offer it up to God.

The second condition of a supernaturally meritorious act is that it proceed from charity, which presupposes the state of grace. The merit and the reward must be proportionate. Merit of the natural order can obtain a reward of the same order, but not a supernatural reward. Nor would faith and hope suffice. There must be charity too, as St. Paul tells us: "And if I should have prophecy . . . and if I should have all faith, so that I could remove mountains, and have not charity, I am nothing." [16] Indeed, without charity our will remains the slave of sin and is turned away from God's will and toward sensu-

---

[14] Matt. 5:3–12.

[15] This point has been defined in contradiction to the Jansenists. Cf. Denzinger, no. 1094: The third condemned proposition of Jansenius: "Ad merendum et demerendum in statu naturae lapsae non requiritur in homine libertas a necessitate, sed sufficit libertas a coactione." *Libertas a coactione* is pure spontaneity, such as exists even in animals, whereas *libertas a necessitate*, or free will, is the principle of a choice that is not necessary.

[16] I Cor. 13:2.

ality or pride. When our souls are deprived of sanctifying grace and charity, they do not live the supernatural life. How then can they produce supernatural fruit? On the contrary, charity calls forth, inspires, and vivifies all the other virtues; and the more charity increases the more merit grows.

The supernatural value of meritorious acts, whether produced immediately by charity or by the virtues which charity inspires, increases with the love of God of which these acts are a sign. It is like offering twice the price of something that is offered for sale. Thus the Blessed Virgin merited more by easy little acts than we do by difficult ones, for there was more love of God and of souls in one of her smiles to a poor old man than there is in our most generous efforts. The meritorious act must, therefore, proceed from charity, that is, it must possess supernatural goodness or be accomplished through love of God.

The third condition of a meritorious act is that it be accomplished during one's earthly life or in the state of passage toward eternity. In heaven we shall no longer merit, but shall enjoy our reward. Nor do we merit in purgatory, for there we are merely purified.

Finally, the fourth condition of merit is that God should have promised a reward for the act which we offer up to Him. Thus He has promised that the just who perform acts of charity will be given an increase of this virtue as well as of the other infused virtues, the gifts of the Holy Ghost, and also eternal life if they die in the state of grace.

These are the conditions of merit: It must derive from a free act, proceeding from charity, performed during one's earthly life, and it must be an act for which God has promised a reward. This being so, what is the value of Christ's merits?

Do Christ's Merits Have Infinite Value in Themselves, Intrinsically, or Solely through God's Acceptance of Them?

Christ's free acts, performed during His life on earth and proceeding from His love of God and of souls, had immense value by the very reason of His eminent charity, which surpassed that of all the angels and saints taken together, since He had received the plenitude of created grace. Yet this eminent charity of Jesus' soul remained a created thing which could not give to His meritorious acts a truly infinite value.

Christ's merits derive their absolutely exceptional value especially from the fact that they were the human acts of a divine person, of infinite dignity. "The blood of Jesus Christ His [God's] Son cleanseth us from all sin," [17] St. John tells us, because it is the blood of the Son of God shed through love of us, for which God has promised this reward, namely, the justification and salvation of all who believe in Christ and who follow Him.

However, one group of theologians, the Scotists, has maintained that Christ's acts of love did not possess in themselves intrinsically an infinite meritorious and satisfactory value, by reason of the divine person of the Word. They held that, on the contrary, it was fitting that these acts be extrinsically accepted by God for our salvation.

Nearly all theologians, on the other hand, admit that the smallest of our Savior's acts of love possesses in itself, or intrinsically, an infinite value by reason of the divine person of the Word made flesh. These acts are called theandric or divine-human, because they are the human acts of a soul personally united to the Word, the human acts of the person of the Son of God. Now, the value of a meritorious or satisfactory act depends not only on the nobility of its object but even more upon the dignity of the person who produces it. In this case, the person of the Word is of infinite dignity. It is the Son of God Himself who is offering Himself up for us.

If the gravity of the offense increases in proportion to the dignity of the person offended, the value of the satisfaction and of the merit increases with the dignity of the person who makes satisfaction and who merits. Our Savior's human actions are united to a divine person by an indissoluble bond, as strong as eternity, in a personal union so close that we can truly say: It is God, the Son, who acts, suffers, merits, and makes satisfaction in the human nature that He has taken on to save us. These reparative acts are most intimately united to God. In

[17] I John 1:7.

consequence their infinite value outweighs the infinite gravity of all mortal sins of all men, which can offend God only morally but cannot touch Him in His substantial and intimate reality.

Hence it is clear that the least of Jesus' merits was more pleasing to God than all the sins of mankind taken together displease Him. Similarly but on the much lower, human level, the expressions of love that are most precious to us are those given to us by the persons to whom we are closest. The smallest act of thoughtfulness by one we love dearly is sometimes enough to make us forget great injustices. This doctrine, without any exaggeration, teaches us to value beyond measure the least of our Savior's actions.

The following objection has at times been raised with regard to this teaching: If all our Savior's acts are of infinite value, it seems that they are absolutely equal and hence Jesus' death on the cross was of no greater merit than His childhood acts. Therefore, the reasoning goes, His death adds nothing to His earlier acts since they were already infinite in value. The Cross would thus appear to be superfluous.

This conclusion, which is so contrary to the Christian approach, results from confused thinking. It can easily be refuted by saying: All Jesus' acts, the least as well as the most heroic, have the same personal value deriving from the union of His humanity with the Word; however, these acts do not have the same objective value, which relates to the object and to the circumstances of these acts. In fact, there is a subordination in the different objects of the virtues. Thus the supreme acts of the Passion which had such a lofty object, such exceptional and painful circumstances, surpassed His preceding acts in objective value, added to the treasure already amassed, filled to overflowing Christ's merits and satisfactions, because these acts represented the ultimate in sacrifice, suffering, and love.

Nothing is superfluous to the love seeking to glorify God to the highest possible degree and to manifest itself to souls in an irresistible manner. Finally, Jesus offered His first acts of love up to His Father not separately but as the beginning of His sacrifice which was to be accomplished in its plenitude on the cross. From the first moment He entered the world He offered up His life *usque ad mortem, mortem autem crucis.* This is what each Christian must do after Christ's example, and especially every religious who professes to live in obedience, chastity, and poverty until death.

Such was the value of Christ's merit. It is a spiritual wellspring from which every human soul can slake its thirst, without ever exhausting its flow. "Where sin abounded, grace did more abound." [18]

What Did Our Lord Merit for Himself and for Us?

He merited for Himself neither the Incarnation nor habitual grace nor the essential glory of His soul, for these gifts are anterior to His merit. These gifts precede His merit and are, as it were, its root. Meritorious acts presuppose grace, charity, and a supernatural knowledge, which in Christ was not faith but the vision of God.

Are we to infer, then, that Jesus merited nothing for Himself? Not at all. He merited His glorious resurrection, His ascension, the exaltation of His name, the expansion of the Church, and the gratitude and love of the faithful. He could have claimed all these things by right of birth, but He chose to obtain them by right of conquest. That is why He said to the disciples of Emmaus: "Ought not Christ to have suffered these things, and so to enter into His glory?" [19] And St. Paul added: "He humbled Himself, becoming obedient unto death, even to the death of the cross. For which cause God also hath exalted Him, and hath given Him a name which is above all names: that in the name of Jesus every knee should bow, of those that are in heaven, on earth, and under the earth: and that every tongue should confess that the Lord Jesus Christ is in the glory of God the Father." [20] Jesus was crowned king of glory only after He had been crowned with thorns. Satan's pride is far more deeply hurt to have been thus vanquished by the humility of our Savior and of the Virgin Mary than to have been immediately crushed by divine Omnipotence, as St. Louis-Marie de Montfort tells us. Our Savior has merited that the power of His name and of the sign of the cross should rout the evil one and deliver souls.

For us Jesus has merited the life of grace and that of eternity, that

[18] Rom. 5:20.   [19] Luke 24:26.   [20] Phil. 2:8–11.

is, all the supernatural aids which lead souls to be converted, to persevere, and to attain their ultimate destiny. "Of His fullness we all have received," St. John tells us.[21] Jesus Himself said: "I am the way, . . . and the life." [22] "If any man thirst, let him come to Me and drink. He that believeth in Me, as the Scripture saith, 'Out of his belly shall flow rivers of living water.' " [23] "He that eateth My flesh, and drinketh My blood, hath everlasting life: and I will raise him up in the last day." [24] Our Savior has merited for us all the effects of predestination, and He could thus say: "My sheep hear My voice: and I know them, and they follow Me. And I give them life everlasting; and they shall not perish forever, and no man shall pluck them out of My hand. That which My Father hath given Me, is greater than all: and no one can snatch them out of the hand of My Father. I and the Father are one." [25]

Jesus merited these great graces for us not merely through a merit of fittingness, as did our Blessed Lady, but in strict justice inasmuch as He was the Word made flesh and therefore the head of humanity. By reason of His divine personality His merits were of infinite value, and because He was head of humanity He could communicate these merits to us just as the head of the human body transmits nervous impulses to the limbs. Thus Jesus merited for every one of us in the same manner as each just man merits for himself. And as St. Peter, enlightened by the grace of Pentecost, told the Jews: "This is the stone which was rejected by you the builders, which is become the head of the corner. Neither is there salvation in any other. For there is no other name under heaven given to men, whereby we must be saved." [26]

The Passion, which merited the salvation of all men, does in fact save all who do not resist Christ's grace. It makes available even to the most debased pagans graces of light, of attraction, and strength. If these men do not resist these graces, they will be led from grace to grace until they attain faith, justification, and salvation. The entire human race was consecrated to the Sacred Heart by Leo XIII at the opening of the twentieth century, so that it might be made more docile

---

[21] John 1:16.   [22] Ibid., 14:6.   [23] Ibid., 7:37.
[24] Ibid., 6:55.   [25] Ibid., 10:27–30.   [26] Acts 4:11 f.

to these graces of light and attraction. The infidel child who after reaching the full age of reason chooses the path of goodness and turns away from evil does so only through Christ's grace.[27]

In evangelized society, in the Church, the Passion makes grace continually available to us through the sacraments—baptism, confirmation, absolution, the Eucharist, extreme unction; it sanctifies the home by the grace of the sacrament of matrimony; it molds the priestly soul by the grace of the sacrament of holy orders. Apart from the sacraments, our Savior sustains us by countless interior inspirations and other helps which inspire us to make good resolutions and confirm us in them. Having once merited these graces for us on the cross, the sacred humanity of our Lord, being the instrument ever united to His divinity, communicates these graces to us with each passing day.[28]

Unbelievers sometimes object: Well, if Christ's merits were infinite, then our own would be superfluous. The reply to this is clear. As the First Cause, far from making secondary causes superfluous, communicates to them the dignity of causality,[29] as God the Author of life creates living beings whereas a sculptor can produce only lifeless works, so does our Savior by His own merits call ours into being and make us work at our own salvation and that of our neighbor. He does not save free beings against their will. We must allow ourselves to be saved by our Savior and we must not resist Him. And precisely because His merits are infinite, He has the power to make us merit with Him and to participate in His redemptive action and to save other souls with Him, through Him, and in Him. Thus it is that He lives again to a certain extent in the saints, and through them proves to the world that He is eternal.

Let us always—and particularly in hours of sadness and temptation—place our trust in the infinite merits of Christ, as does the Church in closing all her prayers with the words, "Through Jesus Christ our Lord." Like the prodigal son and the repentant good thief, even the souls that have gone farthest astray must remember to rely upon Christ's merits. A case in point is that of the penitent who, after confessing his sins for the first time in forty years, heard the priest

---

[27] Cf. St. Thomas, Ia IIae, q. 89, a. 6.   [28] Ibid., IIIa, q. 62, a. 5.
[29] Ibid., Ia, q. 105, a. 5.

ask: "Well, what good have you done?" He answered: "I have kept my faith in the infinite value of Christ's merits, and that is why I have come to confess my sins." Through his faith in Christ this man had touched the depths of God.

Likewise a sorely troubled soul of our acquaintance at times heard our Lord say to her in moments of great darkness from which others seemed to find rays of light: "Your poverty is extreme. But fear not: though you are poor, I am rich, and My riches suffice for you. What could you give Me? Do I not place within you the good I wish to see there? For your part, walk in My presence, for I never leave you." This shows us how closely the mystery of Christ is bound up with the mystery of our own destinies.

❋ XXII ❋

THE LAST SUPPER AND THE EUCHARISTIC HEART OF JESUS

IN REPORTING the events of the Last Supper so as to complete the record presented in the first three Gospels,[1] St. John wrote as follows: "Jesus knowing that His hour was come, that He should pass out of this world to the Father: having loved His own who were in the world, He loved them unto the end." [2] A father who is about to die wishes to leave to his children a supreme proof of his love for them. Often such a father cannot find words to express his love and he remains silent with a silence that is more eloquent than speech. When Jesus was about to die He found not only the words to express His meaning but also the words which would make His meaning a reality, the words of transubstantiation. He gave us the Eucharist as a testament, and in this sacrament He left to us His own divine Person.

The Gift of Self, an Expression of Love

The greatest proof of love is the perfect gift of self. Generosity is essentially communicative, goodness is naturally self-diffusive. St. Thomas goes so far as to say: "It belongs to the essence of goodness to communicate itself to others. . . . Hence it belongs to the essence of the highest good to communicate itself in the highest manner to the creature." [3]

Thus does the sun shed forth light and warmth, thus do adult animals and plants give life to others each after their kind. So too

[1] Cf. Matt. 26:26–29; Mark 14:22–25; Luke 22:15, 20; I Cor. 11:23.

[2] John 13:1.

[3] *Summa*, IIIa, q. 1, a. 1. Also: "Secundum diversitatem naturarum, diversus emanationis modus invenitur in rebus, et quanto aliqua natura est altior, tanto id quod ex ea emanat magis est intimum" (*Contra Gentes*, Bk. IV, chap. 11, initio).

does a great artist conceive and produce his masterpieces, so do the scientist and the scholar communicate their intuitions and discoveries, and share their spirit with their disciples. In the same manner the virtuous man inspires others to virtue, and the apostle, passionately in love with goodness, gives the best of himself to the souls of his fellow men, to lead them to God. Goodness tends essentially to communicate itself to others, and the more perfect a being is the more intimately and abundantly he gives himself.

He who is the sovereign Good, the fullness of being, communicates Himself as fully and intimately as possible by the eternal generation of the Word and by the spiration of the Spirit of love, as revelation teaches us. The Father, in begetting the Son, not only communicates to Him a participation in His nature, His intelligence, and His love, but He communicates to the Son the totality of His indivisible nature, without multiplying it in any respect. The Father gives to the Son to be "God of God, light of light, true God of true God," and the Father and the Son together communicate to the Spirit of love who proceeds from them this same indivisible divine nature and these infinite perfections. Goodness is naturally self-diffusive, and the more perfect it is the more fully and intimately it gives itself.

By virtue of this principle, we have seen [4] that it was fitting that God should not be content merely to create us, and to give us existence, life, intelligence, sanctifying grace, and a participation in His nature. Indeed, it was fitting that God should give Himself to us in person through the incarnation of the Word.[5]

Even after the fall of the first man, God could have willed to re-

---

[4] Cf. *supra,* chap. 6.

[5] IIIa, q. 1, a. 1: "Whether It Was Fitting That God Should Become Incarnate?" (This is the question of the possibility and the fittingness of the Incarnation, rather than the question of its motives, which are analyzed in articles 2 and 3.) St. Thomas answers: "To each thing, that is befitting which belongs to it by reason of its very nature; thus, to reason befits man, since this belongs to him because he is of a rational nature. But the very nature of God is goodness. . . . But it belongs to the essence of goodness to communicate itself to others. . . . Hence it belongs to the essence of the highest good to communicate itself in the highest manner to the creature, and this is brought about chiefly by His so joining created nature to Himself that one Person is made up of these three—the Word, a soul and flesh, as Augustine says (*De Trin.,* xiii). Hence it is manifest that it was fitting that God should become incarnate."

deem us in some other manner,[6] for example, by sending us a prophet who would have made known to us the conditions of forgiveness. But He has done infinitely more; He has willed to give us His own Son in person as our Redeemer. "God so loved the world, as to give His only-begotten Son." [7]

Jesus, priest for all eternity and the Savior of humanity, has also for His part willed to give Himself to us perfectly throughout His life on earth, particularly at the Last Supper and on Calvary. He continues to give Himself to us each day through the Mass and Holy Communion. There can be no greater example of the perfect gift of self than these riches of the priestly and Eucharistic heart of our Lord Jesus Christ. Nor can anything do more to inspire the particular act of thanksgiving which is due to our Lord for having instituted the Eucharist and the priesthood.

The Eucharist should produce in each of us the same effect as the Incarnation produced with regard to humanity in general. For it is through the Eucharist that Jesus gives Himself to each of us.[8]

The Eucharistic Heart of Jesus and the Gift of Self in the Institution of the Eucharist

As God gives His entire nature in the eternal generation of the Word and the spiration of the Holy Ghost, as God willed to give Himself in person in the incarnation of the Word, so Jesus has wished to give Himself in person in the Eucharist. And His priestly heart is a Eucharistic heart for the very reason that it gave us the Eucharist, just as pure air is said to be healthful because it is health-giving.

Our Lord might well have been content to institute a sacrament which was a sign of grace like baptism and confirmation. He has chosen to give us a sacrament which contains not only grace but the Author of grace Himself.

[6] Cf. St. Thomas, IIIa, q. 1, a. 2: "God of His omnipotent power could have restored human nature in many other ways." [7] John 3:16.

[8] Cf. St. Thomas, IIIa, q. 79, a. 1: "Just as by coming into the world, He [Christ] visibly bestowed the life of grace upon the world, . . . so also, by coming sacramentally into man, causes the life of grace."

The Eucharist is thus the most perfect of the sacraments, superior even to holy orders.[9] And it is with a view to the Eucharistic consecration that Jesus instituted the priesthood simultaneously with the Eucharist.[10]

True and generous love, by which we wish others well and do them good, leads us to bend down toward them if they are below us. It inspires us to unite ourselves to them in a perfect union of thought, desire, and will, to devote ourselves to them, to sacrifice ourselves if necessary to make them better, and to encourage them to reach out beyond themselves and attain their destiny.

When our Lord was about to deprive us of His sensible presence, He wished to leave Himself to us in person under the Eucharistic veils. Loving us as He did, He could not bend down any lower toward us, toward the lowliest, the poorest and most wretched. There was no way by which He could unite Himself or give Himself more completely to each of us.

There are times when we yearn for the real presence of loved ones who are no more. The Eucharistic heart of the Savior has given us the real presence of His body, His blood, His soul, and His divinity. Everywhere on earth wherever there is a consecrated host in a tabernacle, even in the most far-flung missions, He remains with us, the sweet companion of our exile. He is in each tabernacle, "patiently waiting for us, eager to grant us favors, yearning for our prayers." He is brought even to repentant criminals about to meet their end.

The Eucharistic heart of Jesus has given us the Eucharist as a sacrifice, in order to perpetuate in substance the sacrifice of the Cross

[9] Cf. St. Thomas, IIIa, q. 65, a. 3 : "The sacrament of the Eucharist is the greatest of all the sacraments." The sacrament of the Eucharist is the most perfect of all because it contains not only grace but the Author of grace Himself. And the sacrament of holy orders owes its greatness to the fact that it is ordained to the consecration of the Eucharist. Cf. *ibid.*, ad 3.

[10] The expression "Eucharistic heart" is, in consequence, superior to the expression "priestly heart." The latter is included in the former. For when Jesus gave us the Eucharist He instituted the priesthood. Moreover, it is permissible to call even the heart of Christ's minister a priestly heart. For instance, we speak of the priestly heart of the Curé of Ars, whereas the expression "Eucharistic heart" can be applied only to the heart which has given us the Eucharist.

on our altars until the end of the world and to apply its fruits to us. And at the Holy Sacrifice of the Mass, our Lord who is the principal Priest continues to offer Himself up for us.

Christ "hath an everlasting priesthood, whereby He is able . . . always living to make intercession for us." [11] He does so particularly at the Holy Sacrifice of the Mass where, according to the Council of Trent, it is the same Priest who continues to offer Himself up through His ministers in an unbloody manner, having once offered Himself up in bloody sacrifice on the cross.[12]

This interior oblation, ever alive in the heart of Christ, is as it were the soul of the Holy Sacrifice of the Mass and gives it its infinite value. Jesus Christ also continues to offer up to His Father our supplications, our reparations, and our thanksgivings. But especially it is always the same infinitely pure victim which is offered up, the body of the crucified Savior, and His precious blood sacramentally shed on the altar so that it may continue to wipe away the sins of the world.

The Eucharistic heart of Jesus in giving us the Eucharistic sacrifice has also given us the priesthood. Early in His ministry He said to His apostles: "Come after Me, and I will make you to become fishers of men." [13] On the night of the Last Supper He told them: "You have not chosen Me: but I have chosen you; and have appointed you, that you should go, and should bring forth fruit; and your fruit should remain." [14] Then He gave them the power to offer up the Eucharistic sacrifice when He said: "This is My body, which is given for you. Do this for a commemoration of Me." [15] With these words He gave them the power of the holy consecration which continually renews the sacrament of love.[16] The Eucharist, sacrament and sacrifice, cannot in truth be perpetuated without the priesthood. That is why for nearly two thousand years the grace of the Savior has brought into being and

[11] Heb. 7:24 f.
[12] Cf. *Conc. Trid.*, Sess. XXII, chap. 2: "Una enim eadem est hostia, idem nunc offerens sacerdotum ministerio, qui se ipsum tunc in cruce obtulit, sola offerendi ratione diversa. Cujus quidem oblationis (cruentae inquam) fructus per hanc incruentam uberime percipiuntur."   [13] Mark 1:17.   [14] John 15:16.   [15] Luke 22:19.
[16] The Divine Office of the Eucharistic Heart emphasizes clearly these different but closely intertwined manifestations of Christ's love for us.

to fruition generation after generation of priestly vocations. And this will continue until the end of the world.

Finally, the Eucharistic heart of Jesus has given itself to us in Holy Communion. Our Savior gives Himself to us as food not so that we will assimilate Him to ourselves, but so that we may become more and more like Him, ever more vivified and sanctified by Him, incorporated into Him. One day He said to St. Catherine of Siena: "I take thy heart from thee and give thee Mine." This is a sensible symbol of what occurs spiritually in a fervent Communion. Our hearts die to their narrowness and selfishness and self-love, dilating and becoming like the heart of Jesus in purity, strength, and generosity. On another occasion, our Lord granted to this saint the grace of drinking deeply from the wound in His heart. This, too, is a symbol of a fervent Communion in which the soul drinks spiritually, so to speak, from the heart of Jesus, from this "source of new graces," "the sweet refuge of the hidden life," "the master of the secrets of divine union," "the heart of Him who sleeps but is ever watchful."

St. Paul had said: "The chalice of benediction, which we bless, is it not the Communion of the blood of Christ? And the bread, which we break, is it not the partaking of the body of the Lord?" [17] And as St. Thomas remarked, when the priest receives the precious blood in Communion he does so for himself and for the faithful also.[18]

The Eucharistic Heart of Jesus and the Daily and Ceaseless Gift of Himself

Lastly, Jesus again and again, day after day, gives us the Eucharist as sacrament and sacrifice. He could have willed that the Mass be celebrated only once or twice a year in certain sanctuaries to which men would travel from afar. Yet the Holy Sacrifice is celebrated perpetually every minute of the day, over the whole surface of the earth, wherever the sun rises. It is the unceasing manifestation of Christ's

---

[17] I Cor. 10:16.

[18] Cf. St. Thomas, IIIa, q. 80, a. 12 ad 3: "The body can be received by the people without the blood: nor is this detrimental to the sacrament, because the priest both offers and consumes the blood on behalf of all; and Christ is fully contained under either species."

merciful love, answering the spiritual needs of each era and of each soul. "Christ . . . loved the Church, and delivered Himself up for it: that He might sanctify it, cleansing it by the laver of water in the word of life: that He might present it to Himself a glorious Church, not having spot or wrinkle, or any such thing; but that it should be holy and without blemish." [19]

This being so, He grants to His Church, especially through the Mass and Holy Communion, the graces she needs at the various moments of her history. In the catacombs the Mass was a source of ever new graces, and so it was during the great barbarian invasions and during the Middle Ages. And so it is today, giving us the strength to resist the great perils that threaten us, above all the atheistic phalanxes which Communism is pouring out over the world to destroy all religion. Despite the sorrows of the present, the interior life of the Church in our time in its highest aspects is indeed beautiful when viewed from above as God and the angels see it.

All these graces come to us from the Eucharistic heart of Jesus who has given us the Holy Sacrifice of the Mass and Holy Communion, and who is ever giving us His blood sacramentally shed on the altar.

Father Charles de Foucauld had a deep understanding of this truth, as he prayed and died for the conversion of Islam and of Moslem lands. This truth is also understood by those who pray with all their souls and have Masses said for lands ravaged by materialism and Communism. A single drop of our Savior's precious blood can regenerate thousands of souls that have gone astray and have dragged others along with them.[20]

Indeed, it is a truth that we too often forget. This cult of the precious blood of the Savior and deep suffering at the sight of it flowing in vain over rebellious souls can do much to turn the Eucharistic heart of Jesus toward His poor sinners—yes, His poor sinners. They are His, and apostles like St. Paul, St. Francis, St. Dominic, St. Catherine

[19] Eph. 5:25–27.
[20] This is what St. Thomas says in the *Adoro Te:*

"Unclean I am, but cleanse me in Thy blood!
Of which a single drop for sinners spilt,
Can purge the entire world from all its guilt."

of Siena, and so many others loved our Savior enough to strive by His side for the salvation of these souls.

When we think of Christ's love for us, we should suffer agonies at the sight of souls turning away from His heart, from the source of His precious blood. He shed His blood for them all, far removed as they might be from Him, even for the Communist who blasphemes and wishes to extirpate His name from the earth. May our Lord, who does not will the death of the sinner, grant through the Holy Sacrifice of the Mass a new effusion of His heart's blood, as it were, and of the blood from His sacred wounds.

There have been saints who at the moment of the elevation during Mass have seen the precious blood overflow the chalice, spill over the arms of the priest as if it would flow into the sanctuary, and be caught up in gold cups by angels who then carried it over the whole world, particularly to lands where the Gospel was little known. This was a symbol of the graces flowing from the heart of Christ upon the souls of unfortunate pagans. It is for them, too, that He died on the cross.

The practical consequence of this truth is that the Eucharistic heart of Jesus is by no means the object of an affected devotion. It is the supreme model of the perfect gift of self, a gift which in our own lives should become more generous with each passing day. Each new consecration should mark for the celebrant progress in his faith, trust, and love of God and of souls. For the faithful, each Communion should be substantially more fervent than the preceding one, since each Communion should increase the charity in our hearts and make them resemble our Lord's more closely and thus dispose us to receive Him more fervently on the morrow. As a stone gathers momentum in its fall toward the earth which attracts it, so should souls tend toward God with increasing speed as they come closer to Him and are more powerfully attracted to Him.

The Eucharistic heart of Jesus yearns to attract our souls to itself. This heart is often humiliated, abandoned, forgotten, scorned, outraged, and yet it is the heart that loves our hearts, the silent heart that would talk to souls to teach them the value of the hidden life and the value of the ever more generous gift of self.

The Word made flesh came among His own, and "His own received Him not." [21] Blessed are those who receive all that His merciful love deigns to give them and who do not by their resistance reject the graces which should radiate through them upon other less favored souls. Blessed are they who after they have received follow the example of our Lord and give themselves ever more generously by Him, with Him, and in Him.

If there is in the midst of even the most benighted pagans a single soul in the state of grace, a truly fervent and renounced soul such as that of Father Charles de Foucauld, a soul which receives everything that the Eucharistic heart of Christ wishes to give to it, sooner or later the radiation of that soul will inevitably transmit to straying souls something of what it has itself received. It is impossible that the precious blood should not in some measure overflow the chalice at Mass and some day—at least at the moment of death—purify those straying souls who do not resist divine attentions or the actual prevenient graces that inspire their conversion. Let us think now and then of the death of the Moslem, or of the Buddhist, or the Communist in our own town who may have been baptized as a child. Each of them has an immortal soul for which the heart of our Lord gave all its blood.

[21] John 1 :11.

❊ XXIII ❊

THE PEACE OF JESUS DURING HIS PASSION

"My peace I give unto you."
John 14:27

IF WE would delve even deeper into the mystery of the Redemption, we must consider how during the Passion Christ's love united within itself two distinct elements. In His love were united the greatest suffering that any human being ever endured during his life on earth and the most perfect peace that can exist even among the blessed in heaven.

These are two apparently contrary effects of the fullness of grace that our Lord received from the first instant of His life: two effects which are, as it were, the two poles of His interior life upon earth.[1]

The Fullness of Grace
and Redemptive Suffering

As we have seen above,[2] this fullness of grace derives from the uncreated personality of the Word made flesh. It is morally proportioned to His dignity as Son of God and also to His mission as universal Mediator. It is absolute plentitude, both intensive and extensive. And there is every evidence that this fullness of grace inclined our Lord to wish to accomplish as perfectly as possible His mission as Savior, Priest, and Victim. Every servant of God, as can be seen in the lives of the founders of religious orders, is inspired by a special

---

[1] This very lofty idea is the core of a book written in the seventeenth century by Louis Chardon, O.P., *La croix de Jésus*, a book which shows that these apparently contrary effects derive from the fullness of grace enjoyed by the Savior and are participated in to various degrees by the members of His mystical body. [2] Cf. *supra*, chap. 11.

269

grace to accomplish as perfectly as possible the mission which he has received. This grace gives him the spirit of his mission, that is, the manner of seeing, judging, feeling, willing, and acting to accomplish it properly. If this was so with the founders of religious orders such as St. Benedict, St. Dominic, and St. Francis, how much more must it have been true of the Savior!

The fullness of grace that our Lord received from the first moment of His human life awakened in Him an ardent thirst for our salvation and a yearning to offer Himself up as a victim to redeem us. *"Amor meus, pondus meum,"* were the words St. Augustine used: My love is like a weight which pulls me toward the beloved object. Christ's love impelled Him to offer Himself up as a sacrifice to save our souls.

This desire found continual expression in our Savior's sermons, and even before that in His first words: "Did you not know, that I must be about My Father's business?" [3]

"And I, if I be lifted up from the earth, will draw all things to Myself." [4] "I am come to cast fire on the earth: and what will I, but that it be kindled?" [5] "With desire I have desired to eat this pasch with you, before I suffer. . . . This is My body, which is given for you. . . . This is the chalice, the new testament of My blood, which shall be shed for you." [6]

This hunger of our Lord for our salvation, this yearning for the cross, correspond to the very motive of the Incarnation: "Who for us men, and for our salvation, came down from heaven," as we repeat each day at the Credo of the Mass.

This desire found ever more powerful expression as the moment of the Passion approached, which Jesus had called "His hour," the hour that had been set by Providence from all eternity and yet interfered in no respect with His own liberty or that of His executioners.

As the hour of the Passion approached, our Lord's will to die for us found ever more forceful expression. In His discourse after the Last Supper, He said: "That the world may know, that I love the Father: and as the Father hath given Me commandment, so do I: Arise, let us go hence." [7]

[3] Luke 2:49.   [4] John 12:32.   [5] Luke 12:49.
[6] *Ibid.*, 22:15–20.   [7] John 14:31.

At Gethsemane His soul was indeed "sorrowful even unto death," but He chose to experience this sorrow to show that He was truly a man and that we, too, may be allowed to cry out in our hours of sadness. He chose to experience this anguish also so that the holocaust might be perfect; and He said to His Father: "Not as I will, but as Thou wilt." [8] Soon afterward, when Peter sought to defend Him with his sword, He answered: "The chalice which My Father hath given Me, shall I not drink it?" [9] This calls to mind His words before entering Gethsemane: "Greater love than this no man hath, that a man lay down his life for his friends." [10] Here was the effect of the fullness of grace which impelled our Savior to desire to accomplish as perfectly as possible His mission as priest and as victim.

In actual fact, as St. Thomas explains,[11] His suffering was the most intense that can be suffered during man's earthly life. He did not of course endure all possible sufferings, for some torments are the antithesis of others. Death on the cross differs from the sufferings caused by weapons or fire. Yet Jesus experienced every form of physical and mental suffering. He suffered in every part of His body, which was but one great wound after the scourging, and which was made to bleed anew when His clothing was torn off before the crucifixion. All these sufferings were made more intense by the delicacy of His constitution, for His was a body miraculously conceived in the womb of a virgin.

Jesus also experienced all the moral sufferings caused by the straying of His people from the path of salvation, by the priests of the Synagogue who were embittered against Him, by the fact that divine justice was striking Him in our stead. This was the most terrible of His sufferings because it was caused by the greatest of all evils, sin, whose gravity and extent Jesus understood better than anyone else. This suffering was as intense as His love of goodness. It was a suffering from which He sought no alleviation but to which He freely offered Himself up, so that He might feel in our stead that hatred of evil which is the essence of contrition.

It has been objected that the desolation of a sinner who has lost

[8] Matt. 26:39.   [9] John 18:11.   [10] *Ibid.*, 15:13.
[11] IIIa, q.46, a.6, c. and ad 4.

grace, such as Peter's after the denials, seem to be greater than that which Christ suffered. For Jesus at least preserved the joy of His innocence. St. Thomas answers as follows: "Christ grieved . . . over the sins of all others. And this grief in Christ surpassed all grief of every contrite heart, both because it flowed from a greater wisdom [by which He knew better than anyone else the infinite gravity of the offense against God and the multiplicity of men's crimes] and charity, by which the pang of contrition is intensified, and because He grieved at the one time for all sins." [12]

We cannot begin to imagine the suffering Jesus must have experienced at the exact and penetrating view of men's crimes. If St. Catherine of Siena was nauseated at the sight of the state of certain souls, how much must our Lord have suffered! For He saw the concupiscence of the flesh and of the eyes and the pride of life just as we see purulent sores on a diseased body.

He suffered from the sight of sin in proportion to His love for God whom sin offends and in proportion to His love for our souls which sin ravages and kills. And He was not content to look upon these sins with profound sadness. He had taken them upon Himself: "Surely He hath borne our infirmities and carried our sorrows." [18] If Mary standing at the foot of the cross suffered because of sin in proportion to her love for God, for her Son, and for us, what then must Christ's suffering have been! The fullness of grace and charity greatly increased in Him the capacity for suffering from the greatest of all evils, an evil which our selfishness prevents us from grieving over.

Peace in Suffering

In spite of His most intense suffering, Jesus maintained a deep peace during His entire passion.

This is evident from the seven last words that He spoke. One of them, it is true, does appear to be a cry of anguish: "My God, My God, why hast Thou forsaken Me?" [14] Calvin chose to see in it a cry

---

[12] IIIa, q. 46, a. 6 ad 4.   [18] Isa. 53:4.   [14] Matt. 27:46; Mark 15:34.

of despair. But such was not the case at all, as shown by the words of trust and thanksgiving which followed: "It is consummated." [15]

These words, "My God, My God, why hast Thou forsaken Me?" are the first verse of a Messianic psalm which fittingly rose to Christ's lips, for it is a psalm in which Jesus spoke in the name of the sinners whose sins He had taken upon Himself.

Here is what psalm 21 says:

O God, my God, . . . why hast Thou forsaken me? . . .

I shall cry by day, and Thou wilt not hear: and by night. . . .

But Thou dwellest in the holy place, the praise of Israel.

In Thee have our fathers hoped: they have hoped, and Thou hast delivered them.

They cried to Thee, and they were saved: they trusted in Thee, and were not confounded.

But I am a worm, and no man: the reproach of men, and the outcast of the people.

All they that saw me have laughed me to scorn: they have spoken with the lips, and wagged the head.

He hoped in the Lord, let Him deliver him: let Him save him, seeing He delighteth in him.

For Thou art He that hast drawn me out of the womb: . . .

From my mother's womb Thou art my God, depart not from me.

For tribulation is very near: for there is none to help me. . . .

For many dogs have encompassed me: the council of the malignant hath besieged me.

They have dug my hands and feet. They have numbered all my bones. . . .

And upon my vesture they cast lots.

But Thou, O Lord, remove not Thy help to a distance from me; look toward My defense. . . .

I will declare Thy name to my brethren: in the midst of the church will I praise Thee.

Ye that fear the Lord, praise Him: all ye seed of Jacob, glorify Him, . . .

Because He hath not slighted nor despised the supplication of the poor man.

Neither hath He turned away His face from me: and when I cried to Him He heard me.

The poor shall eat and shall be filled: and they shall praise the Lord that seek Him: their hearts shall live forever and ever.

All the ends of the earth shall remember, and shall be converted to the Lord.

And all the kindreds of the Gentiles shall adore in His sight.

[15] John 19:30.

Thus does the psalm which began with a cry of pain: "My God, my God, why hast Thou forsaken me?" end in words of trust and praise. Jesus in His dying moments lived this psalm in its entirety with a depth of experience which we cannot begin to fathom.

As for the remainder of Christ's last words, they are all manifestly words of peace, the most beautiful that a martyr-priest can say. Not only do these words prove that the heart of Jesus was full of profound peace. They also show that His was a radiant peace which He communicated to those around Him, to those whom He strengthened at the very moment He was being crucified for them.

"Father, forgive them, for they know not what they do." [16] This was said for His executioners when they were nailing Him to the cross. The martyrs would repeat these words, and first among them St. Stephen obtained through his prayer the conversion of Saul who was keeping the garments of Stephen's murderers.

There is peace also in the words spoken to the good thief, for they promise him heavenly peace: "This day thou shalt be with Me in paradise." [17] After these words, the good thief's cross was no longer merely a punishment, as was the other thief's. It became a reparation which opened the portals of heaven to him. These words were to be repeated again and again by Christ's ministers entrusted with the duty of preparing condemned men to meet their God.

The words addressed to Mary and to John were also words of peace, pouring a gentle balm on their aching hearts: "Woman, behold thy son." [18] By these words Mary became more than ever the Mother of all men personified by John, and mediator and distributer of all graces. "Behold thy mother." [19] These words of mercy produced in John's soul the most respectful and filial affection for Mary, from whom he would receive so many graces for his apostolic ministry.

After saying the first words of psalm 21, Jesus cried out: "I thirst; . . . it is consummated." [20] He thirsted for souls, but He Himself was bringing to them at that moment the living waters of grace. He had the immense joy of consummating the work of the Redemption. There is more joy in giving than in receiving, and Jesus was giving

[16] Luke 23:34.   [17] Luke 23:43.   [18] *Ibid.*, 19:26.
[19] *Ibid.*, 19:27.   [20] *Ibid.*, 19:28-30.

reconciliation with God, profound peace of soul to all men who would accept it, to all who would place no obstacle in its way.

The last word, "Father, into Thy hands I commend My spirit," [21] is, as it were, the consecration of the sacrifice of the Cross which restores all things and brings upon all souls the outpouring of divine mercy.

How did Jesus preserve this profound and radiant peace in the midst of His torments and intense sufferings? Theologians [22] admit that this is a miracle and a supernatural mystery of the order of grace, resulting from the fact that Jesus was at once *viator et comprehensor*, a wayfarer toward eternity and a comprehensor enjoying the vision of the divine essence. This mysterious union of most profound suffering with the most sublime peace has been explained diversely by various theologians.[23]

St. Thomas gives us the truest explanation, one which in spite of its obscurities is very luminous.[24] "If we take the whole soul as comprising all its faculties, . . . His entire soul did not enjoy fruition

[21] Luke 23:46.

[22] Cf. Salmanticenses, *De incarn.*, disp. 17, dub. 4, no. 47.

[23] Some nominalist theologians like Aureolus in the fourteenth century have said that during His passion Jesus suffered only in the sensible part of His soul which is common to both men and animals.—This is contrary to the doctrine of Scripture and tradition, for Jesus suffered above all from sin, a suffering which like contrition is essentially spiritual and even supernatural, in the sense that it derives from charity, from God's offended love and from love of souls who are being lost.

Other theologians have maintained that on the contrary while Jesus on the Cross continued to enjoy the beatific vision, He did not want to continue to enjoy the happiness which this vision normally causes in the highest reaches of the soul. This is the view taken by Salmeron, Melchior Cano and several others.—This opinion is opposed to that of St. Thomas (IIIa, q.46, a.7, and a.8), and appears to be untenable. For it is inconceivable that a soul should see God face to face, should possess Him through this vision and not experience immense joy in the highest of its faculties.

Still others, like Théophile Raynaud, have said: Supreme beatitude and the depths of sadness are contrary to each other, and yet they have been united miraculously in Jesus. To this contention the answer has been made that a miracle cannot be a consummated contradiction. The first two explanations diminish the mystery, and the last ones make a contradiction of it.

[24] In IIIa, a.46, a.7 and 8, St. Thomas first gives an abstract answer which prepares the ground for the solution. He remarks that if we consider the soul according to its essence which as essence is indivisible, it can be said that Christ's whole soul suffered in each part of His shattered body, and at the same time His whole soul, which was the subject of His superior faculties whose highest parts were beatified, rejoiced. But if we would speak in concrete terms we must consider not only the essence of the soul but its different faculties.

. . . by any overflow of glory, because, since Christ was still upon earth, there was no overflowing of glory from the higher part into the lower." [25]

Only the summit of our Savior's human intellect and will were beatified. Jesus willed very freely to abandon to suffering the less elevated regions of His superior faculties and of His sensibility.[26] In other words, He freely prevented the irradiation of the light of glory on His lower reason and on His sensitive faculties. He did not wish that this light and the joy which derives from it should by their irradiance lessen in any way the moral and physical suffering which He had chosen to bear for our salvation. He who was on several occasions to preserve His martyrs from suffering in the midst of their torments, by granting them abundant graces, chose to yield Himself up completely to suffering, so that He might save us by the most perfect of holocausts.[27]

Christ's peace amid suffering reminds us of a high mountain peak whose summit is bathed in sunlight, while its lower reaches are in the grips of a terrible storm. Thus only the uppermost portion of Christ's superior faculties was free from suffering, because He freely yielded Himself up to suffering without seeking any relief in the vision of the divine essence.

There is undoubtedly a mystery in all this. Yet we can at least get a faint idea of it in the case of a penitent. St. Augustine tells us that the truly contrite penitent rejoices because he grieves over his sins, and the more he grieves the more he rejoices.[28]

Christ's suffering and peace, far from being opposed, harmonize very well. His love of God gave Him peace and made Him suffer at the sight of sin. Love of souls also made Him suffer because of our

---

[25] IIIa, q. 46, a. 8, c. and ad 1.

[26] Cf. St. Thomas, *Compendium theologiae*, chap. 232: "Ratio superior Christi plena Dei visione fruebatur. . . . (Sed Christus) permittebat unicuique inferiorum virium moveri proprio motu, secundum quod ipsum decebat."

[27] Cf. St. Thomas, IIIa, q. 47, a. 1: "Christ . . . could have prevented His Passion and death. Firstly, by holding His enemies in check, so that they would not have been eager to slay Him, or would have been powerless to do so. Secondly, because His spirit had the power of preserving His fleshly nature from the infliction of any injury. . . . Therefore . . . He is said to have laid down His life, or to have died voluntarily."

[28] St. Augustine, *De vera et falsa poenitentia*, chap. 13: "Semper doleat poenitens et de dolore gaudeat." Cf. St. Thomas, IIIa, q. 84, a. 9 ad 2.

transgressions and gave Him joy in our salvation. This thought never left Him. Even on Thabor, He spoke of His passion to Moses and Elias, and immediately after His transfiguration He announced to His disciples what manner of death He would die.[29]

The great lesson to be learned from this mystery is that, following in the Savior's footsteps, each of us must carry his own cross if we would participate in the fruits of His cross. There are many crosses that accomplish nothing for the suffering souls that endure them. Such was the cross of the bad thief. By contrast, in union with our Lord, we must carry our cross with patience and even with gratitude and love. Thus shall we gain little by little a deeper understanding of the mystery of the Redemption, and from it we shall receive the fruits of life that endure for all eternity.

[29] Luke 9:31-44.

❋ XXIV ❋

Jesus, Priest and Victim on the Cross

"Christ . . . hath loved us, and
hath delivered Himself for us,
an oblation and a sacrifice to God
for an odor of sweetness."
Eph. 5:2

WE HAVE spoken of the peace of Christ during His passion. In this sublime contrast we are given a glimpse of the depth of His love. There is another contrast that is quite as remarkable: that of divine strength in weakness. During His passion and on the cross Jesus was at once a broken victim, annihilated as it were for our salvation, and the most powerful of priests by reason of His merit and His intercession.

Divine Strength in Weakness

In the Old Testament we find several examples of this strength in weakness in the most beautiful figures of the Christ to come, particularly in the person of Isaac who carried the wood of his sacrifice and allowed himself to be bound on an altar by his father Abraham, in preparation for the immolation. At that moment a voice from heaven was heard saying to Abraham: "Because thou hast . . . not spared thy only-begotten son for My sake: I will bless thee, and I will multiply thy seed as the stars of heaven, and as the sand that is by the seashore . . . because thou hast obeyed My voice." [1] Isaac's greatness lies in the fact that he obeyed with his father and that he allowed himself to be bound on the altar of sacrifice as a victim to be immolated.

[1] Gen. 22:16–18.

Divine strength in weakness is also apparent in another figure of Christ, indeed one of the most touching: Joseph, sold by his brothers, sold out of jealousy because he had prophetic dreams and because he was especially loved of his father Jacob. Joseph, sold for a few pieces of silver, became the salvation of his brothers when he made himself known to them and said: "I am Joseph. Is my father yet living?" [2] Thus was the Savior persecuted through jealousy, because He had a divine message, and was hated by the priests of the Levitical priesthood which was the figure of His eternal priesthood. Thus was He sold for thirty denarii and became the salvation of us all, of all who believe and hope in Him.

The Lord said to St. Paul: "Power is made perfect in infirmity." [3] And the Apostle himself writes: "We preach Christ crucified, unto the Jews indeed a stumbling block, and unto the Gentiles foolishness: but unto them that are called, both Jews and Greeks, Christ the power of God, and the wisdom of God. For the foolishness of God [Christ crowned with thorns] is wiser than men; and the weakness of God [the crucified Savior] is stronger than men." [4]

This remarkable contrast between the power of Jesus and the oppression He endured constitutes the austere and sublime beauty of His spiritual physiognomy. It is something that escapes the eyes of the world and unfolds itself to the saints as they progress in the path of contemplation. If beauty, which is harmony, derives from unity in diversity, the sublime, which is the extraordinarily beautiful, derives from the most intimate unity in the greatest diversity. It is the reconciliation of two extremes which God alone can harmonize.

This mystery has been completely disfigured by two opposing heresies. In the second century the Docetae were scandalized by the passion of the Savior which they considered unworthy of a God, and they declared that Jesus' sufferings had been only apparent. According to them, Jesus had not really suffered at Gethsemane and on the cross, nor had He been a victim. The painful Passion, they said, had been only a sham. To support this senseless contention, which is con-

[2] *Ibid.*, 45:3.
[3] II Cor. 12:9. In this text, according to the Greek, reference is made to divine power rather than to man's virtue.   [4] I Cor. 1:23–25.

trary to the most soundly established facts, the Docetae maintained that the Word had not taken a real body in Jesus, but only the appearances of a body like a ghost. What errors we are led into when we are scandalized by the Cross!

In contrast to this error, there were other heretics later on, like Calvin, who held that Jesus had suffered so very much on Calvary that He had yielded for a moment to despair, and that He had endured the pains of hell at the moment when He cried out: "My God, My God, why hast Thou forsaken Me?" Calvin seemed to think that Jesus redeemed us more through the intensity of His sufferings than through the infinite value of the love with which He endured them.

Thus error swings from one extreme to the other, because men do not know or choose to ignore the culminating point where apparently contrary truths are reconciled. The doctrine of the Church remains on the lofty levels where the diverse aspects of truth are harmonized. It maintains that Jesus on the cross was the most powerful priest by His oblation and the most annihilated voluntary victim. Far more, it holds that divine power has never manifested itself in such a sublime manner as in the passion of the Savior, for this was the greatest action of His life, the consummation of His mission. There is here an admirable law of the spiritual world, which is continually fulfilled in men's souls. "Power is made perfect in infirmity," saith the Lord.

Let us first consider Jesus as victim: the extent of His immolation. We shall then consider the power of the Savior in the midst of this immolation.

Jesus, Victim.
The Extent of His Immolation

Our Lord willed to experience all the sufferings of body and soul which were fitting to His mission as Redeemer and victim. He chose to go through all our trials, to go to the utmost limits of sacrifice in order to expiate our sins and merit eternal life for us by leaving us the example of the loftiest virtues amid the greatest adversity.

He was a victim in His body: His garments were torn off Him, He was mocked, struck, scourged, until His body was one vast wound, He was crowned with thorns and was spit upon. He was treated like a vile wretch, a murderer was given preference over Him; He was nailed to a cross between two thieves. He was given gall to drink, and He was sneered at as He hung dying.

He was a victim in His heart. The affection of His people was taken from Him, this people who eight days earlier when He triumphantly entered Jerusalem acclaimed Him with shouts of "Hosanna, Son of David!" How His heart must have suffered when He cried out in lament: "Jerusalem, Jerusalem, thou that killest the prophets, and stonest them that are sent unto thee, how often would I have gathered together thy children, as the hen doth gather her chickens under her wings, and thou wouldest not!" [5] The world in its wisdom refuses the exceptional gifts that the Lord sends to it. And in giving expression to this suffering Jesus foresaw all the acts of ingratitude that were to come in the future, some even from souls upon whom He would heap the greatest favors.

He was a victim in His innermost soul, for He suffered most intensely from the sight of sin, from the numberless sins He was to expiate, from the deicide that was to be committed through pride and voluntary blindness. Our Lord's soul was crushed by this spiritual and moral suffering inasmuch as it wounded to the quick His charity, His love of God and of souls. He suffered from sin to a degree that we cannot begin to understand: in the measure of His love for God whom sin offends, in the measure of His love for our souls that sin kills. Stigmatists, such as St. Francis of Assisi and St. Catherine of Siena, who participated in these spiritual sufferings, have told us that they are inexpressible.

Our Savior suffered from the sins of all men not only because He understood their limitless gravity, but also because He had taken them upon Himself to expiate them and because He wished Himself to bear the weight of the divine curse due to sin.

Jesus could not have been more completely a victim. There could be no more absolute immolation. We read in Isaias 53:

[5] Matt. 23:37.

Despised, and the most abject of men, a man of sorrows, and acquainted with infirmity: and His look was as it were hidden and despised, whereupon we esteemed Him not.

Surely He hath borne our infirmities and carried our sorrows: and we have thought Him as it were a leper, and as one struck by God and afflicted.

But He was wounded for our iniquities, He was bruised for our sins: the chastisement of our peace was upon Him, and by His bruises we are healed.

All we like sheep have gone astray, every one hath turned aside into his own way: and the Lord hath laid on Him the iniquity of us all.

Jesus as victim understood to what degree God loves goodness and detests evil. "Love is strong as death, jealousy as hard as hell," says the Canticle of Canticles (8:6). The heart of Jesus, victim for sin, endured these rigorous demands of the love of God. Indeed, as St. Paul says, "Christ Jesus . . . emptied Himself, . . . becoming obedient unto death, even to the death of the cross." [6]

The Fortitude of the Savior in His Immolation

It is in this weakness and this annihilation that the power of the Lord is manifest in its fullness. Jesus was indeed a victim. But He was also a priest, and the oblation of Himself which He offered up was of infinite value. As St. Paul says, "The weakness of God [Christ crucified] is stronger than men. . . . But the foolish things of the world hath God chosen, that He may confound the wise; and the weak things of the world hath God chosen, that He may confound the strong, . . . that no flesh should glory in His sight." [7]

David among the prophets, after announcing, "They have dug My hands and feet," added: "All the ends of the earth shall remember, and shall be converted to the Lord." [8] Likewise in Isaias we read: "And the Lord was pleased to bruise Him in infirmity: if He shall lay down His life for sin, He shall see a long-lived seed, and the will of the Lord shall be prosperous in His hand. . . . He hath borne the sins of many, and hath prayed for the transgressors." [9]

The Savior's teaching had progressively brought to light this great law of the supernatural world. From the start, in the Sermon on the

[6] Phil 2:7 f.   [7] I Cor. 1:25–29.   [8] Ps. 21: 17–28.   [9] Isa. 53:10–12.

Mount, He had announced: "Blessed are they that suffer persecution for justice' sake: for theirs is the kingdom of heaven." [10]

In the parable of the good shepherd He clearly announced His sacrifice: "I am the Good Shepherd. The Good Shepherd giveth His life for His sheep. . . . There shall be one fold and one Shepherd. Therefore doth the Father love Me: because I lay down My life, that I may take it again. No man taketh it away from Me: but I lay it down of Myself, and I have power to take it up again. This commandment have I received of My Father." [11] Again He said: "The Son of man is not come to be ministered unto, but to minister, and to give His life a redemption for many." [12] Also: "And I, if I be lifted up from the earth, will draw all things to Myself. (Now this He said, signifying what death He should die.)" [13] Of the sons of Zebedee He asked: "Can you drink of the chalice that I drink of?" [14]

When He instituted the Holy Eucharist, He said: "This is My body, which is given for you. . . . This is the chalice, the new testament in My blood, which shall be shed for you." [15] "Greater love than this no man hath, that a man lay down his life for his friends." [16] Lastly, the priestly prayer which St. John records in his seventeenth chapter is, as it were, the introit of the bloody Mass of the Cross.

We would expect that the apostles, enlightened by all these words, should have understood that the hour of oppression would be the hour of supreme victory. Yet when armed men led by Judas seized Jesus, the apostles, unable to endure this mystery of the Savior's cruel death, abandoned their Master at the very moment when He was about to consummate His work. At that moment they saw only the human side of things and not what God accomplishes in them.

Yet at the very moment when abuse was heaped upon Him and when He was crushed by the weight of our sins, our Lord displayed supreme dignity and invincible fortitude. It was He who determined the course of events, by making even His enemies and the blind fury of the spirit of evil serve the glory of God, and by making of the

[10] Matt. 5:10.   [11] John 10:11-18.
[12] Matt. 20:28; Mark 10:45; Luke 1:68; 2:38; 21:28.
[13] John 12:32.   [14] Mark 10:38.
[15] Luke 22:19 f.; Matt. 26:26 f.; Mark 14:22-25; I Cor. 11:23-25.
[16] John 15:13.

cross with which He was burdened the great means of salvation. He transformed the greatest obstacles into means.

At the time of His arrest, St. John tells us, He asked the soldiers who were with Judas: "Whom seek ye?" "Jesus of Nazareth." "I am He." [17] And at these words they went backward and fell to the ground, as if struck by an invisible force. A few minutes later He said to Peter, who wished to defend Him with his sword: "Put up thy sword into the scabbard. The chalice which My Father hath given Me, shall I not drink it?" [18]

Before Caiphas, He confessed that He was the Son of God and that He would come to judge the living and the dead.[19] Before Herod, He did not answer the questions of the voluptuous monarch who was eager to witness some prodigy.[20] Before Pilate, when asked if He was king of the Jews, He answered: "My kingdom is not of this world. . . . For this was I born, and for this came I into the world; that I should give testimony to the truth. Every one that is of the truth, heareth My voice." [21]

On Calvary He showed His fortitude by His patience and by His heroic constancy. St. Thomas tells us that the principal act of the virtue of fortitude is to endure tribulation, to stand firm under blows, not to be crushed by adversity.[22] Heroic fortitude, St. Thomas says, is connected with the other virtues and must be accompanied by virtues which may seem the most completely opposite, humility and gentleness. This is what the false martyrs lack. This is the fortitude and gentleness that we see in Jesus when they pierced His hands and His feet and when He prayed for His executioners, saying: "Father, forgive them, for they know not what they do." [23]

Christ's gentleness at such a moment is a manifestation of the most complete mastery of self, utter forgetfulness of self for the salvation of souls. Truly Jesus gave up His life as He had foretold in the parable of the good shepherd: "I lay down My life for My sheep. . . . No man taketh it away from Me: but I lay it down of Myself,

---

[17] John 18:4 f.   [18] *Ibid.*, 18:11.   [19] Matt. 26:64.

[20] Luke 23:9.   [21] John 18:36–38.

[22] IIa IIae, q.123, a.6: "The principal act of fortitude is endurance, that is to stand immovable in the midst of dangers rather than to attack them."   [23] Luke 23:34.

and I have power to lay it down: and . . . to take it up again." [24]

This interior oblation is the soul of the sacrifice of the Cross. The sovereign power of the dying Jesus is also apparent in His words to the good thief: "Amen I say to thee, this day thou shalt be with Me in paradise." [25] The oblation also finds expression in these words: "It is consummated." [26] Finally, as St. Luke reports, "the sun was darkened, and the veil of the temple was rent in the midst. And Jesus crying with a loud voice, said: Father, into Thy hands I commend My spirit. And saying this, He gave up the ghost." [27] These last words were the words of the consecration of the sacrifice of the Cross, the supreme expression of oblation.

At that very moment, St. Matthew tells us, "the earth quaked, and the rocks were rent. And the graves were opened: and many bodies of the saints that had slept arose. . . . Now the centurion and they that were with him watching Jesus, having seen the earthquake, and the things that were done, were sore afraid, saying: Indeed this was the Son of God." [28]

To our limited human reason, Jesus on the cross may appear vanquished. On the contrary He is the all-powerful conqueror over sin and Satan. He is the "Lamb of God who taketh away the sin of the world," as His resurrection was to demonstrate in a visible and striking manner: victory over death, which is the consequence of sin, is the sign of victory over sin.

This admirable contrast of power in immolation is to be found in all souls in whom the image of the Crucified is profoundly imprinted: in Mary, Mother of Sorrows, in the persecuted apostles, who were considered "the refuse of this world." [29]

This should teach us the marvelous fruitfulness of suffering when supernaturally endured in union with the Savior. The apostolate of prayer and suffering fructifies far more than we imagine the apostolate of preaching, teaching, and exterior works. As St. Paul exhorts us, let us be "followers of God, . . . and walk in love, as Christ also hath loved us, and hath delivered Himself for us, an oblation and a sacrifice to God for an odor of sweetness." [30]

[24] John 10:15-18. [25] Luke 23:43. [26] John 19:30. [27] Luke 23:45.
[28] Matt. 27:51-54. [29] I Cor. 4:13. [30] Eph. 5:1 f.

It is clear that our Savior's passion was a true sacrifice, the greatest of all sacrifices, as St. Paul explains at length in his Epistle to the Hebrews (chapters 9 and 10). On the cross, Jesus was at once priest and victim, for He was offering Himself up voluntarily.[31] From the time He prayed at Gethsemane until He expired, all His words and acts were expressions of this voluntary oblation which is, as it were, the soul of this sacrifice of adoration, supplication, reparation, and thanksgiving: *"Consummatum est."*

All the sacrifices of the Old Law, from that of Abraham preparing to immolate his son Isaac until the sacrifice of the paschal lamb, were figures of the sacrifice on Calvary, which alone could wipe out sin, for it alone has an infinite value through the person of the priest who offers it up and through the worth of the victim that is offered up.[32]

Jesus on the cross is the victim for sin, by which sin is remitted, the victim of peace which preserves grace, the perfect holocaust which raises us up toward God. This is the holocaust of which all past sacrifices were but the prefigurations.[33] This is the holocaust which will be commemorated and perpetuated in substance until the end of the world in every Mass, at which the Savior will always be the principal priest and the victim truly present on the altar and sacramentally immolated.

St. Paul tells us: "Christ, being come a high priest of the good things to come, . . . neither by the blood of goats or of calves, but by His own blood, entered once into the holies, having obtained eternal redemption." [34] "For Jesus is not entered into the holies made with hands, the patterns of the true: but into heaven itself, that He may appear now in the presence of God for us." [35] The sacrifice of the Cross thus appears as the most perfect of all sacrifices. It is excellent in itself and through itself quite apart from the other sacrifices, and the latter derive their worth wholly from the sacrifice of the Cross.[36]

---

[31] Cf. St. Thomas, IIIa, q. 48, a. 3.   [32] Cf. *ibid.*

[33] *Ibid.*, q. 22, a. 2; Ia IIae, q. 102, a. 3.   [34] Heb. 9:11 f.

[35] *Ibid.*, 9:24.

[36] Of recent years it has been maintained that the sacrifice of the Cross would not be complete without the Last Supper, for it would then lack sufficient and ritualistic expression of the oblation. As a matter of fact the entire Epistle to the Hebrews, and after it tradition and the greatest theologians, notably St. Thomas (IIIa, q. 48, a. 3), point to the

Each day as we assist at the Holy Sacrifice of the Mass let us learn to live by the sacrifice of the Cross which is perpetuated in substance on the altar. Let us especially ask for an understanding of the Cross and for a love of those crosses which Providence has reserved for us from all eternity until we enter heaven. Let us remember this law of Christian life: "Unless the grain of wheat falling into the ground die, itself remaineth alone. But if it die, it bringeth forth much fruit." [37]

Let us often repeat the seven last words of Christ, which are, so to speak, His testament, and let us ask Mary to enable us to understand them: "Father, forgive them, for they know not what they do.—This day thou shalt be with Me in paradise.—Woman, behold thy son. Behold thy mother.—My God, my God, why hast Thou forsaken me?—I thirst.—It is consummated.—Father, into Thy hands I commend My spirit."

Cross, without making reference to the Last Supper, as being the greatest of all sacrifices, and as being excellent in itself and by itself alone. The sacrifice of the Cross is eminently ritualistic, for symbolic reality contains all symbols in an eminent degree, above all when this reality is that of the priest and victim par excellence chosen by God from all eternity. Let us avoid all liturgical formalism here. Symbols have value only in relation to reality expressed through these symbols. Melchisedech has a place in religious history only in relation to Christ. There is a real and complete sacrifice where God and Christ have willed that there should be, where there is interior immolation and oblation manifested by all the words and acts of the victim who offers Himself up. Thus does the Council of Trent (Denzinger, no. 938) speak of the oblation which Christ made of Himself *in ara crucis*, on the altar of the Cross.   [37] John 12:24 f.

❊ XXV ❊

Cʜʀɪsᴛ's Vɪcᴛᴏʀʏ ᴏᴠᴇʀ Dᴇᴀᴛʜ

"And if Christ be not risen again,
your faith is vain, for you are
yet in your sins."

I Cor. 15:17

O N PENTECOST, as the Acts of the Apostles record, Peter, enlightened and strengthened by the Holy Ghost, said to the
Jews: "Jesus of Nazareth . . . being delivered up, by the determinate counsel and foreknowledge of God, you by the hands of wicked
men have crucified and slain. Whom God hath raised up, having
loosed the sorrows of hell, as it was impossible that He should
be holden by it." [1] On the following days Peter repeated it: "The
Author of life you killed, whom God hath raised from the dead,
of which we are witnesses." [2] "Neither is there salvation in any
other." [3]

Thus the Resurrection appears to Peter and to the other apostles
as the definitive confirmation of our faith in Christ. And remarkably
enough, the great adversaries of our Lord had anticipated this. Without knowing it, they served the designs of Providence in a most as-
tounding manner. Just as Caiphas the high priest had said during the
Passion: "It is expedient that one man should die for the people," [4]
so, as St. Matthew reports,[5] the chief priests and the Pharisees remembered that Jesus had said: "After three days I will rise again." Thereupon they "made the sepulcher sure, sealing the stone, and setting
guards." [6] It was these guards, the soldiers, who were struck with ter-
ror at the moment of the Resurrection, at the sight of the angel from

[1] Acts 2:22–24. [2] *Ibid.*, 3:15. [3] *Ibid.*, 4:12.
[4] John 18:14; 11:51. [5] Matt. 27:62–66. [6] *Ibid.*, 27:66.

288

heaven,[7] and it was they who told the priests and Pharisees what had happened.[8]

The resurrection of the Savior was the decisive sign of His divine mission. Peter and the apostles never tired of affirming it. St. Paul said the same thing in his First Epistle to the Corinthians, about the year 55: "For I delivered unto you first of all, which I also received: how that Christ died for our sins, according to the Scriptures: and that He was buried, and that He rose again the third day, according to the Scriptures: and that He was seen by Cephas; and after that by the eleven. Then was He seen by more than five hundred brethren at once: of whom many remain until this present, and some are fallen asleep. After that, He was seen by James, then by all the apostles. And last of all, He was seen also by me, as by one born out of due time. . . . For whether I, or they, so we preach, and so you have believed." [9] Then Paul adds: "If Christ be not risen again, your faith is vain, . . . for you are yet in your sins." [10]

What does Paul mean by these last words? He means that if this is the case, our faith in the risen Christ, which faith is the basis of justification,[11] is vain and false and consequently our sins have not been forgiven.

He also means, as St. John Chrysostom remarks: If Christ is not risen, we have no guaranty that God has accepted His death as redemption. Thus nothing has been accomplished, and the work of salvation is yet to be done.[12]

To help us grasp the inner meaning of these words of St. Paul, as understood by St. John Chrysostom and many other interpreters after him, let us first bear in mind what our faith in Christ must be if we are to be saved. We shall then understand how His victory over death is the great sign of His victory over sin and over the spirit of evil.

---

[7] *Ibid.*, 28:5. [8] *Ibid.*, 28:11. [9] I Cor. 15:3–11.

[10] *Ibid.*, 15:14–17. [11] Rom. 4:25.

[12] St. John Chrysostom says: "Si mortuus non potest resurgere, neque ablatum est peccatum, neque mors est perempta, nec ablatum est maledictum" (*P.G.*, LXI, 335). Cf. Theophylactus and Ecumenius. The latter writes: "Si deletum esset peccatum, utique mors etiam, quae per ipsum erat, extincta esset." In other words, sin is truly wiped out only if its effect, namely, death, is abolished.

What We Must Believe about
Christ's Victory over Sin

We must first of all believe in the existence of God, the author of grace and supreme rewarder.[13] Next we must believe that Jesus, the Son of God, is the Savior, the "Lamb of God, . . . who taketh away the sin of the world." [14] We must fervently believe in the truth of His words: "Come to Me, all you that labor and are burdened, and I will refresh you." [15] I will refresh your souls by extricating them from sin, by giving them the life of grace, the seed of eternal life.

This act of lively faith should be not only a speculative certainty without influence on our lives, but a deep and perpetual conviction which transforms all we have to do or to suffer each day. This act of faith often remains too feeble within us. If in the midst of our troubles we remain depressed, introverted, it is because we do not have enough faith and confidence in Jesus Christ, our Savior.

The apostles were the first to feel on certain days before Pentecost the weakness of their faith. One day during a storm on Lake Genesareth our Lord said to them: "Why are you fearful, O ye of little faith?" [16] They became even more conscious of their frailty during the Passion. Indeed, they had been enraptured by the sublime teaching of the Master, they had seen Him perform miracles, raise Lazarus from the dead, cast out devils, walk on the water. Three of the apostles had even been present at His transfiguration on Mount Thabor. But they also saw Him sad unto death at Gethsemane, and later they saw Him insulted, scourged, spit upon, and even Peter went astray for a moment to the point of denying three times that he knew Him.

What we must believe and what those at the foot of the cross were called on to believe was that the agonizing Jesus was the Savior of souls precisely because of His agony, far more than He had been through His sermons and His miracles. Agony means combat, and Christ's agony was the great combat against the spirit of evil, a combat in which Jesus was completely victorious.

---

[13] Heb. 11:6: "He that cometh to God must believe that He is, and is a rewarder to them that seek Him."   [14] John 1:29.   [15] Matt. 11:28.   [16] Matt. 8:26; 14:31.

He had said to His disciples after the Last Supper: "Have confidence, I have overcome the world." [17] It was on the cross that He won His definitive victory over the gravest of all evils, the most profound evil in the world, namely, sin and Satan.

At the moment of the *"Consummatum est,"* Mary made the greatest act of faith that was ever made on earth. She did not cease for an instant to believe that her crucified Son was the Savior of all men. Participating in the Virgin's great faith were the holy women near her, also St. John, the good thief, and the centurion. In varying degrees they all believed that the work of salvation was consummated in this annihilation of the Victim chosen from all eternity to carry the burden of our sins in our stead.

But few were those who believed it in that supreme hour. The great majority could not bear the death of Christ: *"Fac ut portem Christi mortem,"* are the words of the *Stabat Mater.*

What it was necessary to believe then and what we must still believe is that the object of derision, regarded as the offscouring of humanity, before whom men wagged their heads mocking, is in reality the strength and the life of souls, the one who has overcome the world. What we must believe is that the hour of darkness and shame, when viewed from above, is also the glorious hour of salvation, the most fruitful of all for souls.

At that hour many disciples—as we can see from the words of the disciples of Emmaus—felt themselves weakening, and this can happen to anyone in the face of persecution and hatred. Yet we must believe that the crucified Christ, who seemed totally defeated, was victorious over sin, that He is the one "who taketh away the sin of the world." This mysterious and hidden victory needed to be confirmed by a tangible and overpowering proof that would rekindle the confidence of the disciples. Divine Providence had decided from all eternity that this would be not merely another miracle, but the resurrection of the Lord. What is the reason for this? Because of the very close relation between sin and death. This is one of the great truths of revelation.

[17] John 16:33.

Christ's Victory over Death,
the Sign of His Victory over Sin

In the Epistle to the Romans, St. Paul reminds us that death entered the world as the consequence of sin and that, as Adam was the representative of the human race for its perdition, so Christ is the representative and head of humanity for its salvation and He is the inexhaustible wellspring of grace: "By one man sin entered into this world and by sin death. . . . If by the offense of one, many died, . . . if by one man's offense death reigned through one: much more they who receive abundance of grace and of the gift and of justice shall reign in life through one, Jesus Christ. . . . Where sin abounded, grace did more abound.[18] St. Paul adds: "The wages of sin is death. But the grace of God, life everlasting in Christ Jesus our Lord." [19]

In the actual plan of Providence if Adam had not sinned, if there had not been this disorder, this ruin, this moral corruption which consists in the separation of the soul from God, then there would not have been this ruin, this physical corruption which consists in the separation of the body from the soul. Death is the consequence and the punishment of sin.

Doubtless man is mortal by nature, as the animals are. Yet, through grace the first man had received for himself and his descendants the privilege of immortality, provided he should remain faithful to God. As Genesis records it, when the Lord placed him in the Garden of Eden to cultivate and preserve it, He said: "Of every tree of paradise thou shalt eat. But of the tree of knowledge of good and evil, thou shalt not eat. For in what day soever thou shalt eat of it, thou shalt die the death." [20]

This was but a gentle testing of man's submission, as Boussuet says,[21] a light brake on the exercise of his free will, to make him realize that he had a master, though a most merciful one.

The devil, on the other hand, told him: "No, you shall not die the

---

[18] Rom. 5:12–20.   [19] *Ibid.*, 6:23.   [20] Gen. 2:16 f.
[21] *Elévations sur les mystères,* 6th week, 7th elevation.

death. For God doth know that in what day soever you shall eat thereof, your eyes shall be opened: and you shall be as gods, knowing good and evil." [22] That is to say: you will be able to rule yourselves, with no need to obey. The devil himself had said: "I will not obey."

What happened immediately after the sin of disobedience and pride? As Scripture records it, "the eyes of them both were opened." [23] They acquired the knowledge of good and evil: not the knowledge that enables one to conduct oneself wisely, but the knowledge that is nothing but the bitter experience of evil committed and of its profound difference from goodness and from the holiness they had just lost for themselves and for their descendants.[24] They realized how true had been the Lord's warning to them and how the devil had lied.

Their souls seemed dead within them. For in tasting evil through their pride, they had lost divine life and God's friendship. Their souls had withdrawn from God who gave them life, and God had withdrawn from them. In consequence they lost mastery over their passions. The emotions, until then subject to right reason and to the will, revolted, just as the will had revolted against God. Finally, inasmuch as the soul had ceased to be under God's dominion, the body ceased to be under the soul's governance. Once the soul had withdrawn from God who vivified it, the body separated from the soul, the source of its life. The soul had been untrue to its divine friendship, and God withdrew from the body its wholly gratuitous privileges of impassibility and immortality. Man had preferred nature to grace, and nature's threadbareness was apparent. The human body, thenceforth subject to natural laws, was exposed to winds and inclement weather, to pain, sickness, and death. Until then man had dominated death. The Lord now said to Adam: "In the sweat of thy face shalt thou eat bread till thou return to the earth, out of which thou was taken: for dust thou art, and into dust thou shalt return." [25] The Church reminds us of this every Ash Wednesday.

---

[22] Gen. 3:4-5.   [23] *Ibid.*, 3:7.

[24] The Council of Trent says: "Adam lost for himself and for us both the holiness and the original justice he had received from God." Denzinger, no. 789.

[25] Gen. 3:19.

Death of the body, the consequence and punishment of sin, was also the symbol of sin. For mortal sin is, as it were, the death of the soul. Loss of the life of grace was followed by the loss of physical life. Horror of death should inspire in us a horror of sin, through which death came into the world.

Immediately after the fall of man the Lord promised a redeemer, when He said to the serpent: "I will put enmities between thee and the woman, and thy seed and her seed: she shall crush thy head." [26]

As all the prophecies specify, Jesus eminently represents the posterity of the woman. On Good Friday He conquered both sin and the devil. But this hidden victory, won by the One who might have seemed to be vanquished but who was really a victim for us, was to be manifested by an overwhelming sign. Here we can see the supernatural logic of these mysteries according to the plan of Providence. It was highly fitting that this great sign should be the resurrection of the Savior. If death is the consequence of sin, it was altogether fitting that Christ's victory over death should be the sign of His victory over sin. In other words, Christ's victory over death, proved by His resurrection, means that He was victorious over sin on the cross.

That is why St. Paul wrote to the Corinthians: "And if Christ be not risen again, your faith is vain: for you are yet in your sins." [27] That is to say: we have no guaranty that God has accepted His death as redemption. And St. Paul added that the Savior's resurrection is the guaranty of our own future resurrection: "For by a man came death: and by a man the resurrection of the dead. And as in Adam all die, so also in Christ all shall be made alive." [28] Jesus had said at Lazarus' tomb: "I am the resurrection and the life: he that believeth in Me, although he be dead, shall live." [29] He had also said three times when He promised the Eucharist: "Now this is the will of the Father who sent Me: that of all that He hath given Me, I should lose nothing; but should raise it up again in the last day." [30] This formula recurs several times in this discourse by our Lord, who was called to save both our bodies and our souls and to make us participate in His glorious life.

---

[26] *Ibid.*, 3:15.
[29] John 11:25.
[27] I Cor. 15:17.
[30] *Ibid.*, 6:39–55.
[28] *Ibid.*, 15:21 f.

That is why St. Paul wrote to the Corinthians: "And the enemy, death, shall be destroyed last." [31] "And when this mortal hath put on immortality, then shall come to pass the saying that is written [Osee 13:14]: Death is swallowed up in victory. O death, where is thy victory? O death, where is thy sting? Now the sting of death is sin. . . . But thanks be to God, who hath given us the victory through our Lord Jesus Christ." [32] Likewise the Apocalypse (1:17) tells us that Jesus appeared to St. John and said to him: "Fear not. I am the First and the Last, and alive, and was dead. And behold I am living forever and ever and have the keys of death and of hell." [33] "Write: These things saith the Holy One. . . . He that openeth and no man shutteth, shutteth and no man openeth." [34]

This is the triumph that the liturgy proclaims on Easter Day in the Sequence *Victimae paschali laudes:*

> The Lamb redeems the sheep;
> And Christ the sinless one,
> Hath to the Father sinners reconciled.

> Together, death and life
> In a strange conflict strove.
> The Prince of life, who died,
> Now lives and reigns.

> We know that Christ indeed
> Has risen from the grave:
> Hail, thou King of Victory,
> Have mercy, Lord, and save. Amen.

Let each of us consider how different the history of humanity would be and how different our own lives would be if there had been no Redemption and no Resurrection.

There is every evidence that the victory of Christ over sin is far superior to His victory over death. The former is the very essence of the mystery of the Redemption. The latter is but a sensible sign of

[31] I Cor. 15:26.   [32] *Ibid.,* 15:54–57.
[33] Apoc. 1:17; cf. Heb. 2:14; Apoc. 20:13; Rom. 14:9.
[34] Apoc. 3:7. Cf. Isa. 22:22.

the inward and invisible supernatural mystery. The symbol derives its value from the grandeur of the thing symbolized. The moment of the "*Consummatum est*" was the greatest and most glorious in the whole history of mankind. But this victory was so mysterious, so hidden, that it escaped even the majority of the apostles themselves, and so it needed to be made manifest by an incontestable sensible sign. This was provided by Christ's triumph over death, the consequence of sin. And that is why we celebrate Easter with great magnificence, to honor the great victory won by our Savior on Good Friday. The act of love of Good Friday, which is commemorated at every Mass, far surpasses the corporeal resurrection which is its manifestation.

The apostles were made to see the light. The Savior's death had left them broken, crushed. They were going to return to their earthly occupations and forget the kingdom of God. From the day they knew of the Resurrection, their faith faltered no more. Given still new light through the grace of Pentecost, they scattered over the earth to preach the good tidings; and following their Master's example, they preached His gospel until they were martyred. In the midst of their torments they put all their trust in the glorious Christ, as St. Stephen had done before them, and they trod the same path as he to eternal happiness.

This mystery of resurrection continues in the Church in a certain sense. Jesus made the Church in His own image, and if He allows her to pass through terrible tribulations, He enables her to rise up again and to be more glorious after the mortal blows of her enemies have been struck. This is what happened during the persecutions of Nero, Diocletian, and Julian the Apostate. From the blood of thousands of martyrs sprang up thousands of Christian Churches.

The Church likewise triumphed over the great Arian and Pelagian heresies, which were the occasion of immortal works by the Greek Fathers and by St. Augustine.

During the early Middle Ages the barbarians spread desolation everywhere, but the Church was able to conquer and convert them. In the thirteenth century the Albigensians tried to revive Manichaeism, but great new religious orders arose, and this thirteenth century became the golden age of theology.

In the fifteenth and sixteenth centuries it might have seemed to some people that the Church would perish under the blows of the pagan Renaissance and of Protestantism. Large areas of Germany and England were lost to Catholicism. However, at that very moment there arose in Europe a galaxy of saintly founders or reformers. The Church was established in India, where St. Francis Xavier renewed the prodigies of the apostolic era. In America, Louis Bertrand and Las Casas proclaimed the charity of Christ, and the true reform was being organized at the Council of Trent.

The French Revolution set out to destroy the Church once more. Priests were massacred, religious orders were suppressed, altars were profaned, and the foundations of a new life and a new religion were laid down. But in 1801 the Concordat was signed, the Catholic worship reappeared in the churches. Little by little the dispersed religious orders were re-established, saints like the Curé of Ars called back into being all the vitality of Christianity, and the missions of the Orient, Asia, Africa, and America made astonishing progress.

Thus will it be until the end of time. The mystery of the Savior's resurrection is in a sense reproduced in the Church. The life of the Church is a life that has experienced death and amid the most terrible tribulations finds once again an ever-blossoming youth. This is particularly true of the saints who can say with St. Paul: "I die daily," [35] and who, after experiencing martyrdom of the heart in order to labor for the salvation of souls in union with our Lord, appear more vital than ever and live on in their works that bear fruit for eternity.

Thus is the truth of the Master's words, manifested: "I am the resurrection and the life." [36] "If any man thirst, let him come to Me and drink. . . . Out of his belly shall flow rivers of living water," [37] and "I will raise him up in the last day." [38]

[35] I Cor. 15:31.   [36] John 11:25.   [37] *Ibid.*, 7:37 f.   [38] *Ibid.*, 6:40.

❋ XXVI ❋

THE PRINCIPAL PRIEST OF THE SACRIFICE OF THE MASS

> "Christ . . . always living
> to make intercession for us."
> Heb. 7:25

AFTER His resurrection and ascension, our Savior, who is a priest forever,[1] did not cease to exercise the principal act of His priesthood, and He does this especially through the Holy Sacrifice of the Mass. The Mass is a sacramental sacrifice substantially perpetuating in an unbloody manner the sacrifice of the Cross, of which it is a memorial; and it applies to us the fruits of the sacrifice of the Cross. Such is the doctrine of faith clearly formulated by the Council of Trent.[2]

As the Council explains, the Sacrifice of the Mass is in substance the same as that of the Cross, because it is the same victim, really present on our altars, that is offered up and because it is offered up by the same principal priest.[3] This victim, once nailed to the cross,

---

[1] Ps. 109:4; Heb. 5:6; 7:17.   [2] Sess. XXII, chaps. 1 and 2.

[3] Cf. *Concilium Trid.*, Sess. XXII, chap. 2: "Una enim eademque est hostia, idem nunc offerens sacerdotum ministerio, qui se ipsum tunc in cruce obtulit, sola offerendi ratione diversa. Cujus quidem oblationis (cruentae, inquam) fructus per hanc incruentam uberrime percipiuntur: tantum abest, ut illi per hanc quovis modo derogetur."

St. Thomas had said (IIIa, q. 83, a. 1 ad 1): "As Ambrose says (*ibid.*), there is but one victim, namely that which Christ offered, and which we offer, and not many victims, because Christ was offered but once. . . . For, just as what is offered everywhere is one body, and not many bodies, so also is it but one sacrifice." *Ibid.*, ad 3: "The principal priest at Mass is Christ, who continues to offer Himself up."

Ibidem, q. 22, a. 3 ad 2: "The Sacrifice which is offered every day in the Church is not distinct from that which Christ Himself offered, but is a commemoration thereof." The Thomists say quite generally: "Missa et sacrificium Crucis sunt idem numerice sacrificium quoad substantiam (ratione hostiae oblatae, principalis offerentis, ac finis), non vero quoad modum *oblationis externae* (quae nunc est incruenta, et olim fuit cruenta)." In philosophical terms, the numerical identity of the victim and of the principal priest is

is now offered under the appearances of bread and wine, and is sacramentally immolated by the separate consecration of the body and blood of our Savior, who is present on the altar in the state of death, as it were. Of course His precious blood is no longer physically separated from His body, but we can say that it is sacramentally shed. For, by virtue of the words of the first consecration, only the body of the Savior is present under the species of bread, and formally by the words of the second consecration it is only the precious blood that is under the species of wine.[4]

The Mass is therefore a real sacrifice, but an unbloody one. It is not merely a symbolic sacrifice or the simple re-enactment of a past sacrifice, for the victim is really present and not merely the image of this victim. There is also the real oblation of the victim and not merely a symbol of this oblation. But in this unbloody sacrifice, the real and bloody immolation of Calvary is merely symbolized and commemorated, and its fruits are applied to us. As the theologians say: the Mass is a true, unbloody sacrifice which represents the bloody immolation of the sacrifice of the Cross.[5] Hence the Mass is far supe-

---

far more important than the diversity of the exterior mode of oblation, just as Christ's humanity remains substantially the same, though it is now not able to suffer. It is therefore necessary to preserve as much as possible the terminology of the Council of Trent. It is eminently philosophical and gives admirable expression to this unique case, without losing sight of its elevation and the way it is superior to time. Thus the substance of this sacrifice is perpetuated rather than renewed.

[4] By concomitance, however, of the fact that the body and blood of the glorified Christ are no longer separated, both are present under each of the two species. But, *vi verborum*, formally the words of the first consecration render Christ's body present, and the words of the second consecration, His blood.

[5] The chief objection raised by the Protestants is this: every genuine sacrifice requires essentially a true immolation of the victim offered up. But at Mass there is no real immolation of the body of Christ, which is now beyond suffering. Therefore the Mass is not a genuine sacrifice, but only the memorial of a past sacrifice.

Several theologians, having apparently forgotten that this difficulty had already been examined by St. Thomas and by St. Albert the Great, accepted the major premise without question and were unable to disprove the minor premise by showing that in the Mass a real immolation of Christ's now impassible body takes place.

According to the doctrine formulated by the Council of Trent, it was necessary to distinguish the major premise: Every true bloody sacrifice requires a real immolation of the victim offered up, yes; but this is not true of an unbloody and sacramental sacrifice. And there can be a real sacrifice without a real immolation, for in sacrifice in general the exterior immolation is *in genere signi*, it is the symbol of the interior immolation of the "contrite and humbled heart," and derives all its worth from the latter. As St. Augustine

rior to the sacrifices of the Old Testament, for even the sacramental immolation of the Word of God made flesh is a far more eloquent expression of reparative adoration due to God than was the bloody immolation of the paschal lamb and of all the victims of the Old Law. Moreover, this sacramental immolation is far more efficacious than all the ancient sacrifices.

The Mass is the great memorial of the Passion. Without it, the sacrifice of the Cross would be forgotten and would be lost in the night of passing time. The Holy Eucharist makes it possible for each succeeding generation to preserve a living, daily, and fruitful memory of the sacrifice of Calvary. It makes each of us participate in this sacrifice, if we so desire, through Holy Communion. Thus the source of all graces remains open until the end of the world, and everyone can come to it to quench his thirst.[6]

In What Sense Jesus Is the Principal Priest
of the Sacrifice of the Mass

The Council of Trent says: "*Una eademque est hostia, idem nunc offerens sacerdotum ministerio, qui seipsum tunc in cruce obtulit, sola*

---

says in a text often cited by St. Thomas: "The visible sacrifice is the sacrament or sacred sign of the invisible sacrifice" (*De civitate Dei*, Bk. X, chap. 5). Cf. St. Thomas, IIa IIae, q. 81, a. 7; q. 85, a. 2, c. and ad 2.

Even in the bloody sacrifice, the exterior immolation of an animal is required, properly speaking, as the sign of interior oblation, adoration, and contrition, without which it has no meaning or value whatever. That is why Cain's sacrifice had no value in God's eyes. "*Sacrificium externum est in genere signi*"; cf. John of St. Thomas, *In IIIam*, q. 83, a. 1.

Since this is the case, we can understand that there can be a real and unbloody sacrifice whose immolation is solely sacramental, without any real separation of the Savior's body and blood. This sacramental immolation, the memorial of the bloody immolation of Calvary, is a sign of reparative adoration that is far more expressive than the bloody immolation of all the victims of the Old Testament. St. Augustine and St. Thomas (IIIa, q. 83, a. 1) certainly demand in the Mass nothing more in the way of immolation than the sacramental immolation. See in the article by St. Thomas that we have just cited (arg. *Sed contra*) the important text of St. Augustine.

[6] Moreover, no religion can subsist without a priesthood and without sacrifice. Sacrifice is even the most perfect act of religion, of worship, an act that is at once exterior and interior. And today anyone who considered the sacramental immolation of Christ inadequate and therefore wished to immolate a lamb or kid in a bloody manner, would be considered senseless. There can be only one victim worthy of Christ's priesthood: Himself. And His sacramental immolation on the altar, although merely sacramental, expresses

offerendi ratione diversa." [7] It is the same victim as on Calvary, it is the same priest who offered Himself on the cross and who now offers Himself through His ministers. The only difference lies in the exterior mode of the oblation: on Calvary it was bloody, and here it is sacramental and unbloody.[8]

Is it enough to say with certain theologians [9] that Christ offers up the Mass virtually and not actually, inasmuch as He originally instituted it by commanding that this sacrifice be offered up until the end of the world? Let us not underrate the actual influence of Christ, our Redeemer.

In fact, if during the Mass we pay attention to the words of the double consecration, we see that the priest pronounces them not in the name of the Church but in the name of Christ Himself, whose minister, instrument, and mouthpiece the priest is. When the priest consecrates the bread he does not say "This is the body of Christ," but "This is My body." It is Christ who speaks through the mouth of His minister.[10] Moreover, it is our Lord Himself who now, just as He

---

love of God and hatred of sin far more perfectly than all the bloody sacrifices of the Old Law. It is in actual fact the sacramental immolation of the Word made flesh.

[7] Sess. XXII, chap. 2.

[8] Attention should be given to the more developed text that was first proposed to the fathers of the Council of Trent and subsequently merely abridged. Cf. *Concilii Tridentini Acta*, Pars V, p. 752: Doctrina de sacrificio missae proposita examinanda patribus die 6 Aug. 1563: Caput I, fine: "Quare nemo negare audeat, missam, quo nomine oblationem hanc exprimere communi consensu consuevit Ecclesia, esse opus bonum; est enim ipsius Christi opus, qui simul est offerens et oblatus, sacerdotum tamen ministerio, qui, dum digne sacrificant, opus certe Deo gratum ideoque meritorium exercent."

Caput 2, fine: "Quemadmodum assiduae atque perpetuae Christi preces, quas ipse apud Patrem pro nobis in caelis advocatus existens fundere creditur, nihil potentissimae illi orationi detrahunt, qua in cruce cum lacrimis Patrem pro nobis oravit et 'exauditus est pro sui reverentia' (Heb. 5:7); ita profecto confitendum est, nihil cruento illi crucis tametsi efficacicissimo derogare."

[9] This is the opinion of Father de la Taille, *Mysterium Fidei*, elucid. 9, p. 103; elucid. 23, pp. 295 ff. It was also taught by Scotus, the Scotists, and by Americus. Cf. *infra*, chap. 27.

[10] St. Thomas even makes the distinction, in the case of a valid Mass celebrated by an unworthy minister, between the words that the priest says in the name of the Church and which retain their value, and the words of the consecration pronounced not in the name of the Church but in Christ's own name. He says (IIIa, q. 82, a. 5): "The priest consecrates this sacrament not by his own power, but as the minister of Christ, in whose person he consecrates this sacrament. But from the fact of being wicked he does not cease to be Christ's minister."

St. Thomas adds (*ibid.*, a. 6): "So far as the Mass itself is concerned, the Mass of the

did originally, gives the words of the consecration their transubstantiative value, capable of converting *hic et nunc* the substance of the bread into that of His body, and the substance of the wine into His blood. The Savior's sacred humanity, St. Thomas tells us,[11] remains the conscious instrument, perpetually united to God, to produce the transubstantiation, the real presence, and all the graces that derive from the Eucharist.

At the same time—and this is the point to stress here—Christ, priest for all eternity, continues to offer Himself up sacramentally in order to apply to us the satisfaction and the merits of His passion. In His human capacity, He is the principal cause of this continuing oblation, which is the chief act of His priesthood, the act to which His ministers ought to unite themselves as instruments, becoming each day more conscious of the grandeur of this sacrifice.

The teaching that Christ continues even now to wish to offer Himself up in each Mass is held by theologians in general. What is more, in his encyclical on Christ the King, His Holiness Pope Pius XI has written: "*Christus sacerdos se pro peccatis hostiam obtulit, perpetuoque se offert.*"[12] The words of the Council of Trent, quoted above, are thereby clarified: "*Idem nunc offerens sacerdotum ministerio, qui seipsum tunc in cruce obtulit. . . .*" Having once offered Himself up in a bloody manner on the cross, Christ continues to offer Himself up in a sacramental and unbloody manner through the ministry of His priests.

It follows that even if the Holy Sacrifice of the Mass is celebrated by a bad priest, the consecration is still pronounced in the name of Christ who thereby converts the substance of the bread into that of

---

wicked priest is not of less value than that of a good priest, because the same sacrifice is offered by both. . . . Again, the prayer put up in the Mass can be considered in two respects, . . . inasmuch as the prayer is said by the priest in the Mass in the place of the entire Church, . . . in this respect the prayer even of the sinful priest is fruitful. . . . On the other hand, his private prayers are not fruitful." *Ibid.*, q. 83, a. 1 ad 3. It is evidently on purpose that St. Thomas made a distinction in the Mass between what is done in the name of Christ and the prayers said in the name of the Church.

[11] Cf. IIIa, q. 62, a. 5.

[12] Denzinger, no. 2195. Encyclical, *Quas primas,* December 11, 1925, *De principatu Christi:* "Cum autem Christus et Ecclesiam Redemptor sanguine suo acquisiverit et Sacerdos se ipse pro peccatis hostiam obtulerit perpetuoque offerat, cui non videatur regium ipsum munus utriusque illius naturam muneris induere ac participare?"

His body, and the sacrifice thus retains its infinite value. Even if the minister were in the state of mortal sin, he would still be the instrument of Christ, provided he intended to perform the act instituted by our Lord.

Our Savior is therefore the principal priest at the Sacrifice of the Mass, not only because He participates in it in a remote manner inasmuch as He instituted the Eucharist both as sacrament and as sacrifice; nor merely inasmuch as He once commanded that this sacrifice be offered up in His name until the end of the world. He is the principal priest because He actually participates in it at the present time in two ways.[18] He continues actually to wish to offer Himself up through the ministry of His priests, as the Council of Trent says. In the second place, in His human capacity He is the conscious and intentional instrument, always united to God, that truly produces the transubstantiation and the graces that derive from the Sacrifice of the Mass.

There is no doubt whatever that when the priest at the altar pronounces in the name of the Savior the words of the double consecration, Jesus actually intends them to be pronounced *hic et nunc,* and He Himself gives them their transubstantiative power. If an act of will on the part of the minister is necessary, this is far truer of the principal priest. Moreover, though the minister may at times be a little distracted at the moment of the consecration, our Savior never is. Our Lord continues to intend to offer Himself up in this manner in order to apply to each passing human generation and to the souls in purgatory the merits of His passion and of His death.

There have been saints who have been privileged to see our Savior Himself, and not merely the celebrant, perform the Holy Sacrifice. This is a special grace that reminded them of something that we must all believe: that Jesus is the principal priest of the sacrifice offered up on the altar. In thus continuing to offer Himself up, Christ does not cease to intercede for us,[14] as we read in the Epistle to the Hebrews, which is entirely devoted to the grandeur of His priesthood. We cannot insist too much on this point.

[18] Cf. Salmanticenses, *De Euch.,* disp. 13, dub. 3, nos. 49 f.
[14] Heb. 7:25.

Christ's Interior Oblation Always Alive in His Heart

It is certain and an article of faith that the sacred soul of the glorious Christ never ceases to see God immediately, to love Him above all else, to love us, and to desire our salvation. It is equally certain that Christ in heaven does not cease to adore God and to offer up to Him a thanksgiving that will never end. This is what the Preface of the Mass declares: "It is truly meet and just, right and availing unto salvation, that we should at all times and in all places give thanks unto Thee, O holy Lord, Father almighty and everlasting God, through Christ our Lord. Through whom the angels praise Thy majesty, the dominions worship it, the powers stand in awe. . . . With whom we pray Thee join our voices also, while we say with lowly praise: Holy, holy, holy, Lord God of hosts. Heaven and earth are full of Thy glory. Hosanna in the highest."

This worship of adoration and of thanksgiving will continue for all eternity. It will always be offered up by Christ and by His mystical body.[15] Likewise, it is said of Christ during the Mass, just before the Pater Noster: "Through Him, and with Him, and in Him, be unto Thee, O God the Father almighty, in the unity of the Holy Ghost, all honor and glory, world without end."

Let us call to mind what St. Thomas said concerning Christ's prayer. Does the Savior, now that He is in heaven, continue not only to adore and give thanks but also to pray for us, as He did on earth? In time of need we recommend ourselves to the prayers of the saints. Can we also recommend ourselves to Christ's prayers? It is certain that He no longer merits or makes satisfaction for us, for He has reached the end of His course. He is no longer *viator*, a wayfarer to-

---

[15] However, according to St. Thomas (IIIa, q. 22, a. 5), this worship of adoration and thanksgiving, which will be "the consummation of the sacrifice of Christ," will no longer be a sacrifice in the true sense of the word after the last Mass. For a sacrifice requires an immolation, at least a sacramental one, of the victim offered up, and this sacramental immolation will cease at the end of the world. Likewise, at the present time, Jesus who is really present in our tabernacles does not cease to adore His Father and to give thanks to Him. But these interior acts are not enough to constitute a sacrifice properly so called. Such a sacrifice exists only during the Mass and not because of the simple fact that the real presence lasts afterward in the consecrated hosts.

ward eternity. But does He not continue to pray so that the merits of His passion may be applied to us? It is certain that the Blessed Virgin, who no longer merits for us, continues to pray that her Son's merits may be applied to us. That is what we ask of her each day in the Hail Mary and in the Litany. Why would not Christ continue to pray for us in this same sense?

In explaining St. Paul's words, "Christ . . . always living to make intercession for us," [16] St. Thomas says: "Christ intercedes for us as our advocate,[17] and He does so in two ways: first, by offering up to His Father His manhood which He took on for us and in which He suffered for us. He also intercedes by expressing to His Father His desire for our salvation." [18] St. Thomas presents the same views in his Commentary on the Epistle to the Romans 8:33–35, in explaining the words: "Who shall accuse against the elect of God? . . . Who is he that shall condemn? Christ Jesus that died: yea that is risen also again, who is at the right hand of God, who also maketh intercession for us. Who then shall separate us from the love of Christ?" With the same thought in mind St. John says, "If any man sin, we have an advocate with the Father, Jesus Christ the just." [19]

In the *Summa theologica*,[20] St. Thomas also says: "Since prayers offered for others proceed from charity, . . . the greater the charity of the saints in heaven, the more they pray for wayfarers; . . . and the more closely they are united to God, the more are their prayers efficacious.[21] For the divine order is such that lower beings receive an overflow of the excellence of the higher, even as the air receives the brightness of the sun. Wherefore it is said of Christ: [22] 'Going to God by His own power . . . to make intercession for us.' " [23]

Among the Thomists, Gonet and the Carmelites of Salamanca have

[16] Heb. 7:25.   [17] I John 2:1.   [18] Cf. St. Thomas, *In Epist. ad Hebr.*, 7:25.
[19] I John 2:1.   [20] IIa IIae, q. 83, a. 11.
[21] If we recommend ourselves to the prayers of living persons whom we consider holy, how much more fitting is it to recommend ourselves to the saints in heaven!
[22] Heb. 7:25.
[23] In the Commentary on the Sentences (IV, d. 15, q. 4, a. 6, q^a 2^a, ad 1), St. Thomas says: "Christus in quantum homo, orat pro nobis; sed ideo non dicimus: Christe ora pro nobis, quia Christus supponit suppositum aeternum, cujus non est orare, sed adjuvare, et ideo dicimus: Christe audi nos vel miserere nobis, et in hoc etiam evitamus haeresim Arii et Nestorii."

shown particularly well in their treatment of Christ's prayer,[24] that Christ even now that He is in heaven and even in the Eucharist truly prays for us, so that the merits of His passion may be applied to this or that sinner at the most opportune moment, such as the moment of a happy death.[25] In this sense, when He adores and gives thanks He prays not because of any indigence but through His superabundance and filial piety, in order to render to His Father the worship that is due Him.

St. Ambrose has said: "The risen Christ always defends our cause before the Father."[26] St. Gregory the Great declared: "Christ prays for the Church every day."[27] The interior oblation, that never ceases in Christ's sacred soul, is thus an oblation of adoration, of impetration, and of thanksgiving.

Is this interior oblation, which is ever ablaze in Christ's heart, numerically the same as the oblation by which He offered Himself up in accepting to die for us, from the moment of His coming into the world and especially on the Cross? Some theologians have denied this because, as they see it, the interior act of oblation on the cross was meritorious, whereas the one by which the glorious Christ offers Himself up at Mass as its principal priest is no longer meritorious. Consequently some have thought that Christ offers Himself up at each Mass by a new act.

This view, which would multiply the successive acts of oblation of the glorious Christ, is foreign to the teaching of the great masters and does not seem acceptable for several reasons.

First of all, it is not in conformity with the life of union of the Savior's sacred soul. This is an eminently simple life, through which He attains divine eternity, and in it there is no succession or innovation but solely the immutable continuation of what already exists.[28]

---

[24] *In IIIam*, q. 21.

[25] Cf. Gonet, *De incarn.*, disp. 22, a. 2: "Christus etiam nunc in caelo existens, vere et proprie orat, nobis divina beneficia postulando." Cf. Salmanticenses, Tolet, Suarez, and others.

[26] St. Ambrose, *In Ep. ad Rom.* 8: "Christus resurgens, semper causas nostras agit apud Patrem, cujus postulatio contemni non potest, quia in dextera Dei est."

[27] St. Gregory the Great, *In 5m Ps. poenit.*: "Quotidie Christus orat pro Ecclesia, de quo testatur Ap. Paulus Hebr. 7:25."

[28] Even when we say a decade of the Rosary contemplating, for example, the mystery

Moreover, this opinion that would multiply the acts of oblation in the Savior's soul does not agree with the words of St. Paul: "Christ was offered once to exhaust the sins of many," [29] and: "For by one oblation He hath perfected forever them that are sanctified." [30] Christ does not offer up a new sacrifice, and His minister acts only in His name. It is therefore fitting to state that this unique interior oblation, which was the soul of the sacrifice of Calvary, continues forever in Christ's sacred heart.[31] Moreover, to concede a second act of oblation is to say that the first was inadequate. Lastly, He who is the priest forever must perform a priestly act that lasts forever, with neither interruption nor innovation.[32]

Doubtless this oblation is no longer meritorious, but there is no

---

of our Savior's resurrection, this involves but a single continuous act of our intelligence, an act of lively faith united to an act of love and of prayer. The multiplicity of the Hail Mary's exists only for the inferior faculties, the senses and the imagination.

[29] Heb. 9:28.   [30] *Ibid.*, 10:14.

[31] It must also be remembered that many Masses are celebrated at the same moment and many consecrations occur at the same instant by virtue of the same unique actual will of Christ, although His will is virtually multiple by reason of the different Masses.

[32] It has been objected: What has already been offered up in the most perfect degree and manner possible and accepted cannot be offered up again. For movement ceases at its termination. Christ offered Himself up as wayfarer, and now He no longer offers Himself up.

In accordance with what we have just said, we must answer that the question is not of a new interior oblation but of the continuation of the oblation, as well as of the adoration, thanksgiving, and prayer. Movement as movement (*ut via*) ordained to an end, ceases when this end is reached. But what does not cease is the act ordained to the ultimate end. St. Thomas even says that the act of the gift of counsel (which relates to the means) continues in heaven. Lastly, Christ offered Himself up in a meritorious manner as wayfarer, but, although He no longer merits, He continues to offer Himself up as man and as priest forever by offering up His entire mystical body together with Himself. As Pope Pius XI said: "Christus sacerdos se pro peccatis hostiam obtulit perpetuoque offert" (Denz., no. 2195). This is the significance of the words of the Council of Trent: "Idem nunc offerens ministerio sacerdotum, qui seipsum tunc in cruce obtulit."

The objection has also been made that the love by which Christ gained merit on earth was fitting to Him as wayfarer, and could not therefore be ruled by the beatific vision.

Several Thomists, among them Alvarez, Gonet, and Billuart, have answered: This love could not be ruled by the vision of God considered in itself, which invincibly attracts the will, but it could be ruled by the vision of God inasmuch as He is the reason for freely loving creatures, particularly men to be saved. This love that was both free and meritorious was fitting to Christ as wayfarer. Now it is no longer meritorious. Moreover, even if Christ's love is ruled by infused knowledge, it can continue just as His infused knowledge does. What is more, the act of love of God made by every just soul at the moment of a happy death can continue afterward.

reason why an act that was once meritorious should cease to be meritorious afterward. For example, when a dying man makes a final act of love of God, this act is meritorious. Why, then, cannot this act continue after death in purgatory where there is no longer any opportunity to merit? This spiritual act does not cease because of the simple fact of the separation of the soul from the body. Likewise, when Christ was on earth His act of love of men was meritorious. Why should it not continue, without this modality of merit, after His death? [33] Even here on earth this act of Christ's sacred soul was performed in the light of glory, and He never ceased to enjoy the beatific vision.

This beatific vision, which He always enjoyed on earth, was already measured not in terms of time but in terms of His participation in eternity, as many theologians agree.[34] Why would not the same hold true of the act of love by which Christ's sacred soul loved God and men? [35] Christ's act of love for us was meritorious here on earth.

[33] Undoubtedly the act of the virtue of fortitude, by which Christ suffered heroically, has ceased. But that does not hold for His act of love for us, or even of the interior act of oblation by which He willed first to offer Himself up in a bloody manner and afterward in a sacramental manner.

[34] Cf. St. Thomas, Ia, q. 10, a. 5 ad 1; a. 3 ad 1 and 3. In *Contra Gentes*, Bk. III, chap. 61, he says: "Quod per visionem Dei aliquis sit particeps vitae aeternae. In hoc enim aeternitas a tempore differt, quod tempus in quadam successione habet esse; aeternitatis vero esse est totum simul. Jam autem ostensum est, c. 60, quod in praedicta visione non est aliqua successio, sed omnia quae per illam videntur, simul et uno intuitu videntur. Illa ergo visio in quadam aeternitatis participatione perficitur. . . .

"Haec visio nequidem est in tempore ex parte videntis, quod est intellectus, cujus esse non subjacet tempori, cum sit incorruptibilis, ut supra (Bk. II, chap. 79) probatum est. . . .

"Hinc est quod Dominus dicit (Joan. 17:3): Haec est vita aeterna ut cognoscant te solum Deum verum."

It is not incongruous for an act which is beginning (and even for an act which terminates like the beatific vision *per modum transeuntis* which was probably granted to St. Paul when he was caught up to the third heaven) to be measured by participation in eternity. All that is necessary is that as long as the act continues it be measured not by a fleeting instant of time but by the unique instant of immutable eternity. This can hold true of the glorious Christ's prayer of intercession until the end of the world. As for His prayer of adoration and thanksgiving, it will continue eternally.

[35] Some good Thomists like the Carmelites of Salamanca and several others concede that the free act by which Christ in His capacity as man loved us could be immediately governed by the beatific vision. In God Himself, the free act by which He loves us is governed by the uncreated vision of divine goodness inasmuch as it is the non-necessitated reason for His love of creatures. Cf. St. Thomas, Ia, q. 19, a. 3.

It is no longer meritorious but it can continue without this modality of merit, just as the act of charity of a human soul can continue after this soul has left its body.[36] It is certain that the glorious Christ does not cease to love us, to adore His Father and give thanks and offer Himself up to Him. This interior act of oblation, ever alive in His heart, is the soul of the Sacrifice of the Mass.[37] This sacrifice is in substance the same as that of the Cross, just as the Savior's humanity remains the same, although it is no longer subject to suffering and death.

This truth, superior to theology, belongs to the realm of divine faith. The doctrine that the essence of the Sacrifice of the Mass is in the sacramental immolation actually offered up by Christ, the principal priest, appears susceptible of definition as a dogma of faith.

Let us recollect ourselves under the wings of Christ's great prayer, so that He may present our prayers to His Father and thus increase the value of our adorations, our supplications, our reparation, and our thanksgiving. Let us remember that when Christ offers Himself up in the Masses said all over the world He also offers up His entire mystical body, symbolized by the drop of water poured into the chalice at the beginning of the Mass, to be converted with the wine into His precious blood.

As we become each day more conscious of the human misery within us and around us, let us ask Christ Jesus, priest for all eternity, to save us, to have pity on so many misguided souls, the victims of the education they have received. Let us beg our Savior to hold in His hand all the children who are in danger of being snatched away from Him in Russia, Eastern Europe, and many other lands. And though the evil be great, let us look upon it not with pessimism and discouragement but with the thought that the Savior is stronger than all

[36] Even if the interior oblation of the sacrifice of the Cross could not continue in the Savior's soul after His death, it would suffice for Him to renew it once afterward and then continue it, without renewing it at each Mass.

[37] Just as the beatific vision is measured by participation in eternity, the same is true of the beatific love with which Christ loved His Father and our souls. Moreover, even if the free act of redemptive love was governed by His infused knowledge, it can continue after death just as this knowledge does, especially since the act of redemptive love is the supreme expression of this knowledge.

His enemies taken together, and that His act of love pleases God more than all the sins of the world displease Him.

Made strong by this conviction, let us recall the words of St. Paul: "When I am weak, then am I powerful." [38] "I can do all things in Him who strengtheneth me." [39]

[38] II Cor. 12:10.   [39] Phil. 4:13.

❊ XXVII ❊

THE INFINITE VALUE OF EACH MASS OFFERED UP BY OUR LORD

WE HAVE seen that the Savior is the principal priest at the Sacrifice of the Mass, and that the interior oblation which was the soul of the sacrifice of the Cross continues in the heart of Christ, who desires our salvation and who thus Himself offers up all the Masses that are celebrated each day. What is the value of each of these Masses? A correct idea of this value will help us to unite ourselves more intimately each day to the Holy Sacrifice and to receive its fruits in greater abundance.

It is commonly taught in the Church that the Sacrifice of the Mass, considered in itself, has infinite value, but that the effect it produces within us is always finite, however exalted it may be, and that this effect is proportioned to our interior dispositions. These two points of doctrine merit further elucidation.

The Infinite Value of the Mass

The reason for the doctrine that the Mass, considered in itself, has infinite value, is that it is the same in substance as the sacrifice of the Cross, which has infinite value because of the dignity of the victim offered and of the priest who offered it up, inasmuch as on the Cross the Word made flesh was at once priest and victim.[1] At Mass the Word made flesh continues to be the principal priest and the victim truly present, truly offered up and sacramentally immolated.

But whereas the effects of the Mass that relate immediately to God,

---

[1] The worth of the victim gives the sacrifice an infinite objective value, and the dignity of the person of Christ gives it an infinite personal value, which is more important. When Mary presented her Son in the Temple, this oblation had an infinite objective value, but not an infinite personal value. Christ's oblation of Himself is far superior.

such as reparative adoration and thanksgiving, always occur infallibly
in their infinite plentitude even without our cooperation, its effects
that relate to us are poured forth only in proportion to our interior
dispositions.

At each Mass, adoration, reparation, and thanksgiving of limitless
value are infallibly offered up to God. This is true because of the
nature of the victim offered and of the principal priest, independently
even of the prayers of the Universal Church and of the fervor of the
celebrant.

It is impossible to adore God more perfectly, to better acknowledge
His sovereign domain over all things and all souls, than by the sacramental immolation of the Savior who died for us on the cross. This
adoration is given expression in the words of the Gloria: "Glory to
God in the highest. And on earth peace to men of good will. We
praise Thee. We bless Thee. We adore Thee. We glorify Thee."
This adoration is again expressed in the Sanctus, and still more perfectly in the double consecration.

It is the most perfect fulfillment of the commandment: "Thou
shalt fear the Lord thy God, and shalt serve Him only." [2] These are
the words our Lord used in answering Satan's taunts: "The kingdoms
of the world and the glory of them . . . will I give Thee, if falling
down Thou wilt adore me." [3] Only God's infinite grandeur merits
this worship of latria. At the Mass, the adoration that is offered up
to Him is in spirit and in truth of immeasurable value.

Likewise it is impossible to offer up to God more perfect reparation
for the sins that are committed each day than by the Sacrifice of the
Mass, as the Council of Trent maintains. [4] It is not a new reparation
distinct from that of Calvary. True, the risen Christ no longer suffers
or dies. But, according to the same Council, [5] the sacrifice of the altar,
being substantially the same as that of Calvary, pleases God more
than all the sins of the world displease Him. [6] Just as the Savior's
humanity, now no longer subject to death or suffering, remains substantially the same, thus is the sacrifice of Christ perpetuated in sub-

---

[2] Deut. 6:13.   [3] Matt. 4:8 f.   [4] Sess. XXII, chap. 1.

[5] *Ibid.*, chap. 2, initio, and can. 3 (Denzinger, nos. 940, 950).

[6] Cf. St. Thomas, IIIa, q. 48, a. 2.

stance. The inalienable right of God, the Sovereign Good, to be loved above all else is most perfectly acknowledged by the oblation of the Lamb who takes away the sins of the world.

Finally, it is impossible to give Him more perfect thanksgiving for benefits received: "What shall I render to the Lord for all the things that He hath rendered to me? I will take the chalice of salvation, and I will call upon the name of the Lord." [7] Often we forget to thank God for His blessings, as did the lepers whom Jesus had cured. Only one of the ten came back to thank Him. It is fitting often to offer up Masses of thanksgiving. A pious custom that is gaining favor at the present time is the celebration of a Mass of thanksgiving the second Friday of each month, in reparation for our ingratitude.

Adoration, reparation, and thanksgiving are effects of the Sacrifice of the Mass that relate to God Himself and are infallible. Through each Mass, through the oblation and sacramental immolation of the Savior on the altar, God infallibly obtains adoration, reparation, and thanksgiving of infinite value. This is so because of the dignity of the victim and of the principal priest. The interior oblation that continues ceaselessly in Christ's heart is a theandric act, a human act of His human will, that derives from the person of the Word a value that is truly infinite.

At the moment of the consecration in the peace of the sanctuary, a great surge of adoration rises up toward God. Its prelude is the Gloria and the Sanctus, whose beauty is enhanced on certain days by Gregorian chant, the most exalted, simplest, and purest of all religious chants, or sometimes by magnificent polyphonic music. But when the moment of the double consecration arrives, all is silent. This silence tells in its own way what music cannot express.

It is a silence that mirrors the silence which, according to the Apocalypse (8:1), occurred in heaven when the Lamb opened the book of the seven seals, the book of God's decrees concerning His kingdom.[8] May this silence of the consecration be our solace and our strength.[9]

[7] Ps. 115:12.

[8] "And when He [the Lamb] had opened the seventh seal, there was silence in heaven, as it were for half an hour" (Apoc. 8:1).

[9] "In silence and in hope shall your strength be" (Isa. 30:15).

Thus are the adoration, the reparation, and the *"Consummatum est"* of the sacrifice of the Cross perpetuated in substance. And this adoration that rises up toward God with each daily Mass falls again like a life-giving dew upon our poor earth to fertilize it spiritually. We should never forget that the highest end of the Holy Sacrifice is the glory of God, the manifestation of His goodness, which is the very purpose of the universe. Thus, by one Mass the whole of creation surges up toward its Creator in a prayer of reparative adoration and thanksgiving. If these effects relate to God Himself, there are others that relate to us. The Mass can obtain for us all the graces necessary for salvation. Christ "always living makes intercession for us," [10] and His intercession has as great value as His adoration.

What Effects Can the Mass Produce in Us?

The Eucharistic Sacrifice has infinite value in itself by reason of the dignity of the victim offered up and of the principal priest. Yet the effects it produces in us are always finite because of the limitations of creatures as such and those of our particular interior dispositions as well. There is no disagreement among theologians on this point.

The only disputed question is this: Is the effect of the Sacrifice of the Mass limited not only by our own fervor but also by the will of Christ, so that a Mass that is applied to several persons obtains less graces for them than if it were said for only one of them?

Some theologians [11] answer affirmatively: The effect of each Mass,

[10] Heb. 7:25.

[11] This is the opinion of Scotus, the Scotists, Americus, and several others. It has been reasserted recently by Father de la Taille (*Mysterium fidei*, elucid. 33a), as a corollary of His opinion that Christ does not actually offer up the Masses that are celebrated throughout the world, but merely does so in a virtual manner. We have explained in the preceding chapter why we cannot accept this view, which is contrary to generally approved doctrine.

The relationship of these two questions has been noted several times. Vacant (*Université Catholique*, 1894, XVI, 529) wrote: "The Scotists held that Jesus Christ is the priest of the Eucharistic Sacrifice only because He instituted it and conferred upon priests the power of offering it up. They concluded that two important consequences emerged from this theory. . . . The second is that the Mass, not being an act of the God-man, does not have the same value as the sacrifice of the Cross, that it applies only a part of the fruits of Calvary, and that this application is made by reason of the prayer of the Church and not by reason of an actual offering up of the sacred victim by Jesus Christ Himself."

they say, is limited by the will of our Lord, and consequently a Mass offered for ten of the faithful is less profitable to them than if it were said for one of these faithful. If this were not the case, they add, it would be superfluous to say more than one Mass for the same intention of one particular person.

This reason is really weak, for the person in question may not have all the dispositions required to receive all the desired graces through the first Mass said for him. Moreover, this person must desire eternal life above all else, and cannot ask for it with too much insistence. As for souls in purgatory, the Mass is applied to them by way of suffrage, according to God's good pleasure, the measure of which remains unknown to us, and we do not know when these souls are delivered. It is therefore desirable to have several Masses said for them.[12]

Other theologians, among them many Thomists,[13] follow the inspiration of St. Thomas [14] in saying: The effect of each Mass is not limited by the will of Christ, but only by the devotion of those for whom it is offered up. Thus, a single Mass offered up for a hundred persons can be as profitable to each of them as if it were offered up solely for each individual.[15]

---

[12] Those who hold this opinion have also said that were it otherwise the priest might say one Mass and thereby satisfy for several stipends, something that the Church does not permit. Nor is this reason very compelling, for the stipends are not the price of the Masses but simply a means of subsistence allowed by the Church under certain conditions. Besides, even though a Mass can benefit many persons simultaneously the Church can forbid the priest to receive several stipends for a single Mass.

[13] Cajetan, *In IIIam*, q. 79, a. 5; John of St. Thomas, *In IIIam*, disp. 32, a. 3; Gonet, *Clypeus thom., De Euchar.*, disp. 11, a. 5 no. 100; Salmanticenses, *De Euchar.*, disp. XIII, dub. 6. We disagree completely with what Father de la Taille has written on this subject, namely, his *Esquisse du mystère de la foi* (Paris, 1942), p. 22.

[14] IIIa, q. 79, a. 5, a. 7 ad 2.

[15] St. Thomas says (IIIa, q. 79, a. 5): "Although this offering suffices of its own quantity to satisfy for all punishment, yet it becomes satisfactory for them for whom it is offered, or even for the offerers, according to the measure of their devotion, and not for the whole punishment." St. Thomas sets up no limits except those resulting from the dispositions of the subject. He implies that the love of Christ, the principal priest, has an infinite value.

The Angelic Doctor expresses the same view in IIIa, q. 79, a. 7 ad 2. He says that the Mass, like the sacrifice of the Cross, produces a greater or lesser effect in those who benefit by it according to the measure of their devotion. St. Thomas does not speak of any limit deriving from the will of Christ.

The Council of Trent, which does not assign any limit, declares: "God, appeased by

The reason for this is that the influence of a universal cause is limited only by the capacity of the subjects who receive it. Thus, the sun lights up and warms a thousand persons as well as one in a given area. Now, inasmuch as the Sacrifice of the Mass is substantially the same as that of the Cross, it is in terms of reparation and prayer a universal cause of graces, of light, of inspiration, and of strength. Its influence on us is therefore limited only by the dispositions or the fervor of those who receive it. Like the sacrifice of the Cross, it can thus be as profitable for a large number of persons as if it were offered for a single one of them. The sacrifice of Calvary, which was offered up for all men, was no less profitable to the good thief than if it had been offered up for him alone.

In other words, as the sacrifice of the Cross had infinite value in terms of merit and satisfaction because of the theandric act of love that inspired it, now the Sacrifice of the Mass which perpetuates in substance that of the Cross is of infinite value to apply to us the merits and satisfactions of the Savior's passion.

This explains the Church's practice of offering up Masses for the salvation of the entire world, for all the faithful living and dead, for the Sovereign Pontiff, for national leaders, bishops, without limiting its intentions. In so doing, the Church does not expect to render the Mass less profitable to the one for whom it is specifically applied.

This manner of thinking appears much sounder than the former. It even seems to be a corollary of the accepted doctrine that the Sacrifice of the Mass is numerically the same in substance as that of the Cross, inasmuch as the victim and the principal priest are the same in each of them. There is nothing to justify our limiting the intention of Christ, as He continues to offer Himself up by a theandric act of infinite value, in order to apply to us the fruits of His passion. The limitation is not His doing, but ours. It stems from our own dispositions and fervor. As St. Thomas says, just as we receive more heat from a fireplace the closer we approach it, so we derive more benefit from the fruits of the Mass in the measure that we attend with a spirit of faith, trust in God, love, and piety.

---

this oblation, forgives great crimes, and the fruits of the bloody oblation of the Cross are thus abundantly applied" (Denz., no. 940).

What, specifically, are the effects that the Mass produces in us? The Mass remits our sins, inasmuch as it obtains for us the grace of repentance. If we do not resist this grace, our sins are forgiven.[16] Just as the sacrifice of the Cross obtained this grace for the good thief, the Sacrifice of the Mass obtains it for those who desire it. It is not in vain that the words, "Lamb of God who takest away the sins of the world, have mercy on us," are said before Holy Communion. Who can count the sinners who have gone to Mass and there received the grace of repentance and the inspiration to make a good confession of their entire past life? [17]

Inasmuch as the Mass remits our sins, it follows that it can be offered up even for hardened and impenitent sinners, who would not be permitted to receive Holy Communion. The Holy Sacrifice can obtain for them at least sufficient graces of light and inclination. It can even be offered up, as was the sacrifice of the Cross, for all the living, even for infidels, schismatics, heretics, the excommunicated, provided it is not offered up for them as for members of the Church.[18] Thus St. Paul called for public prayers for all men.[19] And since we can pray for all men, the Holy Sacrifice can be offered up for all men. It is with this in mind that Father Charles de Foucauld, the hermit of the Sahara, often celebrated Mass for the Moslems in order to prepare their souls for the subsequent teaching of the Gospel. Likewise many Masses are now being celebrated for the conversion of Russia.

[16] The Council of Trent, Sess. XXII, chap. 2 (Denz., 940), says: "Hujus oblatione placatus Dominus, gratiam et donum poenitentiae concedens, peccata etiam ingentia dimittit."

[17] A young man who despite his indifference was destined—without knowing it—to become a priest and religious, entered a church one Sunday morning to attend Mass. He was at once conscious that something very great was happening at the altar, but he had in great part forgotten what the Mass is and had only vague memories of the catechism that had prepared him for his First Communion. He saw the priest raise the chalice, and though he had no clear idea of what this chalice signified, he felt that an immeasurable mystery was unfolding before him. This was the moment of his conversion. He then prepared for confession, changed his life completely, and soon afterward became a religious.

[18] However, for the excommunicated *vitandi*, according to ecclesiastical law, the priest can celebrate Mass only in a private manner by praying for their conversion. Cf. Code of Canon Law, can. 2262, #2, 2°: "Sacerdotes Missam privatim ac remoto scandalo pro excommunicato applicare non prohibentur; sed, si excommunicatus sit vitandus, pro ejus conversione tantum."   [19] I Tim. 2:1 f.

The spirit of evil fears nothing so much as a Mass, especially one that is celebrated with great fervor and in which many souls participate with a spirit of faith. When the enemy of goodness meets some insurmountable obstacle, it is because in some church there was a priest, conscious of his own weakness and poverty, who with faith offered up the very powerful host and the blood of our Redemption. It is fitting here to mention that there have been saints who, at the moment of the elevation of the chalice at Mass, have seen the precious blood overflow and trickle down the arms of the priest, whereupon angels gathered it up in golden cups to carry it to distant places and to the souls in greatest need of participating in the mystery of the Redemption.

The Sacrifice of the Mass remits not only our sins but the punishment due to sins that have already been forgiven. This applies to both the living and the dead for whom the Sacrifice is offered up. We can go so far as to say that this effect is infallible. However, the punishment is not always remitted in full, but according to the disposition of Providence and the degree of our fervor. Thus the words "Lamb of God who takest away the sins of the world, grant us peace," are accomplished.

It does not follow that rich men who have left much money for Masses are delivered from purgatory more quickly than certain poor men who could leave nothing or almost nothing, for it may well have been that the latter had smaller debts to pay divine justice, had been better Christians, and therefore participated more fully in the fruit of the Masses said for all the dead as well as in the general fruit of each Mass.[20]

Finally, the Sacrifice of the Mass obtains for us the spiritual and temporal blessings necessary or useful for our salvation. Christ's prayer, as He continues to offer Himself up on our altars, has infinite value. Therefore it is fitting, as Pope Benedict XV has recommended,[21] to have Masses said in order to obtain the grace of a happy

[20] St. Augustine (*Enchiridion*, c. 110), says that the dead participate in the fruits of the Mass in the measure that they have merited on earth, "qui cum viverent, meruerunt ut haec sibi postea prodesse possent."

[21] Letter to the Director of the Archconfraternity of our Lady of Happy Deaths.

death, for this is the grace of graces, the one on which our eternal salvation depends.

This being so, it is fitting when we attend Mass to unite ourselves with a great spirit of faith, trust, and love to the interior act of oblation that continues forever in Christ's heart. He invites us to do so, as the author of the *Imitation of Christ* tells us: "As I willingly offered Myself to God the Father for thy sins, with My hands stretched out upon the Cross . . . even so oughtest thou willingly to offer thyself to Me daily in the Mass, . . . for a pure and holy oblation. . . . Whatsoever thou givest except thyself, I regard not; for I seek not thy gift, but thyself. . . . But if thou wilt depend upon self, and not offer thyself freely to My will, thy offering is not complete, nor will there be an entire union between us." [22] The more closely we unite ourselves to our Lord at the moment of the consecration, which is the essence of the Sacrifice of the Mass, the better will be our Communion, which is a participation in this Sacrifice.

We must answer this call, as the *Imitation* also advises: "Lord, I offer to Thee all my sins and offenses, . . . that Thou mayest . . . blot out all the stains of my sins, . . . fully pardoning me. . . . I offer also to Thee all my good works, though few and imperfect; that Thou mayest amend and sanctify them, . . . and make them acceptable to Thee. . . . I offer to Thee also all the pious desires of devout persons; the necessities of . . . all those that are dear to me. . . . I offer up also to Thee prayers, and this sacrifice of propitiation, for them in particular who have in any way injured me or grieved me. . . . And for all those likewise whom I have at any time grieved, troubled, oppressed, or scandalized, . . . knowingly or unknowingly; that it may please Thee to forgive us all our sins and mutual offenses . . . and grant us so to live that we may be worthy to enjoy Thy grace, and that we may attain unto life everlasting." [23] Let us also offer up our daily difficulties. This is the best way of carrying our crosses, as our Lord asked us to.

Please God that we may have the capacity and strength to renew this oblation at the moment of our death, and to unite ourselves with great love to the Masses that are being celebrated, to unite ourselves

---

[22] *The Imitation of Christ*, Bk. IV, chap. 8. [23] *Ibid.*, chap. 9.

to the sacrifice of Christ perpetuated at the altar! May we thus make of the sacrifice of our life an oblation of adoration, reparation, supplication, and thanksgiving, the prelude for us to eternal life!

When we realize that in some places certain priests must serve three or four parishes, we are forced to conclude that the number of Masses has diminished and it has become much more difficult for many of the rural faithful to attend Sunday Mass. Now, when the faithful gradually cease to attend Mass they progressively lose the meaning of Christianity, the meaning of the things of the spirit and of eternity.

There was a lay saint who, seeing the state of these churches where Sunday Mass was celebrated only rarely, entrusted these parishes to the care of certain saints who had been priests while on earth, in particular the Curé of Ars, so that from heaven they might watch over these shepherdless flocks, intercede for them, and obtain the grace of a happy death for those who died without the sacraments. We should often remember this when we attend the Holy Sacrifice, and inasmuch as every Mass is of infinite value we should pray that the Mass we attend may radiate its graces to those places where the Holy Sacrifice is no longer celebrated, and where the faithful are gradually losing the habit of going to Mass. Let us implore our Lord to call priestly vocations into being in such places. Let us beg Him for priests, holy priests, who become each day more aware of the grandeur of Christ's priesthood, so that they may be its zealous ministers, living only for the salvation of souls. Providence always sends us galaxies of saints in our most troubled times. We must beseech our Lord to send saints into the world who have the faith and trust of the apostles, as in the early days of the Church.

✸ XXVIII ✸

SOVEREIGN REDEMPTION AND ITS FRUITS IN MARY

> "He that is mighty hath done great things to me."
>
> Luke 1:49

THE special manner in which the mystery of the Redemption was accomplished with relation to Mary, the Mother of God, contains such profound harmonies that they long remained hidden even from great theologians and great saints like St. Bernard, St. Bonaventure, and perhaps St. Thomas Aquinas.[1] Now that the Church has made an infallible pronouncement by defining the dogma of the Immaculate Conception, all the faithful can see in this privilege the most eminent form of the mystery of the Redemption. Let us first consider it in the light of the privilege itself, and secondly in the light of its consequences.

The Preservative Redemption

The harmony of a mystery is all the more beautiful when it intimately reconciles things that are apparently most contradictory and

---

[1] It is often said that St. Thomas denied the privilege of the Immaculate Conception. Such a categorical assertion does not seem justified on the basis of a work recently written on this subject by Father N. del Prado, O.P., of the University of Fribourg, *Divus Thomas et bulla dogmatica "Ineffabilis Deus"* (1919). In this work the author shows that St. Thomas made more of a distinction than is generally believed between the body of the Blessed Virgin before the animation, and her person which presupposes the presence of a rational soul within the body. According to the saintly Doctor, the body of the Blessed Virgin before the animation was not preserved from original sin. But with regard to the person of Mary, several reliable authors maintain that St. Thomas neither affirmed nor denied the privilege. Since the Church had not yet made any pronouncement on the matter, neither did he see fit to make. Cf. P. Frietoff, O.P., *Angelicum*, July, 1933: *"Quomodo caro B.V.M. in originale concepta fuerit."*

that God alone can bring together. Thus the mystery of the Redemption, considered in terms of the Savior Himself, reconciles in the sufferings endured through love the most rigorous justice and the tenderest mercy. Therein lies the sublimity of the Cross.

The Immaculate Conception presents a reconciliation of the same order. On the one hand the Virgin Mary, by reason of her birth as a daughter of Adam, was destined to contract original sin. The first man, through his sin, lost original justice for himself and for us. That is to say, he lost sanctifying grace and the privileges that accompanied it. Had he remained innocent, he would have transmitted this original justice to us, together with his human nature.[2] The law that weighs on our fallen nature is universal: human nature is transmitted to all of us by way of generation, but it is transmitted deprived of grace and of the privileges of the state of innocence. Every child is born not merely deprived of sanctifying grace but moreover inclined to covetousness, to disorders of the passions, to error, and subject to suffering and death. "By one man sin entered into this world,"[3] St. Paul tells us. Mary, therefore, by reason of her birth as a daughter of Adam, was destined to contract original sin. How could she, caught in the current of generation, escape the current of sin? And, as St. Peter declares, "there is no other name under heaven given to men, whereby we must be saved" [except that of Jesus Christ].[4] St. Paul also says: "There is . . . one mediator of God and men, the man Christ Jesus who gave Himself a redemption for all." [5] There is no salvation for anyone except through the blood of the Savior, who is the Redeemer of all men without any exception. In this sense Mary needs redemption, just like the other children of men.

St. Thomas lays great stress on this point, for this is a capital dogma of our faith. There is no salvation except through Christ who died for us.

Mary, on the other hand, has been called from all eternity to be the mother of the Savior. The heavenly Father chose her through a

---

[2] The Council of Trent says clearly: "Si quis Adae praevaricationem sibi soli et non ejus propagini asserit nocuisse, acceptam a Deo sanctitatem et justitiam, quam perdidit, sibi soli et non nobis etiam eum perdidisse: an. sit" (Denzinger, no. 789).

[3] Rom. 5:12.   [4] Acts 4:12.   [5] I Tim. 2:5.

love of predilection from among all women, so that in time she should give a body to the Son, only begotten from all eternity. No one but the heavenly Father and Mary can call Jesus, "My Son." The Holy Ghost was to overshadow her and, without sullying her virginity in any way, was to make it possible for her to conceive the Savior. The Word of God, who exists eternally and therefore existed before creation, was to be truly Mary's son, and He was to love her among all creatures as His true Mother.

Could it be that Mary, called to this glorious maternity, should have come into the world bearing the stain of original sin? Was it possible that she who was to be the Mother of the Author of grace should be born deprived of grace? Could she who was to be the Mother of the Word made flesh have been born inclined toward covetousness, disorders of the emotions, and error?

These reasons are so compelling that even the theologians who once doubted the privilege of the Immaculate Conception declared unequivocally that Mary was sanctified before her birth in the womb of her mother, St. Anne. But the Church goes still further and has solemnly affirmed the privilege of the Immaculate Conception, accorded at the very instant when Mary's soul was created and united to her body.

How then can we reconcile these two things that are apparently so irreconcilable: Mary, being the daughter of Adam, must contract original sin; but, being called to be the Mother of God, she must be exempt from any stain whatever, she must escape the universal contagion?

How can these things be reconciled?

We can understand an exception to the law of man's fall, in view of a mission that is unique in the world, a mission that is superior to that of the prophets and apostles. But how was this exception to be accomplished? Was Mary preserved from the common stain independently of the future merits of her Son? Is it possible that Christ, the sole Mediator and Savior of all souls, is not Mary's Savior? Can it be that she does not owe her holiness to Him? St. Thomas rightly placed great emphasis on this point, for he was deeply concerned with safeguarding the dogma of universal redemption.

The Church, in defining the Immaculate Conception, answers: Mary was the beneficiary of a unique mode of redemption, a preservative redemption, and not merely a liberating and reparative redemption. Mary was preserved from original sin because of the future merits of her Son, and this truth reveals to us the deep harmony of the mystery, which long remained hidden even from great saints.

What kept St. Thomas from stoutly affirming the privilege of the Immaculate Conception, not yet defined by the Church at that time, was his fear of contradicting the dogma of the universal redemption of souls by Jesus Christ. He feared he might detract from the Redeemer's glory. And divine Providence seems to have permitted the great doctor to remain in darkness on this point, and with him St. Bonaventure and St. Bernard, because the proclamation of this privilege was reserved for much later, for our era of unbelief and naturalism which denies original sin and the necessity of redemption.[6]

Preservative redemption is one of the marvels of Catholic dogma. To truly understand it we must realize that not only is Jesus Christ Mary's Savior, but that she benefited more than anyone else from His redemptive mission. Herein lies all the grandeur of the mystery. Let us consider it in some detail. Indeed it is fitting that the absolutely perfect Savior should exercise sovereign redemption for at least one soul, the soul called to be most intimately united to Him in His work of salvation. But perfect redemption consists not only in rescuing a soul from sin, but also in preserving it from this sin even before sin has had a chance to sully it. He who preserves us from a mortal blow saves our life even better than if he healed the wound caused by this blow. It is therefore highly fitting that Christ Jesus, the perfect Redeemer, should bestow upon His Mother redemption in all its plenitude: a redemption that is not merely reparative and liberating, but a preservative redemption. It is highly fitting that Mary should not be liberated, purified, cured of original sin, but that she should be totally preserved from it by the future merits of her Son.

Christ's love for His immaculate Mother is immense. At the thought of it our souls should rejoice and soar upward. Only the

---

[6] If these great doctors had made definite pronouncements in favor of the Immaculate Conception, this dogma would probably have been defined before the nineteenth century.

Mother of the Son of God could have this unique prerogative. How fitting that she should have it!

Inasmuch as she had been called to become the Mother of God and the Coredemptrix, the Mother of all men, it was necessary that she be redeemed as perfectly as possible. Being closer than anyone to the stream of grace that pours from the Word made flesh, she received His blessings in their plenitude.

At a time when all truths were being depreciated, when many refused to believe either in original sin or in the necessity of baptismal regeneration, it was fitting that the Church should solemnly define this dogma and that Mary should remind us of all these truths by telling us at Lourdes: "I am the Immaculate Conception." This privilege, far from detracting from the dogma of the universal redemption of souls by Jesus Christ, discloses to us in the person of Mary sovereign redemption in its most perfect form conceivable.[7]

In preserving His Mother from original sin, the Savior gave her an initial plenitude of grace greater than that of all the saints and angels taken together, just as a single diamond may have greater value than a great pile of lesser stones. From this initial plenitude of sanc-

---

[7] Let us note that, since Mary was fully redeemed by Christ, she was not able, properly speaking, to merit the Incarnation even *de congruo.* Why? Because the principle of merit cannot be merited, just as the first cause cannot be an effect produced. It cannot produce itself. Thus the merits of the Blessed Virgin Mary derive from the future merits of her Son as their primary source. Her merits depend on those of her Son not only as on a final cause, but as on an efficient moral cause, foreseen and willed by God. Mary therefore could not have merited the Incarnation.

But having received the initial plenitude of grace through the future merits of her Son, she merited the superior degree of grace which made her the worthy Mother of the Savior. St. Thomas (IIIa, q. 2, a. 11 ad 3) says with admirable precision: "The Blessed Virgin is said to have merited to bear the Lord of all; not that she merited His incarnation, but because by the grace bestowed upon her she merited that grade of purity and holiness which fitted her to be the Mother of God."

Several modern theologians seem to forget this distinction and therefore to misunderstand the great principle that the principle of merit cannot be merited. Some wish to apply in this connection the axiom *"causae ad invicem sunt causae,"* but one must not forget to add *"in diverso genere."* There is certainly a mutual priority of final and efficient causes, but on condition of keeping in mind that they are of diverse orders. The principal root of Mary's merits lies in the merits of Christ, and these latter presuppose the Incarnation. Thus Mary could not merit the Incarnation. It is clear that here we are dealing with the same order of causality. Cf. the commentators of St. Thomas on IIIa, q. 2., a. 11, for example Billuart: "Nullum meritum est aut concipi potest pro praesenti hominum statu, quod non accipiat valorem suum et vim merendi ex Christi meritis."

tifying grace sprang forth in the same eminent degree faith, hope, charity, the infused moral virtues, and the seven gifts of the Holy Ghost. Moreover, this initial plenitude did not cease growing until Mary's death, for no venial sin or imperfection impeded its progress. Because of Mary's unceasing fidelity, the initial treasure increased in a marvelous progression. Just as bodies fall with increasing speed as they approach the earth by virtue of the law of acceleration which is a corollary of universal gravitation, so do souls progress more quickly toward God as they come closer to Him and are increasingly attracted by Him.[8]

This law of acceleration of the progress of souls toward God, which is approximately verified in the lives of the saints especially by frequent Holy Communion,[9] was fully verified in Mary. Whereas Jesus never increased in goodness,[10] since He had been conceived in the absolute plenitude of grace, Mary continued to increase in perfection until her death, until the moment of the final plenitude of grace when her soul entered glory.[11]

It is a consolation to think that there has been one soul that received in its plenitude everything that God desired to give her and that never impeded the pouring of grace upon other souls. There is one absolutely perfect soul which allowed the divine life-giving torrent to flow through her without obstacle. There is at least one soul that never for a single instant failed to measure up to what God desired of her. This is the soul of the Mother of God, the Mother of all men, who watches over them to lead them to eternal life.

This is what we mean by sovereign Redemption, a redemption that

---

[8] Cf. St. Thomas, *In Epistolam ad Hebraeos*, 10:25: "Motus naturalis (v.g., motus lapidis cadentis ad centrum terrae) quanto plus accedit ad terminum, magis intenditur. Contrarium est de motu violento. Gratia autem inclinat in modum naturae. Ergo qui sunt in gratia, quanto plus accedunt ad finem, plus debent crescere." Cf. St. Thomas, Ia IIae, q. 35, a. 6 ad 2: "Omnis motus naturalis intensior est in fine."

[9] In principle, if we fought generously against negligence and every attachment to venial sin, each of our Communions should be substantially more fervent than the preceding one since each of them must not only preserve but increase charity in us and therefore dispose us to receive our Lord with a more fervent will the following day.

[10] Cf. Concilium Constantinop. II (Denzinger, no. 224).

[11] As the theologians say in describing this instant which is preceded by a period of time that can be divided *ad infinitum:* "primum non esse viae, seu primum esse separationis animae a corpore, fuit primum esse vitae ejus gloriosae."

is not merely liberating and reparative but also preservative. This is what motivated the words of the archangel Gabriel when he said to Mary: "Hail, full of grace, the Lord is with thee: blessed art thou among women." [12]

The Consequences of the Preservative Redemption

Did the privilege we have just discussed remove from Mary even here on earth all the consequences of original sin? What happens to us even after baptism which remits original sin and restores us to sanctifying grace with all its accompanying infused virtues and gifts of the Holy Ghost? Even after baptism, there remain in us as a consequence of original sin concupiscence or the roots of covetousness that enkindle our evil passions, inclination toward error or weak judgment that easily goes astray, as well as suffering and death.

None of these evils existed in the state of original justice in which human nature was ennobled by grace and endowed with privileges. The body was perfectly submissive to the soul, the passions to right reason and to the will, and the will was submissive to God. Baptism, while it cleanses us of original sin, leaves the consequences of original sin in us as so many occasions for struggle and merit.

What is so striking about Mary is that the privilege of the Immaculate Conception exempts her from two of the consequences of original sin that are blighting and incompatible with her mission as Mother of God, but her privilege does not exempt her from suffering and death. This is most illuminating.

From the first moment of her life Mary was exempt from every form of concupiscence. The embers of covetousness never existed in her. No movement of her emotions could be disorderly or circumvent her judgment and her consent. Hers was perfect subordination of the emotions to the intellect and the will, and of the will to God as was the case of man in the state of innocence. Thus Mary is the most pure Virgin of virgins, *"inviolata, intemerata,"* the tower of ivory, the most perfect mirror of God.

Likewise Mary was never subject to error or illusion. Her judg-

[12] Luke 1:28.

ment was always enlightened, always clearsighted. In the words of the Litany, she is the Seat of Wisdom, the Virgin most prudent, the Mother of good counsel. All theologians agree that even here on earth she possessed an eminently superior and simple understanding of the Scriptures on the subject of the Messiah, the Incarnation, and the Redemption. She was more intimately initiated into the secrets of the kingdom of heaven than were the apostles. Then too, everything in nature spoke to her of the Creator more poignantly than to the greatest poets. In its simplicity her contemplation was superior to that of the greatest saints, to that of even St. John, St. Paul, or St. Augustine. Mary was above ecstasy. She had no need to lose the use of her senses to become very intimately united to God. Her union with Him was continual. She was thus perfectly exempt from covetousness and error.

Why then did not the privilege of the Immaculate Conception exempt Mary from suffering and death, which are also consequences of original sin? The truth of the matter is that suffering and death, as Mary and Jesus experienced them, were not consequences of original sin, as they are for us. For original sin had not touched them. Suffering and death were for them the consequences of human nature which by its very nature is subject to suffering and to corporeal death just as is the nature of the animal. It was only through a supernatural privilege that Adam in his innocence was exempt from all suffering and from the necessity of dying.

That He might become our Redeemer by His death on the cross, Jesus was virginally conceived in mortal flesh, and He willingly accepted suffering and dying for our salvation. Following His example, Mary willingly accepted suffering and death also, so that she might be united to her Son's sacrifice, make expiation with Him in our stead, and thus redeem us.

And, astonishingly enough, the privilege of the Immaculate Conception and the plenitude of grace she enjoyed, instead of exempting Mary from pain, considerably increased her capacity for suffering. This truth never ceases to arouse the admiration and wonder of the contemplatives. Mary suffered extraordinarily from the gravest evils precisely because she was absolutely pure, because her heart was aflame with divine charity. Yet we in our flightiness are not much troubled by these evils. We suffer because of things that wound our susceptibility, our self-love, our pride. Mary suffered because of sin in the measure of her love for God whom sin offends, in the measure of her love for her Son whom sin crucified, in the measure of her love for our souls that sin ravages and kills. Just as the Blessed Virgin's love for God was superior even here on earth to that of all the saints taken together, the same is true of her suffering. Here on earth, the closer a soul is to God—that is, the more it loves—the more it is destined to suffer. Mary loved the Savior, not only as her beloved Son but also as her Son the legitimate object of adoration, with her most tender virginal heart. The depth of her love made of her the queen of martyrs. As the aged Simeon had prophesied, a sword pierced her soul. The privilege of the Immaculate Conception, far from exempting Mary from sufferings, thus increased them and disposed her so well to endure them that she wasted none of them.

Finally, although this privilege did not save Mary from being subject to death, the Assumption was one of its consequences. Mary, conceived without sin, preserved from all sin, was not to know the corruption of the grave. The Savior was thus to associate her to the glories of the Ascension and to hasten for her the moment of the resurrection of the body.

Such were the consequences of the sovereign redemption which was accomplished in her. Not only was Mary redeemed by the most perfect redemption conceivable, but she has been intimately associated with the work of the salvation of mankind through her love and suffering.

This preservative redemption reminds us of the value of a less exalted grace, but one that is so necessary to us: baptism. Although we are born sinners, we are cleansed of original sin by baptismal grace, which is the seed of eternal life. There is an immense difference between an unbaptized child and one who has received the sacrament of regeneration. And as Mary's initial plenitude of grace never stopped growing within her during her lifetime, so the seed of eternal life should never cease growing in us until the moment of our death. God loves us much more than we realize. In order to grasp the full value of the sanctifying grace received in baptism, we should have to see God. For grace is nothing but a true and formal participation in God's intimate life.

Lastly, the sovereign redemption that we have just contemplated in Mary reminds us of the value of sanctity, and inspires us to pray earnestly, especially at the thought of the spiritual wretchedness of present-day Russia and other vast areas of the world. As the contemplatives tell us, the actual state of the world is at once much sadder and more beautiful than we know. The world desires no more saints, and expels them from persecuted lands. But God for His part wishes to give the world saints of every age and station in life. God wishes to give the world saints, but we must ask Him for them and secure them from His mercy. For a number of years now, Rome has been multiplying its beatifications and canonizations. In moments of great confusion like that of the Albigensian heresy and that of Protestantism, God sent galaxies of saints to carry on His Son's work and to lift up afflicted and tempted souls.

Although the world's plight is grave, let us not view it with discouragement and thereby depress those around us. Let us look at the other pan of the scales with a holy realism, and see in it the infinite merits of the Savior, those of Mary Coredemptrix and Mediatrix, and those of all the saints. This is the supernatural contemplation superior to all science, the contemplation that awakens in us not merely momentary enthusiasm but "the hunger and thirst for God's justice." It tells us that the only genuinely and profoundly interesting thing for us is sanctity and whatever leads us toward it. When this sanctity is incontestable, as in Mary, it becomes manifest to all as the profound reign of God in souls, and it permits us to glimpse even here on earth the grandeur of the mystery of Redemption, that is, the mystery of eternal life given back to souls that are willing to receive it.

❃ XXIX ❃

THE INTIMACY OF CHRIST

> "Can you drink the chalice
> that I shall drink?"
> Matt. 20:22

TO ENTER truly into the depths of the mystery of the Redemption, we must consider the intimacy of Christ, that is, the friendship of predilection He had for certain particularly faithful and generous souls. Among these souls there is one described in the Gospel by these simple words: "the disciple whom Jesus loved." [1] If we would understand the greatness of the Savior's friendship, its wellsprings, its pattern, its tenderness and its strength, as well as its inestimable gifts, we can do nothing better than contemplate His friendship for St. John.

The most beloved of all the apostles must have been perfect for our Lord to love him so much. John's purity delighted Him. Yet it was not John's perfection that attracted the love of Jesus. On the contrary, John's perfection was the effect of Jesus' love for him, Bossuet tells us, just as a fine work of art reflects its author's joy in creation. The love that God the Father and the Son have for our souls does not presuppose that we are lovable. Rather, their love for us implants and increases our lovable qualities by assimilating us to itself. When divine love pours into us, it produces the life of grace in our souls, and it continues to increase this grace in us if we do not set up any obstacles. [2]

Let us see how our Lord, through His friendship, made John re-

---

[1] John 13:23.

[2] Cf. St. Thomas, Ia, q. 20, a. 2: "The love of God infuses and creates goodness." St. Thomas relates his entire treatise on grace to this principle: Cf. Ia IIae, q. 110, a. 1, c. and ad 1: "Whatever is pleasing to God in a man is caused by the divine love."

semble Him ever more closely. Bossuet has remarked that the Savior
gave His beloved disciple three gifts: His cross, His Mother, and
His heart.[3] But it seems preferable to follow the chronological order
in which He bestowed these gifts, for it gives us a better understanding of St. John's progress in grace, and how the beloved disciple
gradually entered ever deeper into Christ's intimacy. At the Last
Supper Jesus gave John His heart. Soon afterward, when He was
dying, He gave him His Mother. And then, to make John's ministry
fruitful, Jesus gave him His cross.

At the Last Supper, Jesus Gave John His Heart

At that moment, all the apostles were ordained priests, received
the priestly character, and also received Holy Communion. But St.
John came closer to the Master's heart, and laid his head on the sacred
heart of the Savior.

When our Lord instituted the sacrament whose purpose is to increase our love of God, He willed that one of His privileged apostles
should be more aware than the others of the beat of His heart, that
would thereafter continue to live in the Eucharist for the consolation
and perfect regeneration of souls.

What interior grace did St. John receive at that moment? We can
get some idea of it when we remember that Jesus' body emitted a
virtue capable of healing the sick. How much more must His heart
have poured forth vivifying grace! Beyond any doubt John received
in that instant a grace of light and love. He learned experimentally
that the Savior's heart lives only for love of God and of souls. He
understood how the Eucharist is the great manifestation of this love
on earth, and that even under its humble appearances it is the very
life of God always present among us. Predestined from all eternity to
be the great doctor of charity, John drank in charity at its very source
and was inspired by the words that were to inspire a holy tenderness
in the faithful until the end of time. So that he might speak more
eloquently of the Savior's love for us, he came very close to the spirit-

[3] *Panegyric on St. John.*

ual fire that burns without destroying and that would transform us into itself.

As St. Paul recalled in his writings that he had been caught up to the third heaven, so St. John remembered that he had rested on the Master's heart. And how the eagle of the Evangelists wrote! He proclaimed the fundamental principles of Christian doctrine to be as follows: God is light and love. It was He who first loved us gratuitously. Our love for Him must be a response to the love He has shown for us, and fraternal charity must be the great sign of our love of God. He summed up his views in his First Epistle: "Dearly beloved, let us love one another: for charity is of God. And everyone that loveth is born of God and knoweth God. He that loveth not knoweth not God: for God is charity. By this hath the charity of God appeared toward us, because God hath sent His only-begotten Son into the world, that we may live by Him. In this is charity: not as though we had loved God, but because He hath first loved us, and sent His Son to be a propitiation for our sins. My dearest, if God hath so loved us, we also ought to love one another. . . . God is charity: and he that abideth in charity abideth in God, and God in him." [4]

This is an abstract of the whole of Christian dogma and morality, reduced to its essentials: love of God and of neighbor, the charity that must inspire and animate all the virtues. "We know that we have passed from death to life, because we love the brethren." [5] This is the great sign of the love of God.

We also have received what John received: the Master's heart. We can receive the Eucharistic heart of Jesus each day at Holy Communion. And if we receive it, if we truly believe in it, we must imitate it. The Savior's heart is open to all the faithful. In His heart we are all united, to be consummated into one. He turns no one away.

If we would enter into Christ's intimacy, our hearts must exclude no one, they must forget the wrongs our neighbors have done us, and be compassionate for the sufferings of others; our hearts must be generous, keeping nothing for themselves, giving their lives for oth-

---

[4] I John 4:7-16.　　　　　[5] I John 3:14.

ers and thereby possessing life all the more securely. Let us remember that God will multiply His blessings to us in the measure that we desire to share them with our brothers. We do not lose truth or goodness when we give them to others. Rather we possess them more securely and in a holy manner.

We should rejoice also in seeing in our neighbor what is lacking in ourselves. Instead of falling prey to jealousy, we ought to rejoice in his qualities, which are ours too in a sense, inasmuch as we are all one in the mystical body of Christ. The hand can rejoice in what the eye sees. Charity thus enriches our poverty. It makes all our goods the common property of all. It appropriates for us in a sense all the gifts of the mystical body of the Savior, and makes us participate in a measure in all the blessings of the City of God.

But to enter even more deeply into Christ's intimacy we must be taught by Mary, for she more than any other creature was privileged to enter into the heart of this sanctuary. That is why, when He was about to die, Jesus confided His Mother to St. John.

John was the only apostle at the foot of the cross. He was there, a heartbroken witness of all the Master's physical and moral suffering. Jesus had invisibly drawn him there to let him hear His last words and to give him a final proof of His love.

Those who are about to die leave to their dearest ones the most expressive testimony of affection. What did Jesus leave St. John, as He was dying? He had nothing left. He had been stripped of everything, abandoned by all. It even seemed that His Father had rejected Him when, as a victim in our stead, He cried out the first words of the psalm: "My God, My God, why hast Thou forsaken Me?" [6] In this state of utter destitution, what did Jesus leave to St. John?

He left him a living memory, the very holy soul whom He cherished more than all other creatures taken together. He left Mary to him. "Behold thy mother," He said to John. And to Mary: "Woman, behold thy son." "And from that hour, the disciple took her to his own." [7]

Contact with Jesus' heart at the Last Supper spiritually vivified John's soul. The Savior's words spoken from the cross also had sacra-

[6] Matt. 28:46.   [7] John 19:26 f.

mental power, as it were. Although He spoke these words on the point of death, He was still strong enough to touch men's hearts and to enrich them as He pleased.

These words created between Mary and John a most intimate bond, analogous to the bond that unites Jesus to His Blessed Mother. They gave Mary a most maternal and deep love that would thenceforth enfold John's soul, and they awakened in John a most filial and respectful love that made him a true spiritual son of Mary.

In this moment of anguish the words of the dying Christ touched their souls to their depths like a gentle balm, soothing their sufferings and their broken hearts. They brought immense consolation to John and to Mary too, for she could see into human souls and, looking into the soul of the beloved disciple, she could see what he himself could not: the living image of the Savior, the image that Mary would make perfect, to render it ever more like its divine model.

And so it happens often in the history of souls. When Jesus seems to draw away to test the confidence of His friends, He leaves His Blessed Mother to them, and He entrusts them to her care. Who can describe all the blessings St. John received from Mary? If St. Augustine and St. Monica had conversations on such an exalted plane, what are we to think of the talks between Mary and St. John?

Through the plenitude of grace she had received, the Mother of God was superior to the angels. The charity ablaze in her heart surpassed that of all the saints taken together. Its lively flame ever aspired toward God, even while she slept, in the words of the Canticle of Canticles: "I sleep, and my heart watcheth." [8]

Blessed with such a supernatural intimacy, how greatly St. John's charity must have grown, especially when he celebrated the Holy Sacrifice of the Mass in Mary's presence for her intentions, and when he gave her Holy Communion! Did he not know that the Blessed Virgin understood immeasurably better than he the sacrifice of the altar which perpetuates in substance the sacrifice of the Cross? Mary did not have the official capacity of the priesthood and she could not consecrate, but "she had received the plenitude of the spirit of the priesthood, which is the spirit of Christ our Redeemer." [9] As uni-

[8] Cant. 5:2.   [9] These are the words of Jean Jacques Olier.

versal Mediatrix and Coredemptrix, Mary never ceased lifting the soul of the apostle up toward God. Thus did He develop great love for the hidden life and become the model of contemplatives.

It was St. John's purity that had prepared him to live in Christ's intimacy. It was his purity, too, that disposed him to inherit Christ's love for Mary, who thus became his spiritual mother in the deepest and truest sense.

Following St. John's example, let us place ourselves under the immediate direction of the Virgin, as St. Louis Marie de Montfort urges. She is our mediatrix before Christ, as He is our mediator before His Father. She will be our counsel and our strength, our defense against the devil. She will increase the worth of our merits by offering them herself to her Son. Let us abandon into her hands the reparative and impetratory value of our actions, our struggles, our prayers, so that she may make them available, according to her good pleasure, to the souls that need them most. Thus to strip ourselves is in reality to enrich ourselves. Under Mary's direction we shall with a much surer step follow the path blazed by the Word, who Himself obeyed her on earth. Then we shall run swiftly on the path of God's commandments, because we shall receive the grace that dilates the heart, in the words of the psalm: "I have run the way of Thy commandments, when Thou didst enlarge my heart." [10] The Blessed Virgin will teach us countless things through her inspirations, as a good mother yields up to her child by a simple look, without need of words, the treasure of her interior life. With her and in her intimacy, we shall make more progress in a few days than during years of personal effort made without her. Thus speaks St. Louis Marie de Montfort, a true spiritual son of Mary as was St. John. [11]

Our Lord gave St. John His heart, He gave him His Mother. What else did He give him to make his apostolic ministry fruitful? He gave him His cross, and progressively made him understand its inestimable value.

Jesus' friendship does not consist wholly in sweetness and joy. It

---

[10] Ps. 118:32.

[11] See his *Treatise on the True Devotion to the Blessed Virgin Mary*, no. 155. Also the summary of this work, entitled *The Secret of Mary*.

is as strong as it is tender. It tends to purify through tribulations, and through suffering to associate souls with itself in the mystery of Redemption.

The apostles did not understand this at first. When Jesus spoke of the foundation of the kingdom of God, the apostles wondered which of them would be first in this kingdom. Then, as St. Matthew records, "Jesus calling unto Him a little child, set him in the midst of them, and said: 'Amen I say to you, unless you be converted and become as little children, you shall not enter into the kingdom of heaven. Whosoever therefore shall humble himself as this little child, he is the greater in the kingdom of heaven.' " [12] The Master had also said on several occasions: "If any man will come after Me, let him deny himself and take up his cross and follow Me." [13] But the apostles did not yet understand the full meaning of the word "cross." They could not accept the idea that Jesus would be crucified. Yet several times He had told them that this would happen.

One day, as He was going up to Jerusalem with them, our Lord again predicted His passion, crucifixion, and resurrection. He wished to implant it more deeply into the mind of John and that of his brother. At that moment the mother of the two apostles approached Jesus and bowed down as if to ask something. As St. Matthew records it,[14] Jesus said to her: "What wilt thou?" She answered: "Say that these my two sons may sit, the one on Thy right hand, and the other on Thy left, in Thy kingdom." Jesus then said: "You know not what you ask. Can you drink the chalice that I shall drink?" Quickly they declared: "We can." He answered: "My chalice indeed you shall drink; but to sit on My right or left hand is not Mine to give you, but to them for whom it is prepared by My Father." That was the day Jesus gave His cross to His beloved disciple.

These words spoken by the Savior, like those spoken on the two other occasions, produced their effects in the disciple's soul. From that moment John no longer sought to be the first. He began to love suffering and humiliation, and this love continued to grow in his heart through the influence of grace.

Jesus was to make John more and more like Himself. He came to

[12] Matt. 18:2–4.   [13] Ibid., 16:24.   [14] Ibid., 20:21–23.

suffer as a victim of salvation, to save us by His agony more than by His sermons. So He united John more and more to His toilsome and crucified life. Bossuet says, "Whenever Jesus comes, He brings with Him His cross and His thorns, and He shares them with those who love Him." As John was His beloved apostle, He gave him the immense grace of loving the cross.

John had at first thought that in order to have an honored place in the kingdom of the Son of God it was necessary to be seated at His right hand and to be clothed in His glory. He was to learn that we penetrate far into this kingdom even here on earth through suffering. He was to learn also how tribulation makes one clairvoyant in contemplating Jesus in the souls of men. Affliction was to open his eyes. He was to understand the profound meaning of the noblest of the beatitudes, the one that is most astonishing to human reason: "Blessed are they that suffer persecution for justice' sake: for theirs is the kingdom of heaven." This kingdom is already theirs here on earth even in the midst of persecution, because of the profound peace that Jesus gives them.

What was John's cross? If we look at things outwardly, it may seem that his was the lightest of all the apostles' crosses. He alone among them did not die in the throes of martyrdom. He did of course suffer persecution. In Rome under Domitian he was plunged into a cauldron of boiling oil. But this oil changed into dew, and he emerged refreshed and purified. He was then exiled on Patmos, where our Lord appeared to him in His glory and revealed His secrets to him, commanding him to write them down in the most mysterious of all the sacred books, the Apocalypse.

Viewed externally, St. John's cross may seem to have been lighter than those of the other apostles. But as Bossuet says, "St. John's cross was inwardly the greatest of all. Learn the mystery and consider the two crosses of our Savior. The one was seen on Calvary, and it seemed the more painful. The other is the one He carried all through His life, and it caused Him far more suffering." [15] Jesus explained to St. Catherine of Siena several times that this interior cross is the desire for the salvation of souls, a desire that was combated by the spirit of

[15] *Panegyric on St. John*, Point 1.

evil, by the spirit of the world, and by covetousness that sweeps millions of souls to perdition. In Jesus' life we can follow the progress of the malice of those who hated Him, thus increasing His thirst for the salvation of souls that was burning and consuming Him. The martyrdom of the heart is often more painful than outward martyrdom, and it can last for years and not merely for a few hours.

It was particularly this interior cross of desire for the glory of God and for the salvation of souls that Jesus gave to St. John. It did not strike at the senses, but it was implanted by God in the depths of his soul together with a very strong desire for the salvation of sinners. To make His apostle capable of carrying this interior cross, Jesus inspired in him the love of suffering which at once quickened the desire to a calm, steady flame, and prevented the soul from finding solace in anything outside of God. Likewise, when certain souls called to holiness find too much natural satisfaction in creatures, our Lord will quickly pour a little bitterness on this satisfaction, and this bitterness far exceeds the pleasure formerly enjoyed. This is a crucifying and purifying grace.

Finally, St. John's interior cross consisted most of all in the heresies that were mutilating Holy Mother Church by denying the divinity of Jesus. How these denials must have tortured the heart of the author of the Fourth Gospel which was written to make known the Word made flesh in all His glory! This interior cross derived from the divisions arising in the new-born Church to the detriment of charity. When the apostle was eighty years old, he had his disciples carry him to the church of Ephesus, and since he could no longer preach long sermons, he merely said: "My little children, love one another." He who in his youth had been called "son of thunder" by our Lord because of his ardor, could now speak only of fraternal charity, the great sign of love of God. He had lost none of his ardor, of his hunger for justice, but it had become more spiritual and gentle. And when his listeners asked him why he always repeated the same thing, he answered: "That is the Lord's command. If you accomplish it, that is sufficient." Such was John's cross; above all an interior cross.

The Lord gives us interior crosses, too. There are three kinds of crosses: those that remain useless, like that of the bad thief; those we carry to make reparation for our own sins and to merit salvation, like that of the good thief; and those that make us think of the Savior's cross, and that we bear in order to labor with Him for the salvation of souls. When we carry a cross well, it in turn carries us. It unseals our eyes and leads us toward contemplation, and helps us to see God hidden in the souls of men. If such a cross sometimes seems very heavy, let us ask our Savior to give us a love of suffering, or at least orient us in the path of suffering.

That is what He desires, since He has given us His heart, a wounded heart. He has also given us His Mother, and one of the greatest graces that our Lady of Sorrows can obtain for us is the grace of delighting in the crosses that the Lord places on our shoulders to purify us and to enable us to labor for the salvation of souls.[16] This is truly to enter into Christ's intimacy and to participate in His hidden and sorrowful life before having a part in His glorious life in heaven.[17]

[16] The expression "to delight in the cross" reminds us that our Lord declared: "There are some . . . that shall not taste death till they see the Son of man coming in His kingdom" (Matt. 16:28). St. Thomas said in this regard (*In Matthaeum*, 16:28) : "Sinners are absorbed, swallowed up as it were, by death, the just delight in death, which is their entrance into eternal life."

[17] To help us enter into Christ's intimacy, let us from time to time reread a hymn composed by St. Bernard of Clairvaux: [18]

> Jesus, sweet is love of Thee
> Nor may nothing so sweet be;
> Nought that man may think or see
> Can have sweetness near Thee.

> Jesus, no song may be sweeter
> Nor thought in heart blissfuller,
> Nought may be felt lightsomer
> Than Thou, so sweet a Lover.

Equally beautiful is a German prayer that has long been sung by the faithful:

> Ich danke dir, Herr Jesu Christ,
> Dasz du fur mich gestorben bist.
> Lass dein Blut und deine Pein
> An mir doch nicht verloren sein.
> O Liebe, o unendliche Liebe Gottes!

Let us repeat with Blessed Nicholas de Flue: "Nimm mich mir, und gib mich dir: Lord, take me from myself and give me to Thee!"

[18] Thomas Walsh, *The Catholic Anthology. The World's Great Catholic Poetry* (New York, 1947), pp. 49 f.

❊ XXX ❊

OUR PARTICIPATION IN THE MYSTERIES OF OUR LORD'S LIFE

> "In My Father's house there are many mansions."
>
> John 14:2

CHRIST'S intimacy takes on different forms that contribute to the harmony of His mystical body, that is, to its variety within its profound unity. In the Church the union of these two factors, unity and catholicity, in the face of so many causes for division, constitutes a permanent moral miracle.[1] For in the Church unity of faith, hope, charity, worship, and government exists despite the diversity of place, time, race, language, customs, and institutions. This is indeed the accomplishment of one of Christ's prophecies, that His Church was to extend to all peoples,[2] and that it would nevertheless remain one[3] in order to lead the souls of every land and every century to eternal life.

It is important to understand the reason for this variety in unity. Diversity of temperament, character, or spiritual cast, is often an occasion for salutary suffering but also for failures in charity, for irritation, impatience, and for arbitrary judgments. In our narrow view we may sometimes wish that all souls were absolutely alike, and

---

[1] The Council of the Vatican (Denzinger, no. 1794) says: "Ecclesia per se ipsam ob suam nempe admirabilem propagationem, eximiam sanctitatem et inexhaustam in omnibus bonis fecunditatem, ob catholicam unitatem, invictamque stabilitatem, magnum quoddam et perpetuum est motivum credibilitatis et divinae suae legationis testimonium irrefragabile."

[2] Cf. Matt. 28:19: "Going therefore, teach ye all nations: baptizing them in the name of the Father and of the Son and of the Holy Ghost." Cf. Mark 16:15.

[3] Cf. John 17:20: "And not for them [the apostles] only do I pray, but for them also who through their word shall believe in Me. That they all may be one, as Thou, Father, in Me, and I in Thee." Cf. Matt. 16:18; John 10:16; Acts 1:8.

341

had the same dominant inclinations as we do. Fortunately that is not the case. The harmony of the Church, as well as that of the religious orders and of religious communities, requires a certain diversity. In the vast fertile plain that is the Church there are a number of hills from which one can look out with the eyes of a St. Benedict, as it were, or of a St. Dominic, or a St. Francis, a St. Ignatius, or a St. Theresa. Our Lord has told us: "In My Father's house there are many mansions."

To gain light on this point we may consider the different forms of holiness that correspond to various dominant inclinations and to different types of trials. Each of these spiritual physiognomies has its own grandeur and beauty. Holiness takes three rather distinct forms, that correspond to the three predominant graces and tend to converge, as trails on different slopes of a mountain all lead to the summit. These three forms of holiness, as we shall see, are eminently present in the sacred souls of Jesus and Mary.

Holiness takes three rather distinct forms that correspond to the three great duties toward God: the duty to know Him, the duty to love Him, and the duty to serve Him. Every Christian must of course fulfill each of these three duties. Yet in the mystical body one must excel in one function and another in some other function.

There are holy souls whose special mission is to love God ardently, and thus to make reparation for the offenses made against Him. They receive early in life graces of love that transform their will and make of it a living power that never ceases spending itself for the glory of God and the salvation of their neighbor.

Other souls are called upon to excel in the contemplation of God, to make Him known, and show us the way that leads to Him. From the start they receive graces of light that increasingly enlighten their intelligence and make of it a beacon to guide the faithful in their progress toward eternity.

Finally, there are holy souls whose mission is essentially to serve God by their fidelity to daily duties in various works of charity. Their memory and their entirely practical activity, under the influx of the theological virtues, are placed continually at the service of God and of their neighbor.

Let us consider each in turn these three forms of holiness that are personified in the three privileged apostles whom our Lord led first to Thabor and then to Gethsemane: Peter, John, and James.

Each of these souls excels naturally in the exercise of one faculty. And as grace perfects nature's good points, it takes hold of this faculty more directly and powerfully, afterward reaching the other, less developed faculties. Grace thus makes use of the resources of our nature for our own perfection and salvation, and constitutes our special supernatural inclination that we must always follow, since it is inspired by God.[4] On the other hand, each of these souls has its dominant fault to conquer, a special pitfall to avoid, and that is why the Lord sends appropriate trials to each one.

Enlightened directors recognize in souls the special supernatural inclination that God has given them and also the dominant fault to be combated. We need to know both of them, the white and the black, in order to understand the trials that God sends us, to derive greater benefit from them, and to avoid making arbitrary judgments of other souls that are going toward the same summit but up another slope. Those who are naturally gentle must become strong, and those who are naturally strong must become gentle. *"Alius sic, alius sic ibat,"* in the words of St. Augustine. There are different paths that lead to the same goal, and even among those traveling in the same direction one may progress more slowly than another and still not be retrogressing.[5]

In the molding of souls the Lord finds a way to make use of every-

[4] St. Thomas (Ia IIae, q. 66, a. 2 ad 2), after showing that all the infused virtues related to charity increase proportionately together like the five fingers of the hand, notes that some saints excel in one virtue and others in another, because they are more inclined in that direction by nature and special vocation or by the attraction of grace: "One saint is praised chiefly for one virtue, another saint for another virtue, on account of his more admirable readiness for the act of one virtue than for the act of another virtue."

[5] Differences in character do not derive, as do differences in temperament, from organic differences. They are distinctive traits of the soul. In the first period of the spiritual life, while the senses still predominate, the temperament is very noticeable. But after the second conversion, or passive purification of the senses, the temperament loses much of its influence, the superior faculties have become much stronger, and therefore the spiritual physiognomy of each one becomes more pronounced. We should beware of artificial classifications, but not of those based on the very nature of the soul and of its faculties. For the different spiritual physiognomies, such as that of the scholar, the man of action, or the artist correspond to the predominant exercise of a given faculty and to the grace that places this faculty at God's service.

thing. He does not deal in the same way with a man of action who is devoured by zeal, a missioner, as He would with a theologian, a St. Thomas, or with a painter like Angelico, a poet like Dante, or a musician like Beethoven. But He makes everything serve for the expression of faith, hope, and charity. He puts Aristotle's logic to work in the mind of a theologian, and the learned harmonies of colors and sounds in an artist. And in the last analysis nothing in the intellectual and sensible order has value except as an expression of God's perfections. Leading to this summit are several slopes, and only what leads to it can have any deep and lasting interest for us. The Office of All Saints admirably takes into account all these variations in holiness as found in the apostles, martyrs, doctors, confessors, and virgins.

The souls in whom the exercise of the will and the ardor of love dominate resemble the seraphim.[6] According to revelation, these superior angels are inflamed with the love that the Holy Ghost communicates to them. It is this love that leads them to contemplate God's sublime beauties. Their spiritual flame generates more heat than light. They sing the canticle: "Holy, Holy, Holy, the Lord God of hosts!"[7] They constitute the supreme order of the first hierarchy of angels. For the highest virtue of those who strive toward God is charity or divine love, which in contrast to knowledge is incompatible with mortal sin.[8]

Likewise, ardent souls are first of all ravished by graces of love. They strive toward the good with zeal and determination, and often ask themselves: "What shall I do for God?" They have a burning thirst to suffer, to mortify themselves, in order to prove their love for God; they yearn to make reparation for the offenses committed against Him and to save sinners. Their desire to know God better is secondary.

This group of souls would, it seems, include the prophet Elias, full of zeal for the Lord,[9] the apostle Peter who chose to be crucified head downward through humility and love for his Master, the great

---

[6] Their name signifies "the fiery ones." They represent divine holiness, and their function is to consume or destroy sin by means of the burning coal of love. Cf. Isa. 6:2–7.

[7] Isa. 6:3.

[8] St. Thomas, Ia, q. 63, a. 7, ad 1; a. 9, ad 3; q. 108, a. 5, ad 5; q. 109, a. 1, ad 3.

[9] III Kings 19:10: "With zeal have I been zealous for the Lord."

martyrs St. Ignatius of Antioch and St. Lawrence, the seraphic St. Francis of Assisi, St. Margaret Mary who from her youth wished to suffer through love and in a spirit of reparation, St. Benedict Joseph Labre the impassioned lover of the cross. Also there were St. Charles Borromeo, St. Vincent de Paul, and countless other apostles and servants of mankind.

All these souls are more outstanding because of their charity, the surge of their hearts toward God, than because of their understanding.

The pitfall of those among them not sufficiently docile to the Holy Ghost would lie in the very energy of their will, which might degenerate into rigidity, tenacity, and obstinacy. This is a dominant fault that is quite visible among the less fervent of these souls. Their zeal is not sufficiently enlightened, nor patient and gentle enough. Some of them may turn too much to active works at the expense of prayer.

The Lord sends these souls trials designed in particular to make their will more malleable, sometimes even to break their will when it has become too rigid. He permits grave setbacks so that their natural ardor may develop into a truly supernatural, disinterested, patient, and gentle zeal. He teaches them to put their trust not in the natural enthusiasm of the heart but in divine mercy that is always ready to help. The Lord humiliates these ardent souls sometimes by permitting them to endure violent temptations, even temptations of despair. This was the case of Elias when he lay down in the desert under the juniper tree.[10] God even permits serious falls, as when Peter denied his Master.

The Lord also sends great aridity to these souls and allows their contemplation to be painful even when it is full of love and merit. Their ardent love burns them, consumes them, and makes them suffer keenly from all the offenses committed against God. He inspires them to expiate or to make reparation.

Thus does God mold these souls that are more ardent than lumi-

---

[10] *Ibid.*, 19:4: "And he [Elias] went forward, one day's journey into the desert. And when he was there, and sat under a juniper tree, he requested for his soul that he might die, and said: It is enough for me. Lord, take away my soul; for I am no better than my fathers. And he cast himself down, and slept. . . . And behold an angel of the Lord touched him, and said to him: Arise and eat . . . for thou hast yet a great way to go."

nous, dominated by the burning zeal of charity, the highest of the theological virtues.

A second group of souls is made of those in whom the exercise of the intellect dominates, rather than of the will. The grace that impels them directly and powerfully toward God is the grace of light. They resemble the cherubim who, the prophets tell us, cluster around the throne of God.[11] These angels, wonderfully enlightened by the eternal Word, are first of all overwhelmed with awe as they contemplate God's beauty, and they are thereby inspired to love Him and to make others know Him.[12] Their spiritual flame produces more light than heat.

Likewise these souls are first enlightened by graces of illumination. They are inclined to rejoice in the contemplation of God, in the great over-all views that are born of wisdom. Their love increases only as a consequence of their enlightenment. They experience in a lesser degree than the first group the need to act, to mortify themselves, to suffer in reparation. But if they are faithful, they attain heroic love for the God who enchants them. The great doctors of the Church belong to this family of souls: among them, St. Augustine, St. Anselm, St. Albert the Great, St. Thomas Aquinas, and many others who through the centuries have been beacons showing humanity the path that leads to God.

The pitfall of the less perfect among these souls is to be content with the lights they receive and not conform their lives to the truths they know. Whereas their intelligence is highly enlightened, their will often lacks ardor. St. Francis de Sales bemoaned this condition in himself, and prayed for the grace of fortitude.

It is not rare for these souls to be given grave interior trials. The night of the senses and of the spirit described by St. John of the Cross leads them progressively to complete selflessness and generous love. The interior trials these souls endure are usually less painful than those of the first-mentioned group of souls. They find consolation in the lights they receive, and they are more strongly attracted toward

---

[11] Dan. 3:55: "Blessed art Thou [O Lord] that beholdest the depths and sittest upon the cherubims." Cf. Ps. 17:11; 79:2; Isa. 37:16.

[12] St. Thomas, Ia, q. 63, a. 7 ad 1; a. 108, a. 5 ad 5.

contemplative prayer. But they must bemoan their lack of energy for quite a while. Their love of truth makes them suffer especially from error, false doctrines that lead men's minds astray. This is at once their cross and a stimulus to labor in making God known.

When these luminous souls have been purified by suffering and remain faithful to the lights that God sends them, they aspire ever more to be united to Him, to lose themselves in Him without falling into self-absorption. A faithful luminous soul will become more closely united to God than an ardent soul that is unfaithful.

There have been great saints like St. Paul, St. John, St. Benedict, St. Dominic, St. Gertrude, St. Catherine of Siena, St. Theresa of Avila, St. John of the Cross, who were both very contemplative and very ardent even from the start. They early combined within themselves the qualities of the first two groups of souls. For that matter, these two types of souls tend to resemble each other more closely as they approach the summit toward which all of them aspire.

Lastly, there are the souls whose particular mission is to serve God through fidelity to daily duty. The faculty they use most is memory combined with activity of a wholly practical order. This group includes the great majority of Christians. Their memory makes them attentive to specific facts. They are enraptured by the history of God's generosity toward man, as recorded in the Old Testament, the Gospels, and the life of the Church. These souls are easily touched by the words of the liturgy and by the outstanding virtues of various saints. Grace adapts itself to their nature and shows them clearly through the maze of their multiple occupations the duty to be accomplished, the neighbor to be helped, and the glory to be given to God.

Only rarely does divine inspiration send them broad over-all views, but it does make them attentive to the various means of perfection. In this way these souls, when they are faithful and generous, attain a practical and personal understanding of the things of God as well as a great love of God and of their neighbor. They are thus able to reach the loftiest levels of holiness.

Their pitfall would lie in becoming too attached to practices that are good in themselves but do not lead directly to God: for instance, certain exterior austerities or vocal prayers. They would then run the

risk of becoming excessively anxious about details, scruples, and becoming unduly attached to methods that are useful at the start but
somewhat too mechanical. These things can prevent the attainment
of intimate union with the Lord.

The trials of these souls generally have less to do with the interior
life and more with the practice of fraternal charity and the exercise
of their generosity. They suffer much from the faults of their neighbors and from the obstacles they encounter in their labors. The great
interior purifications come to them much later than to the souls in
the aforementioned categories. Yet if these practical souls are generous, they also attain an intimate union with God.

These are the three forms of holiness that seem personified in the
three privileged apostles, Peter, John, and James, whom our Lord
took with Him to Thabor and afterward to Gethsemane. All these
souls are called in various ways to the contemplation of the mysteries
of faith and to intimate union with God. The closer they come to the
summit toward which they are striving the more closely they resemble
one another, the more deeply they resemble Christ, without losing
their own individualities.

These three forms of sanctity are to be found in their most eminent
degree in Christ's soul, without any of the imperfections that subsist
in the saints. It reminds us somewhat of the way white light contains
the seven colors of the rainbow. Indeed, no one ever knew God better,
loved Him more, or served Him more perfectly than did Jesus Christ.

Jesus has shown us the excellence of these three forms of holiness
in the three periods of His life on earth: His hidden life, His apostolic
life, His sorrowful life.

During His hidden life in the obscurity of Nazareth, in the carpenter's house, He was the perfect model of fidelity to daily duty in
the performance of acts that were outwardly very modest but inwardly of immeasurable greatness because of the love that inspired
them.

In His apostolic life He shone forth as the light of the world and
told us that those who follow Him do not walk in darkness but shall
receive the light of life.[13] He not merely believed but actually saw

[13] John 8:12.

immediately in the divine essence the things that He taught about eternal life and the means to attain it. He founded the Church, entrusted it to Peter, and said to His apostles: "You are the light of the world." [14] Then He sent them out to teach all nations and to bring the peoples of the earth baptism and the Eucharist.

Finally, in His sorrowful life Jesus manifested all the ardor of His love for His Father and for us. This love was so great as to inspire Him to die for us on the cross. He thirsted to suffer in reparation for the outrages done to God, to save souls, and to consummate the work of Redemption. His thirst for suffering was incomparably greater than that of St. Andrew, St. Ignatius of Antioch, St. Lawrence, St. Theresa, or St. Benedict Joseph Labre. For Jesus' heart is a fiery furnace of charity. No one ever suffered more because of sin, and from His wounded heart come all the graces received by reparative souls, those associated with the great mystery of the Redemption.

Jesus possessed all three forms of holiness without any shadow of imperfection. He was attentive to even the smallest details of God's service, ever fulfilling them with prompt exactitude. He enjoyed the most exalted contemplation, but was never lost in it, as are saints in ecstasy. Jesus was above ecstasy. He could simultaneously see the depths of the divine essence and converse with His apostles concerning the smallest details of their apostolic life. His ardent love and fiery zeal were united to the greatest patience, gentleness, and compassion that inspired Him to pray for His executioners: "Father, forgive them, for they know not what they do."

The holiness of Christ's soul is manifested by its reflection in the souls of His saints, as white light is manifested by the seven colors. The same holds true of Mary, making all due allowances, for she too possesses in an eminent degree all the forms of holiness.

Let us not underevaluate our Lord's life by trying to explain it too much in terms of our own personal psychology. This is how a Jansenist Christ was invented, and then, as a reaction against this view, a liberal Christ. Let us lift our souls up toward Him instead of bringing Him down to our own level. He is infinitely above even our most generous sentiments, and He has no illusions. Though He is far

[14] Matt.

superior to the greatest saints, He is still our perfect model and ceaselessly offers us the grace and strength to follow Him.

The mysteries of Christ's life must in a sense be reproduced in us in the measure that the Savior wishes to assimilate us to Himself and make us participate in His hidden life, in His apostolic life, in His sorrowful life, and finally in His glorious life in heaven. This progressive assimilation is noticeable in the life of a number of saints. Daily meditation on the mysteries of the Rosary can help us to advance ever more securely in this path if we really desire to do so.

The joyous mysteries of Christ's childhood, the sorrowful mysteries of His passion, and the glorious mysteries of the Resurrection and Ascension correspond to the three great acts in the life of a soul: 1. the act of desiring the ultimate end: holiness and eternal beatitude, the thought of which causes happiness and inspires the soul to make its first steps toward God; 2. the act of desiring the means that can enable us to attain this end: fulfillment of the commandments to carry our cross after the Master's example and to follow in His footsteps; 3. the act of finding rest with Him once the goal has been won.

These mysteries of Christ's life must become more and more the food of our souls, the object of our contemplation, so that we can penetrate their depths and rejoice in them. This will be a foretaste, as it were, of eternal happiness. We shall grasp ever better the fact that sanctifying grace is the seed of glory,[15] that a profoundly Christian life is the beginning of eternal life, according to the Savior's own words recorded several times by St. John: "Amen, amen, I say unto you: He that believeth in Me hath everlasting life . . . and I will raise Him up in the last day." [16]

The Meaning of the Incarnation
for Certain Contemplatives

Contemplative souls that are being tested by suffering may find help in the following reflections. After reading a commentary on St. Thomas' thought concerning Providence, one such soul wrote: "When

---

[15] St. Thomas, IIa IIae, q. 24, a. 3 ad 2.
[16] John 6:40, 44, 47, 55; 3:36; 5:24, 39.

I read the first chapters dealing with God's attributes, a black veil descended over all that I read. Only the Deity stood out in relief. It also was wrapped in darkness, but darkness of a different nature from that to be found in the lights of theology. For to me all light is darkness. . . . My soul lives apart, divorced from the sensible portion of me, and does not participate in any way, so to speak, in the celebration of feasts and commemoration of mysteries. The soul gives life to the body, and that is all. The body remains alone, always alone in the presence of these things that are made for the soul and that consequently encounter this human obstacle, inert as a corpse. . . . Then from time to time, but only rarely, a sudden certainty fills my mind, accompanied by an embrace that touches the depths of my soul. At such moments I am sure that I love God with a true love. . . . My walled-up soul (separated from the sensible) thus becomes conscious at times of an abyss and a life of unfathomable depth. It is, as it were, the experimental knowledge of immense but unknown riches; of an incandescent furnace, which neither lights nor warms me; of an overflowing but half-perceived plenitude, for which I hunger but which does not nourish me."

As a matter of fact, the prayer of certain souls that are being subjected to grave trials is almost totally devoid of the intellectual and effective elements normal to prayer. Yet there is in their prayer a consent and abandonment which amounts to saying: "My God, I trust Thee," and which contains faith, trust, love, and true prayer.

Souls in this state may have the same reaction to the preceding pages on the mystery of the redemptive Incarnation. For such souls "all light is darkness" compared to the inaccessible light which they dimly glimpse from afar, especially through the words of the Savior. In fact, the sun is but a shadow by comparison with the intellectual light of the first rational principles. These latter are themselves shadows compared to the supernatural mysteries, as it will some day be given us to see them. And among these mysteries, the redemptive Incarnation is a shadow compared to the Deity which, as it exists in itself, contains eminently, formally, and explicitly all the divine attributes and the three divine persons. The Deity as we know it here on earth contains only implicitly the divine attributes deduced from it. But when we shall see it as it is in itself there will no longer be any need for deduction. We shall see explicitly in the eminence of the Deity, superior to being, to unity, to goodness, all the infinite perfections and the three divine persons.[17] Certain souls have an experimental foretaste of this, as it were, and that is why the superior portion of their souls is never satisfied with anything that can be said about the divine attributes or the personality of the Word, who became man to save us.

The words of St. Thomas are appropriate in this connection: "Matters that concern the Godhead are, in themselves, the strongest incentive to love and consequently to devotion, because God is supremely lovable. Yet such is the weakness of man's mind that it needs a guiding hand, not only to the knowledge, but also to the love of divine things by means of certain sensible objects known to us. Chief among these is the humanity of Christ, according to the words of the Preface, that through knowing God visibly, we may be caught up to the love of things invisible. Wherefore matters relating to Christ's humanity are the chief incentive to devotion, leading us thither as a guiding hand, although devotion itself has for its object matters concerning the Godhead." [18] In other words, it is the Deity particularly that attracts love and devotion; but inasmuch as it is invisible we need to be progressively lifted toward it, starting with things of the senses. Thus the Savior appeared to us first in His humanity, as the way. Later He appeared in His divinity, as the truth and the life. This is what the Preface of the Nativity proclaims: "Because by the mystery of the Word made flesh the light of Thy glory hath shone anew upon the eyes of our mind: that while we acknowledge Him to be God seen by men, we may be drawn by Him to the love of things unseen." This is the perfect way to eternal life.

The state of the contemplative souls we have just spoken of is not solely one of aridity or absence of consolation. It is a state of impo-

---

[17] Cf. Cajetan, *In Iam*, q. 39, a. 1, no. 7: "Res divina prior est ente et omnibus differentiis ejus: est enim super ens et super unum, etc. Est in Deo unica ratio formalis, non pure absoluta, nec pure respectiva, non pure communicabilis, nec pure incommunicabilis; sed eminentissime ac formaliter continens quidquid absolutae perfectionis est, et quidquid trinitas respectiva exigit."

[18] St. Thomas, IIa IIae, q. 82, a. 3 ad 2.

tence, quite different from the natural tendency to sleep. When souls are in this helpless state they can still read a few verses of the Gospel, but they cannot return for the moment to active prayer, that is, discursive meditation.

Active prayer is something like a child's effort to spell and then to read little poems. If the poems were taken away from him and he had to return to his alphabet, he could not do it. He would have no interest or incentive to relearn the alphabet since he knows it already. If the little poems that he loves to read are taken from him, he is helpless to find what he needs.

We have another example of impotence in the preacher who looks at the text of a sermon on the Passion that he preached several years earlier with special fervor. He no longer possesses the grace that would enkindle his notes. He understands the text quite well, he remembers it, but grace does not gleam through. He is like a poet who has lost his inspiration. His soul is like the becalmed water of a lake, or like the leaves of a poplar when there is no breath of wind. It is a dead calm. Whence comes his impression of impotence to preach the Passion as it should be preached. And yet beneath this impression of impotence, or perhaps above it, exists a real thirst to do good to souls and a deep prayer that will be answered in the end. This preacher, who is so thoroughly dissatisfied with his notes, already dominates them. The awareness of his impotence is a sign that he is docile in God's hand. The same holds true for the tested contemplative souls of whom we speak. They feel empty of God, but they are thirsting for Him more than ever.

Father de Caussade, S.J., in his beautiful book, *Abandonment to Divine Providence*, has described this state very well: "Souls who walk in light sing canticles of joy; those who walk amid shadows sing anthems of woe. Let one and the other sing to the end the portion and anthem God assigns them. We must add nothing to what He has completed. There must flow every drop of this gall of divine bitterness with which He wills to inebriate them. Behold Jeremias and Ezechiel: theirs was the language of sighs and lamentations, and their only consolation was in the continuation of their lament. He who would have dried their tears would have deprived us of the most beautiful portions of the Holy Scriptures. The spirit that afflicts is the only one that can console. The streams of sorrow and consolation flow from the same source.

"When God astonishes a soul she must needs tremble; when He menaces, she cannot but fear. We have but to leave the divine operation to its own development; it bears within itself the remedy as well as the trial. . . . Make no effort to escape these divine terrors. . . . Receive into the depth of your being the waters of that sea of bitterness which inundated the soul of Christ." [19]

If the contemplatives of whom we have just spoken no longer seem to understand what they read concerning the mysteries of salvation, it is because they are so eager to pass beyond narrow formulas and enter into the infinite depths of the mystery of God, in His unfathomable love. "O Liebe, O unendliche Liebe Gottes!" The truth is that they are the ones who understand best. While their Holy Communions may seem arid to them, and their poverty extreme, they understand incomparably better than others the sublime words:

> Panis angelicus fit panis hominum.

> . . . .

> O res mirabilis, manducat Dominum
> Pauper, servus, et humilis.

[19] Rev. J. P. de Caussade, S.J., *Abandonment or, Absolute Surrender to Divine Providence*, translated by Ella McMahon (New York, 1945), p. 129.

❊ XXXI ❊

THE GRACE OF CHRIST AND THE MYSTICS OUTSIDE THE CHURCH[*]

Natural Pre-mysticism and Supernatural Mysticism [1]

THERE is much talk these days of certain mystics outside the Church who, without visibly belonging to the true Church of Christ, seem to have lived the life of grace and charity in the superior degree that characterizes the mystical life.

The studies of Louis Massignon [2] and of Asin Palacios [3] on Islam are written from this point of view. These works which contribute mostly documents should be examined with care, and their authors would probably not accept the general conclusions that have been drawn from their works by certain critics.

Emile Dermenghem goes much farther than they in one of his works.[4] In 1930, with regard to several Moslem mystics whom he had studied, he wrote: "All these *çoufis*, thinkers, poets, or saints, have given expression to the great mystical experience: to die to the world in order to live in God, in compelling formulas analogous to those of the Christian Fathers, doctors, and mystics, and often also of the Hindu Vedantists. This would confirm the thesis of R. Guénon on the universality of tradition: *quod ubique, quod semper, quod ab omnibus*, according to the Catholic formula. They repeat incessantly with the Scholastics that creatures have no being except that which

---

[1] The following pages have appeared under this title in the *Etudes Carmélitaines* of October, 1933.

[2] Louis Massignon, *La passion d'Al-Hosayn-ibn-Mansour-al-Hallâj, martyr mystique de l'Islam*, 2 vols., 1922. "*Le Dîwân d'al-Hallâj,*" Journal Asiatique, January–March, 1931.

[3] Miguel Asin Palacios, *El Islam Cristianizado, Estudio del "Sufismo" a Través de las Obras de Abenarabi de Murcia*, 1931.

[4] Emile Dermenghem, "L'Eloge du Vin (Al Khamriya)," Poème mystique de Omar ibn al Faridh, *L'Anneau d'Or*, 1931. Integral translation accompanied by notes, a critical introduction, and a historical and theological essay on Moslem mysticism.

[*] Note that in his first sentence above the author explains mystics "outside the Church" as persons who do not belong "visibly" to the true (i.e., Catholic) Church. This accords with the Catholic teaching that *Extra ecclesiam nulla salus*—"Outside the Church there is no salvation." The term "the Church" always means "the Catholic Church." —*Publisher*, 1998.

they receive from God, and with St. Paul that it is in Him that we have our life, our movement, and our being." [5]

Father Eliseus of the Nativity, O.C.D., commented aptly on this subject: "We do not know what Dermenghem means by 'great mystical experience'; at any rate, the Church will never take this universality of tradition as the sole criterion of truth." [6]

On the other hand certain rationalists and surviving Modernists have been trying to explain even the supernatural mysticism of St. John of the Cross in terms of the natural mysticism which is to be found in varying degrees in all religions and which from their point of view is superior to any single creed. According to this approach, the revelation of the mysteries of salvation as proposed by the Church, the person of our Lord, His example, the sacraments instituted by Him, bring nothing essential to the Catholic but merely a greater security. The essential, they say, lies elsewhere and on a higher level: in a mystical experience that is to be found in the more interior souls of every religion and that is nothing but the natural blossoming of the religious sentiment.

To the theologian, this is one of the most delicate aspects of the very difficult problem of the salvation of unbelievers, and it is becoming more and more acute.[7]

[5] *Nouvelles littéraires*, January 25, 1930. Review of the work by Rev. Bruno, O.C.D., on St. John of the Cross.

[6] *Etudes Carmélitaines*, October 1931, p. 162. "L'Expérience mystique d'Ibn 'Arabî, est-elle surnaturelle?"

[7] Father Clerissac, O.P., had seen how the great problems of the present time culminate in this one. He wrote:

"There is a remarkable fact. I shall not call it the conflict of the great modern tendencies (scientific, social, and mystical), but rather their convergence, inasmuch as they all converge toward a single religion regardless of the aims of those who represent them.

"No doubt the scientific question has existed in every age, although it probably did not in former times imply the philosophical enigmas of the present day nor any problem of history or exegesis.

"Under the various forms of servitude and pauperism, the social question has always haunted us.

"Between the extreme forms of illuminism and quietism, mystical aspirations formerly found many means of expression. But in our own day these tendencies have taken on a special aspect and a new life. Each of them borrows from the other two and communicates to them in return something of itself. Science pretends to be a religion. Socialism desires to be a code of morals and offers itself as a feverish worship of justice. Mysticism in its turn upholds its right to be scientific. Moreover, these three tendencies by their contents and

I. Statement of the Problem
Errors of Extremism to be Avoided

Everybody knows the two radically opposed positions that the Church has rejected as grave errors. One of them is worse than heresy. It does not choose from revelation what it will retain. It denies all supernatural revelation.

On the other hand, naturalism, as it is formulated, for example, by Spinoza and his successors, absolutely denies the supernatural order as well as miracles and the life of grace. It sees in the various religions nothing more than the natural evolution of religious sentiment. Modernism reached this same conclusion by renewing and aggravating the Pelagian error.[8] From this point of view Catholicism is at best the most exalted form of the evolution of religious sentiment; the mysticism described by St. John of the Cross is an interesting form of natural mysticism which is expressed in pantheistic terms by the Buddhists in the Orient, for instance, and in the West by the theosophists who find their inspiration in Jacob Boehme or in Schelling's second philosophy.

their action compete for the attainment in a definite and supreme form either of the experimental knowledge of God or the apotheosis of man. I do not think it is an exaggeration to say that here is the greatest historical event since the invasions of the barbarians. Let us not take this fact to be a simple manifestation of blind forces. Let us beware of the seduction of these tendencies that are everywhere captivating men's minds and hearts. Let us beware of the importance of the inevitable transformations that will ensue."

Indeed, the most recent encyclicals of the Sovereign Pontiff are an answer to these general aspirations of humanity. In particular the encyclicals on Christ the King, on His sanctifying influence on His whole mystical body, on the family and the sanctity of Christian marriage, on social questions, on the necessity for reparation, and on the missions. All these encyclicals center around the reign of Christ over all men. It follows that for religion to maintain the pre-eminence that it must have over scientific and social activity, the interior life of its members must be deep, it must be a true life of union with God. This is manifestly necessary.

[8] Cf. *Bulletin de la Société Française de Philosophie*, May–June, 1925: "Saint Jean de la Croix et le problème de la valeur noétique de l'expérience mystique"; cf. *ibid.*, p. 87, "Remarques," by M. Blondel and J. Baruzi, on the infused character of the contemplation which St. John of the Cross speaks of. See also R. Dalbiez, "Une nouvelle Interpretation de Saint Jean de la Croix," *La vie spirituelle*, 1928: "The integral interpretation of the mystical experience must be theological or else there is no explanation for it whatever." Rev. Benoît Lavaud, O.P., "Psychologie indépendante et prière Chrétienne," *Revue Thomiste*, 1929; also "Les problèmes de la vie mystique," *La vie spirituelle*, June, 1931.

The extreme opposite of naturalism is none other than the pseudo-supernaturalism that appeared under various forms among the predestinarians such as Wyclif, the Protestants, and the Jansenists. They have all maintained that as a result of original sin human nature is so corrupt that every act of the infidel is a sin, and his apparent virtues are but splendid vices deriving from self-love and pride.

In opposition to these last-mentioned errors, Catholic doctrine holds that predestination is not necessary for the performance of even excellent actions, nor are sanctifying grace and infused faith required for an action that is morally good, such as paying one's debts or teaching sound principles to one's children. Fallen man can, without grace, even have a certain ineffectual love of God, the Author of nature, a love consisting of admiration and slight desire, capable of inspiring a naturally poetic soul to describe God's perfections in lyrical terms. Thus the pagans can, without grace, accomplish certain morally good acts. They are also endowed with actual grace by the help of which they can accomplish certain salutary acts that will dispose them to receive habitual grace, the radical principle not only of salutary acts but also of meritorious acts. "To anyone doing what in him lies (with the help of actual grace), God does not deny (habitual) grace." [9]

Pope Pius IX said in effect that those who invincibly or through no fault of their own ignore the true religion but who do what is in their power to observe the natural law can, through an illumination and a grace from God, attain the supernatural acts of faith and charity necessary for salvation. In other words, such persons can receive the life of grace, the seed of glory, and be saved.[10] These men "of good

---

[9] Cf. St. Thomas, Ia IIae, q. 109, a. 6: "Whether a man, by himself and without the external aid of grace, can prepare himself for grace. . . . Now in order that man prepare himself to receive this gift, it is not necessary to presuppose any further habitual gift in the soul, otherwise we should go on to infinity. But we must presuppose a gratuitous gift of God, who moves the soul inwardly or inspires the good wish." Also Ia IIae, q. 112, a. 3: "Whether grace is necessarily given to whoever prepares himself for it. . . . Man's preparation for grace is from God, as Mover, and from the free will, as moved. Hence the preparation may be looked at . . . as it is from God the Mover, and thus it has a necessity—not indeed of coercion, but of infallibility—as regards what it is ordained to by God, since God's intention cannot fail, according to the saying of Augustine in his book on the predestination of the saints (*De dono persev.*, 14) that 'by God's good gifts whoever is liberated, is most certainly liberated.' "

[10] "Notum nobis vobisque est, eos qui invincibili circa sanctissimam nostram religionem

will," in the theological sense of the term, belong to the soul of the Church, as is generally agreed by theologians.[11] *

We can see how Catholic doctrine rises above the diametrically opposed errors: 1. the error of naturalism, which denies the order of grace; 2. the error of narrow pseudo-supernaturalism, which denies that God wishes to offer to all adults the sufficient grace for the accomplishment of the commandments necessary for salvation. Yet a great mystery remains: the mystery of predestination. It is a great grace to belong visibly to the Church, to benefit by its infallible teaching, by the Holy Sacrifice of the Mass, and by the sacraments. Hence the necessity of the missions.

Two Tendencies Relating to the Mystics Outside the Church and the Importance of the Problem

As we have seen, there have been and still are diametrically opposed errors relating to the salvation of unbelievers. Within the limits of orthodoxy one can also distinguish two rather contrary tendencies with regard to those who have been called the "mystics outside the Church."

There are those who are inclined to think that, inasmuch as sanctifying grace, infused faith, and charity can exist in souls that do not belong visibly to the Church, we can also find the mystical life in them more often than has been heretofore admitted, especially when we recognize that this mystical life is the normal blossoming of the life of grace.

This tendency leads to the rather easy admission that certain mystics outside the Church are "authentic" mystics, and even to speak of Moslem, Hindu, Jewish, and other forms of mysticism as if they were, despite their errors, true mysticism. This leads to specific state-

---

ignorantia laborant, quique naturalem legem ejusque praecepta in omnium cordibus a Deo insculpta sedulo servantes ac Deo obedire parati, honestam rectamque vitam agunt, posse, divinae lucis et gratiae operante virtute, aeternam consequi vitam" (Denzinger, no. 1677).

[11] Cf. Dublanchy, *De axiomate: Extra ecclesiam nulla salus*, 1895, pp. 373 ff., and the article "L'Eglise," *Dictionnaire de théologie catholique*. Capéran, *Le problème du salut des infidèles* (theological essay), pp. 80 ff., 92. Edouard Hugon, *Hors de l'eglise point de salut*, 1914, chaps. 1–4.

* Especially since the publication of Pope Pius XII's encyclical *Mystici Corporis* (1943), the concept of belonging only to "the soul of the Church" has been recognized by Catholic theologians as defective and has been superseded by the more correct concept of belonging "invisibly" to the Catholic Church. (See the first sentence of this chapter and third paragraph of this page.) —*Publisher, 1998.*

ments that this or that mystic outside the Church has had authentic supernatural graces, and even very exalted graces, which might be compared to the transforming union, that is, the stage called by St. Theresa of Avila "Seventh Mansion," or at least the stages immediately preceding it. There are at times striking analogies to be sure, as L. Massignon and Miguel Asin Palacios [12] have noted.

But beneath these analogies, the questions of nature and origin remain obscure. And in such a delicate matter, exaggeration, which is contrary to all scientific prudence, would quickly become dangerous as well as easy. On these frontiers of the nature of grace we touch upon the most difficult problems of theology, and scholars who have studied them all their lives may often hesitate to formulate an opinion on them. On the questions about the limits of the two spheres, final judgment can only be the result of a profound knowledge of each of the two domains.

[12] As Maritain remarks (*The Degrees of Knowledge*, p. 337) and also Father Bruno, the case of Ibn 'Arabî discussed by Palacios calls for much greater reserve in judgment than that of al-Hallâj studied by Massignon.

In the April, 1932, issue of the *Etudes Carmélitaines*, pages 139 to 239, Palacios cites striking texts of the "Sharh Hikam" of Ibn 'Abbad Rondi which certainly call to mind what St. John of the Cross writes later on, particularly the following maxims and the commentaries on them: "God often teaches thee in the night of desolation what He does not teach thee in the splendor of the day of consolation. . . . It is therefore fitting that the servant recognize the grace God gives him in the day of anguish" (*ibid.*, p. 152). "Tribulations lead the soul to the presence of God and teach her to converse with Him on the carpet of sincerity. . . . Be convinced of thy own lowliness, and God will help thee in His greatness. . . . Say to thy Lord as thou liest prostrate on the carpet of spiritual poverty: 'O Rich One! Who will help the weak if not Thee?' 'O Noble One! Who will help the worthless if not Thee?' " (*Ibid.*, p. 158.)

We are no less astonished by what is said (*ibid.*, pp. 118 ff.) concerning the virtues of this master. They are described in these beautiful maxims: "He who loves celebrity is not sincere toward God" (*ibid.*, p. 140); "Pray for him who has offended thee, and thy prayer will be heard" (*ibid.*, p. 143); "It is in tribulation that man practices interior virtues, the least of which is more meritorious than mountains of exterior works of virtue" (p. 145); "For those who seek God, days of tribulation should be great feast days" (p. 157).

On the other hand, a person of penetrating vision who is also deeply religious has written to us from his home in Morocco after reading these texts: "Daily experience with the fathmas who serve us has proven to me how circumspect we must be in interpreting their religious vocabulary and in judging their interior life. For example, they repeatedly use the same words as we to signify abandonment to divine will. Yet what an abysmal difference there is between their flabby fatalism and our vital Christian abandonment! This helps me to understand how there may be a deep difference in the source of the most exalted states that are analogous in appearance."

Several thinkers who have formulated reservations that help state the problem with greater penetration and also bring out its importance.

First of all, even admitting that the mystical life is the full normal culmination of the life of grace, this normal summit is still a summit. And because of negligence, spiritual laziness, lack of generosity in trials, and insufficient docility to the Holy Ghost, this summit is rarely attained even in the Catholic Church, even in religious orders. And yet here are available so many supernatural lights, examples, graces, particularly through the sacraments and through daily Holy Communion most of all. How much more difficult it must be to reach this summit when one is deprived of these many aids!

Moreover, as a missioner who is well versed in these matters has recently stated, it is easy when a person chooses wisely—and is it not on choices of this kind that we are depending—to group a large number of texts describing these mystics outside the Church that seem to use terms strikingly similar to those used by St. John of the Cross with regard to the essence of the mystical life. This will lead us to the following conclusions:

a) For all of them the essence of contemplation is indeed the loving, obscure, indistinct, general knowledge with neither form nor image that the Doctor of Carmel teaches.

b) For all of them the practical behavior to be followed during contemplation is a kind of universal *nada*, and consists in abstracting the understanding from any particular notion (*Ascent of Mount Carmel*, Bk. II, chap. 12), and to be occupied with a loving attention in God, without wishing to specify anything (*Living Flame of Love*, *III, 3, 6*).

c) For all of them (and this is perhaps the most remarkable fact) the summit and the perfection of the mystical life exist when the soul totally transformed into its Beloved has become God by participation (*Spiritual Canticle*, Stanza 22).

It seems, therefore, that all these souls meet at the summit regardless of the path they have chosen, whether or not they have enjoyed the help of the infallible doctrine and the sacraments of the visible Church. Do they really meet? This, of course, is a most important question:

If, as we admit, the same sanctifying grace is presupposed in these diverse souls, it follows that, according to the view presented above, everything seems to happen as if this grace sufficed to reach even the highest degrees of supernatural union with God, with no need of having an explicit knowledge of the mystery of the redemptive Incarnation or of receiving the sacraments. (This also presupposes, of course, faith in the two primary truths of the supernatural order, namely, that God, the author of salvation, exists, and that He rewards good works. It also presupposes charity.) This explicit faith in the divine person of the Savior, His example, the sacraments, the teachings and regulations of the Church, would then seem to give the Catholic no more than secondary, not to say accidental, assistance and greater security. The essential, however, would lie elsewhere and on a higher level.[13]

Far more important, it would appear that St. John of the Cross himself defined and described contemplation in a manner that is not specifically Christian and Catholic by notes and definitions that are actually used to "recognize" and "authenticate" the mystics outside the Church. (In reality of course, he founds his mysticism on the fullness of revelation received from our Lord, on the explicit understanding of the mystery of the Cross perpetuated on the altar during the Mass, and on the sacraments, especially on the union with the Savior through spiritual and sacramental communion.) Would this provide

---

[13] That is why the Thomists generally maintain as the more probable the well-known thesis of St. Thomas, IIa IIae, q. 2, a. 7: "Post Evangelium sufficienter promulgatum, fides explicita Incarnationis est omnibus necessaria necessitate medii ad salutem." St. Thomas, *ibid.*, says: "After grace had been revealed, both learned and simple folk are bound to explicit faith in the mysteries of Christ." Cf. IIa IIae, q. 2, a. 8, fine ad 1 and 2. The reason for this is that Jesus Christ is the way to salvation: "I am the way and the truth and the life" (John 14:6). And St. Peter says in Acts 4:12: "There is no other name under heaven given to men, whereby we must be saved." We can be saved only by Christ, by being incorporated in Him, by belonging to His mystical body. This seems to require of adults not only the realization of the mystery of the Incarnation but also an explicit faith in this mystery, an explicit faith in the One who takes away the sins of the world.

However, we can inquire whether the Gospel is to be considered as promulgated in places where it has not yet been preached or where it has been completely forgotten. In any event, true mysticism presupposes at least an implicit faith in the Redeemer.

adequate safeguard for Jesus' words: "I am the way, and the truth, and the life"? [14]

Thus presented, the question is serious. Following the first-mentioned trend of thought which takes on more or less definite forms, would we not, under the influence of present-day syncretism, gradually lose the meaning of true contemplation, which St. Paul calls "the mind of Christ"? [15] This is the question brought up by the missioner we quoted earlier.

The answer will no doubt be given: The doctrine of implicit faith is definitely opposed to this syncretism and does not signify at all that explicit faith and the sacraments have only an accidental value. Father Eliseus of the Nativity has made some apt remarks on this point: [16] "The difficulty originates with regard to faith in the Mediator. The adult can be justified only by believing in one way or another in the redemption that Christ has won for humanity. This faith in Christ the Redeemer has three states or degrees: the explicit knowledge of the mysteries of the Incarnation and Redemption, as we Christians know it; the idea of a mediator between God and man; lastly, the conviction that God in His mercy has provided in some undefined way for the salvation of the human race. This last degree of knowledge of the Redeemer is called implicit faith in Christ and is to a certain extent indistinguishable from supernatural faith in Providence and belief in a God who rewards. . . . To believe that God saves men by whatever means He pleases is to possess an implicit faith in Christ the Redeemer [and according to St. Thomas this was sufficient before Christ's coming]. . . . It is difficult to maintain that conditions have changed for those who lived after Christ's coming but never heard of Him."

[14] In his *Spiritual Canticle*, verse 37, St. John of the Cross says that the mysteries within Christ are called caverns to symbolize their depth and height, that the treasures hidden in Him are like an inexhaustible mine, and that the doctors have discovered only a minute fraction of them. In the *Ascent of Mount Carmel* (Bk. II, chap. 20) he shows that to ask for private revelations is to exhibit disrespect for Christ who has brought the fullness of revelation. The saint lays stress on the divine words of Thabor: "This is My beloved Son, in whom I am well pleased: hear ye Him" (Matt. 17:5). Indeed, St. John of the Cross, like St. Theresa of Avila, maintains that the contemplative must not of his own initiative turn away from the consideration of Christ's humanity.

[15] I Cor. 2:16.

[16] *Etudes Carmélitaines*, October, 1931, p. 162, article cited above.

A serious difficulty remains even for those who accept the view that explicit faith in Christ the Redeemer is not a necessary means since the promulgation of the Gospel. Indeed, there is a vast difference between what is strictly necessary for salvation or in order to avoid damnation and what is required for mystical union with God, especially the loftiest stages of this union.

We are led to ask ourselves if two most important matters are not being left out of consideration.

1. Do we find among these mystics outside the Church the combination of conditions, especially profound purification, requisite for true mysticism, that is, supernatural contemplation and the intimate union with God that results from it?

2. When they are in the state of grace is not theirs a natural mysticism or pre-mysticism, that is, a natural contemplation of God similar to that of Plato and Plotinus, or even of certain Christian Platonists like Malebranche and the most recent ontologists? [17]

If we failed to consider these two points carefully, we should be led, precisely as were the ontologists, to a more or less latent identification of nature and grace, and we should finish by speaking of a universal mysticism which expresses itself in a rather halting manner. Our Catholic mysticism would merely be the most correct form.[18] Not only would this confusion be deplorable for us. It would also be

[17] Rev. Allo, O.P., "Mystiques Musulmans" (*La vie spirituelle*, May 1, 1932, p. 110), cites the words of the Persian Bisthâmi, who, having been transformed by union, cried out in the name of Allah: "There is no God but me. Adore me. Glory be to me! How great is my majesty!" and also the words of Al Hallâj: *"Ana al Haqq.* I am the Truth." "Let us allow," he says, "for Oriental exaggeration. But in Christian lands the Inquisition would have dealt with them. . . . As for their 'pure love,' are we to admire the good woman [spoken of by E. Dermenghem, *op. cit.*, p. 30] who desired to put out the fires of hell with her pail of water and burn heaven with her torch so that God should be loved for Himself alone?" This excellent article by Father Allo should be read in its entirety for its bearing on the question under discussion.

[18] Concerning E. Dermenghem's book, Father Allo writes correctly (*loc. cit.*, p. 114): "We should have wished that the distinguished translator and commentator had put more emphasis on criticism and had made it clear that he grasped the significance of all these differences. As a matter of fact, his very noble confidence in the human spirit enlightened and guided by God, and an almost too 'catholic' breadth of feeling led him to discover everywhere the same effects of divine illumination and to explain everything in terms of a catholicity that can express itself with varying degrees of success. Apparently he saw only shades of difference where there are profound contrasts of color. . . . There are differences in kind, and only one can be the good, true, supernatural kind."

profitless to the souls of good will who even outside the visible Church might seek the true interior life and profound, intimate converse with God. This is clearly a serious question. It is important not to state one's views lightly. Undue haste in reaching conclusions would be particularly dangerous.

As Father Allo says: "At the present time among those given to the study and admiration of mysticism, a perilous syncretism is beginning to take shape. And believers endowed with knowledge and zeal should not close their eyes to this menace. It should be told." [19]

The Difficulties of the Problem

First of all there are the two great inherent difficulties of mystical theology: 1. The object is transcendent, inasmuch as it concerns union with God considered in terms of His intimate life, and not merely known naturally from the outside through the reflection of His perfections in the mirror of sensible things. 2. The subject under consideration is the human individual, of whom the ancients said: the individual is ineffable. Certainly man is not ineffable the way God is, whose intimate life is above the frontiers of intelligibility accessible to us by natural means. Man is ineffable because the human individual is a mysterious composite of spirit and matter, matter that is not very intelligible in itself and that is, so to speak, beneath the frontiers of intelligibility. There can be science only of the general, of the universal, for science is the result of abstraction from individual matter, which is thus in a manner repugnant to intelligibility. From this fact comes the mystery of the individual human composite wherein are perpetually intertwined the acts of the superior faculties, the will and the intelligence, and those of the imagination, the memory, the external senses, and all the emotions or passions that are more or less uncontrolled and either healthy or diseased.

As a result there are "dark nights," fundamentally different but resembling one another on the surface. Some are the product of the deep-seated workings of divine grace, the others are not. Some of these states are mainly neurasthenic and the result of human frailty.

---

[19] *La vie spirituelle, loc. cit.,* p. 117.

These are the difficulties of mystical theology in general and of its application even in fervent Christian and Catholic circles. But these difficulties are greatly magnified with regard to the mystics outside the Church.

We must not forget that there can and does exist a certain natural mysticism or pre-mysticism, midway between true supernatural mysticism and the false mysticism that is evidently diabolical. The indistinct "experiences" of this natural pre-mysticism become the obscure and sometimes poisoned source of the most contradictory systems. It had been said that certain non-Christian philosophies are nothing more than formulations of the mysticism of the savages which has always existed. There are methods of ecstasy that are prehistoric.

Can we be sure that these "experiences" are "ordered toward the truth"? Have we the right to conceive of them in terms of authentic Christian mysticism, rather than in pantheistic terms?

Much has been said about false charity that, sometimes without even being aware of it, has not at all the same formal object as infused charity, yet parades its name. At bottom such false charity is nothing but liberalism or vain sentimentalism. The principle, *corruptio optimi pessima*, is applicable here to an extent which is often unrealized. Though nothing on earth is greater than true charity, which is essentially supernatural, nothing is worse than false charity. Likewise, although nothing is greater than true mysticism, which is the eminent exercise of the three theological virtues and of the gifts of the Holy Ghost that accompany them, nothing is worse than false mysticism. This false mysticism is all the more dangerous to the extent that it takes on the external aspects of true mysticism. One might be tempted to speak of the "soul of truth" within this false mysticism. Yet there may be in it only a "grain of truth" which, far from being its soul, is at the service of the voluntary or involuntary error at the root of this deviation. In what is false *simpliciter* and not merely *secundum quid*, the true is deviated from its goal. These remarks, in direct opposition to theosophy, should not be forgotten.

Insufficient realization that a natural pre-mysticism exists, leads to a falsification, not to say caricature, of the contemplative life. This might be the favorite work of the spirit of lies, which hides as much as possible under the appearances of truth.

A certain modernistic syncretism is inclined to proclaim: "Christ is here" or "He is there." The Gospel tells us: "Do not believe him." [20] From this point of view, Christ would be everywhere except perhaps where He really is.

This gives us an idea of the difficulty of the problem. How can we distinguish a supernatural mysticism which, because of the ignorance of several revealed mysteries, is rather amorphous, from a natural mysticism or pre-mysticism which can exist even in souls in the state of grace? The latter form of mysticism, of course, was that of the Christian Platonists, of whom it was at times hard to say whether they were Platonistic Christians or Platonists with a taste for Christianity. The difficulty is increased by the fact that the mystical vocabulary comes in part from Dionysius and from the Neo-Platonists and therefore does not strictly belong to the Church. Plotinus often speaks of "purification," but in an entirely different sense from that in which St. John of the Cross uses it.

Moreover, this vocabulary is often more one of practical psychological description than is the case with theological descriptions, that is, those written by the light of speculative reason based on revealed principles. It is human language, expressing itself in terms of the "experience" of the contemplative soul. Therefore we should not be surprised that pseudo-mystics use it just as the true mystics do.

In our opinion, these are the chief difficulties of the problem. Some of these difficulties derive from the nature of this mysterious subject. For in it there is the darkness from above, coming from God whose light is inaccessible, and also the darkness from below, which comes from matter, one of the essential parts of the human composite. Between these two darknesses it is no easy task to distinguish true supernatural mysticism from its natural analogies. The difficulty is increased by the fact that the true and the false mystics often use a vocabulary that is rather common to both. It is further increased by the impossibility of seeing and of watching the lives of the mystics outside the Church, who are known to us only by documents that are

[20] Matt. 24:23.

for the most part incomplete. Spiritual directors have difficulty in judging those under their direction on the basis of a few conversations and letters. They often reach conclusions quite different from the ones of those who have lived in close contact with these persons over a long period of time. How much more difficult, then, to pass an exact judgment on the mystics outside the Church under discussion here! But since this question has been presented to theologians and missioners, let us inquire what guiding principles can help solve it.

II. Elements of the Solution

Two theologians who have lived among the Moslems, the late lamented Father Lemonnyer and Father Allo,[21] have indicated several of these elements, as has also Jacques Maritain in his remarkable work, *The Degrees of Knowledge.*[22]

Let us raise our thoughts progressively from the highest degrees of the natural order to the loftiest degrees in the order of grace. We would first consider the work of the imagination and of the rather disorderly emotions on the first ideas on which religious sentiment lives, whether these come from natural reason rising toward God or from religious traditions that have been more or less distorted. This field is unlimited. We have but to think of the sometimes improbable fantasies written even by Christian and Catholic poets, without mentioning the decadents. We shall limit ourselves to the formulation of principles concerning our superior faculties: the intellect and the will.

These principles concern first of all natural contemplation and

---

[21] A. Lemonnyer, "L'Existence des phénomènes mystiques, est-elle concevable en dehors de l'Eglise?" (*La vie spirituelle*, May 1, 1932, pp. 73 ff.). In this article Father Lemonnyer calls to mind the good distinction between "minor mystical graces that may be called 'substitutive' (because of the frailty of the subject or the special difficulties he encounters) and major mystical graces that are called graces of perfection." These latter are the graces which mystical writers usually speak of, particularly St. Theresa of Avila, beginning with the Fourth Mansion or the first passive prayers.

[22] Translated by Bernard Wall and Margot R. Adamson, 1938. See Part II of this work, chapter 5, "Mystical Experience and Philosophy," especially pages 331–36: "Is there an Authentic Mystical Experience of the Natural Order?" p. 331. "First Objection," p. 333. "Second Objection," p. 333. "Third Objection," p. 336; "The Natural Analogies of Mystical Experience," pp. 345–49.

natural love of God to the extent that they are possible in the present state, and then the different forms of superior inspiration that man can receive. It is easy to reduce the guiding principles to these two categories.

Natural Knowledge and Natural Love of God

We must remember that, according to Catholic theological teaching as formulated by St. Thomas (Ia, q. 60, a. 5; Ia IIae, q. 109, a. 1, 2, 3; IIa IIae, q. 26, a. 3), man since his fall [23] can still, without grace, by his natural powers know the existence of God, the author of our nature, he can know the more manifest divine attributes, and he can love God the author of our nature with a natural, inefficacious love. Although this love does not make us renounce mortal sin, that is, does not fundamentally rectify our will and our life, it prompts us to admire God's perfections that are naturally knowable, His infinite wisdom and His goodness.[24] This admiration leads to flights of the imagination which in poetic souls, especially in great artists, find lyrical expression reminiscent of true mysticism. Yet this might really be nothing but a sentimentalism full of deceiving fluctuations, one whose fires soon flicker out.

This natural and inefficacious love of God, the author of our nature, appears more powerful in souls naturally endowed with a vigorous intelligence or a strong will. This is particularly true when natural love of God is united, as in the case of Plotinus, to a love of philosophy, or perhaps to a love of art, or to love of country as in the case of an oppressed people.

In such cases we can easily find a natural prefiguration of the

[23] By this fall, man is born a sinner, "aversus a Deo, directe aversus a fine ultimo supernaturali et indirecte aversus a Deo fine ultimo naturali," for all sin, which is directly against supernatural law, is directly against natural law, which requires us to obey God in everything that He commands.

[24] Cf. the commentators of St. Thomas' treatise on grace, Ia IIae, q. 109, a. 3. Most of them state the question thus: "Whether by his own natural powers and without grace man can love God above all things?" and "Whether man without grace and by his own natural powers can fulfill the commandments of the law?" We have dealt elsewhere at length with this natural and inefficacious love of God. Cf. *The Love of God and the Cross of Jesus*, I, 85 ff.

mystical life that may mislead us if we forget the words of Jesus: "Not every one that saith to Me, Lord, Lord, shall enter into the kingdom of heaven: but he that doth the will of My Father." [25] Nor let us forget that in the actual plan of Providence every man is either in the state of grace or in the state of mortal sin; he is turned either toward God or away from Him. There is no middle ground. Absolute indifference is not possible with regard to God.

Consequently, on the matter of natural analogies to true mysticism we must note what Father Lemonnyer says: "What difference is it to us and what principles can we be expected to present in opposition to the fact that there have been actually observed outside the Church such phenomena as catalepsy, levitation, or luminous radiation materially resembling mystical ecstasy, as well as psychic states more or less analogous to mystical sufferings? Whether these phenomena are normal or pathological, natural or diabolical, they do not necessarily require a divine cause.

"We do not even claim that their appearance is impossible in connection with natural contemplation of a religious object, as Neo-Platonic contemplation could have been, and as can also be Buddhist or theosophical contemplation or any other contemplation that has Christian affinities. This natural contemplation, prepared and sustained by appropriate asceticism, developed through the use of a method and through well-conceived exercises to an exceptional degree of intensity, can have psychic consequences. When temperamental factors are favorable, especially when the imagination and the emotions come into play, there can even be corporeal consequences materially resembling various accessory mystical phenomena, with the exception of levitation. Hallucinations, susceptible of evoking the idea of prophetic visions, can easily be an additional factor." [26] Much could be said on this subject as it concerns the temperament of certain racial groups predisposed to passiveness and fatalism.

Can the natural love of God, which we have just mentioned, attain to what has been called an "immediate seizure of God" which would allow us to speak not merely of a natural pre-mysticism but of a genuine natural mysticism?

[25] Matt. 7:21.   [26] Art. cit., p. 78.

Pantheism, particularly that of Plotinus and Spinoza, gives an affirmative answer. We have explained elsewhere why Catholic theology must answer in the negative.[27] This would be the confusion of nature and grace.

There is a difference in formal object between the dim natural intuition of God known from the outside in the mirror of sensible things without the grace of faith and, on the other hand, the supernatural and quasi-experimental knowledge of God founded on divine revelation and infused faith united to charity and enlightened by the gifts of the Holy Ghost. Only supernatural knowledge can ultimately attain "the deep things of God," as St. Paul says.[28] In other words, it alone attains the intimate life of God, the Deity. First it succeeds in doing this dimly through faith and then it does so clearly through the beatific vision.[29]

Maritain rightly insists on this point:

[27] *The Love of God and the Cross of Jesus,* I, 119 ff.

[28] I Cor. 2:10.

[29] It is precisely because the Deity or the divine essence as such constitutes a formal object that infinitely surpasses the proper object of every created intelligence whether angelic or human, that St. Thomas was able to write (*Contra Gentes,* Bk. I, chap. 3): "Quod sint aliqua intelligibilium divinorum, quae humanae rationis penitus excedant ingenium, evidentissime apparet." The proper object of our intelligence is the intelligible being of sensible things. From this it can naturally rise to the knowledge of the existence of God and of the perfections analogically common to God and to creatures, but it cannot rise to the quiddative knowledge of what the Deity is in itself, the formal object of divine intelligence, nor to the knowledge of what essentially and immediately belongs to this formal object *per se primo.* As St. Thomas says, *ibid.:* "Sensibilia ad hoc ducere intellectum nostrum non possunt, ut in eis divina substantia videatur quid sit, quum sint effectus causae virtutem non aequantes." Nor can the angels know naturally the proper object of divine intelligence: "Non autem naturali cognitione angelus de Deo cognoscit quid est, quia et ipsa substantia angeli, per quam in Dei cognitionem ducitur, est effectus causae virtutem non adaequans." St. Thomas, *ibid.,* no. 2.

Ibid., Ia, q. 1, a. 6: "Sacred doctrine essentially treats of God viewed as the highest cause —not only so far as He can be known through creatures just as philosophers knew Him— that which is known of God is manifest in them (Rom. 1:19)—but also so far as He is known to Himself alone and revealed to others." It is because of this difference in formal object that we maintain in opposition to a recent objection that it can be demonstrated that there is in God an order of supernatural mysteries, that is, mysteries inaccessible to the natural powers of every created intelligence.

That is why St. Thomas says in the passage of *Contra Gentes* that we have just cited: "*Evidentissime apparet.* . . ." If there is a formal object that can constitute a new order, it is the formal object of divine intelligence. We have dealt with this question at greater length in the January, 1933, issue of *La revue Thomiste,* pp. 71–84, and *De revelatione,* Vol. I, chap. 11.

To admit in any degree, even in the simplest imaginable form, an authentic experience of the depths of God upon the natural plane would necessarily imply:

1. Either confounding our natural intellectuality, which is made specific by being in general, with our intellectuality in grace, which is made specific by the divine essence itself;

2. Or confounding the presence of immensity, whereby God is present in all His creatures by the power of His creative might, with the special and holy indwelling of God, that special presence in the soul in a state of grace;

3. Or again muddling up in the same hybrid concept the wisdom of the natural order (metaphysical wisdom) and the infused gift of wisdom;

4. Or finally attributing to the natural love of God what exclusively belongs to supernatural charity.

In one way or another this would be to confound what is absolutely proper to grace with what is natural and of the order of nature.[30]

If vegetative life, the life of the senses, and the life of reason constitute three distinct orders, how much more must we recognize as existing above them the order of truly divine life, superior to the rational life of man and to angelic life!

Thus only can we safeguard the meaning of St. Paul's words: "Eye hath not seen, nor ear heard, neither hath it entered into the heart of man, what things God hath prepared for them that love Him. But to us God hath revealed them by His Spirit. For the Spirit searcheth all things, yea, the deep things of God. For what man knoweth the things of a man, but the spirit of a man that is in him? So the things also that are of God [His intimate life] no man knoweth, but the Spirit of God." [31] What a vast difference there is between knowing the Vicar of Jesus Christ from the outside by what everybody says of him and knowing his intimate life! How much vaster, then, is the difference between knowing God from the outside through the reflections of His perfections in the created order and knowing His intimate life at least dimly through divine revelation!

That is why it has always been necessary for salvation to have explicit infused faith in at least two primary truths of the supernatural order: God, the author of salvation, exists and He is a rewarder.[32] Without this explicit faith we cannot have implicit faith in the other supernatural mysteries.

[30] *Op. cit.*, p. 332.   [31] I Cor. 2:9–12.   [32] Heb. 11:6.

Natural love of God might be efficacious even without grace, if man had not fallen but had remained in a state of pure nature, preferably integral nature. Yet man would not in such a state attain to the "immediate seizure of God." Even the angels would not attain to it by this natural love of God, for, like us, they had to be raised to the supernatural order of grace in order to know dimly at first and then clearly the intimate life of God or the mystery of the Deity.[33] There is an immeasurable distance between knowing God as God, in His intimate life, even in an obscure manner, and knowing God from the outside as the First Being and First Intelligence through the reflection of His perfections in creatures. It is because our natural love of God cannot arrive at this experience of the intimate life of God that we do not speak of a "natural mysticism," but only of a "natural pre-mysticism."

Superior Inspiration and Its Various Forms

But if natural love of God cannot arrive at the intimate experience that is to be found only in the mystical life by reason of the gift of wisdom, it is none the less often difficult in concrete reality to distinguish this natural love from a love born of superior inspiration. This difficulty is greatest in the case of philosophers or vigorous souls in whom the natural love of God is united to another powerful love which is not without grandeur, and when these are accompanied by a certain purifying asceticism such as the catharsis of Plotinus.

It is in such cases especially that a natural pre-mysticism can exist. This pre-mysticism is all the more difficult to distinguish concretely from true mysticism inasmuch as the superior inspiration which we have just mentioned is not always of the same nature.

We shall find, if we read the works of St. Thomas attentively, that he distinguishes at least four kinds of superior inspirations, two of the natural order and two of the supernatural order of grace. They can be reduced to the following table, reading from the bottom up.

[33] Cf. St. Thomas, Ia, q. 62, a. 2.

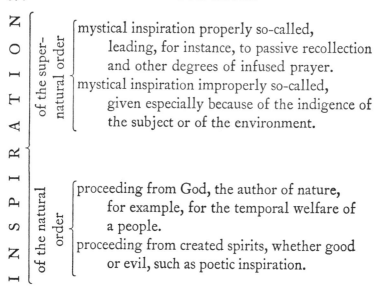

INSPIRATION

of the supernatural order
- mystical inspiration properly so-called, leading, for instance, to passive recollection and other degrees of infused prayer.
- mystical inspiration improperly so-called, given especially because of the indigence of the subject or of the environment.

of the natural order
- proceeding from God, the author of nature, for example, for the temporal welfare of a people.
- proceeding from created spirits, whether good or evil, such as poetic inspiration.

We know there can be inspirations that come not directly and immediately from God but from created spirits, whether good or evil. And sometimes mystics outside the Church have sought contact with spirits.

As Maritain remarks: "The care which St. Thomas took to refute the theories of Avempace, Averroes, and others on the possibility for man of an immediate achievement of the world of pure spirits by intellectual intuition,[34] shows to what point this temptation may prove seductive to philosophers." [35]

It is often forgotten that there can be divine inspiration of the natural order, such as that received by a great philosopher, a great poet, an artist of genius, a lawmaker, or a strategist. St. Thomas speaks of this several times, particularly in Ia IIae, q. 68, a. 1, where he cites chapter fourteen, "On Good Fortune," from *Ethic. Eudem.* 7, 8, written by a Platonist disciple of Aristotle who wrote of the exceptional men who, moved by a divine instinct, do not need to deliberate before doing great things.[36] The end of Plato's *Banquet* and a part of *Gorgias* seem to have been written under the influence

---

[34] *Contra Gentes*, Bk. III, chaps. 41–45.   [35] Maritain, *op. cit.*, p. 340.
[36] See also *Nicomachean Ethics*, Bk. VII, chap. 1, nos. 1–3; St. Thomas commentary, lect. 1.

of an inspiration of this kind. Whence the expression: divine Plato.

We need only call to mind certain leitmotivs of Wagnerian works or certain symphonies of Beethoven to realize that natural poetic or musical inspiration, united to the natural and inefficacious love of God which is possible without grace, can sometimes give the illusion of true mysticism. This illusion will be even more pronounced when the inspiration is received by a soul in the state of grace.

Divine inspirations of the order of grace also occur often enough, but only rarely do they belong to the truly mystical order. First, we must note in souls seeking religious truth the inspiration that leads them to believe supernaturally in the truths that are necessary means of salvation, especially the first two truths: that God (the author of salvation and not only of nature) "is and is a rewarder to them that seek Him." [37] Explicit faith in these two primary supernatural truths contains implicit faith in the others.

St. Thomas even tells us [38] that when a child, even one who has not been baptized, fully reaches the age of reason he must order his life to a good end, and if he does this he receives through grace the remission of original sin. That is to say, he is justified by baptism of desire. In other words, even a non-baptized child who has fully reached the age of reason must choose not only to suit his fancy but efficaciously the path of goodness and he must deliberately turn away from evil. Now, to choose the right path in this way is already to love efficaciously the good more than self, and therefore it amounts to loving efficaciously and above all else the Sovereign Good, God the author of our nature, known at least in a confused manner.

We have seen that fallen man cannot do this without grace.[39] That the accomplishment of this precept be *hic et nunc* really possible, the child then receives a sufficient grace, and if he does not resist it he receives greater assistance. According to St. Thomas, he is actually justified and his original sin is remitted. The text of Ia IIae, q. 89, a. 6, should be compared with the well-known passage *De veritate*,

---

[37] Heb. 11:6.

[38] Ia IIae, q. 89, a. 6: "When he begins to have the use of reason, . . . the first thing that occurs to a man to think about then, is to deliberate about himself. And if he then direct himself to the due end, he will, by means of grace, receive the remission of original sin." [39] Cf. St. Thomas, Ia IIae, q. 109, a. 3.

q. 14, a. 11 ad 1, which the Jansenists forgot.[40] Pope Pius IX speaks
in similar terms in the text quoted at the beginning of this chapter
(cf. Denzinger, no. 1677). God never commands the impossible and
He makes it possible for all adults to fulfill His precepts.

Supernatural love of God is more easily distinguishable in this
case by its efficacy and by the good behavior that it inspires from the
inefficacious natural love that in some respects resembles it. If the
child we have spoken of perseveres in the path of goodness in spite
of all the obstacles that surround him, he will be saved.

Finally, as Father Lemonnyer has remarked,[41] it is important to
remember a distinction that theologians, notably the Thomists, often
make concerning the gifts of the Holy Ghost, which because they
are related to charity are present in every soul in the state of grace.

Among the special inspirations of the Holy Ghost which the gifts
dispose us to receive, some are given us especially because of our
weakness or because of the indigence of our environment, in order
that we may accomplish certain salutary and meritorious acts that
stronger souls or souls in less unfavorable environments might accomplish by the simple exercise of the infused virtues aided by common actual grace. These special inspirations of the Holy Ghost have
been called minor or improperly so-called mystical graces. It is not
unusual for converts to receive them at the moment of their conversion and afterward for a more or less prolonged period of time, to
make up for their lack of preparation.[42]

Other special inspirations of the Holy Ghost that the gifts dispose
us to receive are given to us especially because of the perfection of the
act to be performed. If we do not resist these inspirations, they dispose
us soon to enter the initial mystical stage described by St. Theresa in
the fourth mansion and even in the ones above it. These inspirations

---

[40] "Hoc ad divinam Providentiam pertinet, ut cuilibet provideat de necessariis ad
salutem, dummodo ex parte ejus non impediatur. Si enim aliquis taliter (in silvis) nutritus,
ductum naturalis rationis sequeretur in appetitu boni et fuga mali, certissime est tenendum,
quod ei Deus vel per internam inspirationem revelaret quae sunt ad credendum necessaria,
vel aliquem fidei praedicatorem ad eum dirigeret, sicut misit Petrum ad Cornelium."

[41] *Art. cit.*, p. 7.

[42] Converts also sometimes receive, at the moment of their conversion, genuine mystical
graces and even truly extraordinary graces. Such was the case of Father A. Ratisbonne's
conversion, which calls to mind that of St. Paul.

can be called major mystical graces properly so called. John of St. Thomas, among the Thomists, has made this distinction quite clearly.[43]

The superior inspiration which we have been speaking of occurs in a number of different forms. It can belong to the natural order and proceed from either good or evil created spirits, or from God the author of our nature, as several Greek philosophers have noted, especially the author of *Ethic. Eudem.*[44]

Superior inspiration can also belong to the supernatural order of grace. Apart from prophetic inspiration or other extraordinary graces, it can be mystical in the broad sense or mystical properly so called. Mystical inspiration improperly so called generally follows justification and then becomes the principle of acts that are both salutary and meritorious. But it can precede justification and dispose one toward justification by acts that are salutary but not yet meritorious, inasmuch as the principle of merit is the state of grace and charity.

Above natural acts that may contain a certain prefiguration of mysticism, there is a great diversity of supernatural acts, starting with the first salutary acts and going on to acts that are highly meritorious but still do not properly belong to the mystical order. We believe these are the principal elements of the solution.

The Order of Possibility and the Order of Existence

It is easier to reach conclusions in the order of possibility.

1. True mysticism, which implies or at the very least provides proximate preparation for the quasi-experimental knowledge of God present within us, is possible only for souls in the state of grace. Outside the state of grace there can be a natural pre-mysticism and also diabolic influences. This natural pre-mysticism can exist simultaneously with actual graces that dispose toward salutary but not yet meritorious acts. It can even exist in souls in the state of grace who

[43] Cf. John of St. Thomas, *Cursus theol., De donis, In Iam IIae,* q.68, diss. 18, a.2; solv. obj. no. 6: How the Holy Ghost comes to succor our weakness in the midst of difficulties. Cf. St. Thomas, Ia IIae, q.68, a.2, ad 1 and 3. We have elsewhere discussed the influence of the gifts of the Holy Ghost in the ascetic life, an influence that is frequently latent and only rarely manifest, whereas in the mystical life it becomes both frequent and quite manifest. Cf. *Christian Perfection and Contemplation.* [44] Bk. VII, chap. 14.

perform meritorious acts, as we have seen in particular among Christian philosophers with a Platonist turn of mind.

2. In the actual plan of Providence in which the state of pure nature does not exist, every man is either in the state of grace or in the state of mortal sin. There is no middle ground. Every man is either turned toward God or turned away from Him. In the state of pure nature man would be born with a will not yet converted to God nor turned away from Him, but capable of being converted or of turning away from Him. In the actual state of things, man is born a sinner, turned from his last supernatural end and indirectly from his final natural end,[45] for every sin against supernatural law transgresses natural law at least indirectly. Therefore it is man's duty to obey God in whatever He may command. This means that every man is either turned toward God or turned away from Him. More precisely: every man either loves God efficaciously above all things with a love of esteem (an appreciative love), which presupposes sanctifying grace and charity, or else he does not attain to this efficacious love of God either because of original sin if he does not have the full use of reason, or because of a personal mortal sin.[46] That is why our Lord has said: "He that is not with Me is against Me," [47] and also to the apostles these consoling words: "He that is not against you is for you." [48] Indifference properly so called or absolute neutrality is not possible with regard to the ultimate end. Therefore in the actual economy of salvation every man is either in the state of grace or in the state of mortal sin.

3. The state of grace is possible outside of the visible Church.* It is realized by men who, with the help of actual grace, do what is in their power and thus come to love God efficaciously more than themselves with a love of esteem if not a love of sentiment. "To anyone doing what in him lies (with the help of actual grace), God does not refuse (habitual) grace." [49]

---

[45] Cf. St. Thomas, Ia IIae, q. 109, a. 3, and his commentators of the beginning of his treatise on grace, for the explanation of the thesis: "Utrum homo in statu naturae lapsae nondum reparatae minores vires habeat ad bonum morale (naturale) quam habuisset in statu naturae purae?"

[46] Cf. St. Thomas, Ia IIae, q. 89, a. 6.   [47] Matt. 12:30.

[48] Mark 9:39; Luke 9:50.   [49] Cf. ibid., q. 109, a. 6; q. 112, a. 3.

* Since the phrase "the visible Church" is subject to misinterpretation, this sentence would perhaps be more accurately expressed thus: "The state of grace is possible in souls who appear to be outside the Catholic Church." —Publisher, 1998.

4. Mystical graces improperly so called or minor mystical graces not only are possible outside the visible Church, but they can occur rather frequently in the holiest souls in the state of grace, as a means of making up for the indigence of the environments where God's children find so little help.[50] In this way souls really endowed with good faith and good will in the theological sense can attain a true spirit of prayer, as missioners have often noticed. In consequence these souls may make more or less permanent attempts at attaining God's intimacy, especially if there remain traces of the Gospel in their religious teachings, as in the doctrine of Islam and in some of its traditions.[51] These graces are to be found all the more in environments where, in spite of the errors of the Protestant heresy and of schism, the Gospel is preached and where Christ is loved by souls of good faith.[52]

5. As for mystical graces properly so called or major mystical graces, by which the soul reaches mystical states properly so called as described by St. Theresa of Avila from the fourth mansion on (passive recollection and quietude), they are possible outside the visible Church. For the "grace of the virtues and the gifts" can develop outside the Church, even though this is much more difficult. Yet everything leads us to believe a priori that these mystical graces

---

[50] As Father Lemonnyer remarks (art. cit., pp. 73 ff.): "The minor mystical graces are properly supplementary graces. When God grants them, He takes into consideration need rather than merit. He holds them in reserve as help mercifully granted to weakness rather than as direct means of accelerating progress in perfection. If there are born-candidates for the minor mystical graces, they are these unknown Catholics, members of the one spiritual Church. . . . They lack so many things." *

[51] Cf. Rev. Allo (art cit., pp. 108 ff.): "The Mohammedan contemplatives have deepened and vivified the monotheism of the Koran, which has always been their dogmatic authority. Although they greatly esteemed Christian monks, Christianity's influence on them was much less than the influence of Neo-Platonism. The Indian Vedanta also had its dogmatic authorities. . . . They do not admit the Incarnation, which is a Christian dogma. They deeply venerate Jesus, . . . who was to them the perfect example of transforming union. . . . Although on the whole they were orthodox, they were exposed to the calumnies and persecutions of the literalist theologians, to the point of having their own martyrs, such as the famous Al Hallâj." We can see that in such an environment and in the face of such trials there may well have existed among the best of these souls a certain intimacy with God and genuine inspirations of the Holy Ghost.

[52] These graces must occur even more frequently since the consecration of the human race to the Sacred Heart by Pope Leo XIII at the beginning of the twentieth century. And Mary, the Mother of all men, must obtain the salvation of many sinners.

* The phrase "members of the one spiritual Church" in the last sentence of Note 50 above would perhaps be more accurately expressed as "persons who are spiritually (or invisibly) in the one Church." —Publisher, 1998.

properly so called, already rare in the visible Church, are exceedingly rare in these less favorable environments. Here and there we may find a few instances of what St. Theresa of Avila calls the fourth mansion, but it is doubtful that there is anything more elevated than that.[53]

When we pass from the order of possibility to the order of actuality, it is much more difficult to reach final conclusions.

1. We almost always lack the elements of appreciation necessary to judge the essentially supernatural character of the experiences of the mystics outside the Church. Only the Church could speak with authority on these cases.

2. In order to have even a serious probability, we would be obliged to include among the texts of these mystics outside the Church not only those that have the ring of Christian mysticism but also those that are clearly pantheistic in character, or quietistic, or even erotic, as is the case of many such mystics.

If we were that exacting, the seriously probable cases of true mysticism in these environments would in all likelihood be far fewer and would perhaps be reduced for the most part to short-lived attempts. Let us not forget what St. John of the Cross says even of the most restricted Catholic circles. "God does not raise up to contemplation properly so-called all who desire to attain it by following the way of the spirit. He does not take even half of them." [54] "Why do they not reach this lofty state? . . . [Many souls], as soon as God tests them, flee suffering and refuse to bear the slightest dryness and mortification." [55] If this is true within the visible Church, how much truer must it be on the outside!

3. We should exercise the greatest restraint in judging the numer-

---

[53] Cf. Lemonnyer, *loc. cit.*: "Major mystical graces or phenomena presuppose charity in the way of perfection, a charity called to be effectively perfect. Even in the bosom of the Church, where the grace of Jesus Christ flows with greater abundance, few are the souls whom God favors with these graces after He has disposed them to receive them. We are led to believe that they are even fewer in the vast area where the spiritual atmosphere is less pure and the external means of sanctification are so meager. . . . The existence of the major phenomena of the mystical life remains perfectly conceivable in this portion of the spiritual Church that is outside the visible Church, although there are strong reasons for believing *a priori* that they are very rare." *

[54] Cf. *Dark Night of the Soul,* Bk. I, chap. 9.

[55] *Living Flame of Love,* st. 2, verse 5.

* The phrase "this portion of the spiritual Church that is outside the visible Church" in the last sentence of Note 53 above would perhaps be more accurately expressed as: "these souls who are spiritually in the Church but not visibly in the Church." —*Publisher,* 1998.

ous supposed mystics who are at least tainted by pantheistic monism.[56] No doubt, for the good of souls "of good will" in the scriptural sense, God can make use of natural pre-mysticism, just as He can make use of poetry. St. Paul did this in his discourse before the Areopagus: "In Him we live, and move, and are; as some also of your own poets said: For we are also His offspring." [57] But we do not know to what extent God makes use of these natural flowers for the good of souls.

4. Among the supposed mystics to be excluded would be particularly those who, like the theosophists, wish to possess final beatitude through their natural powers only. For this calls to mind the sin of the angel as described by St. Thomas [58] far more than true mysticism.

5. All things considered, it seems very probable that the natural contemplation so dear to Plotinus and Proclus occurred rather frequently.

Plotinus [59] speaks several times of ecstasy, and says that in order to be united to the first principle we must come to absolute simplicity, and go beyond all reasoning and all multiplicity: "We must wait in silence for the divine light to appear to us, just as the eye turned toward the horizon awaits the rising of the sun over the ocean. . . . Thought can only raise us little by little to the height from which it is possible to discover God. It is like the wave that carries us and lifts us up as it swells, so that suddenly from its crest we are able to see." Lofty as this contemplation may be, Plotinus considers it natural, for our nature proceeds from the One through emanation. It is in the

[56] Yet, as has just been noted, "if the heart is humble and faithful without knowing how to express itself, supernatural grace will be able to take full possession of it, and such a deficiency in doctrinal formulation will become the mute and involuntary homage of the full transcendence of Christian revelation." The prevenient graces and graces of consolation granted to the more conscientious souls in these pagan environments in general do not tend so much to rectify abstract formulas that inadequately express the true aspirations of the mind and heart. They tend rather to compensate for these false notions in the soul's concrete movement toward God, by removing their venom through the void of negative theology, through the spirit of renunciation and abandonment. Thus Eckhart and Rosmini possessed true charity in spite of their erroneous speculative formulas.

[57] Acts 17:28.

[58] Ia, q. 63, a. 3: "It was in this way that the devil desired to be as God . . . by desiring, as his last end of beatitude, something which he could attain by virtue of his own nature, turning his appetite away from supernatural beatitude, which is attained by God's grace."

[59] *Enneads*, 5, 5, 10; 4, 3, 32.

One that we exist and subsist. In this form of pantheism as in the others, we can truthfully say of our nature what Christian doctrine says of grace: it is already a participation in divine nature.

Proclus also says: "The soul that makes an act of intelligence knows itself as well as all contingent beings. But when it rises above intelligence, it is ignorant of itself and also of the contingents. Uniting itself with the One, it finds joy in rest, closed to all knowledge, wordless and intrinsically silent." [60]

We should remember what Ruysbroeck and Tauler say concerning this natural contemplation. The latter says: "If one were to look upon this way [of high contemplation] with abusive liberty and false light, this would be . . . most regrettable. . . . The way that leads to this end must pass by the adorable life and passion of our Lord Jesus Christ. . . . We must pass through this beautiful door by doing violence to nature, by practicing virtue with humility, gentleness, and patience. Know this in truth: he who does not follow this path will lose his way." [61] Of course these words were addressed to Christians, but they show the immense difference between supernatural contemplation and that of Plotinus and Proclus.

In conclusion, let us call to mind the reasons why true mysticism, although it is the normal blossoming of the life of grace, is, like perfect docility to the Holy Ghost, rare even in the visible Church. It is rare even in the religious orders, in spite of the assistance of the sacraments and in particular of daily Holy Communion. The mystical life is a normal development of the life of grace; but it is a lofty summit. Rarely do souls go beyond the fourth mansion, or prayer of quietude. The reason for this is that the mystical life ordinarily requires purity of heart, simplicity of mind, true humility, love of recollection, perseverance in prayer, fervent charity, all of which are attainable when one makes the best use possible of the great means the Church provides; the sacraments, Holy Communion, and when one allows oneself to be molded by the liturgy and the supernatural study of sacred doctrine. This combination of conditions is not often

[60] *Procli opera inedita* (Paris, 1864), col. 171.

[61] Cf. *Sermons de Tauler* (translated by Rev. Hugueny, Rev. Théry, O.P., and Rev. A. L. Corin. Theological introduction by Rev. Hugueny, I, 92 f.).

realized even among Catholics, and therefore it is even less frequent among those who do not belong visibly to the Church.

We do not deny in the least that a pagan can receive sufficient graces that permit him, if he does not resist them, to arrive at an infused faith in the truths absolutely necessary for salvation and for charity.[62] Yet it may be that the "experience of the divine" which we may think we notice in several mystics outside the Church is more often than not a sort of natural pre-mysticism that is profoundly different from the true, essentially supernatural mysticism. If there are certain attempts to attain the latter, these seem to be of short duration or fail to go beyond the lower degrees of quasi-experimental knowledge of God.

This truth can be more clearly understood when these attempts at reaching God are compared with the spirit and the life of the saints, for instance, with what St. Paul says of the life of the apostles: "In all things let us exhibit ourselves as the ministers of God, . . . as deceivers, and yet true; as unknown, and yet known; as dying, and behold we live; . . . as sorrowful, yet always rejoicing; as needy, yet enriching many; as having nothing, and possessing all things." [63] This is true mysticism and the signs that accompany it.

We believe this solution is at once sound enough to fulfill the requirements of the principles and yet flexible enough to respect the different modes by which divine grace acts on men's souls. It avoids the two errors we pointed out at the beginning of this chapter: naturalism and narrow pseudo-supernaturalism like that of the Jansenists. On the one hand it maintains that it is a great grace to be born into the Catholic Church. On the other, it strongly affirms that God never commands the impossible and that He makes it possible for all adults to accomplish the precepts they are called on to obey.

---

[62] St. Thomas even says that it is not impossible that God should work a miracle to confirm a natural truth of religion or the value of a virtue such as chastity. Cf. *De potentia*, q. 6, a. 5, ad 5.

Referring to the vestal who was said by St. Augustine to have carried water to the Tiber in a perforated vessel (*De civitate Dei*, Bk. X, chap. 26), St. Thomas says: "Non est remotum quin sit in commendationem castitatis quod Deus verus suos angelos bonos hujusmodi miraculum per retentionem aquae fecisset, quia si aliqua bona in gentibus fuerunt, a Deo fuerunt." It is true that this extraordinary fact is not a miracle properly so called, for it does not exceed the natural power of the good or evil angels.   [63] II Cor. 6:4-10.

An understanding of the deficiencies of the mystics outside the Church should help those who, according to the expression of St. Paul,[64] are groping for God to find the true life and who can through the grace of Christ, but only through His grace, persevere in it until death.

Let us not forget that at the outset of the twentieth century Leo XIII consecrated the entire human race to the Sacred Heart of Jesus. The effects of this grace should continue to increase with each passing year.

[64] Acts 17:27.

❊ XXXII ❊

E PILOGUE

The Three Births of the Word

THE synthesis of the revelation relating to the Word made flesh is to be found in the Prologue of St. John's Gospel. It is concerned with the three births of the Word which are celebrated each year by the three Masses on Christmas day: His eternal birth, His temporal birth according to the flesh at Bethlehem, and His spiritual birth in the souls of men.

The eternal birth of the Word is clearly expressed in the first and last verses of the Prologue of the Fourth Gospel:

In the beginning was the Word, and the Word was with God, and the Word was God. . . . No man hath seen God at any time: The only-begotten Son who is in the bosom of the Father, He hath declared Him.

These words unequivocally affirm the distinction between the Word (the Son of God) and the Father, and also the divinity of the Word, consubstantial with the Father.

The distinction between these two divine persons is unmistakable from the declaration that "the Word was with God." No one is with himself or in himself. And if there were any doubt whether the expression "the Word" designates a person, this doubt would be removed by verse 18 at the end of the Prologue: "No man hath seen God at any time: the only-begotten Son who is in the bosom of the Father, He hath declared Him." The entire Prologue makes it clear that the only-begotten Son is the Word of God made flesh. The expression "who is in the bosom of the Father" explains the words of the first verse, "the Word was with God."

It is evident also that the only-begotten Son is not the name of a divine attribute but the name of a person, as is the name "Father."

Finally, these two persons are really distinct: The Father is not the Son, for he who begets is not he who is begotten. No one begets himself.

On the other hand, we cannot say: God is not His intelligence, His wisdom, His love. For He is indeed His intelligence, He is wisdom itself, love itself. These essential attributes are absolutely identified with His essence. Yet the Father is not the Son. There is between them a polarity of relationship that does not exist between each of them and the divine essence.

However, the Prologue makes it perfectly clear that the Word is consubstantial with the Father, since it says: "The Word was God." In the Greek "the Word" is clearly the subject of this proposition, as well as of the preceding and following ones. And it is certain that the word "God" is used there in the same full sense as in the preceding proposition, "the Word was with God," and as in the following one, "the same was in the beginning with God."

Moreover, the following verses show that the Word, together with the Father, is the Creator, the author of natural and supernatural life: "All things were made by Him: and without Him was made nothing that was made. In Him was life, and the life was the light of men. And the light shineth in darkness, and the darkness did not comprehend it."

These last words refer especially to the supernatural light needed for believing the truths of faith essential to salvation.

The first and last verses of this Prologue thus show us the profound meaning of the words of psalm 2:7: "The Lord hath said to Me: Thou art My Son, this day have I begotten Thee," and of psalm 109:1–3: "The Lord said to my Lord: Sit thou at My right hand: . . . in the brightness of the saints: from the womb before the day star I begot Thee." We can also grasp a little better what the Holy Ghost wished to express when He inspired the author of the Book of Wisdom: "[Wisdom] is a vapor of the power of God, and a certain pure emanation of the glory of the almighty God: . . . for she is the brightness of eternal light: and the unspotted mirror of God's majesty, and the image of His goodness." [1]

[1] Wisd. 7:25 f.

This prologue, in verse 14, speaks with equal clearness of the temporal birth of the Word: "And the Word was made flesh, and dwelt among us (and we saw His glory, the glory as it were of the only begotten of the Father), full of grace and truth."

This temporal birth according to the flesh was announced by the prophet Micheas: "And thou, Bethlehem Ephrata, art a little one among the thousands of Juda: out of thee shall He come forth unto me that is to be the ruler in Israel: and His going forth is from the beginning, from the days of eternity . . . for now shall He be magnified even to the ends of the earth." [2]

It is the fulfillment of Isaias' prophecy: "For a child is born to us, and a Son is given to us, and the government is upon His shoulder: and His name shall be called Wonderful, Counselor, God the Mighty, the Father of the world to come, the Prince of Peace. . . . And there shall be no end of peace." [3]

Finally, this prologue speaks to us of the spiritual birth of the Word, living in the Church which is His mystical body, in souls of good will: "He came unto His own, and His own received Him not. But as many as received Him, He gave them power to be made the sons of God, to them that believe in His name. Who are born, not of blood, nor of the will of the flesh, nor of the will of man, but of God." [4]

He gave them power to be sons of God by adoption, as He is the Son of God by nature. Our sonship is an image of His, as verse 16 makes clear: "And of His fullness we all have received, and grace for grace. For the law was given by Moses; grace and truth came by Jesus Christ."

Jesus Himself has said: "If anyone love Me, he will keep My word, and My Father will love him, and We will come to him, and will make Our abode with him." [5] He also said: "If you love Me, keep My commandments. And I will ask the Father, and He shall give you another Paraclete, that He may abide with you forever." [6]

The Word, the Son of God, together with the Father and the Holy Ghost, dwells in every soul in the state of grace on earth, in

---

[2] Mich. 5:2-4. [3] Isa. 9:6 f. [4] John 1:11 ff.
[5] *Ibid.*, 14:23. [6] *Ibid.*, 14:15 f.

purgatory, and in heaven. That is, He dwells in the souls of all the just. However, His sacred humanity does not dwell within the souls of the just, but it exerts a continual influence on them, for it is the instrument always united to Divinity that communicates to us all the sacramental and extra-sacramental graces that Jesus merited for us during His life on earth and particularly on the cross.[7] Therefore we can speak of a spiritual birth of the Word in men's souls, or of a silent coming of the Word into souls, as He came into the souls of the shepherds at Bethlehem. It is this silent coming that is honored by one of the three Christmas Masses. In this sense also St. Paul writes: "For in Christ Jesus, by the gospel, I have begotten you," [8] in order to incorporate you into Him, so that you may be in Him and He in you.

We can never thank God enough for the realization of the mystery of the redemptive Incarnation. Often, when we enter a church, we ask for a spiritual or temporal grace for ourselves or for those we love, and sometimes we thank God for this or that particular blessing. Let us not fail to thank Him for the gift of gifts, the blessing which since the fall of man is the source of all other blessings, namely, the coming of the Savior. As St. Paul says to the Colossians: "All whatever you do in word or in work, do all in the name of the Lord Jesus Christ, giving thanks to God and the Father by Him" [9] for all the blessings that have come to us and that continue to come to us daily through His Son. "To Him in glory forever and ever."

The purpose of these pages is to invite souls to the contemplation of the mystery of Christ, who has deigned to become our spiritual food in the Eucharist. It would be difficult to express this contemplation more beautifully than in the words of the great doxology, the Gloria, which is sometimes recited mechanically at Mass, but which delights the souls of contemplatives by the fullness of its meaning. The *Liber Pontificalis* [10] says that Pope Telesphorus at the beginning of the second century (A.D. 128–139) commanded that this *Gloria in excelsis* be recited on the day of Christ's Nativity. When God inspired

---

[7] Cf. St. Thomas, IIIa, q.43, a.2; q.48, a.6; q.62, a.4.
[8] I Cor. 4:15.   [9] Col. 3:17.   [10] Ed. Duchesne, I, 129.

its author He knew that this song of praise would be sung at Mass through the centuries and would be the joy of the greatest believers.

Glory to God

Glory to God in the highest. And on earth peace to men of good will.

The Father

We praise Thee. We bless Thee. We adore Thee. We glorify Thee. We give thanks to Thee for Thy great glory. O Lord God, heavenly King, God the Father almighty.

The Son

O Lord, the only-begotten Son, Jesus Christ. O Lord God, Lamb of God, Son of the Father. Thou who takest away the sins of the world, have mercy upon us. Thou who takest away the sins of the world, receive our prayer. Thou who sittest at the right hand of the Father, have mercy upon us. For Thou only art holy. Thou only art the Lord. Thou only, O Jesus Christ, art most high,

The Holy Ghost

With the Holy Ghost, in the glory of God the Father. Amen.

Let us often contemplate in this Gloria the immense love that God has for us. God speaks. We must answer Him. Let us bear in mind, as St. John of the Cross recommends, that in the evening of our lives we shall be judged by love.

INDEX

Acceleration of spiritual progress, 7: Mary's, 326

Adoro Te, the, 266

Agnoetes, heresy of the, 161

"*Amor meus, pondus meum*," 270

Angels, Christ the head of the, 122 note

Anima Christi, thanksgiving prayer, 132

Announcement of the Savior, 56-77

Apostles, the: Christ according to, 28-36; conversion of, 155 note

Approach to God, acceleration in, 7

Aquinas; *see* Thomas

Assumption of Mary, 329

Author of life, Christ the, 28-36

Baptism of desire, 6, 375

Baptismal formula, authenticity of, 26

Beatific vision, possessed by Christ, 162, 224

Bernard, St.: hymn by, 340 note

Births of the Word, the three, 385-89

Blessed Virgin; *see* Mary

Body of Christ in the sepulcher, 90 note

Bossuet on Christ's priesthood, 246

Caiphas, Christ's affirmation before, 25

Calvin, view of Christ's dereliction, 280

Catechism of Council of Trent on Redemption, 200

Caussade, Father de: *Abandonment to Divine Providence* by, 353

"Caverns," mysteries of Christ as, 11

Charity: inflamed by the Incarnation, 108; power of, 10; superior to hope, 108

Child's obligation to choose God, 6, 375

Christ
according to the apostles, 28-36
the Author of life, 28-36
the beatific vision possessed by, 162, 224
contemplation of, 143-71
controlled emotions of, 180

Christ (*continued*)
daily gift of Himself in the Eucharist, 265
the dead body of, 90 note
divine rights claimed by, 15 ff.
divine sonship of, 20 ff.
doctrine of sublimity of, 146
Eucharistic heart of, 260-68
fortitude of, 282
free obedience of, 179
free will of, 178 note
fullness of grace in, 137, 269 ff.
fullness of virtues in, 139
gift of His cross of John, 336
gift of His heart to John, 332
God's love for, 117
grace of: plenitude of, 138; splendor of, 138
head of the angels, 122 note
His capacity for suffering, 140
His cry of dereliction, 273
His friendship for apostle John, 331 ff.
His love no longer meritorious, 308
His love of God, free or necessary?, 180 note
His obedience free and meritorious, 173
His peace during the Passion, 269-77
His peace in suffering, 272
His prayer in heaven, 234, 236 note, 304: St. Thomas on, 305
His redemptive love, 213-20
His reserve in manifesting His divinity, 14
His testimony on the Redemption, 183-94
His victory over death, 288-97
humility of, 221-29: principle of, 222
human intelligence of, 143-71
human will of, 172-81
impeccable liberty of, 176
impeccability of, 129, 172: and freedom, 174

391

Explains the entire Catholic tradition on the spiritual life . . .

THE THREE AGES OF THE INTERIOR LIFE

by Fr. Reginald Garrigou-Lagrange, O.P.

No. 1073. 1,166 Pages.
2 Volumes.
Sewn Hardbound.
Impr. ISBN-2477.

48.00

(Price subject to change.)

The Three Ages of the Interior Life is one of the greatest Catholic classics on the spiritual life, and it is the masterpiece of Father Reginald Garrigou-Lagrange, O.P. (1877-1964), whom many consider the greatest theologian of the 20th century. Both instructive and inspiring, this book is based squarely on the teachings of St. Thomas Aquinas and St. John of the Cross. Fr. Garrigou-Lagrange has organized and clarified the rich spiritual doctrine found in Sacred Scripture and in the great saints and other Catholic mystical writers. Among the topics covered:

• Infused contemplation as being in the normal way of sanctity • The degrees of contemplative prayer • Discovering one's predominant fault • Healing pride and acedia (spiritual sloth) • Spiritual direction • The active and passive purification of the senses, intellect and will • Retarded souls • The 3 successive "ways" of the interior life—Purgative, Illuminative and Unitive • Understanding the language of mystical writers • The dark nights of the senses and spirit • "Heroic virtue" • The inspirations of the Holy Ghost • The development and flowering of Sanctifying Grace and the 7 Gifts of the Holy Ghost • The spiritual fruits of chastity • The discerning of spirits • The errors of Modernism, Naturalism, Americanism, Jansenism and Quietism and how they deform the spiritual life • The role of spiritual childhood and of True Devotion to Mary • The fruits of Confession and Communion • The charisms (visions, stigmatization, etc.) • Private revelations • True mystical phenomena vs. false or diabolical phenomena.

This work is clear, complete, orthodox and inspiring! A masterpiece in every sense of the word!

U.S. & CAN. POST./HDLG.: If total order = $1-$10, add $2; $10.01-$20.00, add $3; $20.01-$30, add $4; $30.01-$50.00, add $5; $50.01-$75, add $6; $75.01-up, add $7.

TAN BOOKS AND PUBLISHERS, INC.
P.O. Box 424, Rockford, Illinois 61105 • Toll Free 1-800-437-5876

FR. REGINALD GARRIGOU-LAGRANGE, O.P.

Fr. Garrigou-Lagrange, O.P.
1877-1964

Fr. Reginald Marie Garrigou-Lagrange, O.P. (1877-1964) was probably the greatest Catholic theologian of the 20th century. (He is not to be confused with his uncle, Père Lagrange, the biblical scholar.) Fr. Garrigou-Lagrange initially attracted attention in the early 20th century, when he wrote against Modernism. Recognizing that Modernism—which denied the objective truth of divine revelation and affirmed an heretical conception of the evolution of dogma —struck at the very root of Catholic faith, Fr. Garrigou-Lagrange wrote classic works on apologetics, defending the Catholic Faith by way of both philosophy and theology. Fr. Garrigou-Lagrange taught at the Angelicum in Rome from 1909 to 1960, and he served for many years as a consultor to the Holy Office and other Roman Congregations. He is most famous, however, for his writings, producing over 500 books and articles. In these he showed himself to be a thoroughgoing Thomist in the classic Dominican tradition.

Fr. Garrigou-Lagrange was best known for his spiritual theology, particularly for insisting that all are called to holiness and for zealously propounding the thesis that infused contemplation and the resulting mystical life are in the normal way of holiness or Christian perfection. His classic work in this field—and his overall masterpiece—is *The Three Ages of the Interior Life*, in which the Catholic Faith stands out in all its splendor as a divine work of incomparable integrity, structure and beauty, ordered to raise man to the divine life of grace and bring to flower in him the "supernatural organism" of Sanctifying Grace and the Seven Gifts of the Holy Ghost—the wellsprings of all true mysticism. Among his other famous theological works are *The Three Ways of the Spiritual Life, Christian Perfection and Contemplation* (a forerunner of *The Three Ages of the Interior Life*), *The Love of God and the Cross of Jesus, The Mother of the Saviour and our Interior Life*, and *Christ the Saviour*. His most important philosophical work was *God, His Existence and Nature: A Thomistic Solution of Certain Agnostic Antinomies*.

The works of Fr. Garrigou-Lagrange are unlikely to be equalled for many decades to come.